The Columbia Anthology of Japanese Essays

THE COLUMBIA ANTHOLOGY OF
JAPANESE ESSAYS

Zuihitsu from the
Tenth to the Twenty-First Century

EDITED AND TRANSLATED BY

Steven D. Carter

COLUMBIA UNIVERSITY PRESS
NEW YORK

Columbia University Press wishes to express its appreciation for assistance given by the Japan Foundation toward the cost of publishing this book.

 JAPANFOUNDATION NEW YORK

Columbia University Press wishes to express its appreciation for assistance given by the Department of East Asian Languages, Stanford University, toward the cost of publishing this book.

Columbia University Press
Publishers Since 1893
New York   Chichester, West Sussex
cup.columbia.edu

Library of Congress Cataloging-in-Publication Data

The Columbia anthology of Japanese essays : zuihitsu from the tenth to the twenty-first century / edited and translated by Steven D. Carter.
    pages cm
  Includes bibliographical references.
  ISBN 978-0-231-16770-3 (cloth)
  ISBN 978-0-231-16771-0 (pbk.)
  ISBN 978-0-231-53755-1 (e-book)
  1. Japanese essays—Translations into English.   I. Carter, Steven D., editor of compilation translator.   II. Title.

 PL772.C65 2014
 895.64—dc23

                                                    2014012763

COVER IMAGE: Ogata Gekko, title page of *Zuihitsu* (ca. 1886). (Bao Ming Collection)

COVER DESIGN: Milenda Nan Ok Lee

To Charles, Joseph, and Riley

Contents

Acknowledgments

As always, I thank my wife, Mary, for her support. Jeffrey Knott and Benjamin Carter assisted in proofreading. Two anonymous readers for Columbia University Press made a number of helpful suggestions, for which I am duly grateful. Irene Pavitt and Jennifer Crewe of Columbia University Press provided valuable assistance in guiding the project through to completion.

The Columbia Anthology of Japanese Essays

Introduction

This book presents translations of Japanese literary works from the tenth through the twenty-first century that are collectively called *zuihitsu*—a genre of writing that, as Donald Keene notes, "has no close European counterpart"[1] but is generally called "essay" or "miscellany."

Anyone who has attempted to define the word *zuihitsu* can sympathize with the frustration felt by the modern novelist Dazai Osamu in trying to write one:

> Lately I was asked for a *zuihitsu* by a newspaper, so I took courage and set myself to the task. But I kept tearing up whatever I wrote, and even after working on ideas for three or four days, I had ten pages at the most. It seems that I wanted to write a *zuihitsu* so brilliant that I would have readers thinking, "That's it—he has it right!" But after working at it too long, I no longer knew what was what; I didn't even understand what a *zuihitsu* was supposed to be.
>
> I rummaged through my book box and took out two books: *The Pillow Book of Sei Shōnagon* and *Tales of Ise*. I thought that I could use these books to find the *zuihitsu* traditions of Japan. What an imbecile I am.[2]

1. Donald Keene, *Seeds in the Heart: Japanese Literature from the Earliest Times to the Late Sixteenth Century* (New York: Holt, 1993), 1.
2. Dazai Osamu, "The Image of an Author" (chap. 32).

Imbecile or not, Dazai here cagily expresses something fundamental about the *zuihitsu* as a genre: it defies easy definition. And it seems entirely fitting that he should compound the problem by listing one book (*The Pillow Book*) that is almost always defined as a *zuihitsu* along with another book (*Tales of Ise*) that, in modern times at least, is not.[3]

Bookstores generally shelve books by genre—history, religion, science, philosophy, literature, self-help, and so on. In the library stacks, though, one finds a more complicated mix based on a broader range of subject categories and many more subdivisions. And in real life, books pass by like currents in a river, all jumbled together, which is only appropriate since so many books are themselves jumbles of things. As Mikhail Bakhtin and others have demonstrated, this is particularly true of the modern novel, but one may submit that it is even more true of the *zuihitsu*, a supergenre in which one will often find a mix of subgenres, everything from reportage and travelogue to poetry, literary criticism, biography, confession, journalism—and so on, almost ad infinitum.

Perhaps the best way to introduce the pieces gathered together in this book is to quote some of the things said by a few of their authors, beginning at the beginning, with Sei Shōnagon, a tenth-century lady-in-waiting at the Japanese imperial court, whose *Pillow Book* is generally (although not universally) considered to have inaugurated the *zuihitsu* tradition in Japan. For in several passages, Sei makes comments that go far toward defining her method—or, more properly, her antimethod. The first of these is that she has written her "thoughts alone . . . never thinking that anyone would compare my book with other writings or that I would hear people saying I did a passable job,"[4] thus informing us that her book is filled with personal and casual musings rather than anything more formal or scholarly. Second is that she has not restricted herself as to subject matter, writing "whatever occurred to me, for the pleasure of it," and including, she says, "even things that are vulgar or odious."[5] And third, lest her other comments be taken to mean that she has given no thought to her audience, she admits that she has "written about things

---

3. As its title would suggest, *Tales of Ise* (*Ise monogatari*) is generally defined by scholars as a *monogatari* (tale) or as an *uta monogatari* (poem tale).
4. Sei Shōnagon, *The Pillow Book*, final section (chap. 1).
5. Ibid., sec. 134.

that people find amusing and things that are sure to impress."[6] In conclusion, one may put Sei's comments into one declarative statement: she writes personally and casually, for the joy of it, about anything that comes to mind, providing that she thinks it might impress readers. All that one need add to make the statement complete as a description of her approach is that she excludes anything purely fictional.

Sei is true to her own definition. In her *Pillow Book*, we find a dizzying maelstrom of things—anecdotes, based on her own experience or what she has heard from others; lists of things of interest to her, including everything from "Disgusting Things" to "Waterfalls"; reminiscences; homilies and pronouncements of taste; and what in journalistic jargon might be called opinion pieces—all presented with little sense of organization.[7]

It is obvious that many later writers of *zuihitsu* were influenced by *The Pillow Book* and by Sei's ruminations on her project. Yoshida no Kenkō (1283–ca. 1350), whose *Essays in Idleness* is second only to *The Pillow Book* in prominence within the Japanese *zuihitsu* tradition, surely must have had that book in mind when he began his own collection with the words "How foolish I feel when I realize that I have spent another day in front of my inkstone, jotting down aimless thoughts as they occurred to me, all because I was bored and had nothing better to do."[8] Predictably, Kenkō's collection resembles Sei's in presenting a jumble of anecdotes, homilies, opinion pieces, reminiscences, and even a few lists. The relationship was obvious enough that a hundred years later, the poet Shōtetsu (1381–1459)—who loved both books—would say in his own *zuihitsu* that Kenkō's work was "similar in form to *The Pillow Book*."[9]

Sei Shōnagon's statements (and her example) were not the only influence on Kenkō, however. Also important was the eremitic tradition represented by Kamo no Chōmei in "The Ten-Foot-Square Hut" (1212),[10] a work that resembles the Western argumentative essay in presenting a meditation on the uncertainty of human existence with "men and their

6. Ibid., final section.
7. Some textual transmissions seem more organized than others, but the textual history is so confusing that there is no consensus about its "original" form.
8. Yoshida no Kenkō, *Essays in Idleness* (chap. 2).
9. Shōtetsu, *Conversations with Shōtetsu* (chap. 3).
10. There are so many fine English translations of this work (by Natsume Sōseki, A. L. Sadler, Keene, Burton Watson, Helen Craig McCullough, and Anthony Chambers, to give an incomplete list) that I have not dared to produce another one.

houses" as a motif. Chōmei's work would also cast a long shadow, which would fall on later writers from Shōhaku and Kinoshita Chōshōshi to Matsuo Bashō, Natsume Seibi, Shiga Naoya, and Osaragi Jirō. While remaining casual in style, these works are not as desultory in organization or varied in subject matter as *The Pillow Book*; they are also more subjective in tone and more "confessional" in mode. And it should be added that many Japanese writers of *zuihitsu* also read and were influenced by Chinese works in a variety of genres that might also be translated using the English word "essay," including most prominently *pianwen* (parallel prose), *suibi* (miscellanies), *guwen* (ancient prose), and *xiaopinwen* (short classical essays). Indeed, the very word *zuihitsu* is a Japanese rendition of the second of these terms, a literal translation of which is "following the brush." Perhaps this can also account for the works within the general category of *zuihitsu* that resemble what in the West might be called expository prose, represented in this collection by works by scholars such as Dazai Shundai, Motoori Norinaga, and Terada Torahiko.

Still, no formulation is more broadly useful than Sei's in making sense of the *zuihitsu* tradition as it is articulated more generally in the Edo period, which is in many ways the golden age of the *zuihitsu* as a genre. Works like *Tawaregusa* (*Amusements*, 1709), *Mado no susami* (*Window Musings*, 1724), *Hokusō sadan* (*Idle Chats Beneath a Northern Window*, 1801), *Kagetsu sōshi* (*Blossoms and the Moon*, 1803), *Shunparō hikki* (*Shunparō's Jottings*, 1811), and *Unpyō zasshi* (*Clouds of Floating Grasses*, 1843) show the influence of Sei's work (and Kenkō's) in every way imaginable, from their often chatty tone to their eschewing of any unified scheme of organization. Nor is it any surprise that the author of another such work, *Nennen zuihitsu* (*Year by Year: A Miscellany*), Ishiwara Masaakira, writing in 1804/1805, should, when he pauses to say something about the genre in which he is writing, sound so much like Sei and Kenkō: "In a *zuihitsu*, one records things one sees and hears, says and ponders, whether frivolous or serious, just as they come to mind."[11]

Even in the twentieth century, the influence of Sei Shōnagon and Yoshida no Kenkō continues, as is obvious in the case of the perplexed Dazai in his essay noted earlier, who says at one point that "a *zuihitsu* is

11. Ishiwara Masaakira, *Year by Year: A Miscellany* (chap. 17).

not fiction; the writer's words are supposed to be 'raw.' . . . To put it in grandiose terms, I always think of myself as reporting to the heavens the true features of the human story."[12] To be sure, this is not the case for all modern *zuihitsu*, many of which reflect modern assumptions about the self and the personality and read something like memoir or confession, categories that simply did not exist for premodern writers in the same ways. But it is worth emphasizing that the old patterns persist in writers like Nagai Kafū, Uchida Hyakken, and Kikuchi Kan, and even in postwar writers Hiraiwa Yumiko and Dekune Tatsurō. In their *zuihitsu*, we again encounter a casual, sometimes offhand style; a freewheeling attitude toward subject matter; and a commitment to stories that purport to be fundamentally factual and not fictional, remembering Dazai's insistence that "in a *zuihitsu*, fabrications are not allowed."[13] This is the mainstream of the *zuihitsu*, in which, as Linda Chance says, the writer casually invites the reader into his world "to sit down . . . for a long chat."[14] The pose of the writer remains modest and "demure," to use a characterization of Sei Shōnagon by Sakai Junko—who is astute, I think, in wryly characterizing that lady as something close to a newspaper gossip columnist.[15]

That said, the corpus of *zuihitsu* from the tenth century to the present is both diverse and immense. Doing it justice is beyond the power of any single anthology. Most of the works I have chosen for inclusion from the medieval and Edo periods would probably be on anyone's list, except perhaps the short pieces by haiku poets,[16] which are not included in collections of *zuihitsu* but in my opinion should be. But one cannot assume such unanimity when it comes to covering the past 150 years or so, which present us with virtual mountain ranges of works in the genre, not only by literary figures but also by people from many other professions. Some of the names I have included seem inevitable to me: Kafū, Torahiko, Hyakken, Shiga, Kōda Aya, Kawamori Yoshizō, Mukōda Kuniko, Takenishi Hiroko, and Dekune, to name the most prominent ones. In my choices of

12. Dazai, "Image of an Author."
13. Ibid.
14. Linda Chance, "Japanese Essay," in *Encyclopedia of the Essay*, ed. Tracy Chevalier (London: Routledge, 1997), 431.
15. Sakai Junko, "On *Zuihitsu*" (chap. 46).
16. Specifically, Matsuo Bashō, Murata Harumi, and Natsume Seibi. These pieces are usually called *haibun*, or haikuesque prose. Not all of them contain haiku, however, and they so resemble writings by Chōmei, Shōhaku, Chōshōshi, and others that not to include them seemed like a dereliction of duty.

others, as in my choices of specific titles, I have to admit to being guided by my own tastes and interests, which is perhaps not a great sin given the nature of the genre in question. Furthermore, like Osaragi Jirō as he describes himself in "A Bed for My Books," I am one of those people who lives "in a flood of books" and who often finds "what I want to read by rummaging."[17] I cannot claim that my methods in making choices about what to translate have been in any way truly systematic.

One bias that I *did* become aware of early on in the long reading process that led to this book was a preference for things written in a light, humorous vein. When I began reading Japanese literature back in the early 1970s, I got a strong dose of writers like Kawabata Yasunari, Dazai, Enchi Fumiko, Ariyoshi Sawako, and Ōe Kenzaburō—not a cheery bunch, to put it mildly. In time, however, as I read more broadly, I discovered that there was no dearth of light and humorous writing in Japan in any historical period. In this sense, I agree wholeheartedly with Kawamori Yoshizō in his essay "Laughter and Nationality," who rejects the notion that "the Japanese are so serious that they . . . seldom laugh."[18] The evidence of the *zuihitsu* tradition is quite to the contrary, reinforcing Kawamori's contention that "there are plenty of Japanese with a good sense of humor,"[19] as his own essays so delightfully attest. This book is partly intended to emphasize that point—and in that sense to revise, if only slightly, the canon of Japanese literature as it is known in the West. Perhaps because so many *zuihitsu* are in some sense light and frivolous when compared with so-called serious literature, writers of the genre are all too ready to disparage their own work—mere "useless scraps of paper," to quote Matsudaira Sadanobu.[20] Modern scholars of Japanese literature should not be complicit in such a project.

Most of the pieces translated in this book are by people who are in one sense or another writers—poets, novelists, and scholars, mostly. Also included, however, are a few government officials, some monks, a physician, a painter, a physicist, and the owner of a used bookstore (who later became a professional writer). Among the writers, I have included

17. Osaragi Jirō, "A Bed for My Books" (chap. 35).
18. Kawamori Yoshizō, "Laughter and Nationality" (chap. 34).
19. Ibid.
20. Matsudaira Sadanobu, *Blossoms and the Moon* (chap. 16).

zuihitsu both by "serious" novelists and poets and by "popular" writers of everything from period novels and mysteries to television scripts. Did I do this intentionally? My only answer is the one that Sakai Junko puts in the mouth of Sei Shōnagon when she is asked a similar question: "Whatever you say. I haven't thought much about it."[21]

If after reading my collection any readers feel that I have snubbed one of their favorite *zuihitsu* or *zuihitsu* writers, I invite other scholars to remedy the problem. Far too few *zuihitsu* have been translated into English, and I hope that my anthology will be just the first of many.

21. Sakai, "On *Zuihitsu*."

I

BEGINNINGS

The first Japanese literary work to include the word *zuihitsu* in its title is the *Tōsai zuihitsu* (*Musings from an Eastern Study*) of Ichijō Kaneyoshi (1402–1481). Confusingly, however, that book is seldom even touched on by scholars of the genre, mostly, one guesses, because it is a collection of short pieces arranged by topic from earlier works by other people and not by Kaneyoshi himself. Instead, scholars tend to begin their histories of the form with a title from more than four centuries before: *The Pillow Book of Sei Shōnagon*. That said, one must quickly add that, as Konishi Jin'ichi points out, the genre of *zuihitsu* did not yet exist in Sei Shōnagon's day.[1] Yet in some ways, this fact seems entirely appropriate, given the way the *zuihitsu* tradition presents us with such a delightful mix of things that it can be called an antigenre. If *The Pillow Book* raises questions about the identity of the form, then perhaps that is all the better, since it inaugurates a tradition in which there is considerable resistance to any established form.

Written at the highpoint of aristocratic power in the mid-Heian period by a woman in service to an empress, *The Pillow Book* offers intriguing glimpses into the everyday lives of the aristocratic elite and was widely

---

1. Konishi Jin'ichi, *A History of Japanese Literature*, vol. 2, *The Early Middle Ages* (Princeton, N.J.: Princeton University Press, 1986), 257. Elsewhere in the same study, he says, "If we could ask eleventh-century readers what *The Pillow Book* might be, they would no doubt reply, 'A *nikki* [diary], of course!'" (384).

circulated in the centuries to come. That it inspired no other writer of the Heian period—unless we take into consideration collections of tales—to write in a similar way is mystifying. But we can be happy that eventually the poet Yoshida no Kenkō (1283–ca. 1350), with time heavy on his hands, followed Sei Shōnagon's lead in producing his own miscellany, *Tsurezure-gusa*, literally, "Scribbles from Idle Hours," but widely known as *Essays in Idleness*. Kenkō had been a low-ranking courtier in his early years but was disappointed in his social ambitions. The world he reveals is broader in scope than Sei Shōnagon's and more a product of the reclusive life.

Thus a woman and a man, a lady-in-waiting and a cultured recluse, separated by more than two centuries in time, provided the foundation for a literary form that would live on until the present.

The Pillow Book

SEI SHŌNAGON

Outside sources tell us little about Sei Shōnagon, only that she was of the Kiyo-hara lineage, the daughter of Motosuke (908-990), and the granddaughter of Fu-kayabu (precise dates unknown)—both major literary figures—and that she was married for a time and had several children. Our only certain dates for her life come from her famous Makura no sōshi (The Pillow Book) itself, which reveals that in 993 she entered the service of Teishi (976-1001), consort to Emperor Ichijō (980-1011; r. 986-1011), and left court upon or soon after Teishi's death in 1001. Thereafter, Shōnagon—or "Minor Counselor," the name by which she is known in her book, probably because some male relative held that title—lived in relative obscurity. She died sometime between 1025 and 1027, probably in Settsu Province.

Reference works often call her an essayist, but we really have no idea what Shōnagon thought she was writing. Most likely, she thought of her book as a diary of sorts, a place to record important or interesting events from her life at court, along with anecdotes about others, a number of short jottings of a more pedantic and essayistic sort, and her famous lists of the things—tangible and not—that made up her world. Whatever her motives, her precedent would be of supreme importance in the history of the zuihitsu form, influencing, in particular, Yo-shida no Kenkō, Shōtetsu, and Edo-period writers such as Tachibana Nankei and Ishiwara Masaakira, who followed her in producing desultory, seemingly formless works that are hard to categorize.

The numbers of the following selections are from the edition edited by Wata-nabe Minoru (see bibliographic reference at the end of this chapter).

1

In spring—dawn. As daylight steadily spreads, the mountain rims redden and thin streaks of purplish cloud trail off into the sky.

In summer—night. When the moon is out, of course. Also fine is a dark night of jostling fireflies, though I am moved as well by the faint glow of just one or two flitting by. Even rain on a summer night is delightful.

In autumn—evening. Shining brightly, the setting sun approaches the mountaintops, and everything—down to crows hurrying off to roost in sets of three or four, or two or three—stirs the heart. And more captivating still is a line of wild geese, looking tiny in the distance. I will not attempt to describe the feeling one has listening to the sound of the wind and the cries of insects after the sun goes down.

In winter—early morning. The morning after a snowfall goes without saying. But equally pleasing is a white scene of heavy frost—or, if not that, then a brisk cold that has servants bustling about kindling fires in braziers and delivering glowing charcoals. Toward midday, however, when the cold has broken, I find the sight of coals burned down to white ash disagreeable.

4

It breaks my heart to think of parents sending a precious son off to become a monk. What a pity to be dismissed by people like a scrap of wood! For food, he gets dull monastic meals[1] and is denied virtually everything else, even sleep. Being young, he is bound to be curious, yet he is berated for the slightest offense, even for not averting his eyes when offered a peek at a woman.

---

1. Buddhist monks ate vegetarian fare.

Worse still is the life of an exorcist,[2] who truly seems to suffer. How uncomfortable he must feel when, after giving his best efforts, he nods off for a moment, only to hear a voice complaining all he does is sleep.

Of course I'm talking about the past; nowadays monks have an easier time.

26

Things that make the heart race: Baby sparrows in their cage. Passing by a place where a baby is playing.

Burning incense and then lying down to rest. A place on a Chinese mirror that's gone a bit cloudy. A man of consequence who stops his carriage and sends a messenger in.

You wash your hair, put on makeup, and dress up in fine scented robes—an exciting feeling even if you are not going to meet someone.

On a night when you are waiting for someone, you hear the rain, maybe, or something rattling in the wind, and suddenly you are alert.

41

It's a day in the Seventh Month when the wind is blowing hard, the rain is coming down, and the air is cool enough to forget about your fan. What a delight it is at such a time to pull over a thinly padded robe that still smells a little of sweat and get beneath it for a midday nap.

48

Oxen should have a small patch of white on their foreheads—along with bellies, feet, and tails of pure white.

---

2. *Kenja.* Buddhist priests employed to do incantations during times of illness and cast out malignant spirits.

As for cats, I like them black on top, with all-white bellies.

I like my footmen[3] and outrunners lean and on the slim side. The same goes for all the men in my employ, in fact—especially when they are young. Fat ones look too ready to nod off.

A page boy should be small, with well-groomed hair, trimmed up properly and with a nice sheen. He should have a pleasant voice, respond respectfully, and behave smartly.

An ox driver should be a large man, with lots of unruly hair, a red face, and plenty of spunk.

Young people and infants should be chubby. Provincial governors and others of a certain stature should also be well filled out.

Waterfalls: Soundless Falls.[4] Descending Falls.[5] (How splendid to think that the reverend retired sovereign[6] visited there!) Nachi Falls—which

---

3. *Zōshiki*. Low-ranking servants assigned odd tasks.
4. Otonashi no Taki. Located near Kumano Shrine in Kii Province. Shōnagon is doubtless attracted by the witty name more than anything else, here and elsewhere in this list.
5. Furu no Taki. Located in Yamabe, Yamato Province.
6. Probably a reference to Retired Emperor Kazan (968–1008; r. 984–986), who is known to have visited the area on a pilgrimage after taking the tonsure. A site popular with mountain ascetics.

I hear is in Kumano[7]—is most impressive. Rumbling Falls[8] must make a fearsome sound.

68

Things that bear no comparison: Summer and winter. Night and day. A rainy day and a sunny day. A person's anger and that same person's laughter. Old age and youth. White and black. Someone you love and someone you hate. It's the same person, but a man you once loved seems like another person altogether once your feelings have changed. Fire and ice. A fat person and a skinny person. A person with long hair and a person with short hair.

69

In the middle of the night, something disturbs night crows[9] roosting in the trees, and a few tumble from their perches while others hop around in the branches, cawing in sleepy voices, giving a rather different impression than they do in the daytime—and a less unpleasant one.

96

It was when Her Majesty was residing in the Office of the Empress,[10] on a bright moonlit night sometime just after the tenth of the Eighth Month. Having asked Ukon no Naishi[11] to play the lute, Her Majesty was sitting just inside the portico. The others were chatting and laughing, but I sat apart, leaning against a nearby pillar, waiting on my lady in silence.

---

7. Located in Kii Province. Another site popular with mountain ascetics.
8. Identity unknown.
9. "Morning crows" (*asagarasu*) and "night crows" (*yogarasu*) were all just crows.
10. An office within the greater palace compound assigned to support the empress and her entourage, where the empress also had living quarters.
11. A lady-in-waiting at the court of Emperor Ichijō.

"Why so quiet?" asked Her Majesty. "Please say something. Are you so sad?"

"No—I am just looking deep into the heart of the moon," I said.

"That says it all," was her reply.[12]

101

Some men in the Courtiers' Hall[13] sent me a branch of plum, but with the blossoms all fallen, asking, "What do you have to say?"

"How soon have the blossoms scattered!"[14] was my reply.

After this, a whole group of courtiers who had gathered in the Black Door Room[15] began chanting that poem, which His Majesty overheard.

"What a superb response," he declared. "Far better than composing a poem of one's own."

102

One day around the end of the Second Month, the sky grew dark and a few snowflakes appeared, tossed about on a strong wind. One of the groundskeepers[16] came to the Black Door with a message, which I went to receive.

"From Consultant Kintō," the man said and gave me a piece of pocket paper[17] on which I read the final two lines of a poem:

12. An allusion to a famous Chinese poem by Bo Juyi (772–846) that contains the line "Gazing at the river and the whiteness of the moon." The empress's reply—literally, "You have said it"—recognizes both the allusion and the appropriateness of being lost in the moonlight in autumn, the season most often associated with the moon in classical Japanese literature.

13. The southern porticoes (*hisashi*) of the Seiryōden, used by senior courtiers when on palace duty.

14. A phrase from a Chinese poem by Ōe no Koretoki (888–963) recorded in *Wakan rōeishū* (*Songs for Singing, in Japanese and Chinese*, ca. 1013), a collection of Japanese *uta* (thirty-one-syllable poems) and Chinese couplets organized by subject matter that was compiled by Fujiwara no Kintō (966–1041), poet and scholar.

15. Kurōdo no Gosho. A room immediately north of the Seiryōden, the emperor's private chambers. The door between the interior and the room was paneled in blackened wood.

16. Caretakers of the palace grounds, who were often used as messengers.

17. One of the great scholars of the day (see note 14). *Futokorogami* or *kaishi* was the kind of paper used when recording poems for formal events and in correspondence.

Truly the air today
has the feel of spring.[18]

sukoshi haru aru / kokochi koso sure

Yes, I thought, he has captured today's scene well, and began racking my brains for some beginning lines to complete the effort.

When I asked who was with the consultant,[19] the names were all imposing ones, and of course there was Kintō himself, which meant I could not just toss something off. Feeling not up to the task on my own, I wanted to talk to Her Majesty before replying, but she was with the emperor in private, and the messenger was asking me to hurry. I realized that taking too much time would only make things worse, so I gave in, and with a trembling hand scribbled down these lines and sent him on his way:

In a cold sky,
one takes them for blossoms—
swirling flakes of snow.

sora samumi / hana ni magaete / chiru yuki ni

Afterward I was rather downcast, wondering how the men would judge my poem—wanting to have word on the one hand but not wanting to know if it turned out they hated it. In the end all I ever heard was from the captain of the Left Guards[20] (who was a middle captain then), who reported that Toshikata[21] had proclaimed, "Let's make Shōnagon a handmaiden."[22]

---

18. Kintō has sent the last two lines of an *uta*, called the *shimo no ku* (two seven-syllable lines), expecting Shōnagon to cap it with a *kami no ku* (in three lines of five, seven, then five syllables). The full poem would therefore read, "In a cold sky, / one takes them for blossoms— / swirling flakes of snow. / Truly the air today / has the feel of spring." The swirling flakes of snow look so like cherry blossoms that they give the sky the feel of spring.

19. She assumes that Kintō is with colleagues on duty in the Courtiers' Hall.

20. Identity uncertain.

21. Probably Minamoto no Toshikata, son of Takaakira (914–982).

22. *Naishi*, no doubt short for *naishi no jō*, referring to the third tier of women in the Handmaid's Office.

Things that sound better than usual: On New Year's Day, an oxcart, or a
rooster calling. At dawn, someone clearing their throat—and the same
goes for the sound of a musical instrument.

Things that lose by being painted: Pinks. Sweet flag. Cherry blossoms.
Men and women described as wonderful in tales. And as for things that
gain by being painted: Pine trees. Autumn fields. Mountain villages.
Mountain paths.

Winter should be cold and summer hot beyond anyone's experience.

It is in the Ninth Month, and the skies have cleared after a night of rain.
How captivating is the light of the morning sun gleaming in raindrops
fairly overflowing on the plants in the garden. And the way raindrops
cling to half-ravished spider webs in the open-weave fences and the
eaves above, looking like so many strings of white pearls—that is also
charming and beautiful.

As the sun rises higher, dew weighing heavy on the bush clover falls
and the branches recoil though no hand has touched them—a truly captivating sight. Having said that, though, I think it equally interesting that
to other people this may be of no interest at all.

Things with nothing to recommend them: A person who has not only bad
looks but bad character as well. Cleaning starch that has gone rancid.[23]

23. A problematic passage but probably referring to a rice by-product used as a starch in launder-
ing clothing.

People will hate my mentioning such things, but at this late date I cannot restrain myself from recording them.

And should I not mention the bamboo fire tongs used for a parting fire?[24] These things do exist, after all. I never thought anyone would ever read my jottings, so I have decided to just write whatever occurred to me, even things that are vulgar or odious.

148

Disgusting things: The underside of something sewn. Baby mice, still hairless, turned out of their nest. The seams of a leather garment before the lining's been put on. The inside of a cat's ears. An especially filthy-looking place in the dark.

A person of no consequence taking care of a passel of children. A man who has spent a long time looking after a wife he doesn't much care for must feel disgusted.

150

People who seem to have a hard time: The wet nurse of an infant who cries all night. A man involved with two women who gets jealous looks from both sides. An exorcist grappling with a stubborn spirit: he had expected a ready triumph, but things aren't going well, and he bears down even harder so as not to end up a laughingstock—truly a dilemma.

A woman loved by a man who is unreasonably suspicious.

Someone of consequence in the house of a man of high office cannot have an easy time of it—although he still has it easy.

A person upset over something.

157

Things that don't bode well: A flighty young man adopted as a son-in-law neglects his wife and then stops visiting at night.

24. After a funeral, a parting fire (*atobi*) was kindled at the gate after the casket had been brought out. The bamboo tongs used to kindle the fire were associated with death and thus fit only to be thrown away.

A man known for lying puts on a good face nonetheless and is given responsibility for something important.

A sailboat heading off in strong winds.

A person of seventy or eighty years who has been feeling poorly for some days.

159

Things that are close but distant: The Miyanobe Festival.[25] Siblings who don't like one another—or relatives who don't. The twisting path on the way to Kuramadera.[26] The last day of the old year and the first day of the new year.

160

Things that are distant but close: Paradise.[27] The path a boat takes. Relations between people.

171

A place where a woman lives alone moves the heart best if it is forlorn: everything rundown, earthen walls crumbling, pond grass growing in the pond—if there is a pond—and mugwort running rampant in the garden court, or if not that, at least some green grass growing up here and there through the gravel. For such a place to be well kept up and in fine repair, with the gate shut tight and everything in its proper place, is detestable.

177

When I began my service at the palace, occasions for embarrassment were many, and I was often close to tears. Night after night, I would attend

---

25. Held in the Twelfth Month, so actually close to the more prominent festivals of the New Year while being chronologically far from them from the perspective of the yearly calendar, which begins again on the first day of the First Month.
26. In the mountains north of the capital. The path to the temple was a series of steep switchbacks.
27. *Gokuraku.* A Buddhist term.

Her Majesty from behind a low-standing curtain, and she would deign to show me pictures, holding them out to me, though I was so overwhelmed that I could barely bring myself to put forth my hands and receive them. "See what is happening here," she would say, or, "Look at this now, look at that." For light we were using an oil lamp on a low-standing tray, so I felt as if my hair were under a scrutiny more rigorous than in the daytime, but still I put every effort into looking. It was a cold time of year, and the brief glimpse I had of her hands against the backdrop of sleeves of pale rose-plum hue was truly splendid. To one so recently come up from home, so lacking in experience, it seemed nearly beyond belief that the world could have such people in it.

At dawn one day I was anxious to withdraw, and Her Majesty quipped that I was shier than the god of Kazuraki,[28] but still I kept my eyes down, not wanting her to get even a side glance at me, and put off raising the shutters. When some serving women bustled in to put them up, however, she was listening and intervened, sending them away, though smiling at my expense. Then she asked me a few questions and continued trying to draw me out, finally saying, "You must be ready to go home, so run along—but be back early tonight."

No sooner had I begun edging away on my knees than servants were there to put the shutters up, and lo, snow was coming down. A lattice fence stands in front of the Tōkaden,[29] making the garden space seem narrow, and it was beautiful in the snow.

At midday, messengers came one after another, asking me to come up soon and reassuring me that in such a snowstorm I needn't worry about being seen. For her part, the senior lady in my cohort also began to hurry me along. "This is no good—you really can't stay holed up this way. For Her Majesty to favor you this way, to invite you in so conspicuously, why, that is a sure sign of favor. Disappointing her will not do." So, however beside myself with worry, I gave in and went. The fire huts piled with snow were a novel and captivating sight.

There in Her Majesty's rooms sat the usual square brazier, but none of her women were encroaching on her space. Just one senior lady sat

28. Notoriously ugly and shy about being seen.
29. Residence of the empress within the greater palace compound.

nearby. The empress herself had a round brazier of incense wood, lacquered with a pear-peelings pattern.[30] In the next bay, a number of women were crowded around a long brazier with their Chinese jackets pushed back off their shoulders. Seeing them so at ease made me envious. Passing letters about, getting up, sitting down—everything they did was so nonchalant as they chatted away with smiling faces. I was intimidated just thinking about how I could ever get along in such a world. Farther inside, three or four women seemed to be looking at pictures.

After a while, we heard a man in a firm voice announcing that "His Lordship" was arriving. Thinking it would be Lord Michitaka,[31] some women began to ready the room, picking up anything lying about. As for me, I thought I really should leave but was too taken aback to move quickly, so I withdrew a bit farther inside, still curious enough, however, to peek out through a gap in the curtains.

It turned out that it was not Lord Michitaka but rather Major Counselor Korechika.[32] He was wearing a formal robe and trousers of purplish red that stood out beautifully against the snow. Sitting down near a pillar, he said, "These past few days I have been in confinement,[33] but with all this snow I was concerned."

"I should have thought the roads would be 'gone beneath the snow,' "[34] Her Majesty said. "Why did you persist?"

He laughed. "So you would regard me as 'a person of true feeling,' of course."[35]

Such an elegant exchange, I thought—something that had the ring of an old romance.

Her Majesty was wearing white robes, with a scarlet jacket of Chinese damask over them. The way her hair cascaded down was like something I had seen in a painting but never in reality. It all felt like a dream.

30. A reference to *jin*, a kind of wood used to make incense. The pear-peelings pattern was created with flecks of gold and silver.
31. 953–995. Empress Teishi's father.
32. 974–1010. Teishi's brother.
33. *Monoimi.* Usually the result of a divination predicting trouble of some sort if the subject does not stay inside and abstain from certain kinds of activities.
34. An allusion to a famous poem by Taira no Kanemori (d. 990), in *Shūishū* (*Collection of Gleanings*, ca. 1006), poem 251 (topic unknown): "Here in the mountains, / the snow has fallen so deep / that the road is gone. / Who visits today I will deem / a person of true feeling" (*yamazato wa / yuki furitsumite / michi mo nashi / kyō komu hito o / aware to wa mimu*).
35. Korechika obviously picks up on his sister's allusion.

Lord Korechika began to chat and banter with the ladies. Listening to them responding without any hesitation and standing up to his blandishments, I felt almost dizzy and began to go red in the face in spite of myself. Korechika picked up a few nuts and offered some to Her Majesty as well.

Suddenly he seemed to be asking who that was behind the curtains, and, no doubt encouraged by what he heard in response, he stood and came my way. Surely he will pass by, I thought, but then there he was, right next to me, saying something, asking whether what he had heard about me before I came to court was true or not—while I, who had been embarrassed just glimpsing him in the distance, from behind a curtain of state—I simply couldn't believe that I was right there facing him, indeed, that any of this was even happening. Had he so much as glanced at my carriage as he passed by in an imperial procession, I would have put down the inner blinds and hidden behind my fan to be certain I would not be seen. Yet now, here and now, as I sat bathed in sweat and wondering what had possessed me to enter myself into court service—now I was supposed to answer his questions?

Next thing, he snatched away the fan that had been shielding me so well, leaving me ready to cover my face with my tresses but knowing all the while how desperate I must look. Inside, I was hoping he would just go away, but instead he kept examining the fan, asking who had commissioned the painting on it and showing no intention of giving it back— while I sat there with my head down, using the sleeve of my Chinese jacket as a shield, which was bound to get white spots on it and leave my face a piebald mess.

After an eternity, Her Majesty must have realized what an agony I was in, for she said to Korechika, "Come over here, tell me whose writing this might be."

"Give it to me," he said, "and I will take a look."

"No, you come here," she replied.

"But this lady won't let me go!" he said—a witty and fashionable thing to say, but so inappropriate given my status that I felt utterly mortified. Her Majesty then took out an album of draft-style calligraphy and began to look through it with him.

"I wonder about this one?" was the next thing he said. But then he went on, "Let's ask our lady there; surely she will recognize all the fine hands of the day," and continued trying to get an answer out of me, saying the most outrageous things in the process.

As if one such person wasn't enough, now someone announced another, this one also wearing formal robes, and he was an even more lively sort who proclaimed things in comic fashion and got laughter in response.[36] As they regaled my lady with stories about this or that courtier, I thought I must be listening to fantastic beings or angels descended to earth—though as the days went by and I gained experience in service at court, I learned this was not so unusual. All the other ladies looking on must have felt the same way when they began court service, and no doubt they too became accustomed to such things over time.

One day when Her Majesty was talking with me, she asked, "Do you truly care for me?"

I replied most respectfully, "My lady, how could I not?" As it happened, though, someone in the Table Room[37] sneezed loudly, just at that moment.

"Oh, how awful!" Her Majesty said. "You've been caught in a lie—that's all there is to that,"[38] and proceeded to go inside.

"Me, lie about such a thing," I thought to myself, "when my feelings go well beyond merely caring for her? No, it was not I that lied but the sneeze. And who could have done such a horrid thing? Sneezing is not polite, after all, and a person usually exercises more restraint—and at such a time!" But I was still so new to service that despite my frustration I could not bring myself to convey my feelings.

When dawn came, I went back to my room, and soon a letter came, in an elegant hand written on thin, pale-green paper:

How, I wonder—
how could I ever have known
that you had lied—

36. Most scholars identify this person as Michitaka.
37. *Daibandokoro*. The room where food was prepared for presentation to the emperor.
38. A sneeze was believed to be an unconscious attempt to "erase" some impending evil or trouble. The empress jokingly takes it as an attempt to cover up Shōnagon's statement—because, she reasons, it must have been a lie.

if not for the God of Correction
assisting me from the sky?[39]

ika ni shite / ika ni shiramashi / itsuwari o / sora ni tadasu no / kami nakariseba

The note said these were Her Majesty's words. My own reaction was a confused mix of joy and chagrin, and a desire to chastise the woman who had sneezed the night before:

Whether pale or rich,
a flower's hue we must assess
with our eyes.
How dismal to be misjudged—
and by an upturned nose![40]

ususa kosa / sore ni mo yoranu / hana yue ni / ukimi no hodo o / miru zo wabishiki

"Pray present this to Her Majesty," I wrote. "Surely the Diviner's God[41] will judge aright." After I sent the reply back, however, I remained upset and from time to time lamented that that sneeze had come just when it did.

183

The midday heat is beyond bearing and you simply must find a way to escape it, but your fan is doing no good and you're reduced to sticking your other hand in ice water. But then comes a letter on fine paper of a deep red hue attached to some Chinese pinks in full bloom, and you think of how hot he must have been writing it, and realize that his feelings cannot be shallow after all, and before you know it that fan you simply could not do without has been laid aside.

39. Tadasu no Kami. Deity of a shrine located in a grove of trees at the entrance to nearby Kamo Shrine.
40. Shōnagon's response revolves on a pun involving "flower" and "nose"—both pronounced *hana* in Japanese. Shōnagon insists on the steadfastness of her character (flower), complaining that she has been unfairly maligned by whoever sneezed.
41. Shiki no Kami. Enlisted to counter the reference to the god of Kamo Shrine.

What a delight it is, when staying near a broad avenue, to hear something from outside and discover there is a man passing by in a cart with the blinds up, enchanted by the dawn moon, intoning the lines of a poem—"On goes the wanderer, beneath the lingering moon."[42] Hearing a man chanting poems while going by on horseback is also a delight.

At such a place, one may also hear a man chanting, accompanied by the flapping of mudguards, only to discover, when you put your work down and get up to see who it is, that it is just some clod of common birth—truly disappointing.

187

For a man visiting a lady in court service to eat in her presence is just horrid, and the woman who gives him food is just as bad. If the one he loves shows she is ready to offer something, he's obviously going to take it—one can't expect him to close his mouth and turn his face away as if he were repulsed by the idea!

When a man is so thoroughly drunk that he has to stay over, I don't give him a thing to eat, not even warmed-up, leftover rice; and if he should think me heartless and decide never to visit again—well, then, so be it.

If one is at home and someone from the kitchens brings something in, there's nothing for it, but still one wishes they wouldn't.

211

Just after the twentieth of the Ninth Month, I was on my way to do pilgrimage at Hasedera,[43] staying in a flimsy little house. I was so worn out that I soon fell fast asleep, but how moved I was to wake late into the night and see moonlight from a window shimmering whitely on the

---

42. A line from a Chinese poem by Jia Dao (779–843), which Shōnagon probably knew from the *Wakan rōeishū*, poem 416 (see note 14).
43. Located in Sakurai City, modern-day Nara Prefecture.

robes of people sleeping near me. It is at such times that people are wont to compose poems.

215

In bright moonlight, crossing a stream, the ox pulling your carriage splashes through the water, as if shattering crystal into pieces—a delightful sight.

216

Things that are better big: Houses. Provision bags.[44] Monks. Fruit. Oxen. Ink blocks. If a man's eyes are too small, he looks too like a woman—though eyes big as metal bowls are menacing. Braziers. Ground cherries.[45] Kerria flowers. Cherry blossom petals.

217

Things that are better short: A piece of thread for a quick sewing job. The hair of lower-class women. The speech of an unmarried daughter. Lampstands.

223

Taifu no Myōbu,[46] a wet nurse in Her Majesty's service, was departing for Hyūga Province.[47] Among the fans she received as gifts was one that on one side had a scene of sunlight shining brightly on the buildings of a provincial seat and on the other a fine dwelling in the capital deluged by heavy rain—with a poem movingly written in Her Majesty's own hand:

> You must leave us now,
> going off toward the sun.
> But do remember—

44. Used for carrying food while traveling.
45. *Hōzuki.* After removing the pit, people would blow through the shell to make a noise. Evidently used as toys.
46. Identity uncertain.
47. Located in southeastern Kyushu. Read literally, the name means "going sunward."

that here in the capital
the rains will still weep down.

akane sasu / hi ni mukaite mo / omoiideyo / miyako wa hanarenu / nagame
suran to

How much Myōbu must have wished not to leave such a mistress
behind!

224

I was in seclusion at Kiyomizu Temple,[48] and Her Majesty sent a messenger all the way up there just to deliver a note to me. It was written in
draft script, on Chinese paper of reddish hue:

"How often I hear
the temple bell ring at dusk
from a nearby mountain!
Surely she must know
how often I think of her . . .

yama chikaki / iriai no kane no / koegoto ni / kouru kokoro no / kazu wa shiruran

and yet . . ."[49]

You do take your time.
I was traveling, and had neglected to bring any proper paper along, so
I wrote my reply on the purplish-red petal of a lotus flower.

232

Falling things: Snow. Hail. Sleet is unpleasant, but a delight when it falls
with white snow. Snow looks fine on a roof of cypress bark, especially
when it's on the verge of melting. It's also delightful when not much has

---

48. Located up the slope of one of the eastern hills of Kyoto.
49. This phrase continues the sentiment of the poem.

fallen, just enough to fill the grooves between the roof tiles, making them appear like black mounds. Rain showers. Hail, on wood-plank roofs. Frost is also pleasing on wood-plank roofs, or in gardens.

236

Clouds: White clouds, as well as purplish red clouds, black clouds—all are delightful. Rain clouds buffeted by the wind. The greatest delight is when dark clouds gradually vanish in the growing light of dawn—"Hues that depart with morn,"[50] as the Chinese poem says. A thin wisp of cloud in front of a bright, full moon is moving.

245

Truly terrifying things: Thunder in the night. A thief breaking in right next door. If a thief comes into your own house, you're too overcome to stop and think about what's going on. A fire nearby is also terrifying.

248

Surely nothing in this world could be more disheartening than being disliked. Who would be crazy enough to conclude, "Well, let them hate me!" and just give up? Yet the sad fact is that in the natural course of things, at court and even in the family circle, there are those who will be liked and those who will not.

Among the highborn, but also among the lower classes, people are quick to favor a child who is always noticed because of doting parents. And when the child is worthy of such care, it seems so logical that we conclude it couldn't be otherwise. But I find it especially moving when parents fuss over a child who is really nothing special simply because they are its parents.

50. Watanabe Minoru identifies this as a possible reference to another poem by Bo Juyi, in Sei Shōnagon, *Makura no sōshi*, ed. Watanabe Minoru, Shin Nihon koten bungaku taikei 25 (Tokyo: Iwanami shoten, 1991), 272n.15.

I can think of nothing more to be desired than to have the affection of those one serves, of one's parents, and of all others with whom one has dealings in life.

251

People who get angry at gossiping mystify me. How can one not talk about other people, after all? Aside from one's own concerns, the affairs of other people offer the best targets for one's wit.

Still, gossiping does feel mean; and if the victim hears of it, there may be resentment—which can do one harm. Thus when the person is somebody one dare not alienate, one thinks better of it and keeps one's mouth shut—even if in other circumstances one would come out with it and enjoy a good laugh.

279

A taboo or something[51] sends you home the long way around, and you arrive late at night, your jaw clenched and aching against the cold. Yet how delightful it is, as you settle in and pull the brazier close, to stir the fire and find some coals still brightly blazing, with not a burned-out spot to mar them. On the other hand, how hateful it is when you are so lost in conversation that you fail to see the fire's about to go out, and someone rushes in to put new coals in and revive it. If the coals are placed on the outside, with the fire still burning in the center, that is fine; but I find it irritating if someone rakes all the old coals aside, stacks new ones up in a pile, and lights a fire on top.

280

Lots of snow had fallen, yet strangely the shutters were still down. Coals had been stirred up in the braziers, and we were gathered around them chatting.

---

51. Specifically, a seasonal taboo that required one to avoid traveling in certain directions on certain days.

"Shōnagon," Her Majesty said, "is there snow on Kōro Peak?"[52]

She laughed when I promptly ordered the shutters raised and the blinds rolled up.

Some other women said they knew the poem and might have thought to refer to it in their own verses but had not made the connection, concluding that I was just the sort of person who should be in Her Majesty's service.

281

The boys who assist yin-yang masters[53] really know their job. When the master goes out to perform a purification service and begins reading from the scripture, others may slack off, but when the time comes to pour saké or water, the boy will always run over to perform his tasks without being told. I admire how they know the procedures so well that their master need never ask for anything, and I find myself wishing I could find someone so smart for my own employ.

———————

In these pages, I jotted down things I had witnessed and the thoughts of my heart while I was away from the palace at home, with nothing better to do and with no intention that anyone else should ever see what I had written. Because I knew it might prove an inconvenience in some quarters, I meant to keep my book hidden, but in that task I failed, to my own chagrin: the thing has gotten out.

The palace minister[54] presented Her Majesty with a quantity of paper. "What should we write on it, I wonder?" she asked. "In His Majesty's chambers they are making a copy of *The Book of History*."[55]

"Why not make a pillow of it?" I said. She responded by saying, "As you wish, then—take it away," and presented it to me. And so I proceeded to fill the paper—and a nearly endless quantity of it there was—with idle musings, most of them worthless and nonsensical.

52. Again, a reference to a poem by Bo Juyi, in which the speaker lifts the blinds to gaze up at the snow on Kōro (Ch. Xianglu) Peak.
53. Yin-yang masters were employed to perform divinations and purifications.
54. A reference to Korechika (see note 32).
55. *Shizi*, one of the Chinese classics.

For the most part, I have written about things that people find amusing and things that are sure to impress—poems, for example, but also topics like trees, grasses, birds, and insects; and I had thought that what I wrote would be bound to have people jeering at me. "My—it's worse than we thought," they would say, "How wanting she is in taste!" But the truth was that these were my thoughts alone: I simply wrote whatever occurred to me, for the pleasure of it, never thinking that anyone would compare my book with other writings or that I would hear people saying I did a passable job. Yet it seems that some people are saying I have quite put them to shame, which strikes me as strange indeed. I can only conclude that that is the way of the world: when people say good things about what they truly despise and disparage what they truly admire, they only reveal their own want of feeling.

When the middle captain of the left was still known as governor of Ise,[56] he came calling when I was at home, and my book was resting on the mat pulled over for him to sit on. I quickly tried to grab it, but he got ahold of it and took it away, and returned it to me only after quite a long time. It was after that that it began to make the rounds.

[*MAKURA NO SŌSHI*, ED. WATANABE MINORU, SHIN NIHON KOTEN
BUNGAKU TAIKEI 25 (TOKYO: IWANAMI SHOTEN, 1991)]

56. Minamoto no Tsunefusa (969–1023), who served as governor of Ise from 995 until 997.

2

Essays in Idleness

YOSHIDA NO KENKŌ

Yoshida no Kenkō (1283-ca. 1350) was a sometime petty official at the court of Emperor Go-Nijō (1285-1308; r. 1301-1308). After the emperor's death, Kenkō retired from court life and took the tonsure as a Buddhist monk in 1313. Although he was known more as a poet in his own time, it was his collection of essays, Tsurezuregusa (Essays in Idleness)—which began to circulate only posthumously—that secured his reputation in the centuries to come. In time, that collection came to be regarded as a founding text in the zuihitsu genre and an early articulation of what would come to be known—rightly or wrongly—as the so-called Japanese aesthetic of asymmetry, understatement, indirection, and modesty. Kenkō's musings, which touch, usually lightly, on a wide range of topics, show the influence of Buddhist and Daoist thought and Chinese and Japanese poetry at every turn, containing numerous references to specific texts from those traditions. I have noted only a sampling of these references in the footnotes.

Not all of Kenkō's entries are didactic; some of his anecdotes—many of them humorous—are in fact indistinguishable from those found in folktale collections. As is appropriate given the title of the work, Kenkō's style is elegant but not overly ornate. Furthermore, and also appropriately, no easily identifiable scheme of organization informs his jottings, which one can easily imagine as coming into the mind of their author during idle hours, without much planning, although surely not without the exercise of considerable rhetorical restraint.

The numbers of the following selections are from the edition edited by Kubota Jun (see bibliographic reference at the end of this chapter).

How foolish I feel when I realize that I have spent another day in front of my inkstone, jotting down aimless thoughts as they occurred to me, all because I was bored and had nothing better to do.

1

One may conclude that any man born into this world will find a multitude of things to desire.

The position of emperor is too awe-inspiring for words, and so too the princes, down to the last branch and leaf of the imperial tree—all of these being of august status as men not born of human seed. Likewise, it goes without saying that the regent,[1] first of all nobles, is to be envied; indeed, all nobles of sufficient rank to be granted the privilege of acting as escorts at court are truly impressive, so much so that their children and grandchildren retain some of that importance even if they have come down in the world. And on down through the lesser ranks, there are also those who may meet with success according to their various stations and look very self-satisfied, even though in reality they may be of little consequence.

The least enviable of men is the monk. Sei Shōnagon spoke the truth when she said that people think him no more than wood or stone.[2] Even when he is at the height of his influence, ordering people about and making a great display of his power, one cannot consider him that impressive. It is as the monk Sōga said: "Fame is a burden; and the monk who attains it may be transgressing the teachings."[3] The determined recluse is probably a better ideal.

One of course wants a man to be excellent in appearance and to bear himself well, but the man who is easy to listen to, speaks with charm,

1. *Ichi no hito* (literally, "personage number one"), referring to the imperial regent.
2. Sei Shōnagon, *The Pillow Book*, sec. 4 (chap. 1).
3. 917–1003. A recluse who lived on Tōnomine, a peak located on the southeastern edge of the Nara plain, he was known for his wizardry. The source of this quotation is unknown.

and never talks too much is the sort whose company I never tire of. For how lamentable it is when a man one had thought of as quite outstanding reveals himself to be inferior in character! A man's social status and looks are of course determined at birth; but if he resolves to progress in wisdom, what is there to stop him? To see a man of good looks and disposition but no education mixing with men of inferior status and disagreeable appearance who quite outstrip him in talent and treat him as of no account—that is indeed a regrettable sight. It is most desirable for a man to be trained in orthodox learning, the composition of poetry in Chinese and Japanese, and music.[4] Furthermore, it is splendid to observe a man whose knowledge of court custom and ceremony is a mirror for the conduct of others. Finally, the man of breeding is one who is able to write smoothly and in an acceptable hand, who has a voice good enough to lead songs, and who, though reluctant to partake when drink is pressed upon him, does not abstain from drinking entirely.

3

Superior though he may be in every other way, a man who has no capacity for love seems to lack something, like a fine saké cup without a bottom.

For a man in love is a true delight: his sleeves heavy with dew or frost, he drifts along toward no certain goal, taking great pains not to earn the complaints of his parents or the censure of the world; but, for all his trouble, his advances lead only to heartache, and most of the time he sleeps alone, on nights when he sleeps at all.

And yet it is good for a man not to give himself entirely to such pleasures, or to be regarded by women as too easy a mark.

4

One is inspired by the sight of a man who never forgets the life to come and is never lax in his attentions to the Way of the Buddha.

4. *Kangen no michi*, referring to the mastery of a musical instrument such as the koto, *biwa* (lute), or *fue* (flute).

It is best for a man who has suffered some setback not to be quick to shave his head and become a monk; rather, he should close his gate so that no one knows whether he's at home or not, and then pass the days quietly, with no particular expectations for the future.

Middle Counselor Akimoto[5] appears to have said that he wanted to "see the moon of exile—but without committing any crime."[6] One can understand how he must have felt.

7

Life would lose much of its attraction if it went on forever—if man did not melt away like the dew on Adashi Moor or drift off like the smoke over Toribe Mountain.[7] Its very uncertainty gives life its savor.

Look at other creatures, and you will see that none lives as long as man. There are even those like the mayfly, which dies waiting for evening, and the summer cicada, which lives to know neither spring nor autumn. Just being able to live one year to its fullest should be a source of contentment. The man who laments every passing day could go on for a thousand years and still feel it was all the dream of a single night. Besides, since we cannot live forever, what is to be gained by stretching out our years until we have become old and ugly? Long life means an abundance of shame. The best thing a man can do is die before he reaches forty. Once he goes beyond that age, the desire to mingle in society blinds him to proper embarrassment about the figure he cuts; and the affection inspired by his grandchildren in his sunset years makes him want to be spared to see them achieve success. His attachment to worldly things grows stronger and stronger, until he finally loses all ability to appreciate the charm of ephemerality—a most shameful end.

5. Minamoto no Akimoto (1000–1047).

6. This statement is attributed to Akimoto in various early sources, including the mid-Heian miscellany *Kōdanshō* (*Masafusa's Anecdotes*), *Kojidan* (*Anecdotes from the Past*, 1212–1215), and Kamo no Chōmei's *Hosshinshū* (*Awakening to Faith*, ca. 1216).

7. Both places, the first on the western outskirts of Kyoto and the second in Higashiyama, were used as cremation sites in the Heian period.

Nothing exceeds lust in the power to deceive the human heart. And what a foolish thing that heart is!

Scents, for instance, are transitory, and we know that perfume burned into robes lasts only a moment; yet still our hearts thrill at a wonderful fragrance.

The wizard called Kume reportedly lost his power to work wonders after seeing the white legs of a girl washing clothes[8]—something one can believe, since nothing is more beautiful than hands, legs, and skin that are fair, full fleshed, and lustrous.

10

One knows that it is only a temporary dwelling, but still it is a source of pleasure to have a house that suits one's needs and is just what one would like.

At the house where a man of breeding lives in quietude, even the moonlight seems to shine down with greater effect. Though neither modern nor ornate in style, such a place will be surrounded by venerable trees, and in the garden the grass will appear to grow as it pleases, most naturally; the verandas and openwork fences will be joined with exquisite workmanship, and the furnishings, all placed artlessly around the room, will give off an aura of the past, making the place seem comfortable and refined.

On the other hand, a house that carpenters have labored over and polished, full of rare and imposing furnishings, both Chinese and Japanese; a house where everything down to the trees and grasses has been so trained that not a trace of natural beauty remains—now that is truly an ugly and cheerless sight. How could anyone hope to live long in such a place? Just one look is enough to picture it going up in a puff of smoke.

8. Kume was a mountain ascetic. This story appears in various medieval collections of folktales, including *Konjaku monogatari* (*Tales of Times Now Past*, ca. 1120) and *Hosshinshū*. The wizard fell to earth after seeing the girl's legs while he was flying. According to legend, he married the woman but later dedicated himself again to Buddhist stringencies and regained his powers.

One can indeed tell the personality of someone from the sort of place he lives in.

Once the poet Saigyō[9] saw that the Go-Tokudaiji minister[10] had stretched a rope across the rooftop of his house to keep the kites from roosting there. "What would it hurt if kites were to perch there? So this is what the minister is really like!" Saigyō said. It is reported that he never visited the house again.[11] I remembered this incident when I saw a rope pulled along the roof ridge of the Kosaka Palace of the Ayanokōji prince.[12] Upon hearing my story, a man of the prince's household said, "The truth is that crows used to gather on the roof and catch frogs from the pond—something His Highness could not bear to watch." Why, of course, I thought, much impressed. I wonder if the Go-Tokudaiji minister might also have had a good reason.

11

Once, during the Godless Month,[13] I was passing through a place called Kurusu Moor[14] on my way to visit a friend in the hills nearby. Making my way down a long, narrow path covered with moss, I came upon a hut where someone was living a forlorn existence. Save for water dripping from a bamboo pipe buried in fallen leaves, there was not a hint of sound; and chrysanthemum blossoms and autumn leaves scattered about on the altar inside were the only indication that someone was indeed living there.

"Ah, so a man can live even in such a lonely state," I reflected, much moved at the thought. But then, in the garden beyond, I saw a large tangerine tree firmly fenced about on all sides—a sight that quite destroyed

9. 1118–1190. One of the most highly renowned of Japanese poet-monks.

10. Fujiwara no Sanesada (1139–1191).

11. This story appears in *Kokon chōmonjū* (*Things Seen and Heard, Old and New*, 1254), a medieval collection of folktales.

12. Identity uncertain. Perhaps Reverend Prince Shōe, a son of Emperor Kameyama (1249–1305; r. 1259–1274), who lived at Myōhōin, a Tendai-sect cloister.

13. Kannazuki, the Tenth Month of the lunar calendar, when all the gods met at Izumo Shrine and were thus absent from their usual residences.

14. Located probably somewhere in Uji, south of Kyoto in what is now the Yamashina area, although there was a place called Kurusuno north of the capital as well.

the effect of the place and left me thinking, "If only that tree hadn't been there!"[15]

13

To sit alone with a book spread out before you in the lamplight is one of life's greatest pleasures.

Among my own favorite books are the more engaging chapters of *Wen xuan*,[16] the collected poems of Bo Juyi,[17] the sayings of Laozi,[18] and the writings of Zhuangzi.[19] As for things written by scholars of our own country, I find many works of the past very captivating.

22

In all respects, I am drawn to things of ages past. Nowadays, standards of taste grow more vulgar all the time. Even in the fine furnishings crafted by our woodworkers, I am most pleased by those done in old styles.

Even when it comes to letters, I prefer the language I find on old scraps left from long ago. And the same is true of spoken language, which is also getting worse all the time. In the past, people would say, "Forward the coach!" or "Fetch the lamps!"; now they say, "Bring it on around!" and "Light 'em up!" When they ought to say, "Men of the Grounds Bureau—to your posts!" they say, "C'mon, torchers, let's have some light!" And instead of referring to the place where the emperor listens to lectures on the *Sutra of Golden Light*[20] as the imperial attendance chamber, they call it the lecture hall—a sad state of affairs, an old gentleman once lamented to me.

---

15. Opinions concerning what disappoints Kenkō about the presence of the fence vary. Some say that it showed the stinginess of its owner; others, that the imposition of a man-made structure in a natural space ruined the aesthetic effect.

16. *Monzen* (*Selections of Literature*), a large collection of Chinese writings made up of works gleaned from a thousand years of history, beginning with the Zhou dynasty (starting in 1122 B.C.E.).

17. 772–846. The most widely read Chinese poet among Japanese readers in classical times.

18. Legendary Zhou-dynasty (1046–256 B.C.E.) author of the *Daodejing*.

19. Daoist thinker of the mid-fourth to early third centuries B.C.E.

20. Over a period of five days in the Fifth Month, monks from prominent temples came to the place in question to read from the *Kongōmyōsaishōō* (Skt. *Suvarṇaprabhāsa-sūtra*, literally, *Sutra of the Supreme Golden Light*) as a prayer for the safety of the nation and the health of the sovereign.

23

One hears it said that ours is a degenerate time, the age of the End of the Law.[21] Yet how far from that world, how rare a delight is the venerable air that dominates the ninefold imperial palace.

The Open Stage, the Dining Court, the Chamber of This, the Gate of That—such names sound splendid as a matter of course. But at the palace even the names of things that may likewise be found in the commonest dwellings—half shutters, small-plank floors, high sliding doors, and the like—have a most delightful ring. And how splendid it is to hear the command "Prepare for night!" from the Guards' Hall, or the call "Bring the lamps—and make haste, now!" from the imperial bedchamber. At such times, the looks of self-satisfaction on the faces of senior nobles as they go about their duties in the Guards' Hall are to be expected; but to find the same expressions among the minor men of the palace staff is amusing indeed. And what comical sights the same men make when you see them napping here and there on a chilly night! Once the Tokudaiji chancellor[22] declared of the chimes in the Repository of the Sacred Mirror[23] that they made "a most delightful and elegant sound."

25

Our world is a place as changeable as the pools and shallows of the Asuka River: time moves along, things pass away, happiness is overtaken by sorrow; a splendid dwelling becomes a field without inhabitants, while another house stays the same on the outside but has new occupants, leaving us with no one who can share in our reminiscences, as the peach and plum blossoms are unable to speak.[24] And the ephemerality of things is

---

21. *Sue no yo* or *masse*. A period of decline and degradation that many Buddhists of the time believed to have begun in the mid-Heian period.

22. Identity uncertain. Perhaps Tōin Kintaka (1253–1305).

23. The room in the palace where the sacred mirror—one of the imperial regalia—was held in safekeeping.

24. An allusion to a line of Chinese poetry by Sugawara no Funtoki (899–981): "O blossoms of the peach and plum, you will not say how many springs have passed" (*Wakan rōeishū* [*Songs for Singing, in Japanese and Chinese*, ca. 1013], Nihon koten bungaku taikei 73 [Tokyo: Iwanami shoten, 1965], poem 548).

all the more intense at the site where once stood the mansion of a great man of the remote past whose glory we never even saw.

The grand designs of His Lordship Michinaga[25] are still visible in the Kyōgoku Mansion and Hōjōji.[26] But how heart-struck one is to see how time has altered them! When he labored over those buildings, and provided for their maintenance by grants from private estates, he was doubtless convinced that his house would flourish into the distant future as the abode of the emperor's guardians and the chief pillar of the state—never envisioning a time in which the places would fall so completely into ruin. The main gates and the Golden Hall lasted until quite recently; but during the Shōwa era [1312–1317] the south gate burned down, and since then the Golden Hall has fallen over and remains in a state of collapse, with no sign that it will ever be put right again. Only the Muryōjūin survives as a reminder of the past, with its row of nine sixteen-foot Buddhas still inspiring awe.[27] And still impressive are the plaque with calligraphy by Kōzei[28] and the door inscribed by Kaneyuki,[29] whose strokes remain vivid to this day. And the Lotus Hall is still standing as well. But how long will even these last? Here and there in the temple precincts are places that show no such traces of their past, except for an odd foundation stone; today no one knows anything about those places at all.

In all things it is vain to make plans for a future we will never see.

27

How terribly forlorn it is when, after the Abdication Banquet, the three regalia—the Sword, the Necklace, and the Mirror—are formally transferred to the new emperor.[30]

I understand that our recently retired sovereign[31] wrote this poem the spring of the year in which he stepped down from the throne:

25. Fujiwara no Michinaga (966–1027), the most prominent of Heian-period Fujiwara potentates.
26. Both sites of Michinaga's palaces in Kyoto that were in ruins by Kenkō's time.
27. Located in the precincts of Hōjōji.
28. The Chinese reading of the given name of Fujiwara no Yukinari (972–1027), a famous calligrapher.
29. Minamoto no Kaneyuki (precise dates unknown), another famous calligrapher.
30. The transfer of the three imperial regalia was one of the rituals involved in the ascension of a new emperor.
31. A reference to Emperor Hanazono (1297–1348; r. 1308–1318).

Even the groundsmen
who once were in my service
no longer come—
leaving my courtyard unswept,
strewn with windblown flowers.

*tonomori no / tomo no miyatsuko / yoso ni shite / harawanu niwa ni / hana zo
chirishiku*

Preoccupied with all the official functions of the new reign, people
no longer visit the old sovereign, who seems a lonely figure. It is in such
situations that people's true feelings become known.

28

There is no time more moving than a period of national mourning.[32]
　The very appearance of the temporary palace is a poignant sight, with
its plank floors low to the ground, its blinds of rough reed stalks and
valances of coarse cloth, its rustic furnishings. Even the attire of the attendants—down to their swords and decorative sword belts—is different
from usual and most affecting.

29

In times of quiet thought, I realize that of all feelings the most difficult to
suppress is longing for things past.
　After all is quiet, with everyone in bed, I often while away the long
night hours by putting the things around me in order; and as I throw out
notes I would not want left behind, I come across a scrap of calligraphy or
an idle drawing by one who is no longer with us and feel exactly as I did
back then. Or then again I find a letter written by a friend still living but
sent long ago and am moved deeply as I wonder what the occasion might
have been, or in what year it was written. It is somehow sad to think that
the things that have become one's own over time will go on, oblivious
and unchanging, long after one is gone.

32. *Ryōan.* A one-year period during which a reigning sovereign and his court mourned the death
of an imperial parent.

On a morning made beautiful by snowfall from the night before, I sent off a letter to a person with whom I needed to correspond. In reply to my note, which had said nothing of the snow, she wrote back, "Am I expected to consent to the requests of a man so ill-natured that he fails even to ask me how I am liking the snow?" What an amusing thing to say!

Now that the lady is no longer with us, I find even so minor an incident impossible to forget.

32

Once, around the twentieth day of the Ninth Month, I made good on an invitation to visit a certain gentleman and spent the night with him, walking about enjoying the moon. Remembering an acquaintance along the way, the man showed me the woman's house and then went inside. Waiting in the rundown, dew-drenched garden, I caught scent of a most discreet perfume that could not have been prepared for our visit. The snatches of conversation I overheard left me deeply moved.

In good time, my friend emerged from the house. But I was still so taken with the elegance of the scene that I hid myself and watched to see the woman slide open the double doors and gaze up at the moon. How disappointing it would have been had she just locked the door and withdrawn immediately into her rooms! Since she could not have known that anyone would be staying around to watch what she did, her behavior can only have been the result of a practiced sensibility. I heard later that not long thereafter the lady died.

38

What utter foolishness it is to use oneself up in the search for fame and profit, with never a moment's peace, making life a constant toil.[33] Much wealth has a way of consuming life: it is an agent that invites danger, beckons trouble. And after your death, even if you have left behind a pile

33. This whole section is laden with references to Chinese poems and texts such as *Zhuangzi* and *Wen xuan*.

of riches high enough to make a pillar for the North Star, it will bring only grief to your heirs. The pleasures that delight the eye of a foolish man are simply not worth the trouble. A man of sensibility thinks of big carriages, fat horses, and ornaments of jewels and gold as entirely useless things. Better to abandon your gold to the mountains and throw your jewels into a deep pool. Only an utter fool troubles himself over a desire for profit.

Of course, anyone would like to leave behind a name that will last far into the future. But do we call superior only those of high rank and exalted status? No: for we know of many foolish and quite stupid men born into fine houses who, blessed with opportunity, advanced to high rank and lived most glamorous lives; and there are also many sages and holy men who, not meeting with good fortune, resigned themselves to low status and ended in obscurity. Next to desire for profit, desire for a lasting name is most foolish.

Again, one wants to leave behind a reputation for excellence in learning and character. But consider the matter carefully, and you will realize that to love praise really means only that you find joy in the commendation of others. And neither those who praise nor those who condemn last long in this world. Those who have heard what such men have to say are likewise quick to disappear. So whose low opinion should we fear? Whose recognition should we desire? Indeed, it is a high reputation that lays the foundation for slander. No good comes from leaving a high name after one is gone. After a desire for fame and profit, this is the next most foolish thing.

Now, as to those who seek knowledge out of a desire to become wise. I would say that with wisdom comes falsehood, and with great ability comes an increase in harmful passions. True wisdom is not something heard from another or learned through study. And what is true wisdom anyway? What one should do and should not do are part of a continuum. And what are we to call "good"? A man of true excellence has no knowledge, no virtue, no accomplishments, no fame. Who can know of him? Who can make him known? And this is not because he hides his virtue or keeps his stupidity to himself but because he is beyond the realm of wisdom or folly, virtue or vice.

If a man is deluded enough to seek fame and profit, he will end as I have described. All desire must be denied. There is nothing worth talking about; there is nothing worth wanting.

43

Once, toward the end of spring, beneath mild, fair skies, I happened by a noble-looking mansion set well back in spacious grounds, with venerable trees all around and a garden strewn with fallen blossoms that I could not pass by without venturing in for a better look. The southern exposure of the main building was entirely open, with the shutters all down, and there seemed to be no one about. However, going around to the eastern side, I caught sight, through a door left conveniently ajar and a tear in the reed blinds within, of a man of fine features who looked to be perhaps twenty years old. Though at his leisure, he was most dignified and elegant in manner, looking down at a book spread out before him on a desk.

Even now I would like to find out who he was.

52

At Ninnaji[34] there was a certain monk who, although already advanced in years, had never visited Iwashimizu Hachiman Shrine.[35] Regretting this fact, he resolved to go, setting off on foot to make his pilgrimage. He did his obeisances at Gokurakuji and at Kora;[36] then, thinking that that was all there was to the place, he went back home.

Upon returning, he met one of his comrades. "Well," the monk said, "I've finally done what I've been thinking about all these years, and the shrine was more grand than I had heard it to be. But, tell me: Why was it that all the other pilgrims there climbed on up the mountain? I wanted to see for myself, but my intent was only to worship the god, so I didn't go up."

It appears that even in the smallest things it is best to have a guide.

34. A temple located west of Kyoto.
35. A prominent shrine located in Yamashiro Province, not far from Kyoto.
36. Subsidiary temples located at the foot of the mountain on which the main shrine buildings sit.

Here's another story about a monk at Ninnaji.

This happened at a farewell party for an acolyte who was about to go off and become a full-fledged monk. Caught up in the revelry and thoroughly drunk, one of the other monks got up to take his turn at entertaining the group and made to put a three-legged cauldron over his head. Since it would not go on smoothly, he flattened his nose and pushed the cauldron down over his face, and then began to dance around, much to the amusement of all assembled.

After dancing for a while, the monk tried to pull the cauldron off, but to no avail. At this, everyone sobered up and began wondering what to do. First one way, then another, they tried pulling the pot off, scraping the monk's neck until blood flowed; but his neck only swelled up, making it difficult for him to breathe. Then they tried to break the pot, but it would not be broken, and the reverberations were too much for him to bear. Now quite at a loss for what to do, they put a cloak over the three legs of the pot, gave the monk a stick for support, and took him by the hand off to a doctor in Kyoto. Along the way, everyone stared at the monk in wonderment.

What a strange sight the monk must have presented sitting there in front of the doctor! He spoke, but his voice was so muffled that his words could not be made out. "There's nothing in my books about a situation like this," the doctor said. "Nor is there anything about it in the oral teachings." So the monk went back to Ninnaji, where his aged mother and other close friends gathered around his pillow, crying and lamenting his fate—though one doubts that he could even hear them. With the situation getting no better, one man said, "Even if we take off his ears and nose doing it, we have to save his life. Let's just grab on and pull with all our might." So they took dry rice stalks and pushed them up between his head and the metal and pulled as if to yank his head off. In the process, they did leave only holes in place of his ears and nose, but they did at last succeed in freeing him. The story has it that the monk survived in the end but was ill for a very long time.

A house should be designed for summer. In winter, you can stay any-where; but it's hard living in a house that's no good in the heat. Deep water doesn't seem to cool; it's shallow water flowing fast that refreshes. When you're reading tiny writing, a room with sliding door panels pro-vides more light than one with hinged shutters. A room with a high ceil-ing is cold in winter and dark when lit by lamplight. I once heard a dis-cussion in which it was concluded that a house containing some unused space is nice to look at and can be put to all sorts of purposes.

58

Some people say, "If you are dedicated to the Way, where you live makes no difference. What difficulty can it present to your hopes for the next life if after taking vows you stay at home, still mixing with family and friends?" But those who say such things know nothing about how to pre-pare for the life to come. One who aspires to overcome the cycle of life and death can surely have no interest in serving his lord morn and eve, or in the day-to-day business of running a household. The mind is moved by its surroundings, after all: without quietude, the Way is hard to pursue.

People today cannot match the capacities of those of old. Even if they go off into the mountain groves, they need some means of staving off hunger and protecting themselves from storms. How, then, can they not give the appearance of having worldly desires on occasion? Yet it is go-ing too far to say that there is no use in leaving the world, that one may as well not abandon lay life. For even if a man who has entered the Way and turned his back on the world still has some desires, they will not resemble in number or intensity the desires of a man still embroiled in mundane affairs. With his paper bedclothes, his rough hempen robes, his one rice bowl, and his herb broth, will such a man be a drain on others? His demands are easily answered; his heart is quickly satisfied. And even if he does harbor some desires, he is still somewhat shy because of his status, so he will usually retreat from evil and move toward good.

Certainly a man should try somehow to sever his worldly bonds while in this life, in token of his being born a man. He who puts all his effort into worldly gain and makes no attempt to pursue higher understanding is really no different from the beasts.

72

Things that seem common: too many furnishings where one is sitting; too many brushes around an inkstone; too many Buddhas in a home chapel; too many stones and trees and bushes in a garden courtyard; too many children and grandchildren in a house; too many words used when talking to people; too much praise for oneself in a written petition.

Things that don't offend good taste even if numerous: books on a book cart; trash on a trash pile.

74

Like ants they crowd together, hurrying off east and west, running along north and south. Some are noble, others common; some are old, others young. All of them have places to go and homes to return to. At night, they go to bed; in the morning, they get up. But what do they hope to accomplish in their comings and goings? Greed for long life, desire for greater wealth—these are things that never come to an end.

What do they think to gain by preserving their lives? All that awaits them is old age and death, which are quick to come and never rest for a minute, leaving them little to truly enjoy. Yet still there are those who wander in error, fearing nothing. Some stay infatuated with fame and profit because they have never given a thought to their final destination. And then there are the fools who lament their fate, pleading to live on forever because they are ignorant of the universal principle of change.

78

I simply cannot abide people who get ahold of the latest fad and then spread its praises all about. More admirable by far is the kind of man who learns of such things only after they are old news. When a new person arrives at a gathering, some man lacking in both understanding and breeding can be counted on to bring up topics already familiar to himself and his companions, exchanging cryptic phrases and clever glances, with much laughter—all in a way that makes the new person feel completely uninformed.

81

When the painting or calligraphy adorning a screen or a sliding door is clumsily done, one is less critical of the work itself than of the master of the house. For it is all too often the case that a man's accoutrements serve to show the inferiority of his sensibility. By this I don't mean that one must allow oneself only the finest of possessions. Rather, I speak of those who make things tasteless and ugly in an attempt to make them sturdy, or who out of a desire to be original end up filling their homes with useless things that reveal only the fussiness of their owner. The best furnishings are those that seem a little old, are not terribly pretentious, and stand up over time.

82

Once when someone remarked that silk was unsatisfactory as a backing for picture or book scrolls because it showed wear too readily, Tonna[37] replied, "On the contrary, I find that it's only after the silk has frayed at top and bottom and some of the mother-of-pearl has fallen from the roller that a scroll becomes truly attractive." This is an excellent sentiment. In the same way, while most people say that if a set of books is not uniform it is not pleasing to the eye, I am persuaded by the comment of Bishop Kōyū[38] on the subject: "To insist on complete sets of things shows a lack of discernment. Incompleteness is far superior."

Another person has said this: "To want everything uniform and complete shows bad taste. Leaving things imperfect is more pleasing and gives one a future to look forward to. When a palace is built, something is always left unfinished." Indeed, even among the Confucian and Buddhist classics written by the ancient sages, there are many missing chapters.

37. 1289–1372. A contemporary poet and friend of Kenkō's.
38. Precise dates unknown. A monk of Ninnaji who was also a contemporary of Kenkō's.

How many are the things that work within other things to waste and spoil! The body has lice; a house has mice; a country has brigands; the common man has wealth; the man of high station has benevolence; and the monk has his Law.[39]

Once a man went to call on a lady who was living rather despondently in a rundown, out-of-the-way house to which she had withdrawn during a time of personal trial. It was still early in the month, and as the man searched quietly for the house in the dim moonlight, the dogs of the place came toward him, barking so ferociously that they brought out a kitchen maid. She asked him who he was, and he persuaded her to let him into the house.

For a few minutes, he stood on the crude wooden floor in the hallway, wondering how the lady could bear to stay in so wretched a place, until a woman's voice, composed but youthful, said, "Come this way, sir." A sliding door then opened—not too smoothly—and he went inside.

The interior was not in such a sorry state; indeed, it looked very dignified in the glow from a lamp at the other end of the room, whose light, albeit faint, made it possible to see the comeliness of the furnishings. And the scent of incense, which had obviously been burning since well before his appearance, made the place seem a more comfortable one in which to live.

"Shut the gate," someone said, adding, "and it may rain, so pull the carriage in under the gate roof. Then find a place for his men to sleep." This was followed by whispering: "Ah, maybe tonight at least we'll get some rest." Despite the speaker's attempts to be discreet, the quarters were so close that the visitor could not help overhearing.

39. In his fourth and fifth examples, Kenkō echoes the Daoist work *Zhuangzi*, which argues that both the petty man who seeks wealth and the gentleman who cultivates the Confucian virtue of benevolence are equally guilty of failure "to follow the true form of their inborn nature" (*The Complete Works of Chuang Tzu*, trans. Burton Watson [New York: Columbia University Press, 1968], 103).

The night went by, and as the man was relating what had gone on in his life since their last meeting, the first cock crowed. He went on, speaking with great earnestness both of the past and of the future, until the cock crows became more urgent, and more frequent, making him wonder if perhaps the day had already dawned outside. But since the lady's house was hardly the sort of place one needed to leave under cover of night, he took his time. Only when he could see the white of daylight through the crack in the door did he rise to go, choosing final words of parting the lady would not be likely to forget. It was early in the Fourth Month, and the faint dawn light made the treetops and garden plants glow in lovely green hues that impressed the man with their beauty and charm. Even today, he often remembers the scene, and takes care when he passes the house always to gaze at it until the great cinnamon tree above it disappears from sight.

105

It was a time when the unmelted snow in the shade of the north side of my house had turned to ice, and even the shafts of a carriage parked there glistened with frost. The dawn moon shone brightly, although partially obscured. At a chapel in an unfrequented section of the city, a quite proper-looking man was sitting with a woman near the veranda, at the threshold of an inner room. The two were talking, and whatever it was they were talking about, they gave no sign of tiring of it. The woman's face and features were very fine; and her perfume, when a hint of it came to me on the wind, was most charming. What snatches of their conversation I caught left me wanting to hear more.

107

During the reign of Emperor Kameyama, there were some ladies in his service who, convinced that it was the rare man who could give a quick and estimable response to a woman's query, made it a point to test every young man coming to the palace. "Have you ever heard a cuckoo?" they would ask. One man, who I understand went on to become a major counselor, answered, "No. Men of my low station cannot hear such things." The Horikawa Minister,[40] on the other hand, declared, "Yes. I seem to recall hearing one at Iwakura."[41] When they discussed the matter, the ladies deemed the minister's response satisfactory. Of the other man, however, they concluded, "But to say one is of too low a status to hear such things—now that was a bit much."

A man should be taught from his youth how to avoid being laughed at by women. I believe I heard somewhere that it was thanks to the care Lady Ankimon'in[42] took in training him as a boy that the former Jōdoji Regent[43] was so adept at conversation. The Yamashina Minister of the Left[44] once declared, "I'm so ill at ease around women that I have to be on my guard even with serving girls." If there were no women in the world, we could don our robes or wear our caps any way we wanted, and no man would take any care with his appearance at all.

From this one might conclude that women must be splendid beings indeed to make men feel so at a loss. But the fact is that women are by nature perverse—self-centered in the extreme, intensely greedy, and with no concept of reason. Their fickle hearts are quick to follow delusion; and their words flow too easily one moment, only to cease the next when one asks for a response to even the most innocent question. And don't think this silence shows reserve, either, for they may also come forth with the most astonishing things without even being asked. So well devised and highly polished are their statements that you may even think them superior to men in intellect. But when their deceptions come out later, will they ever admit them? No: dishonest and stupid, that is what a woman is. How disgusting it is to see any man following a woman around, trying to gain her favor! Why would anyone let himself be humiliated so? Even if there were such a thing as an intelligent woman, one can be sure that she would be aloof and without charm. Only when you let her wiles become your master does a woman seem attractive and worthy of attention.

40. Minamoto no Tomomori (1249–1316), known as the Horikawa Palace Minister.
41. An area northeast of Kyoto.
42. D. 1286. One of the consorts of Emperor Go-Horikawa (1212–1234; r. 1221–1232).
43. Fujiwara no Moronori (1273–1320).
44. Fujiwara no Saneo (1217–1273).

There are seven kinds of people who make bad friends. First is the man of high and noble station; second is the man still young in years; third is the strong man who never falls ill; fourth is the man who likes saké; fifth is the strong-willed man of arms; sixth is the man who tells lies; seventh is the man who is exceedingly worldly.

There are three kinds of people who are good to have as friends. First is the friend who gives you things; second is the man of medicine; third is the friend who has wisdom.

The most essential accomplishments for a man are, first of all, to be well versed in the classics and knowledgeable in the writings of the sages. Next, a man should have a good hand: even if he does not make calligraphy his chief study, he should learn it for the great help it will be in all other forms of scholarship. Next, a man should study the medicinal arts, for without medicine one cannot provide for one's own health, be of help to others, or fulfill one's duties and filial obligations. Then come archery and horseback riding, two of the Six Arts,[45] and both well worth looking into. Thus training in letters, arms, and medicine is indispensable. Those who gain these skills will never be called useless. Next, since food is what sustains life, the man who can prepare tasty meals has a great advantage. And then comes skill with one's hands, which is useful in all sorts of ways.

When it comes to other matters, however, one must remember that to be skilled in many things is unseemly in a gentleman. Talent in poetry and excellence in music have always been considered elegant avocations that a gentleman should pursue with devotion. In our time, however, we seem no longer to rely on such means to govern the world, just as we recognize gold as the most excellent of metals but deem it less versatile than iron.

45. A list of accomplishments considered essential for the gentleman in ancient China: ritual, music, archery, horseback riding, calligraphy, and ciphering.

When changing something would result in no benefit, it is best not to change it.

Should we look at the blossoms only in full bloom, or the moon only when unobscured by clouds? No: for to yearn for a moon hidden behind rain clouds or to be inside drawn blinds and unaware of the progress of spring is equally moving and a source of great charm. Indeed, boughs on which flowers are about to bloom, a garden strewn with fallen blossoms—these are things that are truly worth seeing. After all, is a poem prefaced with "Going to see the blossoms and finding them already fallen" or "Unable to see the blossoms" inferior to one introduced with "Seeing the blossoms"? To sigh after fallen blossoms or the setting moon is only natural; but only a truly insensitive person would say, "These boughs are bare now—there's nothing left to see."

In everything, it is beginnings and endings that are of greatest interest. Does love between a man and a woman refer only to when they are together? To suffer misery when one must give up before ever meeting the object of one's affections; to lament a pledge that has come to nothing; to stay up through a long night alone, with one's thoughts as far away as the clouds; to sit in a reed-choked house thinking of the past—this is what love really means. Rather than gazing out on a moon shining unimpeded over a thousand leagues, it is more moving to wait for the waning moon near dawn, when it takes on a greenish hue. And certainly nothing could be more moving than to see moonlight shining through cryptomeria branches deep in a wood, or to look at the moon as it hides behind masses of clouds that have just brought rain showers. The way the moonlight on scrub oaks makes the leaves glisten as if wet is striking indeed, making one wish for a friend of fine sensibility to share it with, and for a quick return to the capital.

And do we really see the moon and blossoms only with our eyes? One is more certain to be captivated when staying inside the house in springtime, or imagining the autumn moon from one's bedchamber. For the man of breeding never flaunts his tastes and is reserved even when deeply impressed. Only a rustic shows his admiration with no restraint. When he goes to see the cherry blossoms, he works his way forward through the throng, his eyes so fixed on the blossoms that he has not a glance for those he pushes aside; then he drinks his saké, composes some linked verse, and leaves, thoughtlessly breaking off a big branch to take home with him. At a spring, he has to soak his hands and feet; when there's snow, he gets down on it and leaves his footsteps behind. Never is he able to enjoy anything from a proper distance.

Such people have a curious way of watching the Kamo Festival.[46] "The procession's slow in coming," they say. "There's no use sitting here on the stand waiting." So off they go to a shack at the rear to amuse themselves by drinking, eating, and playing *go* and backgammon. But they leave someone to keep a lookout for the procession, and when he calls out, "It's coming!" they all rush back, nearly knocking one another down in their resolve to get to their places and miss nothing. "Would you look at that! Look what's coming!" they say, remarking on everything that goes by. Then, after one group has passed in parade, they say, "Tell us when the next group's coming!" and get down from the stands again. Such people seem to come only to see the processions themselves. The highborn of the capital, in contrast, occasionally nap, showing no desire to see everything. Their servants are up and down, serving their masters, but even those in attendance on the high ones, seated behind their masters, never lean forward in an unseemly manner or make an effort to see everything that goes by. [Final paragraphs omitted.]

140

A wise man will not leave any treasures behind after his death. If he has saved things of no worth, he will seem ridiculous, and if he has stored things of value, he will appear to have been vain and silly. And it is particularly regrettable if he has left a vast array of things behind, for there are sure to be those who will cry, "I'll have this!" and start bickering over his

46. More properly called the Aoi Festival. One of the premier events of the court calendar, held in the Fourth Month at Kamo Shrine.

goods—a most undignified scene. Certainly, it would be better to pass on whatever things he has decided should go to particular people while he is still alive. There are, of course, some few things that one cannot do without in one's daily life; but otherwise one is better off owning nothing.

145

When the escort Hada no Shigemi[47] said of the Shingan of Shimotsuke, of the North Guards,[48] "His is the face of a man who will fall from his horse; he should take care," no one believed he could be right. But Shingan did indeed fall from his horse and die. Then people thought that the words of Shigemi, a man expert in the art of reading faces, must be as sure as the words of the gods.

When someone asked him just what in the man's face boded such a fate, however, Shigemi replied, "I could see that his seat wasn't too firm in the saddle, and he liked unruly horses; that's why I made the pronouncement. Have I ever been wrong before?"

146

When Abbot Meiun[49] asked a face reader whether his countenance boded danger from weapons of war, the face reader replied most respectfully, "Yes, I fear it does." The abbot went on, "What sign is it that you see, then?" To this the man replied, "Why, a man of My Lord's status should have no fear of being killed in such a way; that you even asked me the question is itself a sign that there may be danger to come." As it turned out, the man was right: it was an arrow that did the abbot in.[50]

47. In service to Retired Emperor Go-Uda (1267–1324; r. 1274–1287).
48. Identity unknown. The North Guards (Hokumen no Bushi)—so called because their guard quarters were located in the northern section of the palace—were the personal guards of the retired emperor.
49. 1115–1183. The head priest of the Tendai sect.
50. The abbot was killed by a stray arrow in 1183 during a battle in which he had imprudently become involved.

Recently, some people have been saying that a man who has too many burns from moxa treatments is ritually unclean and should forbear from participation in Shinto rites, but in the regulations I find no evidence of such a rule.

149

One mustn't put the new antlers of a deer up to one's nose and smell them. There are little bugs inside them that crawl in through your nose and eat your brain.

150

People who aim to master an art seem to say to themselves, "While I'm still not too good at this, I'll keep it to myself and not let anyone know what I'm doing. People will be more impressed if I practice in private and show myself only after I've developed true skill." But anyone who says such things will never learn a single art well. For it is the man who mingles with the masters even as a beginner, undaunted by ridicule or laughter, always pushing ahead coolly—it is that man, even if he has no special gift from birth, who will not stumble along the way or become too casual in his attitude. As the years pass, such a man will surpass one with natural gifts but no dedication, in the end arriving at a higher level of performance, expanding his talent constantly, and gaining the high opinion of the public as an artist of matchless reputation.

There are some who are recognized by the whole world as experts who in the beginning were thought clumsy, and who indeed had faults. But by strictly following the standards of their art, dedicating themselves in selfless toil, they attained acceptance as authorities, serving as teacher to many. This is true in all the arts.

The man who would follow the ways of the world should first learn to sense the mood of the moment. A word spoken out of turn will grate on the ear of the listener, offend his sensibilities, and lead to no good end. Thus one would do well to recognize such exigencies. But falling ill, bearing children, and dying—these things alone follow no schedule; untimely or not, they cannot be put off. The truly crucial events—being born, taking on years, going through changes, the final dissolution—these flow on like the waters of a raging river, stopping never for a moment, continuing always on course. And in the same way, when it comes to the truly important things—whether in lay life or after one has taken holy orders—one should not stop to consider the prevailing moods but instead stride on without hesitation.

Summer doesn't begin only after spring has ended, nor does autumn come only with summer's demise. Rather, in time the spring itself begins to feel like summer; and in summer, autumn already appears. Then autumn suddenly turns cold, and it is the Tenth Month, the first month of winter—but with weather again springlike as the grass turns green and buds swell on the flowering plum. And even with falling leaves, it isn't that new growth comes out after the leaves have fallen, but rather that the leaves fall because of pressure from below. So great is the pressure from within that the opportunity comes and is taken with the greatest speed. Even more rapid, however, are the changes of human life—birth, aging, illness, and death—compared with which the seasons follow a determined order. For death does not wait for a convenient time; it may not even attack from the front but steal up from behind. We all know that death must come; the problem is that it comes when we feel no urgency to prepare for it, when we are not expecting it, just as when a high tide surges in over tidelands that seem broad until the sea rushes in.

Pick up a brush, and you end up writing something; pick up an instrument, and you want to make music. Pick up a cup, and you think of saké; pick up dice, and you think of gambling. The mind always follows what the hand touches. It is for this reason that we should not engage in sinful pleasures for even a moment.

If by chance we glance at a line of holy writ, we somehow end up reading on, perhaps even correcting an erroneous notion of many years. And if we had never opened the book, would we have ever realized our mistake? This is the value of chance stimulation. For if you sit before the altar, beads in hand, sutra open, you may accumulate merit despite a general lack of devotion; and if you sit in meditation—even with distracted thoughts—you may find yourself moving toward a sense of concentration without knowing it.

Phenomenon and essence are not two things, but one. If we are true to the outward form, the inner reality cannot fail to mature. Thus it is wrong to declare such things empty formalities; they deserve praise and respect.

164

People meet, and there's never a moment of silence. Always there is talk. And if you listen to what is being said, it's all useless jabber: the rumors that are circulating, gossip about people, good and bad—all of which is harmful to both those talking and those being discussed, and does no one any good. When people talk like this, they don't realize that what they say profits no one.

166

Watching people strive to attain success reminds me of people making a snow Buddha on a spring day; they take pains to decorate it with precious metals and pearls, and then build a pavilion to display it. But will there be enough time to place their Buddha on the altar? Too many men wait for success in the same way, supposing they have plenty of time, while beneath them life is melting away like snow.

172

When a man is young, his body overflows with energy, his heart is easily moved by things, he is full of passion. He throws himself into danger as he might toss a jeweled ball to the ground, almost wanting it to shatter. So much does he love the beauty of women that he seems ready to waste his fortune in pursuit of it, only to relent and cast all that aside, debasing himself in the mossy robes of the priesthood. In an excess of bravado, he gets into a fight, then feels ashamed and ends up envying the very man he has attacked. Thus his affections change from day to day, always unsettled. He loses himself in lust, is moved by the kindness of another, commits himself to good works; then he risks his future chasing after the example of those who have thrown their lives away—not thinking for even a moment that he might want to live safe and long. Pulled along by his whims, he makes a scandal of his life that may well be talked about for years to come. Yes, leave it to the young man to ruin his life.

When a man grows old, his spirit, too, loses vitality. He is impassive, easygoing, and never excited by things. Because his heart has arrived at a natural state of serenity, he engages in nothing not needful, he cares for his body and thus does not suffer from ill health, and he is mindful not to cause anyone trouble. The old man surpasses the young man in wisdom, just as the young man surpasses the old in beauty of appearance.[51]

189

Today you had planned to do one thing, but something else comes up and takes the whole day. The person you've been waiting for is detained, but someone you hadn't expected shows up instead. Something you had confidence in goes awry, but something you had no hope for works out. The task you worried over comes off without trouble, but the task you thought would be easy proves to be difficult. As the days go by, what happens bears no resemblance to what you had anticipated. It's that way for any year; it's the same for a lifetime.

But just as you start to think that things never turn out as planned, something does and you feel more at a loss than ever. The only way we can be sure of things is to realize the truth: that all is uncertainty.

---

51. The first part of this passage shows the influence of a passage in book 16 of the *Analects*, where Confucius characterizes youth as an "unsettled" period of life when men are particularly susceptible to "the attraction of feminine beauty" (*The Analects*, trans. D. C. Lau [New York: Penguin, 1979], 140).

If there's one thing a man is better off without, it's a wife. I am impressed to hear of a man who has "always lived alone,"[52] and if I learn later that he has gone to so-and-so's as a son-in-law or taken some woman in to live with him, he comes down in my estimation. People are bound to deride him, saying, "He's decided for himself that his woman is something fine, but she's really not so special!"[53] Or, if the woman is fine indeed, "Look at him carry on; why, it's as if he'd got his own little guardian Buddha!" And it's worse if the woman really runs the house.[54] Soon they have children, whom she spoils and frets over disagreeably.[55] Even after the man dies, she goes on, becoming a nun and mocking her man's memory with her wizened form.

No matter who the woman is, if a man spends dawn to dusk with her every day, he will grow tired of her and hate her in the end—in which case the woman, too, is left dangling in thin air. So to live separately, visiting the woman on occasion, makes for a more secure relationship, and one that will stand the test of time. To come unannounced and stay the night is sure to make one's visits seem something special.

191

Only a person of no feeling would say that things lose their beauty at night. On the contrary, it is at night that all rich fabrics, decorations, and colors are most delightful. In the daytime, one can appear in simple, subdued apparel; but at night, showy, bright clothing is best. And personal appearance is also shown to greatest effect in lamplight, just as

---

52. The quotation is from the "Butterflies" chapter of *The Tale of Genji*, referring to Genji's brother, Prince Hotaru, who after his wife's death chooses to live alone. See Murasaki Shikibu, *The Tale of Genji*, trans. Edward Seidensticker (New York: Knopf, 1976), 421.

53. The words are those of Lady Rokujō in the "Evening Faces" chapter of *The Tale of Genji*, when she is angry about the attention Genji is paying to Yūgao, a lady of much lower rank than herself. See ibid., 71.

54. A reference to a comment made by the guards captain in the famous "rainy night discussion" in "The Broom Tree" chapter of *The Tale of Genji*, when a group of young men are chatting on the topic of the ideal wife. See ibid., 25.

55. A reference to a scene in the "Evening Mist" chapter of *The Tale of Genji* in which Yūgiri shows impatience with his wife, Kumoinokari. See ibid., 689.

voices speaking in the dark, taking care not to be heard, are most elegant. Scents and sounds, too, are especially delightful at night.

I find it particularly pleasing when on a night of no special significance a man comes to a mansion well into the evening dressed in the finest attire. And since those among the young who pay close attention to such things are always observant, young people—especially at times when they might be tempted to let their guard down—should take great care with their appearance, making no distinction between normal and special occasions. How charming it is when a gentleman stops to groom his hair after dark, or when a woman, late into the evening, slips out of sight, takes out a mirror, and touches up her face.

202

One hears it said that Shinto rites should not be performed during the Tenth Month—the Godless Month—but I can find no such stipulation anywhere. There's not a word about it in the classics. It may be that this name was given only because there are no Shinto festivals during that month.

There are those who say that during the Tenth Month all the gods gather at Ise Shrine,[56] but no source for that idea exists. If there were any foundation to it, certainly that month would be a festival time at the Grand Shrine; but there is no such tradition. And historically, though there have been many imperial processions to shrines during the Tenth Month, most of them turned out not to bode well for the future.

204

When a criminal is to be beaten with rods, he should be tied to a torture device. No one now knows what such a device should look like, or how to tie a man to it.

---

56. The foremost of all Shinto shrines, dedicated to the Amaterasu, the Sun Goddess.

When the ground was being prepared for the building of the Kameyama Palace,[57] workers hit upon a grave mound that contained great numbers of serpents all coiled up together. "They must be the gods of the place," someone said. The whole matter was reported to the emperor, who sent out an official query asking what should be done. Everyone said, "It would be a hard thing to dig them out if they've been occupying the place for a long time." Only Minister Sanemoto[58] disagreed: "The serpents live in the emperor's realm; why would they want to put a curse on the place where an imperial palace is to be built? The gods and spirits do not engage in evil deeds. Stop your worrying. Just dig the snakes out and let them go." So the workers destroyed the tomb and released the snakes into the Oi River. No curse ever ensued.

209

Once a man lost a suit over a rice field and, out of spite, dispatched men with orders to harvest all the rice from the field in question. When the men stopped at the first field along the way and began reaping, someone said, "This isn't the right field. What do you think you're doing?" The men replied, "Well, we've really got no business taking the rice from the other field either. Since we've come to do something unreasonable anyway, why shouldn't we do our reaping anywhere we please!" Their logic was most amusing.

211

We can rely on nothing. It is because the foolish man trusts in things that he so often ends up full of hatred or anger.

If you have power—don't depend on it: the man of strength is first to fall. If you have great wealth—don't depend on it: riches can vanish in

---

57. Built at the command of Retired Emperor Go-Saga (1220–1272; r. 1242–1246) at the foot of Mount Kameyama in the Saga area, west of the capital.
58. Tokudaiji Sanemoto (1201–1273).

an instant. If you have learning—don't depend on it: even Confucius was rejected by his age. If you have virtue—don't depend on it: even Yan Hui[59] met misfortune. Nor should you rely on the affection of your lord, whose retribution may strike swiftly. And don't put faith in servants: they can betray and abandon you. Don't trust in anyone's goodwill: sometime it must change. Don't trust agreements either: sincerity is rare.

If you depend neither on others nor on your own state of being, you can rejoice at good fortune and not be bitter at bad. With open space left and right, you will suffer no impediment; with distance behind and ahead, your way will not be blocked. In a narrow passage, things get crunched and broken. When a man has too little latitude for thought, he runs into other people, gets into fights, and loses; but when he has room and is at ease, not a hair of his head suffers.

Man is the most marvelous of all creatures in heaven and on earth. And if heaven and earth know no bounds, why should man's nature be any different? When we are open and unconstrained, joy and sorrow will not impede us, and no one will cause us trouble.

212

The autumn moon is a thing splendid beyond compare. Any man who fails to recognize this, thinking the moon is the same in all seasons, must be lacking in sensitivity indeed.

218

Foxes bite people. Once an attendant at the Horikawa Mansion[60] was bitten as he slept. And a low-ranking monk at Ninnaji, passing by the main hall at night, was attacked so ferociously by three foxes that he drew his sword and ran two of them through while trying to defend himself. One of them died on the spot; the other two got away. The monk had bites all over him, but he escaped serious injury.

59. Yan Hui, Confucius's peerless disciple, died young.
60. The residence of Minamoto no Michitomo (1171–1227), who was known as the Horikawa Major Counselor.

Any man who persists in visiting a woman against all odds, despite the obstacles presented by "those observant fisherwomen of Shinobu Bay" and "the watchmen of Kurabu Mountain," must indeed have the most profound feelings for her and will share with her unforgettable memories.[61] On the other hand, it can only be embarrassing to a woman if he is accepted by her parents and siblings without the least complication.

And what a waste it seems when a woman suffering financial hardship announces that she will yield "if a stream beckons," provided only that the man—be he an unseemly old monk or a vulgar easterner—has money, and then goes off to be greeted in a new house, unknowing and unknown.[62] How will the two ever begin a conversation? By contrast, those who can reminisce about the pains of a long courtship, when they "met despite mountains between," will never run out of things to talk about.[63]

When people are brought together by an outsider, there is bound to be a great deal of unpleasantness. Even in the case of a woman of high birth, if she goes to a man of lower status who is ugly and advanced in years, the man may think to himself, "What reason could they have for throwing away such a fine woman on the likes of me?" and then conclude that she must be of inferior character. Then again, he may feel embarrassed by his own mean figure in his wife's presence—a most miserable situation.

The man who has never paused beneath a hazy moon on a night heavy with the scent of plum blossoms, or who has no fond memories of the sky near dawn when he went out into the dew near his lady's hedge—that man had best not fall in love at all.

61. Both *shinobu* (translatable as "hide" in this case) and *kurabu* (partially homophonous with *kurashi* [dark]) suggest covert trysts. It is unclear whether Kenkō is alluding to specific poems.
62. An allusion to a poem by Ono no Komachi (fl. ca. 850), in *Kokinshū* (*Collection of Ancient and Modern Times*, ca. 905), poem 938: "In this forlorn state,/I grow weary of life:/if a stream beckoned,/I would gladly cut my roots/and, like duckweed, float away" (*wabinureba/mi o ukikusa no/ne o taete/sasou mizu araba/inamu to zo omou*).
63. The quotation is probably an allusion to a poem by Minamoto no Shigeyuki (d. ca. 1000), in *Shinkokinshū* (*New Collection of Ancient and Modern Times*, ca. 1205), poem 1013: "All those watchful eyes,/thick as the thickly wooded hills/at Tsukuba Mountain—/will not deter one whose heart/burns with longing so strong" (*tsukubayama/hayama shigeyama/shigekeredo/omoiiru ni wa/sawarazarikeri*).

Men find themselves caught up in cycles of prosperity and adversity for the sole reason that they are too concerned with pursuing pleasure and avoiding pain. Pleasure is liking something so much that we become infatuated with it. And we seek such things endlessly. Our foremost pleasure comes from fame, of which there are two kinds: praise for our deeds and praise for our artistic accomplishments. Our next chief pleasure comes from lust, and our third from appetite. No other desires exceed these three. They all result from a backward view of things and are the sources of much trouble. To not pursue them at all is the best course.

243

When I turned eight years old, I confronted my father with this question: "What sort of being is a Buddha?" My father said, "Why, a Buddha is what a man has become." So I went on: "How does a man become a Buddha?" My father replied, "Through the teachings of a Buddha." Then I asked, "And the Buddha that taught the man—what sort of being was it that taught him?" He replied, "Well, he became a Buddha through the teachings of the First Buddha." I asked, "And what sort of Buddha was that First Buddha, the one that first taught how to become a Buddha?" At this point my father said, "I suppose he must have fallen down from the sky, or popped up out of the earth," and began to laugh.

Much amused, he said to the people around, "When the kid pressed me for an answer, I didn't have one!"

[TSUREZUREGUSA, ED. KUBOTA JUN, SHIN NIHON KOTEN BUNGAKU
TAIKEI 39 (TOKYO: IWANAMI SHOTEN, 1989)]

II

THE LATE MEDIEVAL ERA

In the late medieval era (1350–1600), literacy was still confined to the social elite, although that term should be understood to include an increasing number of men (along with some women) of the warrior ranks, clerics, samurai, and even some petty officials—who collectively might be characterized as an emerging middle class. Although still holding high title and rank, which gave them cultural authority, the old aristocracy had less real political and economic power than their colleagues in the great warrior houses, and in these years demand for literary services (lecturing, copying and editing texts, and presiding at poetic gatherings, for example) and participation extended well beyond the confines of Kyoto into the provinces.

The four works presented here nevertheless come from men of great prominence associated with the capital and its culture—two professional poets, an imperial regent who was also a major scholarly figure, and an anonymous writer who must likewise have been of high birth. As was always the case in the period in question, texts were circulated in handwritten manuscript; only much later were they reduced to the "vulgar" form of print.

These four *zuihitsu* display great variety in style and subject matter. The first, by a *waka* poet and teacher, reads like intimate "chats" shared with disciples, mostly involving poetry. The second is a set of admonitions, in appropriately high and hortatory diction, offered to a shogun by a former imperial regent. Then comes a set of two short pieces by a master of linked verse (*renga*) that are personal in tone but written in an ornate style designed to display high (often Chinese-inspired) rhetoric and mastery of arcane vocabulary. The final essay is similar to those by Sei Shōnagon and Kenkō in including not only expository pieces but also amusing stories (presented as factual).

Conversations with Shōtetsu

SHŌTETSU

Although born into a low-ranking samurai family, the man we know by the Bud-
dhist name Shōtetsu (1381-1459) was placed in a monastery at a young age and
spent his whole life as a Zen monk. In his early twenties, however, he chose to
pursue poetry as his Way, becoming in time one of the premier poets of the late
medieval era and leaving behind the single largest personal collection of poetry,
Sōkonshū (The Grass Roots Collection), *in the premodern Japanese canon.*

In addition to poetry, Shōtetsu left behind a travel record, a short critical
work on The Tale of Genji, *and the large miscellany* Shōtetsu monogatari
(Conversations with Shōtetsu). *Although not usually included in the category*
of zuihitsu, *the last of these is a desultory work that has all the qualities we*
usually associate with the zuihitsu *as a genre. From his comments in* Shōtetsu
monogatari *and the existence of a manuscript of* Tsurezuregusa (Essays in
Idleness) *in his own hand, we know that Shōtetsu knew that text and had great*
admiration for Yoshida no Kenkō, whom he described as a "poetic genius of the
first order." The following selections present Shōtetsu's ruminations on various
dimensions of the artistic culture of his time. That his comments are often more
prescriptive than descriptive is an indication that the text was intended less as a
memoir than as a set of suggestions for his students.

The handwriting of Retired Emperor Fushimi[1] in his letters is like a withered tree, with no outward beauty at all. Since he took no pains over his calligraphy, his style should not be imitated by ordinary people.

———————————

Among my recent poems on the topic "Snow on the Mountains at Dusk," I think this one turned out well:

As evening falls,
even the clouds hang back
in hesitation—
before the trackless snow
of the plank bridge on the peak.[2]

watarikane / kumo mo yūbe o / nao tadoru / ato naki yuki no / mine no kakehashi

Now, it is unlikely that the clouds would in actuality be unable to cross "the trackless snow," but as it is the way of Japanese poetry to attribute feelings to insentient things,[3] I have presented the clouds as deliberately passing over the bridge morning and evening. In the brightness of snow piled up deep and white, the clouds cannot tell that dusk has come and seem just to hover, hesitating to move on. One often sees such scenes when gazing out at the gathering dusk on mountains deep in snow where clouds slowly drift above. Attributing feelings to the clouds in this way makes plausible the poetic idea that they are "hesitating" to cross the bridge. Also, since I say there is no sign even of human footprints, one can imagine that the clouds too would forgo crossing.

One might think it better to have said, "There are no tracks upon the snow" [*yuki ni ato naki*], but that would be inferior. I believe the phrase "the trackless snow" gives a better impression, my reason being that,

1. 1265–1317; r. 1287–1298. A prominent poet, calligrapher, and patron of the arts.
2. *Sōkonshū*, poem 3986.
3. *Mushin naru mono*. Things without human feeling, particularly animals and plants.

while there can be no such things as footprints left by clouds in reality, my phrase "in hesitation . . . before the *trackless* snow" can mean that the clouds *too* have left no tracks. So between "there are no tracks upon the snow" and "the trackless snow," it is the latter that presents the more beautiful scene.

Thus we see the ineffable charm and elegance of the style of "moving clouds" and "swirling snow"[4]—as in scenes of snow blown about by the wind, or spring haze drifting across cherry blossoms. A poem that has something of indescribable mystery about it is a superior poem. Such a poem has been compared to a beautiful lady who is grieving but does her grieving in silence, since saying nothing despite one's sadness is unusual. The same thing happens when a little child of two or three brings an object to a person, saying, "This, this"—knowing what it wants but being unable to express itself clearly. The best poems are those that leave something unsaid.

A poet should not work at book learning[5] but rather gain a clear understanding of the nature of poetry—"a clear understanding" meaning to be enlightened.[6] This is the kind of person who goes on to become a skilled poet.

When reading over old poems, I muse over whether a given poem would best be described as being in, say, the style of mystery and depth[7] or in the lofty style.[8] I may also ask myself, "Suppose I tried using the words of this poem in one of my own—could I hope to produce anything as fine as this?" When pondering the poems of the masters, what one should do is study carefully each poem and ask someone about any places one doesn't understand. And one must realize that at formal occasions

4. The styles of *kōun* (moving clouds) and *kaisetsu* (swirling snow) are treated as subcategories of the style of *yūgen* (mystery and depth) in a number of medieval critical works associated with the great medieval poet-scholar Fujiwara no Teika (1162–1241).
5. *Saigaku*, referring to poetic lore and scholarly study, in contrast to practice (*keiko*) and the nurturing of a proper sensibility.
6. "To be enlightened" translates *satoru*, a word that conventionally refers to Buddhist enlightenment. The idea ultimately derives from the writings of the great medieval poets Fujiwara no Shunzei (1114–1204), his son Teika, and Teika's son, Tameie (1198–1275).
7. *Yūgentai.* An ideal established in the era of Shunzei and his students that remained important throughout the medieval period.
8. *Taketakaki yō.* Characterized by elevated diction and grand imagery.

like poetry gatherings, those who do not go beyond leafing through other people's papers and poem slips, without actually understanding their poems, will not advance in poetic accomplishment. Nor will those who, having had a poem explained to them by the author, conclude, "Well, it must be as he says" and abandon the subject even though they still fail to comprehend the poem.

Of course, it is difficult to admit when one does not understand a poem. Ryōshun[9] said that when poets gather together, the best training is to leave off composing in order to discuss and criticize their work together. Again, to have the experience of participating in a single poetry contest where judgments are made by group decision is far more valuable than composing a thousand or two thousand poems alone. Since in such settings people are criticizing one another's poems and expressing their opinions about them, it may be that another person will understand a poem in a way different from how one interprets it oneself.[10]

It is said of Ryōshun that it was after he heard this poem by Reizei Tamehide[11] that he became Tamehide's disciple:

> How rare a thing
> is a friend of true feeling
> in this world of ours!
> Alone, I listen to the rain
> all through an autumn night.[12]

aware shiru / tomo koso kataki / yo narikere / hitori ame kiku / aki no yosugara

The idea "Alone, I listen to the rain / all through an autumn night" actually begins the poem, since it is when listening to the rain alone through

9. Imagawa Ryōshun (1326–1417?), a warrior-poet associated with the Reizei school of poetry who was one of Shōtetsu's teachers.
10. Ryōshun makes similar comments in *Ryōshun isshiden*, comp. Sasaki Nobutsuna and Kyūsojin Hitaku, Nihon kagaku taikei 5 (Tokyo: Kazama shobō, 1956), 179–82.
11. D. 1372. Heir of the courtly Reizei house, descendants of Fujiwara no Teika, and a major figure in courtly poetic circles.
12. A corroborating story about an almost identical poem appears in Imagawa Ryōshun, *Rakusho roken*, ed. Takanashi Motoko, Karon kagaku shūsei 11 (Tokyo: Miyai shoten, 2002), 108–9.

an autumn night that the speaker realizes how rare a thing it is to find a friend of true feeling. Had he had such a friend, he would doubtless have been invited out somewhere to spend the night in conversation, and therefore would not be listening to the rain in this way. The fact that he is left with nothing to do is particularly affecting, in my opinion.

Also, if the poet had written, "Alone, I listen to the rain *at midnight, in autumn*," the experience would have ended there. The essential thing is that by leaving it as "*all through* an autumn night," the poet does not bring the experience to an end but implies, "As I listened alone to the rain all through an autumn night, *what I realized was . . .*" It is in this sense that "Alone, I listen to the rain / all through an autumn night" is actually the beginning of the poem. If "Alone, I listen to the rain" had come at the end, the poem would have been nothing out of the ordinary.

Ryōshun used to say, "In my youth, when I was undergoing training in linked verse, I thought that instead of writing a great many bad verses I ought to try composing five, or even as few as three, that satisfied me, so I produced only a small number of verses.[13] His Lordship the regent[14] heard about this, and when I presented him with some of my work, he gave me a good scolding in the comments he appended at the end: 'I hear you have recently cut down on the number of your verses in the hope of producing some good linked poetry. That won't do. You may polish up one or two verses and think they are extremely good, but in the eyes of an expert they will still be the efforts of a beginner and be no good at all. While you are still a novice[15] you should produce as many verses as possible and with as little effort as you can, and eventually you will become an expert as a matter of course.'"

In a letter written at a time when I was making a deliberate effort to compose good poems, Ryōshun remonstrated with me in turn. He would

---

13. Ryōshun in fact discourages young poets, in particular, from composing lots of poems in the hope of producing a few good ones, in *Ryōshun isshiden*, 185.

14. Nijō Yoshimoto (1320–1388), a high-ranking courtier who was one of the most prominent poets of the day.

15. *Shoshin.* The religious connotations of the word are no doubt intentional.

often mention His Lordship the regent's instructions and say, "This is an example of stern kindness."

————————

A poem on the topic "Spring Love":

> In dusky light,
> I thought I saw the dim form
> of the one I love—
> there too as a memento
> in haze 'round the dawn moon.[16]

yūmagure / sore ka to mieshi / omokage no / kasumu zo katami / ariake no tsuki

The idea of this poem is that at dusk, when the spring haze spreads over everything, the poet catches a glimpse of someone, and thinking that it may be the one he longs for, cherishes that image carefully in his heart. Then the sight of the moon in the sky at dawn reminds him again of that vision, thus becoming a fragile memento. The imagery of thin clouds wreathing the moon and haze trailing across the cherry blossoms is not put into words but instead expressed through an atmosphere of mystery and depth and gentle elegance. Such things lie outside the words of the poem.

————————

Whatever it may be about, a poem by a skilled poet will display some special element of treatment that holds one's interest. Seeing this, the novice may feel envious and try to compose something similar himself, only to produce a jumble of nonsense—something so absurd that when asked what it means, he must answer, "I'm afraid I don't understand it myself." One must be careful about this sort of thing. While still a novice, a person should simply sit down with his fellows and compose poems that are straightforward and easy to comprehend. Imitating an accom-

16. *Sōkonshū*, poem 4443.

plished master before reaching some level of achievement oneself will make for results that are laughable.

———————

It is a good thing to look through treatises and handbooks—when one is not composing poetry, that is. But when one is going to compose a formal poem, one should resolutely put such things away and work without them. Those who look at the old handbooks as they go along, composing poems a piece at a time, are bound to end up borrowing too much[17] or producing nothing of worth. What's more, if composing in this fashion becomes a habit, one will be unable to produce a formal poem in any other way.

Long ago, there were court ladies who would write their poems lying down, while others would trim the lamp to make for a fainter light, and then consider their work after putting themselves into a melancholy mood.[18] Saigyō[19] spent his whole life either traveling about and composing poetry while on religious pilgrimages or else opening the door on the north side of his hermitage a crack and writing as he gazed out at the moonlight. Teika[20] used to remove the shutters on the south side of his house, sit in the exact center of the building where he could see far off to the south, and—dressed in strictly correct attire—work on his poems. This was good practice so that his mind would not fail him when he had to compose poems for formal occasions at places such as the imperial palace or the chambers of the retired emperor. Shunzei[21] would always throw just the top part of a shabby court costume over his shoulders and compose poems huddled against a brazier of paulownia wood.[22] Never, not even for a moment or two, would he relax and stretch out at his ease.

———

17. The Japanese word here is *dōrui*, referring to poems that come too close to repeating what has been done in poems of previous ages.

18. Inada Toshinori notes a reference here to a passage in the medieval poetic treatise *Guhishō* about the court ladies Izumi Shikibu (fl. ca. 970–1030) and Kunaikyō (d. 1204?), in *Shōtetsu monogatari*, ed. Inada Toshinori, Karon kagaku shūsei 11 (Tokyo: Miyai shoten, 2002), 167n.12.

19. 1118–1190. A famous monk-poet.

20. See note 4.

21. See note 6.

22. Inada identifies a reference here to the early medieval treatise *Kirihioke*, in *Shōtetsu monogatari*, 167n.15.

As for the rest of us, I have found that the poems I have written on just waking from sleep and other such times have invariably proved on later inspection to be no good.

Michikaze,[23] Sukemasa,[24] and Yukinari[25] have been termed the skin, flesh, and bones of calligraphy.[26] Michikaze wrote in a style that pierced the bone to the marrow, Sukemasa in the style of the flesh, and Yukinari in a style corresponding to the skin, it is said. The three men lived in more or less the same period of history. Toward the end of Michikaze's life, Sukemasa appeared; toward the end of Sukemasa's life, Yukinari appeared.

Retired Emperor Fushimi adopted the calligraphic styles of Michikaze and Sukemasa, but for writing Japanese kana,[27] he developed something entirely his own. In the few examples that still survive of kana penned by Michikaze and Yukinari, the lines are full of gaps, like the footprints of a mouse. Kana in which the symbols are joined together in a beautiful, rounded style was the innovation of Retired Emperor Fushimi. From this time on, the whole court imitated his "palace style." Among others, Retired Emperor Go-Fushimi[28] and the retired emperor of the Hagiwara Cloister[29] adopted Retired Emperor Fushimi's style.

The calligraphy of the Rokujō Palace minister, Lord Arifusa,[30] in particular, was patterned exactly after Retired Emperor Fushimi's handwriting. Failing to realize this, a great many people treasure examples of his calligraphy, thinking they are by Retired Emperor Fushimi himself. The kana of the two men is particularly similar. Arifusa is said to have been

---

23. Ono no Michikaze (894–966), who was famous for his cursive style.

24. Fujiwara no Sukemasa (Sari; 944–998), who was noted for his elegant brushwork, which was often characterized as uniquely Japanese—as opposed to Chinese—in its features.

25. Fujiwara no Yukinari (972–1027), a favorite of the potentate Fujiwara no Michinaga (966–1027), who was credited with a precise, flowing style that is often contrasted with the bolder, more "masculine" style of Michikaze.

26. In *Yūgaku ōrai* by Gen'e (1279–1350), although probably known to Shōtetsu through the poetic treatise *Guhishō*. See *Guhishō*, comp. Sasaki Nobutsuna and Kyūsojin Hitaku, Nihon kagaku taikei 4 (Tokyo: Kazama shobō, 1956), 295.

27. The Japanese phonetic syllabary, as opposed to Chinese characters, the traditional focus of calligraphy.

28. 1288–1336; r. 1298–1301. A son of Fushimi's.

29. Retired Emperor Hanazono (1297–1348; r. 1308–1318), another son of Fushimi's.

30. Rokujō Arifusa (1251–1319).

an ancestor of the Koga lineage.[31] He was originally called the Zenrinji Middle Counselor. The Shimizudani[32] and other lineages also descend from him.

Michikaze and Sukemasa perpetuated the calligraphic styles of the Han dynasty, but the calligraphy of Retired Emperor Fushimi shows mastery of both Chinese and Japanese elements. When compared with examples of the handwriting of Ziang[33] and Jizhi,[34] the character of the brushwork is exactly the same. In its blending of both Chinese and Japanese elements, Retired Emperor Fushimi's calligraphy gives an impression similar to that of a room with a set of three scrolls by a Chinese monk hanging in the alcove—with an ensemble of incense burner, flower vase, and candlestand in antique bronze—together with Japanese folding screens covered with polished gold or silver foil. The handwriting of Shōren'in[35] is like a room fitted out with slatted blinds, sliding doors, and folding screens of polished gold and silver, with all the objects and accessories of Japanese origin.

The handwriting of Retired Emperor Go-Kōgon[36] as seen in his letters shows an honesty without pretense, delicate and beautiful; but when it is placed side by side with that of Retired Emperor Fushimi, it cannot match the latter's withered elegance and nobility.[37] Go-Kōgon's style is like a fine court lady seated within her curtains, whereas Fushimi's is like a handsome man in formal court dress proceeding toward the southern pavilion in the imperial palace. Looking in on the lady behind her curtains, we see her beauty and gentle elegance. But if it is a matter of appearing in public, the man in formal court dress has a superior dignity and splendor. Such is the character of Retired Emperor Fushimi's hand.

31. A court family descended from the Murakami Genji lineage.
32. The Shimizudani house specialized in calligraphy in Shōtetsu's own day. However, that lineage descends not from the Murakami Genjis but from the Saionji branch of the Fujiwara.
33. Zhao Mengfu (1254–1322), a calligrapher and painter of China's Yuan dynasty (1271–1368).
34. Zhang Jizhi (1186–1266), a calligrapher of the Southern Song dynasty (1127–1279) whose work was very influential in Japan.
35. Emperor Fushimi's son Son'en (d. 1356), who served as abbot of Shōren'in, one of the ruling cloisters of the Engakuji branch of the Tendai sect.
36. 1338–1374; r. 1352–1372. Son of Emperor Kōgon (1313–1364; r. 1331–1333), who was himself the son of Go-Fushimi.
37. *Karabite kedakaki.* A positive appraisal less ambiguous than Shōtetsu's first mention of Fushimi's style.

During impromptu sessions[38] held after formal poetry gatherings, the poem slips of the younger participants are written last and submitted first. When old and young are in attendance, one or two inkstones are pushed from one person to the next, the elders and seniors writing first and the younger ones in the lowest seats writing last. Nevertheless, the young people should be first to pass in their poem slips to the master of topics. No matter how quickly they may come up with their poems, junior members should not write them down before the senior members have finished. This rule must be scrupulously observed. Elders may ponder their poems as long as they like, but for the younger members in the lowest seats to take a long time over their poems and be slow in turning them in is extremely bad manners.

As far as reading the poems to one another is concerned, in the old days they did not do as they do today, with everyone showing everyone else his poem written on a piece of folded paper. Instead, people sitting next to each other would ask each other's opinions and offer criticisms—saying, "I'm not sure what you are trying to say here," and so on. A far cry from what goes on today, when there is such a hubbub that impromptu meetings have become chaotic and unpleasant affairs.

Shunzei's house was at the intersection of Fifth Avenue and Muromachi.[39] After Teika's mother[40] died, he went to visit Shunzei there, only to find the autumn wind blowing desolately about the place, and Shunzei too—whenever it was—looking sad and forlorn.

Upon returning to his own house at First Avenue and Kyōgoku,[41] Teika sent the following poem to his father:

38. *Tōza.* After a formal meeting at which poets presented poems composed on topics that had been passed out beforehand (*kendai*), people would often compose poems—again on topics—but this time on the spot.
39. Gojō (Fifth Avenue) running east to west and Muromachi, north to south.
40. Bifukumon'in no Kaga died in 1193, at around age seventy.
41. Ichijō (First Avenue) running east to west and Kyōgoku, north to south.

No moment of respite,
not for the dew, nor for my tears,
at a dwelling
where autumn wind comes calling
for one who is no more.[42]

tamayura no/tsuyu mo namida mo/todomarazu/naki hito kouru/yado no
  akikaze

The poem is a most complex and deftly wrought composition, indescribable in its intense feeling and sadness. The word *tamayura* means "a moment." The whole poem, from beginning to end, is deeply moving, but
where it says "calling for one who is no more," it sounds particularly
forlorn.

Shunzei's reply was,

Autumn has come,
and the wind blowing by
is cooler now.
Yet still my dewdrop tears
are falling thick and fast.[43]

aki ni nari/kaze no suzushiku/kawaru ni mo/namida no tsuyu zo/shino ni
  chirekeru

One finds it difficult to understand why Shunzei responded in such an
offhand way.[44] For Teika's part, since the lady was his mother, it is only
natural that his poem should be so moving and sad, so heartrending. As
for Shunzei, the lady *was* his wife, after all; but because he was already
old himself, it would not be seemly for him to say that he was "sad" or

---

42. Teika's poem appears in *Shinkokinshū* (*New Collection of Ancient and Modern Times*, ca. 1205), poem
788, under a headnote that identifies it as having been composed "one stormy day in the autumn after
his mother's death, when he went to the house where she had once lived."
43. Shunzei's poem is recorded as a reply to Teika's in the latter's personal anthology, *Shūi gusō*
(*Worthless Poems of the Gentleman in Waiting*), poem 2775.
44. *Sugenage ni*. The point is that Shunzei's composition presents straightforward description,
without rhetorical adornments.

"disconsolate,"[45] and so he simply says that the season is autumn and the wind has cooled down, just as if nothing were out of the ordinary, making for a fine effect all the same.

In poetry there are many vexations. Winding up loose ends and thinking of the future, I must conclude that things never turn out as one would wish. If one continues to compose poems of the sort that everyone else considers good, one must remain forever at that ordinary level. On the other hand, when one writes poems whose essence is profound and difficult,[46] others fail to understand them, and that is frustrating. No doubt what is generally called good would seem to be good enough, I suppose.

Among connoisseurs[47] of poetry, there are a number of different kinds, just as there are among connoisseurs of tea. Among the latter, for instance, are people who possess beautiful tea utensils, who take pleasure in collecting china cups, Tenmoku bowls,[48] tea kettles, water jars, and all manner of tea articles. In Japanese poetry, their equivalent is those who are equipped with elegant inkstones, desks, poem slips, and pocket paper;[49] who always compose a complete set of verses; and who choose fine places for their poetry meetings. Such men are like *chazuki*—connoisseurs of tea.

Next come *chanomi*, tea drinkers—people who may not be particularly concerned about their utensils but are ready for a bout of tea tasting, no matter where they are. If it is Uji tea, they will sip it and say, "This is from the third picking," or "This tea was produced around the first day

---

45. Buddhism taught all people—especially those like Shunzei, who had taken orders—to put worldly ties behind them.

46. *Yūen*. A term of praise that expresses the highest level of art in Shōtetsu's poetics and that would go on to become central to the poetics of his disciple, the *renga* master Shinkei (1406–1475).

47. *Suki*. A word that implies amateur status but often more than amateur dedication.

48. Ch. *tianmu*. Bowls of black or persimmon-colored glaze produced in Zhejiang, China.

49. *Kaishi*. The paper on which poems were recorded at gatherings, its name deriving from the custom of carrying the paper inside the breast pocket of one's robe.

of the Third Month." Or with Togano'o tea, they will be able to tell by taste whether it is from the tea gardens of Tobata or the tea gardens of Saga. Those who are able to recognize where a tea is from by tasting it, in the manner of Yamana, the former officer of the imperial guards,[50] then, are called tea drinkers. The equivalent of such men in poetry is those who are able to tell the good from the bad, who know whether a given word may or may not be used in a poem, who understand whether a given poetic conception is correct or incorrect, who can accurately rate people's poems as of high or low quality. Such men are thoroughly versed in the very essence of poetry and should be ranked on a level with tea drinkers.

Finally come *chakurai*, tea guzzlers. As long as it is tea, it means nothing to them whether it is crude and coarse or of the best quality—they just go on swilling it down by the bowlful with no notion of whether it is good or bad. Such men who drink great quantities of tea are the tea guzzlers. Their equivalent in poetry is those who have no discrimination in diction and no regard for the good or bad in poetic ideas, who are not particular whether they associate with skilled poets or unskilled ones but go on forever pouring out verse simply because they like to write it. These men are of the same sort as the tea guzzlers.

As long as a person belongs to one of these three categories of amateurs, no matter which one, he may take his proper place at a gathering.

Chiun[51] used to say, "As for me—I'm one of the tea guzzlers."

———————

Ietaka[52] gained a name as a poet only after the age of forty. Prior to that, he had composed quite a number of poems, but it was only after he turned forty that he was accorded any honor or praise. Tonna[53] was over sixty before he achieved a reputation in the Way.

50. Possibly a reference to Yamana Tokihiro (d. 1435).
51. Ninagawa Chikamasa (d. 1448), a prominent poet and one of Shōtetsu's disciples.
52. Fujiwara no Ietaka (1158–1237), a famous contemporary of Fujiwara no Teika's.
53. 1289–1372. One of the preeminent poets of the fourteenth century.

Thus even the masters of old did not gain fame and honor when they were novices. Name and reputation are won by dint of accumulated achievement in training and connoisseurship. How absurd it is, then, for men of the present day to think to rival Teika or Ietaka after producing only one or two hundred poems! It was Teika himself who wrote, "A man who doesn't keep walking will never reach his destination."[54] It's like what they say about going to the Kantō or Kyushu: it will take a number of days, but people always want to get there with a single stride as soon as they have decided to go. If a man is a dedicated connoisseur, pursuing the Way unremittingly day and night—if he composes one poem after another lightly and easily but always pressing forward to the next one—then he is bound to arrive at some interesting results sooner or later, quite naturally and without deliberately straining for success.

Of course, there are contrary cases. His Lordship the Kyōgoku Regent,[55] who died at the age of thirty-seven, was by nature so skilled a poet that he still produced some compositions of the highest excellence. Yet can one not surmise that if he had lived to the advanced age of eighty or ninety, he would probably have produced many even more valuable poetic treasures? The same is true of Lady Kunaikyō,[56] who died in her twentieth year. She, too, in the course of time, would doubtless have benefited from continued practice and discipline, even though she was such a natural talent that she won fame and honor nevertheless. Those born with skill and talent achieve accuracy and precision when they are still novices, so that it is not as necessary to wait for the improving effects of discipline.

People who do not have such inborn talent arrive at natural understanding and enlightenment only through months and years of unremitting practice. Above all, there is nothing more precious and essential than dedication. In ancient times as well, men who were devoted to poetry were allowed access to secret transmissions on the *Kokinshū*[57] and

54. In *Gukenshō*, a medieval text commonly attributed to Teika but probably written by someone else of a slightly later generation, perhaps one of his own descendants. See *Gukenshō*, comp. Sasaki Nobutsuna and Kyūsojin Hitaku, Nihon kagaku taikei 4 (Tokyo: Kazama shobō, 1956), 358.

55. Go-Kyōgoku Yoshitsune (1169–1206), a major poet of Teika's era.

56. D. ca. 1204. A court lady.

57. *Collection of Ancient and Modern Times* (ca. 905). Normally such secret teachings were allowed only to the nobles in the poetic houses.

had their work included in imperial anthologies. As long as a man is a true connoisseur, how can the time of enlightenment fail to come?

[*SHŌTETSU MONOGATARI*, ED. HISAMATSU SEN'ICHI, NIHON KOTEN BUNGAKU TAIKEI 65 (TOKYO: IWANAMI SHOTEN, 1961); *SHŌTETSU MONOGATARI*, ED. INADA TOSHINORI, KARON KAGAKU SHŪSEI 11 (TOKYO: MIYAI SHOTEN, 2002). THE TRANSLATIONS ARE SLIGHTLY MODIFIED VERSIONS OF THOSE IN *CONVERSATIONS WITH SHŌTETSU*, TRANS. ROBERT H. BROWER, ED. STEVEN D. CARTER (ANN ARBOR: CENTER FOR JAPANESE STUDIES, UNIVERSITY OF MICHIGAN, 1992)]

4

To Unify the Nation and Restore Civil Society

ICHIJŌ KANEYOSHI

Ichijō Kaneyoshi (Kanera; 1402–1481) was born into one of the senior Fujiwara lineages and served as imperial regent three times during his long career at court. Active as a poet and scholar as well as a government official, he was a stubborn advocate of courtly customs and ideals in an age when they appeared to be in jeopardy. During the Ōnin War, he had to flee Kyoto, finding refuge in Nara with one of his cleric sons who was serving as the abbot of a temple there. When Kyoto—or what was left of it—finally returned to peace after ten years, he returned to court and did all he could to restore the rites and traditions of his heritage.

Kaneyoshi was a prolific poet who also wrote scholarly commentaries on court classics such as The Tale of Genji *and essays. The one translated here, "Bunmei ittōki" (To Unify the Nation and Restore Civil Society, 1480?), is a short hortatory work enjoining the young shogun Ashikaga Yoshihisa (1465–1489) to obey six specific commandments, each treated separately. The essay seems to have been written at the behest of the shogun's mother, Hino Tomiko (d. 1496), who evidently hoped that it would inspire the young man to a strong sense of duty as he assumed his official responsibilities.*

PRAY TO THE BODHISATTVA HACHIMAN

This you must do because, humble though you may be in station, you have taken upon yourself a public trust by assuming the lauded title of barbarian-subduing shogun. Doubtless the injunction to rule the sixty-six provinces of the Japanese nation has come to you by karmic fate—and by the bounty of your parents. Remember, then, that if you fail in governing the land and restoring tranquility to the world, your appointment will have been in vain. What is required, therefore, is that you pray for the goodwill of Hachiman[1] that he may grant you dominion—and offer that plea not so that you can thereafter do as you please.

This past decade we have watched as everyone—nobles and warriors, priests and laymen, men and women—endured sorrow and pain while their hard-won properties were plundered. Moved by compassion, then, you must rely solely on the profound favor of the gods and determine to pursue the Way uprightly, if only you may obtain the authority to do so. The hearts of the constables[2] of the many provinces you must pacify, enjoining them to compassion and promising swift punishment to any who do not mend their ways. If you return the world to tranquility, your greatest desire in this life will have been satisfied, and you will be known by later generations as Honored Shogun, higher praise than which human memory cannot bestow.

Now: if you would seek to act in accordance with the will of Hachiman, you must begin each morning by washing your hands and cleansing your mouth and, facing south, offering up the sincerest of prayers. As sure as the gods exist, they will hear your pleas. Then your commitment, if maintained properly before the world, will be observed, inspiring fear of judgment and also shame over any who resort to brute force, and thereby

---

1. The Shinto god of war, whom the Buddhists had adopted as a bodhisattva. He was the titular deity of the Minamotos, the clan from which Yoshihisa's Ashikaga clan descended.

2. *Shugo*. Originally, appointees of the shogunal government entrusted with policing powers over local jurisdictions. By Kaneyoshi's time, many had become independent and unruly warlords whose pacification he saw as a necessary step toward a restoration of the old order.

leading the hearts of the constables to improve as a matter of course. After that, unifying the nation will be as easy as keeping hold of what is already in your hands.

HONOR YOUR PARENTS

High or low, no one is born without parents. The inner teachings of the Buddha, and the outer scriptures of Confucius—both of these declare the weighty debt owed to our fathers and mothers.[3] Buddha teaches that even if every day of our lives we were to walk around Mount Sumeru carrying our fathers on our right side and our mothers on our left, still we could never repay our filial obligations.[4] Confucius teaches that we receive our very bodies—frame, hair, skin, and everything else—from our parents, and that the beginning of filial piety is to do ourselves no injury[5]—meaning that since we obtained our bodies from our parents, we walk the way of filial duty first of all by guarding against even the tiniest bruise. Suffering bodily harm makes one's parents grieve, while taking care of oneself is a filial act that spares them worry.

We are also taught that children who fail to correct their parents' mistakes are themselves being unfilial. At such times, a child should approach the parent respectfully and with kind words and a cheerful countenance offer correction. And if that attempt fails, filial duty demands that the child persist in the effort, whether by tears, displays of sorrow, or even feigned anger, until the parent reforms.[6]

The punishment for being unfilial toward your parents is coming to appreciate what that means later, when your own child is unfilial toward you in turn. Holding one's behavior to the standard of scripture in this matter may be a challenge, but surely the principle involved is one that all can comprehend.

3. The Confucian classics were referred to as "outer scriptures" (*geden*) in comparison with the "inner teachings" (*naikyō*) of Buddhism.
4. A quotation from *Xiao jing* (*Classic of Filial Piety*), traditionally attributed to Confucius.
5. Another quotation from *Classic of Filial Piety*.
6. Confucius, *The Analects*, trans. D. C. Lau (New York: Penguin, 1979), 74.

ESTEEM HONESTY

Among Buddha's teachings is one that says, "Be honest, and reject expediency,"[7] and in his vow Hachiman also declares that the gods reside with the honest man. To be honest means to be straight of heart. The acts of a crooked-hearted man will inevitably be crooked. When dealing with others, you must therefore recognize good men for their goodness and reward their labors, while recognizing the wickedness of the wicked and administering punishment accordingly. That is what is meant by honest government maintained by a man of honest heart.

There is no better metaphor for honesty of heart than that of a mirror. For when a person of fine countenance looks into a mirror, those good looks are reflected back, while an ugly face looking into a mirror sees also an ugly face. This is why one of the truths of Buddha is expressed by use of the mirror as a symbol—"All knowledge—reflected in the mirror of wholeness."[8] The true form of the gods is also embodied in the form of a mirror.[9]

UPHOLD COMPASSION

The character *ji* in the word *jihi* means to "save from suffering" while the character *hi* means to "endow with joy." Buddha's vow is to save all living beings from suffering and grant them joy; that is the meaning of compassion. In the outer scriptures, the word is *jin*, "benevolence," meaning love for human beings. The words may be different, but the meaning is the same.

Tame a bird or an animal as a pet, and you will come to feel compassion for it. How much more so should you bestow pity on all men! This indeed is the way of a benevolent lord. For more than ten years now, people of high and low station have been forced from their homes, countless

---

7. *Shōjiki shahōben*. Most traditions teach that the *Lotus Sutra* allows for the use of "expedient means" provided they lead to the right ends, but some argue that this is an incorrect interpretation and that honesty should be valued above expediency.

8. *Dai'en kyōchi*. One of the four truths that one achieves at the time of enlightenment, according to the teachings of the bodhisattva Nyorai.

9. Along with the sword and the necklace, the mirror was one of the three ancient Japanese imperial regalia.

thousands of them suffering hunger and cold. Those who commit such acts of aggression, heedless of principle and in defiance of the Way, do so because their hearts are devoid of compassion. How awful it is that they fail to comprehend even the principle of righteous acts leading to enlightenment![10]

PURSUE THE ARTS

Here I need scarcely mention the Way of the bow and horse, as it is the way of your own house. Beyond that, you should pursue the Ways of Japanese poetry, *kemari*,[11] and other arts, according to your own preferences. Lord Yoshimitsu[12] went so far as to serve as inner comptroller at the Sechie Festivities[13] and pursued even the Ways of music and singing. That he went to such lengths, however, was because of his intense personal affection for the arts. In all such matters, you should let occasion dictate how far you allow your intimates to become involved.

Saké is called the lord of joy,[14] and surely there is no harm in everyone imbibing in connection with festive occasions. Remember, however, what the *Analects* say: "He set himself no particular limit, but never drank to excess."[15] Saying that "he set no limit" implies that some people can hold their liquor and some cannot, and that there are no firm laws concerning the matter; but "never drank to excess" means that one should not drink to the point of losing one's senses. When you are thoroughly enjoying yourself and in high spirits, and realize that you are drunk, the best thing is to go to bed. Many a mistake comes from drunkenness. When a colleague gets drunk and commits some offense, then, refrain from correcting him while he is still intoxicated. Greater benefit will come if you wait until he has sobered up and is himself again. Then you can ask if he

---

10. *Shuin kanka.* In other words, enlightenment comes about through proper training. Kaneyoshi uses the term here to suggest that political leaders should be responsible for their actions.

11. A game played with four players on a "court" defined by four trees that involved keeping a ball in the air as long as possible.

12. Ashikaga Yoshimitsu (1358–1408), the third Ashikaga shogun, was one of the most courtly shoguns and even seems to have had imperial ambitions.

13. A banquet held at court in early spring.

14. *Kanbaku.* A partial homophone of *kanpaku* (imperial regent).

15. Confucius, *Analects*, 103.

remembers what he did and enjoin him to exercise more caution in the future.

SET YOUR MIND UPON GOVERNANCE

When all is said and done, nothing should be of greater import to you than the proper conduct of government affairs. In recent years, some have forced their way into the domains of temples and shrines and taken control of them, their hearts set only on violence, giving no thought to the harm they do their reputations in future times. What a regrettable thing it is to bring shame on the memories of a house that has stood for loyal service over generations! The lives of these men are their own to live, of course, but do they give no thought whatsoever to their descendants? This is why under no circumstances should you neglect matters of governance.

When someone ignores your orders, it would seem reasonable to later turn a deaf ear to that person if he comes to you with a request. When your own heart is at peace, however, it should make no difference to you who is to blame and who is not. Yet as the saying goes, "What one person casts aside, another picks up." People with all kinds of violent intentions will arise, and this must not be allowed.

Now that you have handed down your first judgment as shogun,[16] no great labor need be expended in administering justice through your representatives on easier cases. In matters involving only one party, adjudication can be left to commissioners, with you merely attaching your seal to the orders. In a case that demands judgment between parties, it should be an easy matter to direct two or three men to judge between the suitors and determine which side has the stronger argument. If something is misunderstood or not noticed initially, a verdict can always be changed upon appeal. There is nothing new in this; such things have happened since ancient times. When you are dealing with more weighty matters, on the other hand, it will not do to neglect things

16. Yoshihisa had performed the ritual of "first judgment" (*go-han hajime*) in the Twelfth Month of 1479, when he was fifteen years old.

for even a few days, and to abandon things altogether would make a mockery of your office.

There are many other things that I could touch upon, but space being limited, I will stop with these admonitions.

["*BUNMEI ITTŌKI*," IN *SHINKŌ GUNSHO RUIJŪ*, VOL. 21
(TOKYO: MEICHŌ FŪKYŪKAI, 1997–1998)]

5

Cottage of Dreams *and* Three Loves

SHŌHAKU

Shōhaku (also known by the sobriquet Botanka [Peony Flower]; 1443–1527) was born in Kyoto, into the Nakanoin lineage of the Fujiwara clan. As a younger son, however, he had little hope of making a career at court and so took the tonsure at a young age, later pursuing a career as a poetry master. Among his teachers were a prominent monk of the Rinzai sect of Zen and the linked-verse master Sōgi (1421–1502).

Accomplished in both the classical uta *(the thirty-one-syllable form that was the primary genre of the courtly tradition) and more modern linked-verse forms, Shōhaku was able to maintain strong ties with the aristocracy and also attract the attention of powerful patrons among the military elite, who became his primary patrons. He spent his middle years in a small dwelling he named the Cottage of Dreams in Ikeda, Settsu Province, which he describes in the first of the following two short essays: "Muan no ki" (Cottage of Dreams) and "San'aiki" (Three Loves).*

Cottage of Dreams

Sōshitsu[1] made the China trek,[2] and while he was there had a calligrapher friend of his named Zhonghe write out the words "Cottage of Dreams," which he kindly brought back to me—an unexpected gesture that moved me greatly.

> How awe-inspiring—
> to think that even far off
> in Cathay
> a brush has proclaimed the name
> of my "Cottage of Dreams."[3]

> *kashikoshi na / morokoshi made mo / fude ni sae / kikite somekeru / yume no iori*

I also showed the Chinese calligraphy naming my cottage to my colleague Sōho.[4] Impressed that Sōshitsu had not forgotten about me, even as he sojourned in a foreign land, I wrote,

> Incomparable
> is the bond I share now
> with one in China—
> seen only in the brushstrokes
> of my "Cottage of Dreams."[5]

> *mizukuki ni / kakeshi chigiri ya / tagui naki / minu morokoshi no / yume no iori o*

1. Identity unknown.
2. *Totō su*. Monks often made the journey to China to study.
3. This poems appears in Shōhaku's personal anthology, *Shunmusō*, Shikashū taisei 6 (Tokyo: Meiji shoin, 1976), poem 2076.
4. Identity unknown.
5. *Shunmusō*, poem 2077.

This is how my hut looks: on four sides it is walled in by pines and flowering trees, and in the front garden stands a large boulder that resembles a crouching dragon or a ferocious tiger. Also mixed in are stones from the seashore. Up against my eaves is a rose plum[6] I had transplanted from far-off Ashiya[7] years ago whose branches form an arbor thirty or forty feet wide. Next to the rose plum is a well, where a rope dangles down several yards, and above that is a paulownia whose canopy makes for a good place to escape the heat.

Each season brings flowers to my countless varieties of trees, the sight of which, morning and evening, helps me forget I am old. Which is why I call my studio the Cottage of Flowery Delights.

A dream, and no more—
yet in my declining years
my heart finds solace
in summer's final blossoming
among mountain rocks and trees.[8]

yume nagara / kokoro wa tomeshi / oiraku no / natsu sabikinuru / yama no iwaki ni

Three Loves

Here dwells a recluse—still in the world, adhering neither to Confucianism nor to Buddhism, leaving his appearance up to nature. For years, I lived in the ninefold enclosures of the capital at Kyoto,[9] but more recently I erected this cottage in Inano in the land of Tsu,[10] which I have dubbed Cottage of Dreams, taking for myself the name Peony Flower.

6. *Kōbai.* A flowering plum with red blossoms, sometimes called rose plum.
7. The southeastern corner of what is now Hyōgo Prefecture.
8. *Shunmusō*, poem 2078.
9. The imperial court.
10. An area along the Ina River in Settsu Province. Shōhaku appears to have moved there sometime in his early forties and stayed there most of the time until moving to Izumi Sakai in 1518.

This may seem presumptuous, I fear, but I mean only to declare the unity of all things.[11]

In enjoying blossoms, appreciating scents, and loving wine, I am no different from everyone else. Past to present, these three have been favored by stalwarts and sages, and who from the oldest village elder to the tenderest youth does not feel the same?

Since long ago in my own youth, which I spent beneath the moon shining down on the imperial precincts, I have lamented the passing hours of each spring evening, traveling from time to time into the mountains of Yoshino in search of the haunts of Saigyō[12] and going on to nearby provinces to bask in the light of places of renown.[13] To even the smallest grasses along the pathways I have been attentive: overlooking not even the briar rose where it languished on the fence of a rude peasant's hut as I made my way through the lush growth of summer, and beckoning with my sleeves to even a solitary blossom remaining on a frost-blighted moor. Especially have I been moved in a dawn glowing red as the brocades of Chengdu as I reclined beneath spring breezes blowing through groves of peach and damson plum. Like Zhuangzi, I gave up my life to a butterfly dream,[14] and I could only weep when I reflected on my times.[15]

For me, it is aloe that is the fundament of scents, and I am fond of the scents that have a long history in this country—the famed Ranjatai, Red Dust, and Middle River.[16] When it comes to blends, I use Plum Blossom, Lotus Leaf, and New Pillow, and employing the various house teachings that I have received, I do my own blending—a little more of this, a little

11. *Banbutsu ittai*, a fundamental Buddhist doctrine. Jōan's version of "Three Loves" connects Shōhaku's choice of the peony for his sobriquet with a story about the Zen monk Nanquan (784–834) teaching a disciple the principle that all things are one by pointing to a peony in his garden and saying that it was no different from a dream. See Kidō Saizō, *Rengashi ronkō* (Tokyo: Meiji shoin, 1973), 2:532.

12. The great monk-poet Saigyō (1118–1190) left behind scores of poems about Yoshino, the headnotes to which make it clear that he traveled there often.

13. *Na aru tokoro*, referring to famous places in poetry.

14. An allusion to the famous story in which Zhuangzi falls asleep, dreams that he is a butterfly, and then wakes up, never sure again whether he was a man dreaming that he was a butterfly or a butterfly now dreaming that he is a man. See *The Complete Works of Chuang Tzu*, trans. Burton Watson (New York: Columbia University Press, 1968), 49.

15. An allusion to one of the most famous poems by the Chinese poet Du Fu (712–770). See "Spring Prospect," in *The Columbia Book of Chinese Poetry: From Early Times to the Thirteenth Century*, trans. and ed. Burton Watson (New York: Columbia University Press, 1984), 225. No doubt, Shōhaku is also referring to the degradations of his own time, which was the beginning of what would later be called the period of Warring States.

16. All three of these incense blends use aloe wood as their primary ingredient.

less of that.[17] On a rainy night, pillowed with a visitor, or in the daytime, to the accompaniment of wind in the blinds, I mingle scents with poetry. In moments stolen from worldly troubles, I do little else.

I have sampled the wines of the Chinese and the barbarians, and also sought out the Kneaded Silk of Kyushu, the Chrysanthemum Flower of Kaga, and the superb brew of Amano, trying everything from thick to thin.[18] With one cupful, I banish a thousand cares, or get thoroughly drunk as I repair my spring robes.[19] It is saké that has helped me withstand wind and cold, reaching a fine old age. Once in a while I even dance, and then dance some more, returning my heart to the days of youth.

Shōjū of Kenninji[20] is the venerable priest from whom I received my name, and his successor, Jōan,[21] is also an old friend. I asked him to write something on these three virtues, and he complied, titling his piece "Three Loves." His words were so extraordinary that I am at a loss to describe the effect they had on me. But as a certain young man has importuned me to write out a version easier to read,[22] I have picked up my brush and done as he desired.

["MUAN NO KI," IN GUNSHO RUIJŪ, VOL. 17 (TOKYO: ZOKU GUNSHO RUIJŪ KANSEIKAI, 1959–1960). I HAVE ALSO CONSULTED H. MACK HORTON'S TRANSLATIONS IN SONG IN AN AGE OF DISCORD: "THE JOURNAL OF SŌCHŌ" AND POETIC LIFE IN LATE MEDIEVAL JAPAN (STANFORD, CALIF.: STANFORD UNIVERSITY PRESS, 2002), 165–66]

17. Perfume blending had been an art form for centuries before Shōhaku's time and was still widely practiced among courtiers and the high-ranking military. The first two scents mentioned here are among the classical Six Scents. The nature of the scent that Shōhaku refers to as *niimakura* (New Pillow) is unknown.

18. Many regions were known for their distinctive varieties of saké. Shōhaku mentions one from the southern island of Kyushu (*nerinukizaké*); another from Kaga, modern-day Ishikawa Prefecture; and another from Amano in Kawachi Province, present-day Osaka

19. Here Shōhaku alludes to two poems by Du Fu, both written in praise of wine. See H. Mack Horton, *Song in an Age of Discord: "The Journal of Sōchō" and Poetic Life in Late Medieval Japan* (Stanford, Calif.: Stanford University Press, 2002), 348.

20. D. 1498. Younger brother of the warrior-poet Tō no Tsuneyori (1401–1484). Kenninji was a Rinzai Zen temple located in the eastern hills of Kyoto.

21. D. 1536. A son of Tō no Tsuneyori's who became head priest of Kenninji after Shōjū. He wrote an inscription for a portrait of Shōhaku that gives us some of our most basic information about the poet's life.

22. Jōan's piece was in Chinese.

6

A Tenbun Miscellany

The Fujiwara Lay Monk

Tenbun zōsetsu (A Tenbun Miscellany) *is a collection of stories, interspersed with topical essays, that dates from the Tenbun era (1532–1555). Everything we know about the text's author—the Tō (Chinese reading of "Fujiwara," the name of a lineage) Lay Monk (late sixteenth century)—comes from the colophon of the work, which says that he compiled his collection during a time of quiet seclusion, completing it in 1553; that his work is based on chats he had with various people; and that he hopes his work will at least amuse readers of later times. Not all his entries are humorous, but they are generally light in tone, preparing us for similar collections to come in the Edo period, when many so-called* zuihitsu *were actually compilations of amusing anecdotes and stories.*

An Old Fox Knocks at the Door

Tales of foxes knocking at people's gates have been around for a long time. There's no way to determine whether they are true or not, so everyone just passes the stories down.

This past summer, at a house near Horikawa,[1] a knocking came at a certain door every night, just before daybreak, waking the residents from sleep. Intrigued, the owner of the house got up, went out, and opened the door, hoping to find out who it was. But there was no one there; all around was quiet and entirely deserted. The doors of the shops along the street were shut tight, and it didn't look like it could be an outsider.

After this happened four or five more times, the man was fed up, so one night he stayed up on the lookout, and, sure enough, just at the usual time a hairless old fox showed up.

"Aha!" the owner thought. "So that's who it is."

As the owner watched from his hiding place, the fox turned, stood with his back against the door, and knocked on it with his head.

The man thought this awfully funny, of course, and would have started laughing had he not restrained himself. After a while the fox ceased knocking and left.

The next night, the man sat waiting inside the door until late at night, and when the knocking started, he swiftly opened it and grabbed the fox as he fell over the threshold onto his back.

When daylight came, he found that the fox was not an ordinary fox at all but ancient and quite large. Some people said, "Ugh—kill the thing," but the man thought it would be unkind to take the animal's life over a bit of harmless mischief, so he just told the fox repeatedly not to knock on doors anymore and let him go.

The fox cried out twice by the gate as he was going off and then vanished.

What an amusing thing for a fox to do!

A Coward in Nara

A priest at Kōfukuji[2] says there is nothing one can do for someone who has suddenly been overwhelmed by fear.

---

1. The name of both a canal running north to south in Kyoto and the street alongside the canal.
2. One of the largest and most powerful Buddhist temples in Nara. The city had been the capital of the imperial government from 710 to 784 and remained a prominent noble enclave.

In Nara lived a carpenter who after careful thought concluded that the world is in such an uproar these days, with trouble lurking around every corner, that being in a city offers no safety and the only thing you can do is keep your place locked up tight. After the hour of the evening bell had come, the four or five people who made up his household would not open the door to anyone who came knocking, no matter what the errand, but would only talk through the door.

One night a thief came, and the carpenter heard him pushing on the door and working on the latch and knew what was up, so he picked up a hand lance, swung it around to make ready, and went over to the door, planning to kill the intruder as soon as he got inside. As he waited, he bore up as best he could while his hair stood on end, his legs began shaking, and all the power went out of his arms. When at long last the thief pushed the door open a crack and began to stick his head through, the man yelled, "Thief—I've seen a thief!"—but then just stood there, with the lance still in his hand.

Taken aback by the shouting, the thief said, "Yes you have!" and ran off into the night.

The other people in the house thought the master had really shown his stuff and came running with lanterns, but found the carpenter standing there with his hair undone and the lance in his hand but no sign of a dead thief.

"What happened?" they asked.

"That thief got lucky," the carpenter said. "I thought I'd run him through, but he got away. I guess my words got out before my lance. No matter, though. I did the job; he won't be back again."

Thus dismissing the matter, the carpenter went back to bed, but in his sleep he kept calling out, "Ah—I see him, I see him!" in a voice so distraught that his wife finally shook him awake and asked what he was saying.

"Oh my—that thief—that thief's got me scared silly," he replied.

The next day, the carpenter got the chills and then later was burning up with fever. His wife rushed out to get a doctor to examine him. The doctor gave him an herbal medicine, but still his fever persisted, and he just lay there groaning and saying, "Oh, that thief—he's a scary one, a scary one for sure."

After all his medicines had failed, the doctor said, "I've treated many people suffering with fevers before, but this is the first time I've seen anyone come down with a fever out of fear. I don't think anyone but the thief himself can cure it. So go find him, and beg *him* to help."

With that, the doctor left. Other doctors heard the story, and not a one of them would even try to help. After a while, the family got a venerable Shingon Buddhist priest to come and pray over the carpenter, but he too failed to produce results.

Time went by, and for fifty days the man lay there, not succumbing to death, until his fever left of its own accord and he returned to his senses. People all over town heard the story and had a good laugh about it.

"If you live long enough," the priest said, "you do hear the strangest stories."

Two Merchants at a Roadside Chapel in the Eastern Hills

Recently I was at Kiyomizu Temple on a pilgrimage.[3] As I left, heading across the mountain from behind the temple, I saw two or three men who looked to be merchants stopping for a break at a roadside chapel. Hiding myself nearby, I listened as they chatted and laughed about the world, very much at their ease.

One of them said, "Just look at the world these days. People are like dogs at one another's throats, as if they weren't even human beings. When they come across someone who looks vulnerable, they cut him down and strip him of his clothing. It's outrageous. I guess it must be because we're in the Days of Decline—the way no standards apply anymore between master and servant, or between friends. And the weak, they're the ones who suffer. That's not all, though—the way monks behave is also deplorable. Listen to what goes on in temples around the capital, and you see how bad things have gotten. A priest will pretend that some woman is family and shack up with her, or hide her in a house somewhere and visit all the time—the variations are endless. Then, with such a reputation for weaknesses of the flesh, it appears that they eat meat and fish,

---

3. Located, then and now, up a slope in the eastern hills of Kyoto.

too.[4] Or the chief priest of a temple will retire and say he's turning it over to a disciple, when it's really his son—it's shameless. He wears the three robes,[5] so people spend their precious money entertaining him and make him the guest of honor at their parties. You have to wonder what's going on."

The other man then said this: "Well, look all you want for a good person in the world—you won't find a single one. You may not see it in their faces, but inside they're all rotten. And it's not just priests who are bad. No, if you hold Buddhism in high regard, expecting much of priests is pointless. They have lots of faults, but as long as they're keeping up appearances, you should just pretend you don't notice. Ears are for hearing, noses for smelling, mouths for eating, tongues for tasting good and bad—and all of us, high and low, are the same. The role of our private parts, male and female, is to propagate life, and that is vital. So if you're talking about someone whose faculties are all in order, you can't blame a priest just because of his passions—that would be heartless. After all, it looks to me like it's *because* they're priests that they try to cover up for their sins. What's so bad about that, next to stripping people of their clothing out in broad daylight?"

The two men laughed and then parted ways, one going east, one going west.

Treasured Words from Lord Nijō Masafusa

A certain man invited Lord Nijō Masafusa[6] to his house to serve him tea, and Masafusa went discreetly, with just a couple of attendants to accompany him.

After the meal was over, when Masafusa was praising the tea utensils, one by one, he said, "This kettle here—this is one I am not acquainted with. If you own this, you must surely have other treasures as well. Be

4. Buddhist regulations required priests to be celibate and to refrain from eating meat.
5. *San'e*. Priests wore three different kinds of robes: one for going out, one for performing devotions, and one for resting and sleeping.
6. 1496–1551. An imperial regent and the head of one of the most prestigious lineages of the Fujiwara clan, albeit at the nadir of aristocratic power.

that as it may, what an extraordinary fragrance the kettle produced when the water was steaming. Just what can you tell me about it?"

The owner replied, "You are a fine judge of quality. The piece is called a Nine-Ringed Kettle. Until medieval times there were a lot of them around, but these days it's a rare find."

"Ah," Masafusa said, "then this is that Moroyasu's doing[7]—the design he had cast after the pattern of the rings at the top of a pagoda. And if that's what's behind it, I'm not interested. I appreciate your intentions, of course, but no—I'd feel almost heartless to have any regard for something made by such a villain."

He had his tea made with water from a quite ordinary kettle and would have nothing to do with the Nine-Ringed piece, so the story goes. Quite an example of simple, refined good taste.

The Akamatsu Preceptor's Manual for Warriors

In Nisonji[8] in Ōmi is a scroll that claims to be a copy of a military manual by the Akamatsu preceptor.[9] In it appears a group of "Admonitions for Warriors" said to have been transmitted from a goblin[10] to Kuro Hōgan[11] when he was in Kurama.[12] It contains the following items:

- Take heed when you pass your first urine in the morning. If it is frothy, it is a good sign; but on days when it is not, take extra care in what you do.
- When you are headed out somewhere, you should drink warm water, tea, and saké, in that order, before leaving. Whatever the beverages, if they come around in proper order, it bodes well—go ahead and

---

7. Kō no Moroyasu (d. 1351), brother of the infamous Moronao (d. 1351), both of whom figure as villains in stories and plays of the late medieval and Edo periods.

8. The location of this temple is unknown.

9. Probably Akamatsu Norisuke (1314–1372), a warrior in service to the Ashikaga shoguns.

10. *Tengu.* Category of creatures with beaks, wings, and human bodies that were associated with mountains such as Kurama, where they transmitted esoteric knowledge and skills to initiates.

11. The nickname of Minamoto no Yoshitsune (1159–1189), the younger brother of Minamoto no Yoritomo (1147–1199) and a prominent warrior in his own right. Legends about him and the Kurama *tengu* appear in many medieval stories and plays.

12. A mountain north of the capital, which is the site of a temple of the same name.

be on your way. If they come around in reverse order, though, don't leave.

- If you cannot see your reflection in broth, don't eat it.
- A vertical line at the tip of the nose bodes ill. If it is greenish in color, it means someone is preparing to do you harm. If it is purplish, someone is planning to poison you.
- Spit in your hand and look to see if the spit is frothy. If it is, that's a good sign; if not, that's a bad sign.
- Sometimes red blotches will appear on your palms. That indicates you have suffered a pollution. You should purify yourself and concentrate your thoughts on the bodhisattva Miroku.[13]
- If your palms or that place between your balls and your anus itches, something bad is going to happen. But if it's the palm of your right hand that itches, that's a good omen.
- Sometimes your ears will suddenly ring. During the hours of the Rat, Tiger, Dragon, Snake, Horse, and Monkey, ringing bodes well; but during the hours of the Ox, Rabbit, Ram, Cock, Dog, and Boar, it bodes ill.
- If you take your pulse at your neck and your wrist at the same time, and they are in harmony, that's a good sign. But it bodes ill if they are different—as if life were at odds with itself.
- If a weasel crosses your path, it's fine if he's going to the left, but if he's going to the right, you shouldn't take that path.

I recorded this in phonetic script so that not just warriors but others too may treasure its precepts.

Saint Kūya Saves Morouji

Major Counselor Morouji[14] was one of the most trusted courtiers of the Engi emperor,[15] whom he served in every way. Each morning, he parted

---

13. Skt. Maitreya, "the Benevolent One," also called the Buddha of the future, who will come to earth in ages hence, bringing universal enlightenment.
14. Fujiwara no Morouji (913–970), who was indeed a major figure at court.
15. The Engi emperor—emperor of the Engi era (901–923)—was Daigo (885–930; r. 897–930).

the mists going to the palace; each evening, he went home with the stars above his head. So busy was he administering worldly affairs, in fact, that he did nothing in preparation for enlightenment or the next life.

But the time came: he was stricken with illness and about to die. Regretting that he had accumulated no merit, he sent a messenger to Saint Kūya[16] lamenting his fate. Kūya wondered what he could do for such a person but said that he would at least go and see him, and returned with the messenger to Morouji's house.

When he saw that Kūya had come, Morouji put his hands together and pleaded, "I have done no good deeds and must certainly descend to hell. Please, find a way to help me!"

From the moment he arrived, the people standing by had been wondering what Kūya might say, but he merely asked for paper and ink, wrote something down, and said, "Put this in the coffin, and after he dies cremate it along with the body." Then he left.

Not long thereafter, Morouji passed away, and they put the letter in his coffin before cremation. After four or five days, when they were extracting the bones, they found a letter in the ashes, with no evidence of having been burned at all.

Thinking this most curious, someone picked up the letter and opened it, discovering that it was not Kūya's letter, but rather a note addressed on the outside "To the Honorable Saint Kūya, from the Palace of King Enma."[17]

They opened the note and read, "Major Counselor Morouji's bad deeds are undeniable, and he deserves to be sent screaming down to hell; but because of the high regard we have for Your Eminence's intercession, we have sent him on to the Tusita Heaven.[18] Most Respectfully."

All those who heard of this were moved to tears and spoke of Kūya with even greater reverence.

Among the lives of priests are many stories of this sort.

---

16. 903–972. A Tendai monk and the founder of Saikōji in Kyoto.
17. Skt. Yama. The underworld judge who consigns people to their appropriate fates.
18. *Tosotsuten*. The paradise of the bodhisattva Miroku.

Secret Transmissions on Grafting

A certain physician said this: "Taking grafts from a tree and spreading them here and there is a fine practice. The fruit from grafted trees is bigger and tastes better, and in the case of a tree that is ill and rotting, grafting a branch onto another tree will preserve its flowers and fruit into the future, even if the original tree dies. The cherry tree at Kōsetsuji[19] was grafted from one at Urin'in Temple[20] that was dearly loved by Emperor Uda.[21] Thus the virtue of grafting is that it brings joy to the eyes of people of a later day and inspires fond feelings about the past. Isn't this how that tree loved by Saigyō,[22] the tree that withered and died in the end, is still in its glory today? If not for this technique, the beloved trees of earlier times would no longer exist. No doubt those who came up with this idea did so against our own day of decline.

"I saw in a Chinese book that if you put musk on the bark of a graft, its fruit and flowers will end up rich and fragrant. It appears that people of other countries went so far as to experiment even in such matters. But in our country, that kind of thing is unheard of. Surely more possibilities must exist, but we lack the inventive spirit to pursue them. Instead, we trundle along, entangled in the demands of the moment, never concentrating our thoughts. And one hears that a lot of fine ideas never got written down."

[*TENBUN ZŌSETSU*, ED. YOSHIDA KŌICHI, KOTEN BUNKO 628
(TOKYO: KOTEN BUNKO, 1999)]

19. The location of this temple is unknown.

20. A Tendai temple located in Murasakino, north of Kyoto. Like many temples on the outskirts of the capital, it began as an imperial retreat.

21. 867–931. In 896, Emperor Uda made a pilgrimage to the temple and later wrote a Chinese poem about the experience.

22. 1118–1190. A famous monk-poet. The cherry tree referred to here may be the one at his hut in the western hills of Kyoto that is featured in the Noh play *Saigyōzakura* (*Saigyō's Cherry Blossoms*).

III

THE EDO PERIOD

With the establishment of the Tokugawa shogunate around 1600, Japan entered a new era of peace and economic stability that had a profound impact on every dimension of Japanese life, including literary discourse. Urbanization and rising rates of literacy made for new audiences that new genres of fiction, poetry, and drama, in particular, sought to accommodate. For the first time, books were being published in a thriving literary market.

In this new world, *zuihitsu* writing blossomed as never before.

Most of the dominant intellectual discourses of the new age are represented in the following pieces—the majority of which are by poets, Confucian scholars, Nativist scholars, and government officials. But also found here is a sheaf of anecdotes and preachments by a prominent painter (Shiba Kōkan), a miscellany (à la Yoshida no Kenkō) by a physician (Tachibana Nankei), a selection of jokes and anecdotes by a Buddhist priest (Anrakuan Sakuden), and a group of stories by the wife of a provincial samurai (Tadano Makuzu). Furthermore, the authors do not always restrict themselves to their own disciplines. Thus Matsudaira Sadanobu, senior councilor (*rōjū*) to the shogun, offers not a treatise on government but elegant musings on rain, cherry blossoms, and cautionary anecdotes about predicting the weather and the wisdom of always "doing things well," while Natsume Seibi, a haiku poet, presents not an essay on poetics but a narrative of his move into a new house in his declining years.

What the works of the Edo period present is thus diversity in style, voice, and subject matter. In more mainstream genres, writers were bound by fairly strict conventions, but not so in their essays, where they could indulge their own interests and proclivities. In most cases, the works they produced in this way were not commercial. Instead, they were—to hark back to Kenkō once again—the products (rhetorically, that is) of idle hours and vagrant interests or by-products of more serious discourse.

7

Laughs to Keep You Awake

ANRAKUAN SAKUDEN

Anrakuan Sakuden (Sakuden of Anraku Cottage; 1554-1642) studied at Zenrinji in Kyoto and eventually ended up as chief priest at Seiganji, also in Kyoto. In 1619, he was given imperial permission to don purple robes, one of the highest honors available for a cleric. His circle of friends included prominent poets, such as Matsunaga Teitoku (1571-1653) and Kinoshita Chōshōshi, as well as the tea master and garden designer Kobori Enshū (1579-1647). After retiring from Seiganji, he constructed a tea house, which he called Anrakuan (Peace and Pleasure Cottage). He is especially known for his humorous writings and is indeed often regarded as the originator of rakugo—a form of comic monologue that remains popular in Japan. He left behind collections of poetry in a variety of forms but is best known for the zuihitsu *collection Seisuishō (Laughs to Keep You Awake), which he presented to the governor-general of Kyoto in 1628.*

Sakuden's anecdotes involve people from all classes and all walks of life— daimyo, samurai, court aristocrats, scholars, poets, and priests, but also gamblers and thieves. Many of his stories are about people of earlier times, but just as many are about life in the present. His humor ranges from the light and whimsical to the bawdy, including everything in between.

Dumb Disciples

The stupidest disciple in all Japan had this to say behind his master's back: "The old man is always scolding me for something, but lately he's said three things that make no sense at all. The first is about all the pains he's taken trying to make me into a proper human being—which would be fine if I'd been born a dog. But the fact is I was born a man, and he can't take credit for it. The second is how angry he is that I show no appreciation for the effort he's put into teaching me the scriptures, which would be a reasonable complaint except that I don't remember a single verse of what I learned and can't very well be grateful for what I've completely forgotten. And the third is about my attitude toward all the worldly things he'll be leaving me—the temple, the furnishings, and everything. But I don't feel any gratitude for that. If he's so peeved, let him take everything with him when he goes! Not a one of his three big complaints makes any sense."

> "Ill treatment too
> should with gratitude be met"
> —so the saying goes.
> A man without gratitude,
> why he's no man at all.

ada o sae / on nite mukuu / iware ari / on o wasururu / hito wa hito kawa

———————

There was a disciple who was incredibly dense. His master would host a tea gathering, and while the tea was being served people would engage in small talk, guessing one another's ages. But the disciple was likely to mistake someone who was thirty or forty for being fifty or sixty, and be laughed at.

The master couldn't stand listening to this anymore, so he confronted the disciple. "I suppose there really is no cure for stupidity,"[1] he said, "but listen: no one wants to take on years, so the thing to do is always say people look younger—and take care never to say that someone has gotten old."

The next day, the disciple was sent on an errand. When he met the lady of the house, who was holding an infant in her arms, he asked, "And how old is the child?"

"Not even a full year yet," she replied. "He's a newborn."

"Oh," the disciple said, "I must say, though—he looks even younger than that!"

Far off the Mark

Despite coming down with a disease in his own eyes, an eye doctor was still boasting that his medicine was the best around. "Use it once, and the mists will clear; twice, and your cataracts will disappear," he noised it about.

"Why hasn't it worked on your own eyes, then?" someone asked.

"Ah," he said, "but that's what I mean. My medicine is so miraculous that it's stopped the disease at my cheeks. Otherwise, it would have gone all the way down to my chin!"

Just Judgments

On Mount Hiei,[2] the young men of Kitadani loved snow, which in their belief surpassed all other things in beauty, while the young men of Minamidani thought that cherry blossoms provided the most beautiful of all sights.

Things went on like this for a while, and before long people on both sides began to attribute feelings where there were none and

---

1. A Japanese proverb, *ukke ni kusuri ga nai.*
2. Site of the Enryakuji complex.

arguments broke out. Some spoke ill of cherry blossoms; others bad-mouthed snow.

Those on the side of snow said, "Let's get those louts who praise blossoms and pommel them good!"—while those on the side of blossoms said, "Let's catch the idiots who praise snow and bash them!" Both sides got more and more worked up, until the uproar on the mountain was something quite out of the ordinary.

Lord Nishisanjō Shōyōin[3] was told this and made a special trip up the mountain.

"To be fond of snow is entirely reasonable," he said.

If these were blossoms,
not every branch would bloom
at the same time.
What can truly compare, then,
to snow in the light of dawn?[4]

hana naraba / sakanu kozue mo / aru beki ni / nani ni tatoen / yuki no akebono

"But I can also understand how people are moved by cherry blossoms."

If this were snow,
I would endlessly be brushing flakes
from my sleeves.[5]
In a blizzard of blossoms
I cross over Shiga Pass.

yuki naraba / ikutabi sode o / harawamashi / hana no fubuki no / shiga no yamagoe

"Hereafter, stop contending over which is superior and get along. You're in the same bedroom, so get together,[6] and apply your efforts to your studies."

---

3. Sanjōnishi Sanetaka (1455–1537), a famous poet and scholar.
4. In other words, the snow is superior to blossoms in that it covers all the branches at once.
5. Because blossoms do not drench one's sleeves, one need not brush them off.
6. Here Sanetaka borrows the syntax of a Buddhist injunction to suggest that the young priests might better spend their time "getting together"—a reference to sexual relations—instead of arguing.

After calming them down in this way, he returned home.

On the seventh day of the Seventh Month of 1602, a skinny, swarthy laborer with a bamboo basket on his back, leaning on a bamboo walking stick, passed by on a street in Kyoto.

"What a sight!" people said. "Rumor has it that of late the lid of hell's caldron has come off, allowing sinners to roam free as spirits. I wonder if he's one of them?"

At this point, the man approached a shop and asked how much it would be for a melon.

"Two coppers," came the answer.

Since he had only one copper, the man asked the merchant if he might consider charging only that much and think of it as a good deed.

"As you wish," the merchant said, and the man took the melon and quickly gobbled it down, top to bottom. But when the man looked for the coin, it had fallen off somewhere, leaving only the money string hanging there.

"Mister melon seller, please show some mercy and just let me go," the man pleaded, but the merchant was a callous sort. "That's enough; you're no different from a pickpocket," he said, and called his neighbors over. They chased the skinny man into the courtyard of the governor-general's house and recounted all that had transpired. The laborer also explained his plight.

After listening to their stories, the governor of Iga[7] said, "I'll have to examine the facts here. In the meantime, turn the man over to the melon seller and have him feed him his two meals a day. And you neighborhood people—you be sure to guard the man carefully. If you don't, I won't spare you the consequences." He then sent them all home.

The people thought that this was a lot of fuss for one copper and were annoyed at the bother it caused them, but they found a small room, shut the man up in it, and fed him his daily meals.

Six or seven days went by without a judgment, until the people got fed up and went to ask for a decision. To this, the governor replied, "Sorry,

7. Itakura Katsushige (d. 1624), the governor-general (*shoshidai*) of Kyoto at the time.

I've been awfully busy. Here it is, the time of the Lantern Festival,[8] and the offense involves a single melon. I should have handed down my judgment right away, but I stretched things out because I resented the hardheartedness of the melon seller. When you see someone starving, you should invite him in and give him something to eat. Instead, you seize the helpless man and say, 'Off with his head!' over one silly copper. I kept you waiting in order to teach you a little compassion. Now, hurry up and let the poor man go."

Hearing this, the people sitting there all bowed their heads, every one of them moved to tears.

In Yadamachi of Kyoto lived a man and wife. The husband died first, and the wife spent her days grieving until the first full year after his death had passed by. Then she called in her son—the heir of the house—and his younger sister and talked with them about their father.

Holding back tears, she said to the son, "You have received the headship of the house and your inheritance, so please follow your father's wishes now and give this residence and the little else that remains to your sister, and find a husband for her."

To this the son replied, "The inheritance I got wasn't that much, and I'm not about to hand over this house or any of my wealth," and stormed out of the room.

Later, the son sent a message declaring that he was going to take the house, which made the mother so angry that she said she would refuse to turn it over, even if it came to burning it down in spite. The neighborhood got involved at this point, but when they tried to relay the demands of the mother to her son, it did no good.

The son then wrote a list of his complaints and took it to the governor-general, who carefully considered the son's statement but became very angry before even getting to the point where a hearing of the parties could be held.

---

8. Urabon. The Festival of the Dead, held midway through the Seventh Month. The implication is that at such a time, people might show a little more kindness.

"Filial piety is the foundation of all virtue, and the lack of it is the source of all evil," he said. "Even if what your mother asked were unreasonable, you would still obey her, all alone and old as she is, if you understood the first thing about what it means to be dutiful. As the saying goes, 'When a parent goes crazy, the child must go along.'[9] What's more, in this case I think your mother's reasoning is entirely sound. To defy your father's will and go against the order of things by being unfilial in your reaction to your mother's commands—that is just not right. Indeed, I'm so concerned that having someone like you in the city may lead others astray, I think I want you out of town, and I mean now. Stay around, and I'll take care of you—you can be sure of that."

The son vanished without uttering a word.

———————

One day, the wood roofing of a house on Ayanokōji Street was being replaced. The woman of the house went up to the roof and somehow tripped and fell off just when the neighbor lady next door was standing right under her—striking her so hard that her neck broke and she died.

The husband of the dead woman just kept insisting that this had all been done intentionally and wouldn't listen to reason. So he went to the governor-general.

The governor of Iga[10] said, "You persist, so we'll do this—since as luck has it we have a model to follow. Let's just put the wife of your neighbor right where your own wife was standing, and then you go up on the roof yourself and fall down on this woman you hate so much and kill her."

The man went home speechless.

———————

In Heian City, a man had put some clothing in a pawnshop, and when he went to reclaim it, he saw places where a mouse had been nibbling. This distressed him so much that he begged the owner to make amends in

9. The *Analects* imply that a filial child should "shield" his parents from harm, no matter what the circumstances. See Confucius, *The Analects*, trans. D. C. Lau (New York: Penguin, 1979), 121.
10. Again, Itakura Katsushige (see note 7).

some way, even if only by charging a little less in interest; but the pawn-broker would not listen. He did, however, kill a mouse and give it to the man, saying, "Here is the guilty party who nibbled at your things in the storehouse. So there—he's been punished."

The customer was very dissatisfied with this and went to the governor-general to explain his case, which resulted in an order from Taga no Bungo.[11]

"It was indeed the mouse who was the thief. The house he belonged to should therefore be confiscated."

All the pawnbroker's goods were taken and given to the customer.

Spoken Too Soon

Someone asked a man walking with a limp, "Is one of your legs shorter than the other?"

"Why no," the man replied, "one is *longer* than the other."

————————

A band of thieves got done with a job and gathered in an unfrequented place to divvy up their loot.

"Hey," one of them said, "that washcloth of mine's gone missing. What's going on?"

One of the men shook his head and said, "I can't believe it. Why, surely there's no one here who looks like he might steal!"

————————

One morning, even before dawn, a young man opened the door and was heard to say, "Wow, a lot of snow has fallen!"

The master heard him and asked, "And just how much?"

"Well, it's about six inches deep," came the answer, "but as for width, I can't say."

11. Taga Takatada, who served as governor-general at the time of the Ashikaga shogun Yoshimasa (1436–1490).

That's the Way the World Is

An old lady was standing by the roadside, weeping, as if overcome by some great sadness. A passer-by asked her what had happened to choke her so with tears.

"It's that man there. As I look at him, going off in formal robes of dark blue, his umbrella on his shoulder, and bamboo clappers[12] in his breast pocket, I just know he must be a preacher. Thinking about all the sad feelings in his breast, my heart goes out to him, and I drench my sleeves."

> An ordinary man
> is what I behold, yet see
> the Buddha—
> Buddha who, for all that,
> is an ordinary man.

> *tada ari no / hito o miru koso / hotoke nare / hotoke to iu mo / tada ari no hito*

> If that's how it is,
> I will weep, then, and make tears
> my offering—
> I who at Tanabata[13] time
> have only tears to give.

> *iza saraba / naite tamuken / tanabata ni / namida yori hoka / mi ni mo araba ya*

———————

When Muan[14] was living in Tsu,[15] Sakai Province, so many people had asked for poems on the beginning of spring[16] that he had told his servants

---

12. *Sasara.* Such clappers were used by mendicant monks to attract attention.
13. The Festival of the Herd Boy and the Weaver Maiden, which in Japan is associated with the Festival of the Dead, or Obon. It is traditionally celebrated on the seventh day of the Seventh Month.
14. Botanka Shōhaku (1443–1527), a master of linked verse.
15. Ancient Settsu Province, modern-day Osaka.
16. People attending various festivities had to produce poems, which a poetry master like Shōhaku would often compose for them.

very firmly, "I don't care who comes asking, tell them I'm indisposed and can't oblige." Then he settled down to get a little rest.

But on the morning of the fifth day of the New Year, while he was sleeping, the servant came in and quietly asked his master, "A certain man has come asking for a hokku[17] on the subject of 'The Day of the Rat.' What should I say?"

"Haven't I already told you . . . ?" the poet began to scold the servant.

"I know," the man said, "but he's brought three thousand coppers as a gratuity."

"Well, in that case," Muan replied, "I'll get up and compose a verse right away."

The Finest of Feelings

Suddenly a man lost his love for his wife and sent her packing. Without a complaint, she prepared to leave. When some women friends came to say good-bye, they asked, "You really don't deserve this treatment. Isn't there anything you'll take with you?"

"No," she answered, "what could be more dear to me than my husband? If I'm going off without him, there isn't anything else I want to take along."

Overhearing this, the husband felt such inexpressible sadness that he ended up staying with her until death.

———————

In Izumi Province, Sakai, there lived a writer named Sōchin.[18] He had copied out *The Tale of Genji* twenty-three times and was at the "Morning Glories" chapter on his twenty-fourth time when he passed away. Botanka[19] was so moved by his dedication that he wrote the following as a memorial:

17. The first verse of a linked-verse sequence.
18. A master of linked-verse, he lived in Sakai, not far from Shōhaku's place in Settsu Ikeda.
19. "Peony Blossom," one of Shōhaku's sobriquets.

As he set to write,
he must have had in his heart
a vow from before:
to perish that very moment—
dew on the morning glory.

fude ni somi / kokoro ni kakeshi / chigiri ni ya / orishimo kieshi / asagao no hana

―――――――――

A man and wife who had gotten along for a long time had a senseless argument, and the man told her to get out. On the day she was set to leave, the rain was falling down hard as friends of hers gathered.

"This rain is really awful," someone said, but the wife replied,

If it rains, let it—
and let clouds gather too!
Even if the sun
comes out to clear the skies,
my sleeves will not be dry.

furaba fure / kumoraba kumore / teru totemo / nurasade yukan / sode naraba koso

When the husband heard this, he was so sad that he didn't want to let her go. And someone else there, quietly listening, remembered that the poem was one that Izumi Shikibu[20] had written when she was in Tango Province.

―――――――――

At the time of the governor of Echizen, there was a very dedicated samurai named Takatada,[21] who although it was winter had only a thin kimono

20. A famous court poet of the eleventh century in service to Empress Akiko. This story comes from *Shasekishū* (*The Sand and Pebbles Collection*, 1283), which says only "a certain person" and not Izumi Shikibu.
21. Identity unknown. A similar story appears in two medieval folktale collections: *Konjaku monogatari* (*Tales of Times Now Past*, ca. 1120) and *Uji shūi monogatari* (*A Collection of Tales from Uji*, early thirteenth century).

to wear. One snowy day, he was commanded to write a poem and asked what the topic should be.

"On being naked," was the reply, so he intoned,

White flakes of snow
pile up on my naked skin,
falling on and on,
with no sign at all
they will soon melt away.

hadaka naru / waga mi ni kakaru / shirayuki wa / uchifuruedomo / kiesezarikeri

So moved was the governor that he gave the man the robe he himself was wearing, and the wife, too, felt so sorry for him that she presented him with a fine robe of light purple.

————————

When Lord Sanjō Sankōin was just sixteen years old, he drew the topic "Reminiscing" to write a poem about for an event at court.[22]

"This is going to be difficult," he said, which made everyone look at him with great anticipation. Since no one offered that it would be all right for him to write on a different topic, he finally said,

As I think fondly
of a past that for me
is not so long ago—
I can understand the tears
of those who have grown old.

hodo chikaki / waga mukashi sae / koishiki ni / oi wa ika naru / namida naru ran

————————

In the town of Gifu, Mino Province, there lived a poor master of linked verse named Sōko. He was always putting things into pawn at the house

___

22. Sanjōnishi Saneki (1511–1579), a grandson of Sanetaka's and himself a court poet. After a formal poetry gathering, topics were "drawn" by all participants for extemporaneous composition.

of a rich man named Horiike, and then every year lacked the funds to redeem anything. As he was wondering what to do about getting a jacket as winter approached, he wrote this poem and sent it to the rich man:

What kind of river
flows through your storehouse?
I must wonder.
The things I put in pawn there
never flow out again.

kura no uchi ni / ika naru kawa no / aru yaran / waga oku shichi no / nagarenu
   wa nashi

Reading this, the rich man took pity and said, "His feelings are like those of Huiyuan[23] of Mount Lushan,[24] who received saké for a poem he composed." The story goes that he then took everything Sōko had in pawn and returned it to him.

Tipplers

During the reign of Lord Yoshimasa,[25] the fifth generation after Ashikaga Takauji,[26] saké was banned both inside and outside the capital city. However, a man named Man'ami—a curator[27] in service to the shogun—must have been drinking, for as he knelt before Yoshimasa his face looked as red as if it had been lacquered.

Lord Yoshimasa said, "From the look of your face, you've been drinking saké."

"Oh no, My Lord," replied Man'ami, "it's just that—well, it's so cold outside that on my way in I warmed myself in front of the fire."

---

23. 334–416. One of the founders of the Pure Land sect in China, he lived on Mount Lushan.
24. A famous mountain in China that was the site of many Buddhist temples.
25. Ashikaga Yoshimasa, the eighth Ashikaga shogun (see note 11).
26. 1305–1358. The first Ashikaga shogun.
27. *Dōbōshū*. The designation given to monks who served as stewards in the arts, assisting at shogunal events and collecting and maintaining artistic wares.

"Is that so?" said Yoshimasa. "Then come over, and let's see if I can smell it on you."

The man had to go forward, of course, so he did.

"No doubt about it," said the shogun. "You're ripe as a rotting persimmon."

"Yes, My Lord," Man'ami said. "You are precisely right. The fire where I warmed myself was burning just that—persimmon wood!"

At a drinking party, after the dancing and revelry were over, a man who was thoroughly drunk recklessly headed for home. Stumbling along, he made some headway. It being the end of the Eleventh Month, however, the canal was covered over with a coat of snow and frost, and as he attempted to cross it, his steps went awry and he ended up falling into deep water. Before long, he was in up to his neck. But, despite being half drowned, he started to fall asleep and didn't even realize that he was beginning to freeze.

At his house, they began to wonder why he was so late, seeing as everyone else had come home, so they got a group together and went off to the canal, where they saw a head out in the water.

As they headed out to him, breaking the ice on the way and calling to him, he replied, "Who's that, beating on the door in the middle of the night? Rude bastard!"

Silly Secrets

When Yoshitsune[28] was on his way to the Kantō, he took lodging one night in a roadside house. Benkei[29] asked the lady of the house how many children she had.

---

28. Minamoto no Yoshitsune (1159–1189), a famous general at the time of the Genpei Wars in the early 1180s. Branded a rebel by his brother, the shogun Yoritomo (1147–1199), he fled to the deep north, where he eventually committed suicide.
29. Yoshitsune's faithful retainer.

"My husband has six, and I have six, so altogether we have nine," she answered.

This seemed to make no sense, so he made slow progress wondering about the matter as he traveled on the next day, until he figured it out: the man had had three children of his own from a previous marriage, as had the woman from her first marriage, and then the couple had had three more children together. This would mean that the man had six children himself, and the woman six as well, but would make for a total of only nine.

A certain guest made everyone nervous. Among other things, he demanded to be brought saké. The servant, a boorish sort named Chiyo, proceeded to ask the proprietor in a rather loud voice, "Mistress, shall I bring him the cheap stuff, or the good stuff?" This put such a damper on things that the mistress called the servant over and chided her, saying, "You shouldn't say that out loud right in front of a guest!"

Then one day the heir of the house, who was just five or six years old, got away from his tenders and tumbled down the well. The same Chiyo quietly walked over to the mistress and whispered into her ear, so that no one could hear, "Mistress, the little master has just fallen into the well."

Off the Mark

In the neighborhood of a roof-tile maker lived a family with the ugliest daughter in the whole world. At the age of twenty-four or twenty-five, the girl died, and the tile maker went over to call on the parents, in tears.

"But why should *you* be so upset?" he was asked.

"Oh," he replied, "it's just that now I'll be without a model to use for my gargoyles!"[30]

30. *Onigawara*. Used as decorations on roof gables.

Bishop Jie[31] was from Ōmi Province. When he was the Tendai abbot, the day came for ordinations, and people gathered, just as always, waiting for the abbot to come out and perform his task. But midway there, he turned around and withdrew to his chambers.

Wondering what might be going on, his attendants and other officers said to him, "You are postponing a very important ordinance that is always undertaken on this day—and for no good reason. It simply won't do," and then went on to berate him.

Novices from all over the country had come, expecting to be ordained, but the abbot only sent a messenger from Yokawa saying that the ordinations would be put off until a later date. And when those assembled asked why they were being put off,[32] the servant said only, "I don't know. He just told me, 'Quickly, now—go and make the announcement.'"

Still uncomprehending, all the monks left the mountain. But that very afternoon, a great wind descended upon the south gate, which collapsed. Had the monks still been there, people realized, they all would have been killed.

At a Loss for Words

A handsome young novice came into service at a temple. The interest of the priest there was piqued, and he sneaked into the room where the young men always slept. Another young man heard him and followed behind in secret. When the priest in turn heard footsteps behind him, he flattened his arms out against the wall, and spread his legs out, too.

31. Ryōgen (912–985), the chief priest at Enryakuji on Mount Hiei, which was the foremost of all the monasteries of the Tendai sect. This story is taken almost verbatim from *Uji shūi monogatari*. See D. E. Mills, *A Collection of Tales from Uji: A Study and Translation of Uji shūi monogatari* (Cambridge: Cambridge University Press, 1970), 358.

32. Suzuki Tōzō notes a reference here to a passage in *Mencius* in which a messenger from a certain king comes to ask him to stay, in Anrakuan Sakuden, *Seisuishō*, ed. Suzuki Tōzō (Tokyo: Iwanami bunko, 1986). Mencius gives an enigmatic answer that sends the man back, disappointed. See *Mencius*, trans. D. C. Lau (New York: Penguin, 1970), 93.

Seeing this, the young man following him said, "What do you think you're doing?"

"Me? Why, I'm—aah—I'm just pretending to be a spider!" the priest replied.

––––––––––––––

Once there was a man who came to a house whenever the master was away. The wife told him, "Sneak down from the roof—I'll have a ladder ready. If my husband should come home, I'll just say, 'That must be a cat walking on the roof,' and then you make a meow sound."

So things were all arranged. But when the master really did come home one night, he heard something and said that it sounded like a man walking on the roof. "No," the wife said, "lately there's been a big cat walking around up there." But the man on the roof was so taken aback that he forgot what he was supposed to do and instead, in a very faint voice, came out with—"That's right, I'm a cat."

Rapid Replies

The monk Tonna,[33] dressed in his religious robes, was looking at the sights in the imperial palace compound when someone from inside one of the rooms there asked, "Where might this monk at his devotions come from?"

"From the Kantō," Tonna replied, and then was asked,

What are your memories
of the East so far away?[34]

nanika azuma no / hate no omoide

To this, Tonna replied,

33. 1289–1372. A poet and scholar who was famous as a quick study.
34. The question is in the form of one-half of a linked-verse couplet.

In the capital
the first thing one must tell of
is Fuji's snow.

miyako nite / mazu kataru beki / fuji no yuki

After this, Tonna was invited inside and ascended without any conces-
sion to protocol, eliciting the following:

Those in the lower estate
seem not to fear those above.

iyashiki mono wa / ue o osorezu

To this, Tonna replied immediately:

Floating waterfowl
tread on the reflection
of the moon.[35]

mizutori no / ukabeba tsuki no / kage fumite

In Kyushu, there was a man named Kiyama who was skilled at linked
verse. On the fifteenth day of the Eight Month, he said that he had
written a hokku[36] that included the line *tsuki mo nashi* [no sign of the
moon].

"That won't do; it just won't do," said Jōha.[37] "Not here beneath the
full moon of autumn."

"Please listen to the whole verse before you decide," the man said.

35. The poem suggests that appearances are deceiving: just as the waterfowl only appear to be
floating directly on the moon, it only appears that the monk is not conscious of being in the presence
of someone of high social rank.
36. The first verse of a linked verse had to be true to the surroundings and the season at the time.
37. Satomura Jōha (d. 1602), the most prominent linked-verse master of the day.

No sign of the moon—
only an orb shining bright
as the noonday sun.

tsuki mo nashi / hi o sono mama no / koyoi kana

———————

As Confucius[38] was walking down the street, he met a boy eight years old or so who asked him, "Which is farther away—the place where the sun goes down or the capital?"

Confucius answered, "Where the sun goes down is far away, while the capital is close by."

To this the boy replied, "I can see where the sun goes down, though, while the capital is beyond my sight. So I think of the sun as nearby and the capital as far away."

"What a bright little boy," Confucius exclaimed, and declared that the boy was really extraordinary.

[*SEISUISHŌ*, ED. SUZUKI TŌZŌ, 2 VOLS.
(TOKYO: IWANAMI BUNKO, 1986)]

---

38. The original story—somewhat different in details—appears in *Liezi*. See *The Book of Lieh-tzu: A Classic of the Tao*, trans. A. C. Graham (New York: Columbia University Press, 1960). Anrakuan probably knew the version that appears in the folktale collection *Uji shūi monogatari*. See Mills, *Collection of Tales from Uji*, 369.

8

On Ōhara

KINOSHITA CHŌSHŌSHI

Kinoshita Chōshōshi (born Kinoshita Katsutoshi; 1569-1649) was a samurai in service to Toyotomi Hideyoshi (1536-1598). Eventually, he became lord of Obama castle in Wakasa. After Hideyoshi's death, he found himself on the losing side in the conflicts that brought Tokugawa Ieyasu (1542-1616) to power and was obliged to take the tonsure at the young age of thirty-two. For nearly forty years thereafter, he lived in the eastern hills of Kyoto, moving to the foot of Oshio Mountain west of the capital in 1640. His time there was spent on literary and artistic pursuits. Among his friends were the most famous literati of the day, the poets Hosokawa Yūsai (1534-1610), Matsunaga Teitoku (1571-1653), and Reizei Tamekage (1612-1652), as well as the garden designer and architect Kobori Enshū (1579-1647) and the Confucian scholar Fujiwara Seika (1561-1619). Unusually for one of his era, however—and despite his close relationship with orthodox poets like Yūsai—he looked for inspiration to earlier and less-conventional poets such as Kyōgoku Tamekane (1254-1332) and Shōtetsu (1381-1459).

Chōshōshi's essay "Ōhara no ki" (On Ōhara) was written in 1640, after his move to Oshio Mountain, an area that had anciently been known as Ōharano. The piece presents a description of his life there, albeit one studded with allusions to earlier works in both Chinese and Japanese and heavily dependent on the models of earlier recluses, especially Kamo no Chōmei (d. 1216)—whose famous "Hōjōki" (The Ten-Foot-Square Hut) Chōshōshi alludes to several times—and the monk-poet Saigyō (1118-1190).

At the foot of Oshio Mountain stands a temple. Vivid still is the name Shōjiji, inscribed on a plaque written by Michikaze.[1] In front of the abbot's quarters is an old cherry tree said to have been planted by Saigyō. How movingly those half-rotten old limbs, which never forget spring, remind one of ancient times! The priest in charge of the place, one Chūkai, is a friend of mine.[2] He is a disciple of a famous priest said to be associated with Genkōin.[3]

Behind the temple, there is superb scenery. A curious cherry tree with five trunks grows there, big enough that one could hide an ox behind it. In some ways, it resembles a shrine oak.[4] At first, I wondered how it had escaped the carpenter's axe long enough to grow to such a size, but then I saw the truth: all things truly *do* live out the years granted them by heaven. To go back again in search of a tree that was useless as lumber yesterday is pointless, after all.[5] One can only chuckle and move on.

Living beneath that tree is an old man who takes it for shelter.[6] Where he comes from, I do not know; he has no name. Looking out upon the flowers in bloom, he composed a poem, for himself alone:

Who knows the heart
of one living deep in the hills?
Only the blossoms.
So it is with you, yon cherry tree—
that I shall converse.[7]

yama fukaku / sumeru kokoro wa / hana zo shiru / yayo iza sakura / monogatari sen

1. Ono no Michikaze (894–966), one of the most famous ancient calligraphers.
2. D. 1645. A friend also mentioned in Chōshōshi's personal anthology of poetry, *Kyohakushū* (*Draining the Cup*, 1649).
3. Location unknown.
4. *Shareki*. A tree set aside as sacred within the precinct of a shrine, sometimes graced with a torii.
5. An allusion to a story told in *Zhuangzi* about carpenters who come upon an immense tree that they conclude is of no use because otherwise it would never have been spared long enough to grow so old. See *The Complete Works of Chuang Tzu*, trans. Burton Watson (New York: Columbia University Press, 1968), 63–64.
6. Chōshōshi himself.
7. *Kyohakushū*, Shinpen Kokka taikan 9 (Tokyo: Kadokawa shoten, 1992), poem 1789.

It was to this area, the site of her clan deity, that the Nijō empress once came on pilgrimage. She was still known as the mother of the crown prince then, and in her entourage was Lord Narihira,[8] who in a poem once hinted at a certain dream of the past by referring to "what happened in the age of the gods."[9] Also nearby is a shrine to the Kasuga deity.[10]

The walls have ears, as the saying goes, and some child in the village must have heard about the monk's poem. In time, the cherry tree was being hailed as You, Yon Cherry Tree. Most amusing.

The only person who ever calls on me is Kinnori.[11] Reizei Tamekage,[12] who serves as imperial librarian, is so busy with official duties that he has forgotten me altogether. As he copes with the burdens of his station, I think of him off in the clouds[13] and feel more keenly the sadness of a departing spring we cannot lament together.

From limbs I just saw in bloom, the blossoms scatter; then comes the thick growth of green leaves and frail shafts of moonlight spilling through them, more touching even than when seen through trees in autumn.[14] Garden and fence[15] enclose a stand of pines where hardly a single human shadow passes by.

8. Ariwara no Narihira (825–880), a famous poet.
9. A reference to a poem in *Ise monogatari* (*Tales of Ise*), sec. 76: "Today the god / of Oshio Mountain / in Ōhara / must remember what happened / in the Age of the Gods" (*Ōhara ya / oshio no yama mo / kyō koso wa / kamiyo no koto mo / omoiizurame*). In section 76, Narihira is an old man, hinting at old memories to the woman who was his lover in times gone by.
10. The main shrine was in Nara. This one, in Ōharano, was a subshrine located closer to the capital.
11. D. 1647. One of Chōshōshi's disciples.
12. 1612–1652. The head of the lower Reizei house at the time, a lineage descended from Fujiwara no Teika (1162–1241).
13. People of court rank were referred to as *kumo no uebito* (people of the clouds).
14. An allusion to an anonymous poem in *Kokinshū* (*Collection of Ancient and Modern Times*, ca. 905), poem 184: "Gazing at moonlight / spilling down through gaps / between the branches / I feel it deep within my heart— / yes, autumn has come!" (*ko no ma yori / morikuru tsuki no / kage mireba / kokorozukushi no / aki wa kinikeri*).
15. An allusion to a poem by Bishop Henjō (816–890), in *Kokinshū*, poem 248, written when the crown prince, who would later become Emperor Kōkō (830–887; r. 884–887), visited Henjō's mother's house: "Around a dwelling / where buildings are in ill repair / and the owner grown old, / garden and fence are now / no more than an autumn moor" (*sato wa arete / hito wa furinishi / yado nare ya / niwa mo magaki mo / aki no nora naru*).

My hempen robes are coming apart at the shoulders;[16] my skirts are tattered and torn[17]—but who is to notice? The sight of me leaning on my staff to get around must be comical indeed. When I'm tired of walking, I just lie down and make the grass my mat—happy if there is a rock nearby to serve as a pillow. All sorts of things come to me as I sleep, which I relish as much as that king did his anthill.[18]

From spring on, the fields appear to be all the same green, but autumn colors weave a richer brocade.[19] Beneath the evening sky, how could the bitter cries of insects, the tears of deer yearning for their mates, and the dew on the bush clover not wrack the body and pain the heart? Filling my bamboo flask with sagely brew,[20] I never miss a chance to enjoy the flowers, each in its season.

Once someone lived here, where there is now only a fading memento, a grave mound covered in pines.[21] "When I die, place my remains here," I say, and plant a cherry tree that I hope may remind people of me when I'm gone. The grove has a hoary look and is quite large, and when I think of those who will gaze on the scene of blossoms blooming there, snow-white, in a world I shall never know, I mumble a pathetic prayer that they do not forget the one who lived here long before.

Deep down in a gorge a stream goes by, coursing over Donkey Back Boulder.[22] In the summer, we float saké cups on it; and we never tire of

16. An allusion to a poem in Man'yōshū (*Collection of Ten Thousand Leaves*, ca. 759), poem 1265: "With the new year, / a new guard in hempen robes / goes to his island— / where there will be no one to repair / tears in the shoulders of his robes" (*kotoshi yuku / niijimamori ga / asagoromo / kata no mayoi wa / tare ka torimimu*).

17. An allusion to the famous "Dialogue Between Poverty and Destitution" by Yamanoue Okura (660?–733?), in Man'yōshū, poem 892, which refers to a "coat hanging in tatters like so many strands of seaweed" (*nuno katakinu no miru no goto wawakesagareru*).

18. An allusion to an incident in a Tang-dynasty (618–906) fantasy in which a man gets drunk, falls asleep under a pagoda tree, and dreams that he has spent twenty years living a life of luxury in a grand kingdom, only to discover after awakening that the kingdom was an anthill.

19. An allusion to an anonymous poem in Kokinshū, poem 245: "In springtime / the grasses looked all the same— / all of them green. / But in autumn they bloom / in hosts of different hues" (*midori naru / hitotsu kusa to zo / haru wa mishi / aki wa iroiro no / hana ni zo arikeri*).

20. Saké.

21. An allusion to a poem by Retired Emperor Tsuchimikado (1195–1231; r. 1198–1210), in *Mandai wakashū* (*Poems of Myriad Ages*, 1248), a collection of waka compiled by Hamuro Mitsutoshi (1203–1276): "Who could it have been / that lived here in the past? / —leaving behind / only a robe of moss / cast down upon the stones" (*mukashi tare / sumikemu ato no / sutegoromo / iwao no naka ni / koke zo nokoreru*).

22. Rojōgan. Evidently a name given to the boulder by Chōshōshi himself, alluding to a statement by Zheng Qi, a minor poet of the Tang dynasty.

drinking from its waters with our cupped hands.[23] In the winter, on a snowy morning, I think of what Zheng Qi said about the bridge over Ba River[24] and then consider my own back-broken poems and am overcome by tears.

> What ever became
> of his ideas, long ago,
> on a donkey's back?
> Here, snow caps the boulders—
> blossoms in flowery dawn.[25]

> *usagi uma no/mukashi no nozomi/ika naran/iwao ni mo saku/hana no akebono*

"Ideas for poems come to you on a donkey's back"—that is the truth. When one arrives at the most superb places, though, words won't suffice: they are beyond description.

———————————

The sages of the past left teachings on how to compose poems, but they tell you little. In the case of poets writing from the time of the *Shinkokinshū*[26] onward, one must not borrow even a single word from the masterpieces that have been most praised for their rarity and excellence,[27] for in the Way of poetry to do so is a sin worthy of death. And even more so when it comes to the works of one's own contemporaries.

23. An allusion to a poem by Ki no Tsurayuki (ca. 872–945), in *Kokinshū*, poem 404, composed when he bade farewell to someone with whom he had been talking near a rocky spring on the Shiga Mountain road: "As when a traveler / seeks in vain to slake his thirst / at a mountain spring / soiled by drops from his cupped hands— / so, unsatisfied, I part from you" (*musubu te no / shizuku ni nigoru / yama no i no / akade mo hito ni / wakarenuru kana*).

24. When he was in government service, someone asked Zheng Qi about his recent poems, and he said, "Ideas for poems come at Ba Bridge, in snow or wind, or on a donkey's back." The implication is that those involved in worldly affairs are not in the right frame of mind to compose good poems. The bridge over the Ba River, east of Chang'an in Shaanxi Province, was the place where people in the capital said farewell to departing travelers.

25. *Kyohakushū*, poem 1790.

26. *New Collection of Ancient and Modern Times* (ca. 1205), the eighth imperial anthology of *uta* (the thirty-one-syllable form that was the primary genre of the courtly tradition).

27. A reference to the preface of *Eiga taigai* (*Essentials of Composition*, after 1221) by Fujiwara no Teika (1162–1241). See "Eiga no taigai," in *Karonshū, Nōgakuronshū*, ed. Hisamatsu Sen'ichi, Nihon koten bungaku taikei 65 (Tokyo: Iwanami shoten, 1961), 114.

Who would fail to respect the writings of the Kyōgoku Middle Counselor?[28] Let all praise them, then, for esteemed they should be!

Poems composed by worldly men are concocted with lies, in order to gain a reputation for skill.[29] By contrast, Saigyō's poems all came from his experience on pilgrimage to distant places, recording the truth of what he saw. He let his mouth choose proper words, not concerning himself with style; yet the total effect was one of natural dignity.

> From branches
> in fields gone to seed
> above a cliff,
> a dove calls out for his mate—
> adding to the evening chill.[30]

furuhata no / sowa no tatsu ki ni / iru hato no / tomo yobu koe no / sugoki yūgure

This is the kind of poem one should try to compose.

Just composing a poem is no challenge; the challenge is producing something that carries meaning. To do this, one must concentrate completely on the poem, undistracted by anything else, and learn from the examples of the man who stole brocade in the open market[31] and the man who loved cicada wings.[32] Do that, and the ideas and words that you produce will be imbued with spirit and will make people take notice. Above all, do not waste your mind endlessly straining for ideas. In *Fūgashū* there is a poem:

28. Fujiwara no Teika, author of a number of critical treatises, most prominently *Kindai shūka* (*Superior Poems of Our Time*, 1209), *Maigetsushō* (*Monthly Notes*, 1219), and *Eiga taigai*.

29. Teika is quoted in some texts as saying that he was a mere versifier (*utazukuri*) who "constructed" poems, as opposed to his father, whom he praises as a true poet (*utayomi*). The word *jōzu* is sometimes used in Edo-period poetic discourse as a pejorative.

30. *Shinkokinshū*, poem 1674, by Saigyō (1118–1190), one of the most highly renowned of Japanese poet-monks.

31. An allusion to a story in the Daoist classic *Liezi* (*Master Lie*, ca. fifth century B.C.E.) in which a man steals money in a crowded marketplace. When asked why he did something so foolish, he replied, "I wasn't paying any attention to the people around; I was just looking at the money" (*The Book of Lieh-tzu: A Classic of the Tao*, trans. A. C. Graham [New York: Columbia University Press, 1960], 180–81).

32. Another allusion to *Liezi*. In this case, Confucius asked a man how he was so successful at catching cicadas, and the man replied that he concentrated on nothing under heaven except cicada wings. See ibid., 45.

A clear sky—
and branches richly hued
on a moonlit night.
Awakened by the wind,
a cicada cries out—just once.[33]

sora harete / kozue irokoki / tsuki no yo no / kaze ni odoroku / semi no hitokoe

This poem describes a scene just as it is[34] and yet achieves a total effect never created before, which is just what one wants in a poem.

Searching for the headwaters of poetry, one comes upon a place where grasses float on a pure stream beneath towering boulders covered with moss—moss of the sort a man called Genbin[35] wore for his robes. He wrote this poem:

In the countryside
grasses float on waters so pure!
Better, then,
not to dwell in the dust
of the bustling capital.[36]

*totsukuni wa / mizukusa kiyomi / koto shigeki / miyako no uchi wa / sumanu
masareri*

Truly spoken.

————————

Off I go to cut rushes, pull up reed-flower sprouts, and pick violets. I clamber up the peak to gather wasabi, some of which the boy I take along

33. *Fūgashū* (*Collection of Elegance*, 1344–1346), poem 421, by Retired Emperor Hanazono (1297–1348; r. 1308–1318).

34. *Ari no mama no keiki.* The concept is taken directly from the Kyōgoku-Reizei school of late medieval times.

35. D. 818. A devout monk who cast aside all concerns for rank and advancement and lived as a hermit in the mountains.

36. A similar poem appears in the folktale collection *Kokon chōmonjū* (*Things Seen and Heard, Old and New*, 1254). See *Kokon chōmonjū*, ed. Nakajima Etsuji (Tokyo: Kadokawa bunko, 1975), 1:140.

crams amusingly into a bamboo box.[37] Legs tired from walking up steep slopes, I break off a few branches of pasania and spread them to take a moment's rest at the base of a rock, in the shade of wisteria—familiar in color. Now and again comes the sound of a tree being felled, from who knows where; then storm winds seem colder, their fearsome echo raising the hairs on my head.

Realizing that I am late, my woman sends the servant girl with food. No sooner do I see it in front of me than I spy some horsetail[38] and rock-pear berries.

When I get back home, the house is in an uproar, wondering what kept me. "The path was steep, and I lost my way, so I got more tired out than usual," I explain.

"Well, that's no one's fault but your own," my woman laughs, almost beside herself.

At one time, clouds raise a tower on the peak;[39] at another, mists erect an eightfold fence. A rainbow bridge appears, traversing the sky,[40] and I wonder for whose benefit such endless delights are intended. From before its season, I await the cuckoo's call and wonder at the lack of feeling of the one who said, "Unexpectedly a cuckoo calls . . ."[41] In some ways, my place resembles Chōmei's foothills, except perhaps in being blessed with a better place to break and bundle firewood.[42]

What a pitiful state! An old man, nearing eighty, I am ever awake in the night, so frustrated with never being sleepy that time and again I get

37. In "Hōjōki," Kamo no Chōmei also describes taking walks with a boy. See Kamo no Chōmei, "An Account of My Hermitage," in *Classical Japanese Prose: An Anthology*, ed. Helen Craig McCullough (Stanford, Calif.: Stanford University Press, 1990), 389.

38. The text here says *tsutsuji* (azaleas). Since azaleas are not edible, Ueno Yōzō posits a scribal error and suggest instead *tsukushi* (horsetail), in Kinoshita Chōshōshi, "Ōhara no ki," in *Kinsei kabun shū*, ed. Matsuno Yōichi and Ueno Yōzō, Shin Nihon koten bungaku taikei 67 (Tokyo: Iwanami shoten, 1989), 1:44n.19.

39. An allusion to a Chinese rhapsody by Lu Ji (261–301) on "Clouds."

40. An allusion to a poem by Li Bo (701–762).

41. A reference to a poem by Fujiwara Sadayori (995–1045), in *Goshūishū* (*Later Collection of Gleanings*, 1086), poem 162, composed upon hearing a cuckoo call at the end of the Third Month: "Unexpectedly / a cuckoo cries out / before spring's end. / This year I need not wait / to hear its first call" (*hototogisu / omoi mo kakenu / haru nakeba / kotoshi zo matade / hatsune kikitsuru*). Waiting for the first call, Chōshōshi suggests, is a crucial part of the experience—and also a way to show one's sensitivity.

42. In "Hōjōki," Chōmei refers to the place where he lives as *toyama* (foothills) and notes that he extended the eastern eaves of his cottage to provide a place to break up and burn firewood, available in abundance nearby. See Chōmei, "Account of My Hermitage," 388.

up, then lie back down—praying childishly, "Send dawn swiftly, Lord of Night!" Through my window spills light from the moon setting on the mountain rim—but even that is no symbol for my advancing years.[43] Already I am a resident of the yellow springs.[44] Surely the very monkeys crying out from the mountain gorges will admit the sadness of my lot.[45] Yesterday I closed my pine door in the shadow of Eagle Peak in the eastern hills;[46] today I am a peasant picking dropwort in the paddy lakes on the slopes of Ōhara. Was the past a dream and the present a reality? Is the present a dream and the past a reality? I don't know.[47] I do recall that someone long ago met Zhuangzi and wanted to ask the same question about the butterfly.[48]

["ŌHARA NO KI," ED. UENO YŌZŌ, IN *KINSEI KABUN SHŪ*, VOL. 1, ED. MATSUNO YŌICHI AND UENO YŌZŌ, SHIN NIHON KOTEN BUNGAKU TAIKEI 67 (TOKYO: IWANAMI SHOTEN, 1989)]

43. At the end of his essay, Chōmei compares himself to a setting moon. He was in his late fifties when he wrote "Hōjōki," whereas Chōshōshi wrote his essay in his early seventies.
44. The next world.
45. The cry of the monkey was considered to be especially gut-wrenching.
46. Earlier in life, Chōshōshi had lived in the Ryōzen area of the eastern hills.
47. The phrase "I don't know" (*shirazu*) is another reference to Chōmei, who at the beginning of his essay says, "From whence do they come, and whither do they go, all who are born and then die? We don't know. And for whose benefit do they labor their hearts to make temporary dwellings that bring pleasure to the eye? This too we do not know" ("Account of My Hermitage," 380).
48. *Zhuangzi* records a brief parable of sorts in which the author falls asleep, dreams that he is a butterfly, and then wakes up, never sure again whether he was a man dreaming that he was a butterfly or a butterfly now dreaming that he is a man. See *Complete Works of Chuang Tzu*, 49.

9

Haikai Prose

MATSUO BASHŌ

Matsuo Bashō (1644-1694) is perhaps the most famous of all Japanese poets. While now known primarily for his haiku and travel journals, in his own day he was a master of linked verse (haikai renku) who had disciples all over Japan. He was born and raised in Iga Ueno in the Kansai area but moved to Edo in his twenties to become a haikai master. Although struggling at first in a very competitive market, he eventually developed his own practice and became one of the most prominent masters of his or any age. In contrast to the work of many of his contemporaries, Bashō's work made explicit allusions to such earlier figures as Saigyō (1118-1190) and Sōgi (1421-1502). In this sense, he tried to retain a strong sense of connection to earlier cultural traditions while responding to the demands of his own age.

In addition to haiku and linked verse, Bashō left behind a number of fine examples of haibun (haikai prose). This subgenre of haikai is seldom included in Japanese anthologies of zuihitsu—though for no good reason. Certainly similarities to works by Kenkō, Shōhaku, Chōshōshi, and—later—Higuchi Ichiyō and Shiga Naoya are enough to justify inclusion here. The selections date from his last ten years and are presented in chronological order.

In Praise of Mount Fuji

Kunlun,[1] Penglai, and Fangzhang[2] are abodes of wizards, heard of from afar. Yet here before my eyes is Fuji's peak, towering above the earth, girding heaven, so vast it seems a cloudy gate for sun and moon, displaying myriad sights, ever changing. Poets cannot encompass it; wordsmiths cannot describe it; nor can painters prevail: they cast their brushes aside. The wizard of Gushe Mountain[3] himself would fail to capture it in word or image.

Clouds and mist
in a brief instant reveal
a hundred scenes.

kumokiri no / zanji hyakkei wo / tsukushikeri

Rebuke for a Recluse

Silly old man! Ever bothered at visitors, vowing to see no one, to take no callers, time and time again, till a moonlit night or a snowy morning comes and makes you want a friend—when it's too late.[4] In silence you sit, drinking saké, putting questions to your own mind, chatting with yourself.[5]

1. A range of mountains running east and west between Central Asia and Tibet, as well as a mythological place.
2. Penglai and Fangzhang are mythological places in China.
3. An abode of wizards mentioned in *Zhuangzi*. See *The Complete Works of Chuang Tzu*, trans. Burton Watson (New York: Columbia University Press, 1968), 33.
4. An allusion to a poem by Bo Juyi (772–846), in the Heian-period anthology *Wakan rōeishū* (*Songs for Singing, in Japanese and Chinese*, ca. 1013), poem 734, that speaks of missing friends most at times of snow, moon, and blossoms. See *Wakan rōeishū*, ed. Kawaguchi Hisao, Nihon koten bungaku taikei 73 (Tokyo: Iwanami shoten, 1965), 239.
5. In "Hōjōki" (The Ten-Foot-Square Hut), Kamo no Chōmei describes a similar scene in which, in his loneliness, he asks himself questions. See Kamo no Chōmei, "An Account of My Hermitage," in *Classical Japanese Prose: An Anthology*, ed. Helen Craig McCullough (Stanford, Calif.: Stanford University Press, 1990), 392.

You open the door, look out at the snow, and take up your saké cup or pick up your brush, only to put it down again. Foolish old man![6]

I drink my saké,
and then can't get to sleep
this snowy night.

sake nomeba / itodo nerarenu / yoru no yuki

Year's End

In times past, even the wisest of people had trouble forgetting their hometowns, it would seem. As for me: well, here I am just four years into my decline[7] and already I get nostalgic at the slightest excuse and just have to go see my brothers and sisters, who are also getting on.[8]

Beneath the rain-filled skies of early winter I departed, moving along through snow and frost, arriving in the mountains of southern Iga[9] at the end of the Twelfth Month. If only Father and Mother were still alive, I thought, remembering the past.

In my hometown—
my cord of life[10] brings tears
at year's end.

furusato ya / heso no o ni naku / toshi no kure

6. In the preamble to *Tsurezuregusa* (*Essays in Idleness*), Yoshida no Kenkō describes himself with the predicate *monoguruoshi*, meaning "foolish" or "eccentric." See Yoshida no Kenkō, *Essays in Idleness* (chap. 2).

7. Bashō was forty-four years old at the time, four years into old age according to traditional thinking.

8. He returned to Iga to visit his family in the same year. His journey is recorded in *Oi no kobumi* (*Notes from My Backpack*, 1690–1691).

9. Bashō's birthplace of Iga Province was located just south of the Suzuka range.

10. It was common for a child's umbilical cord to be kept by his family as a memento.

Pilgrimage to Kōya

Into the recesses of Kōya[11] I go, to a place where sacred sites abound, where the lamp of the law never goes out, where monks' quarters cover the ground and tile-roofed chapels stand in rows. Spring blossoms—instant heirs of salvation—seem to set the tranquil, hazy skies aglow; the cries of monkeys and birds wrench one's insides. In silence I worship before the ossuary of Saint Kōbō,[12] deep in my own thoughts. Gathered in this place are the mementos of multitudes, from the hair of remote ancestors to the white bones of recent loved ones. So many of them, I think to myself, shedding more tears than my sleeves can contain before finally they stop.

> Father, Mother—
> that's who I long for
> when pheasants cry.[13]

chichi haha no / shikiri ni koishi / kiji no koe

Abode of Purity

Mountains are tranquil, nurturing one's true nature; waters move, a salve to the emotions.[14] Chinseki of the Hamada clan[15] resides between tranquility and movement. Because he has beheld every fine sight, intoned elegant words, cleansed himself of impurities, and washed away the dust of the world, we call his dwelling Abode of Purity. Above his gate on a

---

11. A mountainous area in the northern part of present-day Wakayama Prefecture, it is the site of Kongōbuji, a large temple complex of the Shingon sect of Buddhism.

12. Kōbō Daishi (Kūkai, 774–835), founder of the Shingon sect in Japan.

13. A haiku restatement of a famous *uta* by the priest Gyōgi (688–749), collected in *Gyokuyōshū* (*Collection of Jeweled Leaves*, 1313–1314), poem 2627, when he visited the great Buddhist enclave at Kōya.

14. An allusion to the *Analects*. See Confucius, *The Analects*, trans. D. C. Lau (New York: Penguin, 1979), 84.

15. D. 1737? One of the chief disciples of Bashō's last years. He lived in a cottage on the southern shore of Lake Biwa, in the castle town of Zeze.

banner he has written, "Schemers, no entry here!"—ingeniously adding another category to the ones in Sōkan's madcap poem.[16]

Chinseki's dwelling is modest, a square hut of two *ma*,[17] patterned after Rikyū[18] and Jō'o[19] but with none of their regulations. For his amusement, he has planted trees and arranged stones. His dining area has Seta and Cape Kara for left and right wings, with the lake in between and Mount Mikami in front. As the lake resembles a koto in shape, the echo in the pines harmonizes with the waves. Mount Hiei and Hira's high peak appear off to the side, with Mount Otowa and Mount Ishi standing at each shoulder. On Mount Nagara, cherry blossoms serve as ornament, and Mirror Mountain shines in the moonlight. Daily the scenes change, lighter makeup one day, thicker the next. From this the artist within can learn too: from the constant changing of the wind and clouds.

> From four shores
> blooming cherries converge—
> on Biwa's waves.

> *shihō yori / hana sakiirete / niho no nami*

A Rhapsody on Crows

Small crows have one name; large crows, another—the magpie and the large-bill. For sharing food with parents, the crow earns praise and comparison with Zengzi.[20] When visitors approach a house, he announces them; it is he who spreads his wings across Heaven's River as a bridge

---

16. An allusion to a famous comic poem by Yamazaki Sōkan (d. mid-sixteenth century): "The best don't come, / the next best come but don't stay, / while the worst stay on. / And those who stay on two nights— / they're the worst of the worst" (*jō wa kozu / chū wa kite inu / ge wa tomaru / futayo tomaru wa / gege no ge kyaku*).

17. One room, two mats in size.

18. Sen no Rikyū (1522–1591), a tea master known for developing the *wabi* (spare and simple) style of the tea ceremony.

19. Takeno Jō'o (1502–1555), Rikyū's teacher.

20. The word translated in the heading as "rhapsody" is *fu*, referring to a Chinese literary genre, whose usage here he probably intended as tongue in cheek. Young crows are known to regurgitate food and feed it to their parents. Zeng Shen, one of the youngest disciples of Confucius, was known for his loving dedication to his parents.

for the stars.[21] At year's end, the crow studies the spring wind and moves his nest if need be. In snowy dawn there is a chill in his voice, and his dusk journey to his nest is a thing of beauty to writers[22] and for painters a favored theme.

So the crow has signal virtues—among the ranks of the ravenous, that is. Count up his crimes, though, and there is less to praise and more to blame. The large-bill in particular is of a twisted disposition: he is contemptuous of the eagle's wings and unafraid of the hawk's talons, and his meat is not as tasty as wild goose or his call at all like the warbler's. In his caws, men feel ill tidings, from which misfortune and trouble are sure to follow. On farms, he raids chestnut and persimmon trees and makes a wasteland of fields and crops, knowing nothing of farmers' labors—or makes off with the eggs in sparrows' nests, takes frogs from ponds to gobble up, and is there waiting to feed on a corpse or tear at the guts of a fallen ox or horse. Why, one even hears of crows losing their lives attacking squid on the sea or trying to fish like cormorants—ever greedy for spoils, never seeking knowledge!

When a man is like you, Master Crow—dressed in ink-black but full of rank desires—we call him a priest for hire.[23] Preachers hate him, and the laity shun him too. So be on your guard: you may end up on the end of Yi's arrow yet.[24] Or lose your place among those vaunted Three Birds of the Sun.[25]

Moving My Plantain

Chrysanthemums once flourished along an eastern fence;[26] bamboo once lorded over a northern window.[27] As for peonies—debates arise over

21. According to Chinese tradition, the Herd Boy (Altair) and the Weaver Maiden (Vega), allowed to meet over the River of Heaven (Milky Way) just once a year, on the seventh day of the Seventh Month, crossed to meet each other on a bridge of magpie wings.
22. Sei Shōnagon, *The Pillow Book*, sec. 1 (chap. 1).
23. Epithet for a monk who sold his knowledge or services for money.
24. Hou Yi, a legendary Chinese archer at the time of the sage-king Yao (traditional dates 2353–2234 B.C.E.).
25. An old legend said that three golden birds lived in the sun.
26. An allusion to the Chinese poet Tao Yuanming (365–427), who was fond of chrysanthemums.
27. An allusion to an anecdote about the Chinese poet Wang Ziyu (more formally known as Wang Huizhi; d. ca. 388), who was so fond of the bamboo around his mountain hut that he referred to it as the lord of the place.

whether red or white is best, and they are thus sullied by worldly attitudes. Lotus will not take to ordinary soil, will not blossom in waters impure.

Some years back, when I moved to this place, I planted a plantain, which must have taken to its new surroundings, for from its buds grew so many leaves that it took over my garden space, almost obscuring the eaves of my thatched roof. This is why people began calling my place Plantain Cottage.[28] So loved was the plant by old friends and disciples that they had me cutting off buds and roots to send them here and there for years.

Then came the year when I decided to take a walking trip into Michinoku.[29] As I prepared to abandon my hut, I moved the plaintain against the fence next door and asked the people nearby to keep the frost off it and shelter it from the wind; I even left them a silly note about it. With thoughts of the long journey ahead filling my breast, I thought the plant would end up like Saigyō's pine, "left all to himself."[30]

Those five years I was away, I missed my friends and my plantain. Finally, though, came the time for tearful reunion.[31] Now, midway through the Fifth Month, with the scent of orange blossoms not far off, I renew my friendships in a new place close to the site of my old dwelling. It is a three-roomed hut, thatched just right with grasses, boasting a finely smoothed cypress pillar, a proper swinging door of bamboo, a thick fence of reeds, all opening on a pond to the south—which explains why it's called Water Tower. The site faces Mount Fuji, and the gate is arranged not to obstruct the view. The branches of the Sumida River meet nearby, and their currents run deep and still, like the Qiantang[32]—making the place so perfect for enjoying moonlight that early in the month I already find myself worried about clouds and rain in the evening.

---

28. Bashō first moved from central Edo to his cottage across the Sumida River in 1688. The next spring, a disciple gave him a plantain, or *bashō* plant, the name by which his cottage and he himself would later be known.

29. A reference to the poet's journey of 1689, which would become the basis for *Oku no hosomichi* (*The Narrow Road of the Interior*).

30. An allusion to Saigyō's (1118–1190) *Sankashū* (*Mountain Home Collection*), poem 1450: "If again I tire / of the life I live here / and move away, / then left all to himself / will be my faithful pine" (*koko o mata / waga sumiukute / ukarenaba / matsu wa hitori ni / naran to suran*).

31. He returned to Edo in 1691.

32. The Qiantang flows through Zhejiang Province, emptying into the sea at Hangzhou.

It was in hopes of such good views of the moon that I moved my plant here. Its leaves are broad now, large enough to fully cover a koto. Some of them are battered and broken, reminding one of the wounded tail feathers of a phoenix; others are like wind-damaged fans. Flowers bloom here and there, but not in bright colors, and the stems are thick, but not so thick as to invite the woodsman's axe—just like those trees in the mountains that are no good for lumber, and the more laudable for it.[33] The monk Huai Su[34] wrote words on plantain leaves, and Zhang Zai of Hengqu[35] was inspired by the example of their growth to put more effort into his studies. Taking neither of these courses, I just amuse myself in their shade, all the more attached to them for the way they are vulnerable to wind and rain.

On Parting from Kyoriku

Only last fall we met, and here we are at the beginning of the Fifth Month preparing for reluctant good-byes. Anticipating our parting, Kyoriku[36] came knocking on the door of my hut, and we spent a whole day in quiet conversation.

His loves are painting and poetry, so I asked him, "Why are you so fond of painting?" His answer was, "For the sake of my poetry." Then I asked, "Why are you so fond of poetry?" and he said, "For the sake of my painting." While learning two things, then, he is really involved in just one. Truly it is said, "To be skilled at many things is unseemly in a gentleman."[37] His two vessels are in purpose one and the same.

In painting, he is my master; in poetry, I teach him as a disciple. His painting is so profound in spirit and his brush technique so superb, however, that it takes him to depths I shall never see. My poetry, on the other

---

33. An allusion to an anecdote in the "Mountain Tree" chapter of *Zhuangzi* in which a woodcutter spares a tree because it is not the right shape or size to be useful as lumber, a situation that strikes Bashō as a good model for the recluse. See *Complete Works of Chuang Tzu*, 209–10.

34. 737–799. A calligrapher who was so poor that he was reduced to writing on leaves instead of paper.

35. 1020–1077. A scholar who was born in the Hengqu area of Shaanxi Province.

36. Morikawa Kyoriku (1656–1715), who became one of Bashō's foremost disciples.

37. Confucius, *Analects*, 97. See also Kenkō, *Essays in Idleness*, sec. 122.

hand, is fire in summer and a fan in winter, a thing so contrary that ordinary people have no use for it.

But at least we have the poems of Shunzei[38] and Saigyō, even the most offhand of which are full of emotion. I believe it was Retired Emperor Go-Toba who said, "There is truth in their words, accompanied by deep feeling."[39] So to Kyoriku I say, "Trust the retired emperor's words, and stay on the straight and narrow. As Saint Kōbō says in his teachings on calligraphy, 'Don't mimic what the masters left behind; rather seek what they sought.'"[40]

"The Way of Poetry is just the same," I say, lantern in hand, as I see my guest out through my gate and bid him fond farewell.

An Argument for the Reclusive Life

The gentleman abhors desire, which the Buddha put at the top of the list of his five proscriptions.[41] Yet love is hard to push aside and inspires the deepest of feelings. Lying beneath the plum trees in the gloom of Kurabu Mountain,[42] you are taken by unexpected scents; and if Stealthy Gate has no guard, there is no telling what mistakes may ensue.[43] How many men have lost their homes and then their lives to women of the floating world, cast adrift on waves that served as pillows! But even they deserve forgiveness sooner than old men who, still greedy for more time, torment their spirits with concern for appetites and money, unable to discern the perils of desire. "For a man to live to seventy years is a rare thing,"[44] and one's prime lasts but two decades and a little more. When

---

38. Fujiwara no Shunzei (1114–1204).

39. Go-Toba (1180–1239; r. 1183–1198) says similar things in *Go-Toba no in gokuden* (*Ex-Emperor Go-Toba's Secret Teachings*). See Robert H. Brower, "'Ex-Emperor Go-Toba's Secret Teachings': *Go-Toba no in Gokuden*," *Harvard Journal of Asiatic Studies* 32 (1972): 35–36, 41. See also *Karonshū, Nōgakuronshū*, ed. Hisamatsu Sen'ichi, Nihon koten bungaku taikei 65 (Tokyo: Iwanami shoten, 1961), 145–50.

40. Kōbō Daishi (Kūkai). This is a paraphrase of what Kūkai says in *Shōryōshū*, a collection of his writings compiled by a disciple after his death.

41. The five commandments proscribe murder, theft, adultery, lying, and desire. There is no evidence that the Buddha ranked one above another.

42. A famous landmark in Yamashiro Province. "Lying beneath the plum trees" is meant to suggest a secret meeting between lovers.

43. An allusion to *Tsurezuregusa*, section 240, where Kenkō uses similar images to speak of the difficulties—and joys—of clandestine meetings between lovers. See Kenkō, *Essays in Idleness*.

44. An allusion to a poem by Du Fu (712–770).

old age arrives, it is like the dream of a single night. Then comes the downhill slide into your fifties and sixties as you waste dreadfully away—until there you are, awake in the night, waiting for morning, hoping for who knows what. The more foolish one is, the more plagued one will be by thought.

"Great ability increases harmful passions,"[45] so it is said. Anyone achieving excellence in an art must end up in vain striving. Relying on such things for a livelihood means abandoning your heart to the world of desires and appetites, drowning there as in a canal between rice paddies, with no way to return to life.

What one must do, then, is follow the teachings of the sage Nanka:[46] rid yourself of all concern over profit and loss, forget about your years, and go into retirement, which is the true joy of old age. Visitors mean senseless banter; going out means interfering in others' affairs. Zūn Jing shut his door;[47] Du Wulang locked his gate.[48] Make friendlessness your friend and poverty your treasure. So counsels this stubborn old man of fifty, writing advice to himself, first of all.

[*MATSUO BASHŌ SHŪ*, ED. IMOTO NŌICHI, NIHON KOTEN
BUNGAKU ZENSHŪ 41 (TOKYO: SHŌGAKUKAN, 1972)]

45. A quotation from *Tsurezuregusa*, sec. 38. See Kenkō, *Essays in Idleness*.
46. Another name for Zhuangzi.
47. A man of the Three Kingdoms period (ca. 220–ca. 280) who was famous for closing his door to the world and spending all his time reading books.
48. A man of the Song dynasty (960–1279) who reputedly stayed inside for thirty years without ever coming out.

10

Amusements

AMENOMORI HŌSHŪ

Amenomori Hōshū (1668-1755) was a Confucian scholar from Ōmi Province (modern-day Shiga Prefecture). He began studying medicine under his father, a local physician, but eventually decided on a career in Confucian scholarship instead. After his father's death in 1684, he went to Edo, where he studied Korean and Chinese and prepared himself for an academic career.

In 1693, Hōshū gained a position as a scholar-official on the island of Tsushima, off the coast of Kyushu, and spent the rest of his public life there in government service, traveling to Korea frequently. He composed Chinese poetry and late in life also composed poetry in Japanese, leaving more than ten thousand poems when he died. Tawaregusa (Amusements, 1789) is a rambling series of instructive anecdotes, preachments, and tidbits of advice informed by the author's reading of the Chinese classics and works of history.

Records say that in China, in times of great famine, people eat one another. In this country, one never hears of such a thing. Someone said this is because we refrain from eating even the flesh of birds and beasts. Since the birds and beasts are messengers of the gods, one should not eat their progeny; and if gold or silver is found in a mountain, even greedy people don't dig it up if birds and beasts are occupying the place. One can only hope that things will remain this way forever.

"In the world, all things work together." So the saying goes, and the Way ratifies the statement. A nation cannot stand with only a capital and no countryside, and in the same way the Middle Kingdom could not have progressed on its way without the barbarians. In everything from the use of medicines on down, great and small assist one another. Whether a nation is noble or common derives from the number of its great men and small men and whether its customs are good or bad. One should therefore not be proud just because one was born in China, or be ashamed just because one was born a barbarian. When we hear a foolish man call someone "a country bumpkin among country bumpkins," we deride him, and by the same token we should not call China the Middle Kingdom without any justification.

"Cherry trees have short lives. I wonder why this is so?" someone asked. I replied, "It's because they have so many flowers. They are no match for the pine or the cypress. What a fortunate example of the principle that governs heaven and earth! From this, we learn that a country or a house that flourishes in excess will not last long."

When asked what they think on a certain issue, people in council are so afraid of their superiors and so busy glancing at others around them that as soon as anyone at the top says, "This is what I think," they all go along, no one dissenting. Upon hearing an opinion, people of wisdom surely should have more to say than that they have no thoughts of their own. Thus while such a gathering may appear to be a council, it is in fact not. One wishes that we would learn from the example of China, where everyone writes their ideas down and presents them for consideration.

Whenever there is a disturbance in the world, bands of brigands arise. By brigands, I don't mean normal thieves but farmers who are forced to form leagues and rise up in rebellion. Every year, the tax burden grows heavier, and since appealing to the authorities for help brings only punishment, they try to get by but reach the point where they can't support their wives and children and are forced to rise up. This in turn leads to various other uprisings, and before long domains large and small are doing as they please, and a huge disturbance ensues. It's just like people who are weakened physically falling prey to a hundred competing diseases and perishing—the most horrific of extremes.

The cause of the heavy tax burden is, of course, the extravagance of leaders. By extravagance, I don't mean just fondness for show and wealth, however, but rather lack of government action to keep expenditures within income levels, as circumstances demand. When officials, high or low, have no way to succeed on established tax revenues, they turn to exploiting the people.

When a government is established, of course, a spirit of frugality generally prevails: tax revenues are more than enough to meet expenses, and benevolent government is carried out quite naturally, with those above enjoying abundance and those below living well. A happy scene, to be sure. But as time goes by, first fifty years and then a hundred, burdens become heavier, and without anyone taking notice, limits are exceeded and the people below begin to suffer. One example of how it happens is this: in the beginning, the upper classes use simple wares for containers, but before long these give way to lacquerware, then to inlaid lacquerware, and then to things decorated in silver and gold. In clothing, people wear cotton in the beginning, but then move on to pongee, then to silk, and after that they go on to develop a liking for damask and other fine Chinese fabrics, in the end donning even woolens and other such things[1] and other products from barbarian lands. And since we are not talking about a few cases, how could incomes ever hope to cope with such endlessly rising expenditures?

Now, during all this time, there are learned lords who should know it is the responsibility of government to prohibit such excesses, but they concentrate so much on trivial matters that they fail to realize when

---

1. The meaning of this last term, *kumuchu*, is unclear.

the larger things are getting out of hand and are therefore of no use in averting disaster.

A certain daimyo built his house facing east, but as time went by more and more people said south-facing homes were better, so when a fire destroyed the house, he took the opportunity to rebuild it facing south. In time, however, more and more people were saying that east-facing homes were actually better, so after another fire occurred, he rebuilt it facing east again. Lately, people are saying again that south-facing homes are better, so if there is a fire, he will change things around again.

One thinks that things would be better another way, decides to leave one place to go to another, to stop doing this and start doing that—always in a state of confusion. But what one thinks will be one's heart's desire never turns out to be. The best thing is to forget about it all and do what is appropriate to one's situation.

There was a man who lamented his child's wickedness, scolding him day and night.

"Back when you were young," someone asked the father, "did *you* always submit to your parents' commands in every thing?"

After a minute he replied, "No, I did not."

"This is why the proverb says that years are the best medicine. After he takes on some years, you won't need to concern yourself so much."

Later on, that same someone took the child aside and said, "Did you hear about the argument that took place between some people passing on the road the other day—when a younger man struck an older one?"

"That's unsettling," the young man said.

"All right then. When you hear about the suffering of an older person who isn't your father, then you think it's unfortunate. Yet you don't have any consideration at all for your own father, your own flesh and blood, who is suffering day and night," the man said. "I don't get it."

The boy's face turned red, and he had nothing to say. Someone said that after this, the father and son got along much better.

When he has knowledge of something, a physician should tell the truth, good or bad, regardless of whether it makes people unhappy. Sad to say, however, there are very few physicians who do things this way.

A man sent his son up to the capital to make him a physician. Since the young man had no good clothing, his father wondered what to do and lamented the situation in a letter to a Tendai monk with the title "dharma seal."[2]

The monk said, "I find it fascinating that China and Japan are alike in not expecting physicians to wear fine robes. Remember, too, that the Buddha did not dress extravagantly and was not highly regarded by most people. Rather than outward decoration, one should think about inward decoration. Once when I was in the capital, the innkeeper told me about a man from Bungo[3] who had come to that city for the first time. He had no attendants and only a tattered umbrella and leather sandals of the shabbiest sort. But he had such good manners that soon he was well thought of and attracted many admirers, so that now he is counted among men of high repute. Isn't being loyal and trustworthy in word and prompt and respectful in action superior to outward decoration? If people say good things of your son and not bad things, he will surely gain success." Very laudable words.

A person from China told me this story:

A man who was talking with his friend as they passed by the foot of a mountain saw a wooden placard there that said, "A tiger from these mountains is eating people. To the one who kills the tiger we offer 100,000 *kan*."[4]

2. *Hōin.* The highest honorary title, usually given to those who had served long years as bishop (*sōzu*) or in some other way accumulated merit.
3. Present-day Ōita Prefecture.
4. One *kan* was the equivalent of a thousand copper coins.

Overjoyed, the man rolled up his sleeves and was about to head off when the people around him said, "Don't you value your life?"

"If only I could have that fortune," he said, "I wouldn't begrudge losing my life."

An amusing example of a foolish man's aspirations. But think of how those who accumulate wealth, with no thought of the resentment and censure of others, or of the ever-growing excesses that in the end endanger their health and destroy their houses: How is that different from what happens in this story? The way Xi Yuan, emperor of the Han, hoarded tribute,[5] becoming more and more alienated from the people and never realizing that his own virtue was fading away; or the way Dong Zhuo hoarded the grain of Shensi and failed to realize that someone was setting fire to his own belly[6]—these are painful stories. This is why someone once declared, "When wealth is gained, the people are lost."[7]

———————

In every nation, there are diaries and journals in which people record things. As the years pile up, so do the words, enough to make a draft ox sweat, or to fill the room to the ridgepole. Yet for the most part, people write down only whether the day is cloudy or clear. Rare indeed are those who write in detail, discussing arguments and matters having to do with government and human affairs.

When something dubious takes place, we often ask people of advanced years to help us make up our minds. At best, though, those people have only fifty or sixty years of experience. If our records were more substantial, it would be like having at our disposal people who had been around several hundred years. Perhaps one of the reasons our country cannot compete with China in terms of knowledge is because we don't keep good records.

5. Xian Di (181–220), the twelfth and final emperor of the Later Han (25–220), was known for his excesses and eccentric behavior.

6. Dong Zhuo (d. 192), a military leader of the Later Han who built storehouses in Shensi and stored thirty years' worth of grain there. His assassins set fire to his belly, and legend has it that his body was so fat that it burned for days.

7. "Moral and Social Programs: The *Great Learning* [*Da xue*]," in *A Source Book in Chinese Philosophy*, trans. and comp. Wing-tsit Chan (Princeton, N.J.: Princeton University Press, 1963), 93.

How wondrous and strange is the world of human affairs! It is truly impressive that the Chinese keep such detailed records. Yet some people get ideas from those records and then commit great wrongs. From the vantage point of this country, there seem to have been so many such lords and ministers that at times one wonders if it might be better to have no records at all.

During times of upheaval, men of valor and violence are highly esteemed, it would seem. A man who kills people and robs them out of personal rancor is a great sinner, of course, but in every country there are killers employed in secret in order to work violence. In my younger years, the ways of the era of warfare persisted,[8] and such things still happened occasionally. At the time of the Duke of Zhou,[9] it was said that one should not share the world with those who had offended one's parents, and this led to an era of strife—which is one way in which our country has not gone as far as China. Yet still it was a time when it had become popular to accept destruction and invite rebellion.

Nowadays, there is no place in the Eight Islands[10] where grasses do not sway gently in the breezes of a peaceful reign that has brought unity to all. Such being the case, anyone whose parent has been murdered should be able to seek the facts and ask for justice. For some reason, though, the government instead leaves the matter up to the children, giving them the right to carry out capital punishment.[11]

When someone kills his lord, punishment extends down even to his parents and elder brothers. This goes too far, in my opinion.

8. From the late fifteenth century until the establishment of the Tokugawa government around 1600, Japan was in a period of protracted regional warfare that would later be called the period of Warring States.
9. A semilegendary figure of the era known by his name, which began around 1100 B.C.E.
10. Another name for Japan.
11. Edo government policy allowed for family members to secure government permission to carry out vendettas (*katakiuchi*) against a person who had taken the life of a parent or in some cases a lord.

Anyone who takes public wealth entrusted to him for private gain is the same as a thief. He should be dealt with according to the Song law that says, "For corrupt officials—public execution."[12]

This is the way to raise infants: from the time they can crawl, get a mat out and let them crawl about to their heart's content; then when they can stand up, let them run around as much as they wish. Obey the adage that says not to dress babies in underwear and skirts of silk, instead dressing them in thin fabrics that let them feel the wind and the sun. And let them play outside. And when it comes to food, let them eat what they want, only not to excess. Do all this, and they will not fall ill but grow up healthy and strong.

Too often, children born into wealthy houses are left to the constant care of nursemaids who are so worried that the children might catch cold or get a bellyache or injure themselves that they pile layers of soft clothing on them, measure out every morsel of food, and when they begin crawling about, quickly pick them up and keep them inside all the time. This means that their legs develop slowly, they stay skinny and stolid, and fall prey to unusual maladies—all of which retards their growth.

Physicians should tell wet nurses and also nursemaids that when they think a child shouldn't do something because he might injure himself, they should stop thinking only of his body and keep their mouths shut. Also, some of these people foolishly think that high-class infants are somehow different from children of the lower classes. But all people, high and low, are born with the same blood—how could they be different?

I think of the old saying "To love too much—that is the cause of doing harm,"[13] and can't help but feel sad.

---

12. Historical records do indeed record such a punishment. See Amenomori Hōshū, *Tawaregusa*, ed. Mizuta Norihisa, Shin Nihon koten bungaku taikei 99 (Tokyo: Iwanami shoten, 2000), 77n.10.

13. An allusion to a statement in the biography of Li Si (ca. 280–208 B.C.E.), in *Shiji* (*Records of the Historian*), by Sima Qian (145–86 B.C.E.).

A man who had children in his old age was so taken with them that he would put a screen up around them and play with them day and night. It happened to be summer, and the heat was unbearable. But still he took them outside and played with them, one after the other. After about thirty days, they all turned yellow as with jaundice, took ill, and died.

How unfortunate that the man didn't understand that if the heat was too much for adults, it would be even more so for infants—that he didn't realize how his love for them could be the cause of doing harm. This kind of thing should never happen again, one may think, but similar things happen all the time.

Someone told me that when the surface of rocks gets wet, one knows that rain is coming. When popular songs are the rage, one can be sure that the military is in a sorry state.

A man who is proud of his capacity to drink is sure to die young, and a country given to extravagance is sure to suffer destruction before long.

If government is left in the hands of someone who neglects to take care of himself, that country will fall swiftly when there is trouble.

When men of skillful words are popular, the people are sure to be unrighteous. And no man can be successful with a jealous woman in his house.

The saddest of all sad things is when a person born with strong insides and a sturdy frame, someone who could easily live a hundred years if he only took care of himself, dissipates his life with saké and pleasure and dies young. Someone born without talents, no matter how intent he is on living until there is snow on his brow, no matter how hard he tries or how much he laments his misfortune, never gains a name outside his hometown; while, in contrast, someone born gifted does well but spends so much time on vain pursuits, cracking the whip on his horse, that he ends up a dead and rotting trunk—a sad fate.

In this world of ours, there is nothing more painful or trying than poverty. No matter what he wants, a man without power cannot get it. Thus someone in favored circumstances should be grateful in every way, thinking always of others and striving to be benevolent—which, if he is, will have a righteous influence down to his children and grandchildren. If he has the chance to make his house a righteous one and does not, however—if he cares only for the accumulation of things pleasing to the appetites—his descendants will know nothing but wanton behavior, for as the proverb says, "Not three generations do the mighty last." Things piled up in a storehouse encourage only excess and will in the end be cast aside.

Since heaven and earth began, only a few rulers can be said to have sustained their lands and peoples. One would wish that those born into ranks difficult to achieve would govern so well that their fame would go down in the records and be honored for a thousand, even ten thousand, years. How sad it is that so few rulers have such ambitions, instead letting their time pass to no avail.

There's nothing so good as learning, but also nothing so awful. A man of upright character who gains learning is like a powerful man studying judo: the more he learns, the more worthy he becomes. But when a man of questionable character gains learning, it is like a powerful man addicted to pleasure and liquor studying judo—the more he learns, the more evil he becomes. In China, officials who passed the civil service exams and progressed into the ranks had, of course, done a great deal of learning. Yet, among their number are many who even today are remembered as evil men who harmed the people and led the nation astray. So one cannot say that obtaining learning will necessarily work to the good. Zhuangzi says, "The Confucians rob graves according to *The Odes* and ritual,"[14] and that's not just bombast.

14. *The Complete Works of Chuang Tzu*, trans. Burton Watson (New York: Columbia University Press, 1968), 296. The criticism is aimed at the hypocrisy of those who quote ancient texts while engaging in wicked behavior.

Someone asked me, "What kind of person governs well?" I replied, "One whose work produces results, who is deeply compassionate, who shows deference and respect for his vassals—he is one who will govern well. It has nothing to do with accomplishment in literature."

Someone once said, "If one gathered together scholars of renown and let them govern, the nation would be at peace and the people at ease."

But another man said this: "Had not Yao and Shun[15] been in power, even Hou Ji, Xie, and Gao Yao[16] would have had difficulty maintaining governance. The fact is that scholars, though they may not be selfish, still defend their own points of view, and because among those points of view there are various irreconcilable differences, they cannot be unified as one. So if there is no wise lord to judge their merits, arguments will only increase and that will be the end of it. In China, the Luo and Shu factions[17] are known to this day for the fine scholars they produced, but they ended up arguing and never coming to agreement—which shows the way the world is. Yet neither am I suggesting that we should turn government over to ordinary men who know nothing about either the past or the present."

When it's small, we call it an encampment; when it's large, a castle. In China, a stone wall is built around the castle, and not only officials but also artisans and merchants and others are allowed to live inside it, as one knows from the example of the fortress at Chang'an.[18] Of course, after the fortress is established, the populace may grow and some of the latter end up living outside the walls, but the original intent is to have all the people live inside to keep them safe from any harm.

15. Legendary rulers of China in remote antiquity.
16. Ministers of agriculture, education, and justice during the legendary times of Yao and Shun.
17. A reference to various scholarly factions of the late eleventh century.
18. Capital of the Han, Sui, and Tang empires.

In our country, we refer to the place where the governor of a province lives as a castle. Within, there may be two or three enclosures, but these are only for samurai, with others such as artisans and merchants all living outside the walls—which means that if there is an assault, many of them are burned out of their homes or injured.

One wishes that on this issue we would learn from China, although there are good and bad points to be considered, I suppose.

———————

The word "samurai" means "servant." Zigong had this issue in mind when he asked Confucius, "When is it that a man may be called a servant?"[19] In China, it is scholars who are given the title of servant, while in our country it is those who serve with bow and arrow. In one case valor is honored, in the other learning, but both are servants in the sense that they don't go in the same box with farmers, artisans, or merchants, but instead do their work for the government.

———————

Chinese poems and Japanese poems are no different, deep down. Some people say they can write Chinese poems but have trouble writing Japanese poems, and this seems to be true. We use our own words in Japanese poems, after all, and thus when someone writes a poem, both he and those who read it somehow feel that it doesn't measure up; but since a Chinese poem uses Chinese words, even if one puts it together without much care, it seems to work, and both the person who wrote it and those who read it praise it as something impressive. This is why they say that writing Japanese poems is hard but writing Chinese poems is easy. If a Chinese person were to write a Japanese poem, he would probably say, "Writing Japanese poems is easy, but writing Chinese poems is hard."

Anyone who says writing Chinese poems is easy doesn't know much about Chinese poems, while anyone who says writing Japanese poems is easy doesn't know much about Japanese poems. Neither is easy. And the same is true when it comes to writing prose.

19. A quotation from the *Analects*. The Master's answer is, "A man who has a sense of shame in the way he conducts himself and, when sent abroad, does not disgrace the commission of his Lord" (Confucius, *The Analects*, trans. D. C. Lau [New York: Penguin, 1979], 121).

Looking at a book written by someone wanting to condemn the Way of the Buddha, I found that the author had merely dredged up a lot about the evil deeds of priests without getting to the heart of the Buddhist Way itself. In the same fashion, one could write about the bad actions of the Confucian sages and condemn their teachings accordingly. One can discern substance from shape and know the source by its water, but people who judge by the fray along its edges without learning about the thing itself are annoying.

Our leaders have seen fit to ban the teachings of Deus,[20] and this is something for which we should be grateful. At the end of the Hōei era [1704–1711], a man named Itaria[21] came to Yakunoshima. He was sent to Nagasaki,[22] though it had already been decided that he should be put to death. Since there were those who wanted to look him over first, however, he was taken to the Kantō at the beginning of the Shōtoku era [1711–1716] and put in prison there. At that time, men of curiosity and learning went to meet with him and asked him in great detail about his country. "His teachings differ from those of the Buddha only in name and aren't really worth looking into; but he is a man of extraordinary character, unforgettable," some of them said. It was decided that it was too dangerous to let a sorcerer lead them astray in this frightful way, so three years later, when it became known that he had secretly converted some of those watching over him, he was put to death.[23]

There was a man who lived in the countryside of Ōmi[24] who had gained a reputation over time. Someone came to visit him in his rude little hut in a grassy meadow. Opening the door, the visitor saw a man of over forty

20. Christianity.
21. An Italian Jesuit priest, Giovanni Battista Sidotti (1668–1714), who arrived in Japan in 1708.
22. The only government-sanctioned foreign colony in Japan during the Edo period was a small island named Dejima, located in Nagasaki harbor.
23. Sidotti was held in confinement underground and died seven months later.
24. A veiled reference to Hōshū himself.

years reading a book spread out before him and knew this must be the man he was looking for.

"I have heard of you by reputation," the visitor said.

"Come in, then," the recluse said, and served him tea in a most unusual fashion. After a while, the visitor asked, "Confucians make the world their business, while the Daoists try to forget it and the Buddhists to escape it. Which of these ways would you think of as yours?"

"If hearts are calm, then everything will conform to its proper principle," he replied.

"And what is it that leads to order, and what to disorder?" the man asked.

"Always these things result from what goes on in the bedchamber of the person at the top," he said.

The other man thought this such an interesting response that he stayed on for twenty days, chatting about things old and new, before going home.

[*TAWAREGUSA*, ED. MIZUTA NORIHISA, SHIN NIHON KOTEN BUNGAKU TAIKEI 99 (TOKYO: IWANAMI SHOTEN, 2000)]

11

Window Musings

Matsuzaki Kanran

Matsuzaki Kanran (also known as Hakukei and Gyōshin; 1682–1752) was a Confucian scholar in the service of the Sasayama clan of Tamba Province. Born in Edo, he spent much of his time there, traveling also to the Kansai region on various administrative assignments. In his last years, he turned over responsibility as head of the Matsuzaki house to his son Kankai (1725–1775)—who became an even more prominent Confucian scholar—and devoted himself to his studies. In addition to scholarly works on Confucian classics and government, he left behind a collection of poems and several volumes of essays in Japanese.

    Mado no susami *(Window Musings) is a collection of randomly organized anecdotes and short cautionary tales and essays based on what he gleaned from his reading and conversations with friends and acquaintances over the years. The book appeared in 1724 and was followed by an addendum (*tsuika*).*

After being destroyed in a fire, the Satsuma mansion[1] was going to be rebuilt just as before, but the old retainer in charge of the project, who

---

1. The Satsuma domain comprised what is now the western half of Kagoshima Prefecture in Kyushu. The mansion refers to the residence of the daimyo in Edo.

was called the Shimazu Guardsman,[2] wanted windows put everywhere, inside and out. As this would be rather expensive, a number of people asked whether it might not be best to consult the people back in Satsuma before proceeding.

"Back home, the young men are used to living in wide-open spaces," he said in reply. "Then they come far by land and sea and are cooped up here for more than a year, suffering a melancholy that I am sure is hard to bear. The least we can do is give them windows that let them amuse themselves by looking at people passing on the street. How else can we make life bearable for them? If the expense is too great, I'll donate it from my own stipend. Then I can at least feel that I have helped them persevere."

Windows were put on every floor of the house, high and low. According to Taura Kengyō,[3] who told me this story, everyone in the province was very impressed with the depth of his desire to comfort the young men.

It was during the Genroku era [1688–1704], when Major Counselor Kujō, son of Lord Regent Sukezane,[4] was just twelve or thirteen years old. His father gave him an incense burner of celadon that was one of the treasures of the house, which the young man kept next to where he always sat—that is, until one day a young servant accidentally knocked it over and broke it.

The father of the servant was fearful and distraught: "The burner was something highly treasured by the regent, which he gave to his son because he loves him so. When he hears about this, who knows what he will choose as a punishment. Why, he may well lock my boy up."

In response, the young lord said, "Not to worry, nothing of that sort will happen. I have a way to deal with the problem."

A few days later, the regent came to visit.

2. Shimazu Tatewaki. *Tatewaki* was an honorific title given to an accomplished samurai.
3. The title *kengyō* was given to officials in the Mōkan (Bureau of the Blind), a government office for blind musicians, masseurs, and acupuncturists.
4. Kujō Sukezane (1669–1729). His son was Kujō Morotaka (1688–1712).

"Where is the lion?[5] Didn't I say it was something so fine that you should keep it right here on your shelf? Please do put it out on display."

"Because of what you said," the young lord replied, "I was taking the thing down from the shelf last night to admire it, and dropped it. Now it's in pieces. Since you had stressed how valuable it was, I was chagrined over my mistake and decided not to bring the matter up if you didn't ask about it, but you have, so I have to confess."

"No," the regent said, "I can't believe you would make such a mistake; it must have been one of your servants." But the son just kept insisting that it was he who was responsible, and so the incident came to an end.

The father of the servant boy said that even his life would not be enough to repay the young lord's kindness. Later, the regent heard what had really happened and declared that his son was truly shameless, the story goes.

Another time, the regent came over for a gathering, and the rice was too hard. "You should punish the cook—he must be a dolt," he said, and was very put out.

The young lord replied, "Recently I ordered him to make the rice more firm, instead of soft like before; later I told him I would inform him if there were any complaints—but I'm afraid I forgot to tell him."

The house steward said that the people there all praised the young lord as a man of deep benevolence whose way of taking pity on people was a model for all.

Slandered by Uesugi Norizane, Ashikaga Mochiuji was branded a rebel by the shogun Yoshinori, who commanded Uesugi Kiyokata and Isshiki Kunai Shōsuke to attack Mochiuji at Kamakura.[6] After Mochiuji had committed suicide, the attacking force was closing in on the residence of his heir. As attackers pressed in from all sides, the heir's men were all being

5. Probably a reference to a lion-shaped figurine adorning the lid of the incense burner.
6. Acting as shogunal deputy in the Kantō, Uesugi Norizane (1410–1466) ordered the attack on Ashikaga Mochiuji (1398–1439) in 1439 upon the instructions of Ashikaga Yoshinori (d. 1441). The conflict has traditionally been referred to as the Eikyō Uprising. Both Uesugi Kiyokata (Norizane's younger brother) and Isshiki Kunai Shōsuke (Yoshitsura; d. 1440) were in the attacking force.

killed. Among the assailants was one samurai stronger than the others and very skilled in the use of weapons who got into the inner courtyard and cut down seven or eight men.

As Mochiuji's heir, too, was doing himself in, a pet monkey he doted on was there beside him, weeping—until suddenly the animal got up and ran into the courtyard, jumped up on the shoulders of the strong samurai, and gouged out both the man's eyes before running away. Strong though the samurai was, he collapsed and was taken and killed by the heir's men.

Thus even a monkey sensed when its master was in dire straits and went to take on his enemies. How much more so a man, if one is always kind toward him, will be sure to feel devotion.

When a certain lord was so disappointed at an inept samurai that he was about to let him go, someone chided him. "A lord should make use of men the same way a good carpenter makes use of wood, knowing that there is no such thing as a large tree that can be used for veranda boards or a slender tree that can serve as a girder. In a tree, a monkey may have the power of a bird, but in the water he can't compete with fish. A unicorn can run across any plain but cannot match foxes and badgers for leaping between crags in a mountain gorge. Put Tadanobu[7] or Benkei[8] on a horse with a sword in his hand and no enemy can stand against him, but give him a spade instead and he won't compare with a single farmer.

"Men who enjoy mimicking a rooster's crow or a dog barking are not the smartest of people, surely; but the man who helped Lord Mengchang escape from Qin at Hangu Barrier accomplished a feat more than worthy of a warrior.[9] No one likes a samurai who can do little more than put on

7. Satō Tadanobu (1161?–1186), one of the fiercest defenders of Minamoto no Yoshitsune (1159–1189). His exploits were the subject of countless stories, plays, and pictorial representations throughout the Edo period.

8. D. 1189. The closest friend and protector of Minamoto no Yoshitsune.

9. When Tian Wen, lord of Mengchang, was trying to escape from the state of Qin, he was assisted by one of his men, who tricked the border guards into thinking that it was nearly dawn by mimicking a rooster's call. The incident is alluded to in Sei Shōnagon's *Makura no sōshi*. See *The Pillow Book of Sei Shōnagon*, trans. Ivan Morris (New York: Columbia University Press, 1967), 2:114n.637.

a sad face and weep, but such behavior helped the Kusunoki bring peace to the world in a time of trouble.[10]

"So: if you fail to grasp a man's strong points and simply dismiss him as incapable, or force a man to do something beyond his capabilities and then send him away as a lost cause, you will never find men you can use, nor ever realize your potential as a warlord," the man said, impressing the lord greatly.

This must be the meaning of the saying "Use a man according to his capacity."[11]

————————

In Edo, only Yoshiwara, Shinagawa, and Senju are designated as prostitution districts, and I have never heard of any others. When Gokokuji[12] was built, some fine teahouses were constructed there, complete with women of pleasure, but the government immediately outlawed them and tore the places down. Despite all the clamor, however, new houses kept appearing. When Nezu Shrine was built during the Shōtoku era [1711–1716], for instance, prostitution areas appeared there, too, just as they had around Gokokuji. The government outlaws them, but still they crop up.

Midway into the Kyōhō era [1716–1736], such houses began to appear in the Tawaramachi area of Asakusa, and since then they have spread all the way to the bridge at Shitaya, encroaching on Honjō, Fukagawa, and other areas without any inhibition. At first, the magistrate's office closed some of them down, but it was like keeping flies off food.

I have heard that it has been this way in Kyoto since long ago. Here it was not like this until the Genroku era, when the districts began popping up everywhere. I guess that's the way of the world.

10. Lugubrious incidents involving Kusunoki Masashige (d. 1336) and his son Masatsura (d. 1348), both supporters of the Southern Court, abound in Edo-period drama and fiction. Both were considered men of high sensibility as well as fearsome warriors.

11. A reference to the *Analects*. See Confucius, *The Analects*, trans. D. C. Lau (New York: Penguin, 1979), 122.

12. A temple of the Shingon sect founded in 1681 in the Bunkyō area of Tokyo.

Haikai poetry began as an amusement after *renga* sessions in the times of Sōgi[13] and Moritake,[14] it is said. Thinking of it as a popular form, people employed even the most vulgar words and felt it all right to delve into new and unprecedented subject matter. Knowing all about prostitutes, farmers, boatmen, teamsters, gamblers, and beggars became a matter of pride, and haikai practitioners alluded even to the most unspeakably vulgar things.

This is something in which a person of proper feeling should not participate. It teaches people of high station about only the basest of things, into which they may regrettably find their interest drawn. One would hope, therefore, that from such things the nobility, at least, would turn away.

It happened in a commercial district in the castle town of Matsuyama, in Iyo Province.[15] The son of a certain household went home with his mother's younger sister, who had come for a visit. The plan had been that he would stay the night, but as dusk came on he said that he was going to return home.

Hearing this, the boy's aunt said, "It's almost sundown, and you'll have to go over a *li*[16] in darkness—and with no one to see you off, since the men aren't back from the fields. Why not wait till first thing tomorrow?"

"I had intended to stay, but suddenly I have the feeling that I must return home," the boy said. Then he hurried away.

It was fully dark when he arrived home. As he came up to his house, however, he noticed that there were lots of lamps burning inside and went up to the window to take a peek. There he saw seven or eight rough-looking men, their faces all painted black, gathered together.

13. 1421–1502. The most famous of all masters of "serious" linked verse.
14. 1473–1549. Another master of linked verse. He was known as one of the first true champions of unorthodox (haikai) linked verse.
15. Modern-day Ehime Prefecture.
16. A traditional Chinese unit of distance, now standardized at 1,640 feet.

Thinking this most strange, he went down the alley to the back of the house, looked through the window, and saw his mother cowering in fear as she prepared food by the hearth.

In a whisper, he called to his mother. "What's going on?" he said. "When I got back and looked in the window, something strange seemed to be up."

His mother explained very quietly that just after dark ten thieves had broken in, killed the boy's father, tied up all the servant men, and ordered her to prepare food for them, which she was doing because she had no other choice. She added that five or six of the men were in the storehouse.

"All right," the boy said. "Get me the rifle, some ammunition, and fuse cords. Then when you present the food, put the trays out so that all the men are lined up in a neat row."

The mother did as he said and lined the trays up, and as they were eating the boy stuck the rifle in through the window, aimed, and fired a round that brought all five of the men down at once. The other men were thrown into a panic and fled, but the evidence on the five dead bodies made it easy to apprehend them. All were executed by the lord of the province, and the boy was made a samurai.

A man of over ninety years from Matsuyama told me this story. It appears that it took place in the Enpō era [1673–1681].

Seven men from Imagawa Village were delivering seventy ryō[17] in coin to the headman, ostensibly toward payment of the annual tax, but after a few minutes, one of the seven pulled out a sword and killed the headman. Seeing this transpire, the headman's wife filled the coal scoop with hot coals from the brazier and dumped them over the attacker's head, which immobilized him and took the other men completely by surprise. Although they tried to lift him up and help him away, the fire was so hot that he was unable to move before officials from the magistrate's office and some other villagers showed up, bound the men, and sent them off

17. The term ryō generally referred to large, oblong gold coins.

into custody. Everyone commented on the wife's quick thinking in a dire situation.

————————

I think it was at the time of the fire of the Meireki era.[18] When the residence of one Hotta Masakiyo, vice-governor of Ueno, was in danger, his men put such great effort into fighting the fire that the buildings escaped damage. Yet Masakiyo did not appear to be all that pleased.

"You men are like my hands and feet, and each is precious to me. Suppose the buildings *had* burned: Would it have been such a loss? I appreciate your efforts, but for you to have been injured would have been truly disloyal. That is why I am not pleased. Remember this in future."

The men all felt that this was a most extraordinary command.

————————

Among ancient blades of renown, nine of ten have nicks in them; it is inferior blades that are flawless. This is how value is determined in the Hon'ami house.[19] If one is trying to determine utility, nicks and breaks are the only thing to consider. Looking for a pearl of pure white is a mistake.

Yuasa[20] says that most of the swords used in the era of Warring States that have come down to us are damaged in some way, and I think he must be right. The father of Takebayashi Tadashichi[21] was a samurai who fought in many battles and distinguished himself at Shimabara.[22] The famous sword that he used, which had been passed down to him, had lost much of its edge, but he used it over and over again, employed it all through the Shimabara campaign, and then had it sharpened and used it again, all without any trouble, according to Honda.[23]

18. 1655–1658. The fire took place on the eighteenth day of the First Month of 1657. It burned much of the central area of the city and caused more than 100,000 fatalities.
19. A samurai house tracing its lineage back to the fourteenth century. In the beginning, the family's specialty was the repair and sharpening of blades, but in later years it became famous for appraisal and authentication.
20. Yuasa Jōzan (1708–1781), a Confucian scholar and government official.
21. 1672–1703. One of the famous Forty-seven Rōnin.
22. The Shimabara Uprising (1637–1638), when the government put down a peasant rebellion led by Amakusa Shirō (1621–1638) and other Christians at Shimabara in Kyushu.
23. Honda Shigetsugu (1529–1596), a vassal of the Tokugawa house.

When it comes to people, too, a person with no faults may be all very fine but is rarely of much use. People with flaws make the best heroes. It stands to reason that if one overlooks their faults and makes use of them, many men will accomplish much. These days, there are lots of people who mar the edge of a blade in secret in order to make up for it having no nicks, but what they end up with is something that looks right only on the surface, like a doll of papier-mâché, so the story goes.

———————

A masterless samurai living in the Honjō district taught utai[24] in his spare time. He had two young daughters by his wife, but a rumor was going round that his wife was carrying on with a young man who came for lessons, and one of the samurai's close friends told him in private that the stories were true.

Hearing this, the samurai replied that this was something that had to be handled delicately, a difficult matter, yet that he understood.

Shortly thereafter, when the young student was down sick for a time, the husband went to a place called Funabashi in Shimōsa[25] and visited a man who tamed foxes and arranged to pay him two ryō in gold if he would come to a certain place on the next day with a fox on a leash.

The utai class met the next night, with lots of students in attendance, as usual. As the night grew late, while the class was still going on, the sound of fighting came from out in the street. Everyone got up and went out with lamps, finding the master there, standing next to a fox he had killed. When asked what had happened, he replied that he had come out and found a young man standing there, peeping in from the street, so he had cut him down.

After this incident, people began to say that the whole thing had been the workings of a fox. Some days later, the samurai went to his father-in-law's place and told him the whole story, saying that had he let the truth out, a scandal would have ensued, perhaps making things difficult for his

24. The chanting of Noh librettos, a hobby of the time.
25. Modern-day Funabashi, Chiba Prefecture.

two children, so he had taken care of things by stratagem. Nevertheless, he demanded a divorce, which was arranged.

———————————

A troop captain in Tsugaru[26] committed an offense and was put under house arrest, with the order that anyone visiting him would be punished, but one of his men kept climbing over the roofs each night to bring him saké and other things. When someone informed the lord of what was going on, however, the latter was so impressed that rather than punishing him he judged the man to be a paragon of devotion, a true example of heroic loyalty. Furthermore, he concluded that anyone who could inspire such dedication must be a man of deep affections himself and forgave the captain his offense.

———————————

The wife of a recluse named Ginza no Gotō was a compassionate woman who was very kind to her husband's mistress. Over the years, in fact, the wife treated the mistress like her own sibling, providing clothing and furnishings equal to her own and always dealing with her as a friend. When the wife took ill, however, the mistress kept messengers busy corresponding with a master of the dark arts, and one of the messages went astray somehow and got into the husband's hands. "It appears that the illness is progressing," the note said, "so please put even more effort into your incantations."

When word of this got to him, the husband was furious. He told his wife, "Over the years you have been so open and considerate, to the point that I felt guilty at times. To repay your kindness in such a senseless way is simply unforgivable. If not for the scandal it would cause, I would put her to death. Instead, I will dismiss her and tell her to leave immediately."

The wife, however, felt pity for the mistress. Over and over again, she pleaded with her husband, saying that a woman's heart was a foolish thing, that what the woman had done was not unheard of, and that to think of the mistress falling into dire straits after so many years was more than she could bear. Her suggestion was that he give a house in

26. In ancient Mutsu, now Aomori Prefecture.

Asakusa to their youngest son and place the woman there as his mother. In the end, this is just what the husband arranged.

We praise people merely for a lack of jealousy, but surely rewarding villainy with compassion is even more remarkable.

One day, a blind man on his way to Kyoto to take the tonsure showed up at the country home of a lowly foot soldier in Kii Province.[27] It was getting dark, and since it would be difficult to go on and find an inn, the man asked for lodging. He seemed so pathetic that the soldier let him stay for one night.

The next day, after the traveler had taken his leave, the soldier's wife went into where he had been sleeping and found that he had left behind a pouch with two or three hundred gold coins in it.

Showing the pouch to her husband, the woman said, "If he has lost this, he will have to give up his plans to become a priest, and that will put him in a bad way. You must get it back to him—and quickly."

Before she was even done speaking, the man took off running. After two or three *li*, he came to a precipice above a mountain stream and found the traveler there in a meditative pose.

"It's just as I feared," the soldier thought, calling out before arriving by his side.

"What are you doing?" he asked.

"I have lost the money I needed to become a priest," the traveler said, "so my hopes have been dashed. Since I have no more reason to go on living, I thought I would throw myself in this river. I was just reciting a sutra before being on my way."

"I thought so," the soldier said. Then he explained how his wife had found the money and how he had nearly worn himself out running after him. Then he handed over what had been lost.

The traveler was so choked with tears that he was unable to give a proper reply. He offered profuse thanks, saying that he would not forget this act of unexpected compassion as long as he lived. Then he departed, and they never heard from him again.

27. Present-day Wakayama Prefecture.

Years later, an official of Kii was on business at Mount Kōya,[28] and as he was seeing the sights he came upon a stone stele six or seven feet[29] high on which the name of the foot soldier had been inscribed. The blind man had risen to the position of head of the Bureau of the Blind. The stele said that he had erected the monument as a prayer for the foot soldier. The story was such an unusual one that when the official returned home he told people about it, and eventually the lord of the province heard about it as well. He had the soldier called before him and after hearing the details was himself so impressed with the man's honesty that he elevated him to samurai status.

When Kanran first came to Edo he had no friends here, so he had taken lodgings in a back alley near Nihonbashi.

On the night of the last day of the Twelfth Month, a merchant came to the house next door demanding to be repaid money that was owed him. There was much talk back and forth, but the man next door was broke and simply couldn't pay off the debt, so the argument went on and on. Hearing the conversation, Kanran quickly went over and introduced himself as a traveler who had just arrived in the place.

"I've been listening to the argument and can't stand it anymore," he said. "As it happens, I have a little money leftover from my trip, which I will give you to pay the man with."

This surprised the neighbor, of course, who told the story to people and made a name for Kanran. He hadn't done the deed as something for people to learn about, but the fact is that what he did in secret got him his reputation.

Ishikawa Jōzan fought in the Genna campaign[30] as Hachirō Saemon Naomoto, accumulating merit as a warrior by attacking before the vanguard

28. Site of a prominent temple complex located in Kii Province.
29. The Japanese measure mentioned here is *shaku*. One *shaku* is approximately one foot.
30. Jōzan (lay name Kaemon; 1583–1672) is remembered as an important figure in Kyoto intellectual circles. The Genna campaign, also known as the Osaka campaign, was fought in the spring of 1615, the first year of the Genna era (1615–1624).

of Ieyasu's men, which impressed everyone, high and low.[31] Since doing this had meant committing the serious offense of disobeying a direct order, however, he was dismissed and ended up going into seclusion in the eastern hills of the capital. He wrote this poem before leaving the city to which he would never return:

Never again
shall I cross Semi River—
whose ripples
of clear water shame me
with the wrinkles of old age.[32]

wataraji na / semi no ogawa no / kiyokereba / oi no nami sou / kage mo hazukashi

Some years back I saw the tower at Shisendō,[33] which looked to be a most serene dwelling place. Jōzan's poems are said to be without peer in his generation. He was a true practitioner of both the martial arts and letters. And he must have retained his bravado late into life, for once when a certain merchant who had gone to see him said something inappropriate, he killed the man with his sword. The merchants of the area got together and complained to Governor-General Itakura Shigemune,[34] who after hearing them is reported to have chuckled and said, "When a man says something to give offense to a Great Mountain, this is what he should expect. It amounted to suicide!" and pursued the matter no further.

———————

The daughter of a merchant in the Kanda area[35] lived with her mother and a man who had been adopted into the household as her husband. When the first husband died, another was brought in.

31. He rode into the enemy camp the night before a planned morning attack, against the orders of Tokugawa Ieyasu (1542–1616) himself. Tradition says that he did so in order to fulfill his mother's wish that he prove himself to be a master spearman, following in the footsteps of his deceased father.
32. In other words, the ripples on the water would be reflected back as the wrinkles of old age on his face.
33. The Hall of Poetry Immortals, a residence—later a temple—that Jōzan began building in 1641 and where he lived until his death three decades later. The tower referred to was doubtless the Tower for Whistling at the Moon, a second-story structure designed for moon viewing.
34. 1586–1656. One of Tokugawa Ieyasu's closest retainers, he was made governor-general of Kyoto in 1620, succeeding his own father.
35. A district in Edo.

The daughter was always unfilial toward her mother, so much so that the husband worried what the future might bring. Then he learned that his wife had a lover and was even more at a loss. But as he was wondering what to do, his wife came to him one night and said that her mother was so stubborn and difficult that even the neighbors hated her and asked him to lure the old woman out somehow and murder her in secret.

The husband had been expecting something like this, so at first he refused the idea but in the end went along. A few days later, he invited his mother-in-law out to visit Asakusa Temple, and when he came home in the evening and his wife asked him what he had done with the old woman, he said that after considering various stratagems, he had finally killed her in secret at Hashiba River and thrown her body into the water. He then took out his dagger and showed the blood still on it to his wife, who was overjoyed at how well her intentions had been realized.

The next day, the wife went to the commissioner's office and accused her husband of killing her mother, and when the police went to get him and examined his dagger, there was blood on it. But then the husband related everything that had happened, explaining that he had been suspicious all along and that he had actually left his mother-in-law at the house of a relative in Asakusa and put fish blood on the dagger.

When the old woman was brought forward for questioning, it turned out that all was as the husband had said and the case was cleared up completely. The wife was executed.

This happened in the first year of the Enkyō era [1744–1748]. Such stories are always incomplete, but I have set it down just as I heard it.

In the Genroku era, there was a surgeon named Tominaga Han'i, who was already old by then and had a fine reputation. He was a brave man and very forthright.

It was when I was about twelve or thirteen, I think, at the time when they were just starting to adjust currency values. People were chatting somewhere, and Han'i turned to me.

"You are young and will be here to see things far into the future. From now on, I predict that things will become more and more scarce and the truth more and more a rare thing. By the time you get to fifty or sixty, the world will be in dire straits."

When asked why, he replied, "Coins of gold and silver are the foundation of all material value. When they lose their integrity, people too begin to lose their foundations and seek only profit. And because they are brought up that way, the virtues that have prevailed until now must change and everything go to lies."

It seems that he was exactly right.

———————

Han'i went to the public bath and was soaking in the water when a townsman got in with him. As Han'i was slender of build and short, the man was disdainful and rude.

"Hey, old man, how about giving me a scrub?" he said.

"Why, of course," Han'i said, and began to scrub the man down. While he was doing so, the man let his guard down and began to chat.

"Let me wash your feet, then," Han'i said, and when the man lifted his legs to be washed, Han'i grabbed him hard by the balls.

At this, the man changed his attitude and began to apologize, but Han'i would have none of it and was about to kill him. So intense were the man's entreaties, however, that Han'i only told him never to come to that bathhouse again, had him write out a promise to that effect, and let him go.

———————

Among the *kyōka* of Bishop Inkai[36] is this one:

Don't compose poems
in Japanese or Chinese,
or play at linked verse—

———

36. 1613–1689. *Kyōka* refers to humorous or bawdy *waka*. Inkai was the adopted son of Kazan'in Sadayoshi and the author of poetry collections and other works.

then at least you won't suffer
from any sleepless nights!

uta yomazu / shi mata narazu / renga mo senu / hito no nezame ya / mata nakaruramu

Very astute, I think.

———————————

A wealthy village elder of Kamakura admired the monk Munan so much that he built him a cottage and treated him with great respect. After a while, however, the elder's daughter became pregnant, and when he pressed her, she said she was in her predicament because of the monk, whom she said had been visiting her in secret. Furious, the elder went directly to Munan's place.

"Here I am treating you with the greatest respect," the old man said, "and all the while you're carrying on with my daughter! It's too much! Get out, and I don't care where you go."

Munan bore this abuse without saying a word, left, and moved in with a close friend living in Yuki no Shita[37] who still trusted him enough to put him up in a vacant temple and provide for his needs.

After a while, the elder's daughter confessed to him that she had accused the monk only because she thought her father might be less harsh in his punishment since he held Munan in such high regard. The truth was that she had been having an affair with another man for a long time and had never been visited by the monk at all. The elder then called his daughter's lover in and got the full story.

Greatly upset, the elder knew that somehow he had to atone for having accused the monk unjustly and cursed him on top of that, so he ran right out and made his way to Yuki no Shita and offered a tearful apology. Munan just smiled and appeared to bear no grudge at all.

"Now that I have apologized," the elder then said, "would you consider coming back to my place?"

"Why, of course," said the monk, and the two went back to the elder's cottage. It appears that no doubt ever troubled the elder again.

———

37. A neighborhood in Kamakura.

Once when Kanze Tayū[38] was out on the street, he heard someone chanting lines from a Noh libretto in the house next door and decided to try to silence him by chanting himself, and sure enough, after a moment the chanting stopped.

Some nights later, when he was staying at an inn, again there was someone chanting, and the people with Tayū asked him to do as he had before.

"I'm not sure I would succeed," was his reply. When they asked him why, he said, "In the earlier case, the chanter was actually quite good, so that when he heard my voice he listened carefully and was embarrassed to proceed. Tonight's chanter is not good enough to discern good from bad and wouldn't understand no matter how long I tried."

This is true in all things. Not only in this case, but in many others the saying "You strike it—but it produces no echo" applies.

———————

When Matsumae,[39] governor of Izu, was a district magistrate, his friend the painter Kaihō Yūchiku[40] came to visit. It was a winter day, and Matsumae had set out a beautiful arrangement of rose plum blossoms, which were in full bloom at the time. Yūchiku praised them, saying that no one but a governor-general or someone of noble station could enjoy the first flowers of the season in such a way.

Matsumae said nothing in reply but instead began to shed tears, leading his friend to worry that something must be wrong. After a time, however, he did reply: "You have spoken wisely. It is as you said. For someone as unworthy as I to be honored with high office and enjoy such a level of power is not something to idly forget. My position is one of considerable importance, and to be appointed to it is certainly beyond what I deserve. I was so overcome with gratitude and chagrin just now that I couldn't hold back the tears."

38. A master of the Kanze lineage of Noh.
39. Most likely Matsumae Yoshihiro (d. 1731).
40. 1654–1728. Son of the more famous Kaihō Yūsetsu (1598–1677).

It is said that afterward the people of Kyoto talked about his fine character for years.

Since ancient times, there has been a tradition of the dead returning to life after three days. When a servant girl in a certain house died in an epidemic, she was put in the usual barrel and taken to the temple, but because rain made it difficult to dig a grave for her, the barrel was left in a closet for the time being. The next day, someone wearing a white coat came staggering out to the altar, sending the young acolytes fleeing in surprise. When the chief priest went in to find out what was going on, it turned out that the girl had come back to life, pushed the lid off the barrel, and gotten out. After eating some food, she recovered completely. Since her head had already been shaved, she became a nun and left the world.

There are many cases of this sort, which one hears about from time to time.

According to a samurai from Satsuma, when Lord Yoshihiro[41] was encamped in Korea, one of his soldiers who had gone into a gorge to cut fodder was taken by a tiger. It grabbed him gently by the neck and carried him into the mountains, toying with him as a cat does with a mouse.

Time passed by, and as the man slipped into unconsciousness, the tiger lay down on top of him and went to sleep. When later he came to himself again, the man gently rubbed the belly of the tiger, who remained asleep on top of him, until it began to snore. Then—still lying there—he took off the rope he had around his waist, tied one end around the tiger's balls, and, after making sure that the animal was still asleep, tied the other end around a big tree nearby. When he proceeded to run back the same way he had come, the tiger was so taken aback and enraged that it leaped over the gorge, tearing off his balls and dying on the spot.

41. Shimazu Yoshihiro (1535–1619), one of the greatest generals of Toyotomi Hideyoshi's (1536–1598) Korea campaign.

The man skinned the beast and presented the pelt to the lord of the province, who used it for the lid of a container that is still in service, it is said.

In his old age, the minor captain Sakura Toshikatsu[42] was asked by a man who was about to take up his duties as governor of a province if Toshikatsu might do him the honor of coming to enjoy tea.

Toshikatsu and his men all thought this a promising invitation and decided that they would go together on the appointed day. Before they left, though, Toshikatsu met with his men and told them that they should eat before going.

When the day came, Toshikatsu went with his band of old retainers and was met at the gate of the house by the governor himself, who greeted them happily and ushered them into his study. Shortly after, they all went into the tea house, where they found a stack of five small boxes of rice crackers, along with a toothpick on the lid of each box. Soon the governor served them tea, after which they all chatted briefly before the men thanked their host and went home.

In *Essays in Idleness*, Kenkō writes of the frugality of Ashikaga Yoshiuji[43] when he was visited by the Saimyōji lay monk,[44] which is indeed admirable. But do people realize that there are those today whose ways differ little from those of long ago?

Lord Karasumaru Mitsuhiro[45] spent all his time in a single room of ten tatami mats filled with open books. He kept two of the four sliding doors open. In the room were one desk, an inkstone, and a fan box designed for three fans in which he kept brushes. For years at a time, no one else ever

---

42. Doi Toshikatsu (1573–1644), one of the great daimyo of the early Edo period, later an elder (*rōjū*) in the central government.

43. 1189–1254. One of the most prominent generals in the service of the Hōjō government at the time.

44. Hōjō Tokiyori (1227–1263). The incident is recorded in Yoshida no Kenkō, *Tsurezuregusa* (*Essays in Idleness*), sec. 216.

45. 1579–1638. A court noble and poet.

went into the room, so that a depression was worn into the place where he sat and dust covered everything. For public occasions, or even when he attended court, he put his inkwell in the fan box and carried it himself in the palanquin and right into the meeting room.

Mitsuhiro was called to service in Edo for three years, where he is said to have lived on the Takakura estate. When he heard that he was going to return to Kyoto, the steward who had watched over things for him in Kyoto thought that in Edo his master must have become so used to having a lot of space that having a storehouse right next door would feel oppressive, so he tore it down. The storehouse contained treasures that had come to Mitsuhiro as gifts over many years. Each thing was taken into the study, catalogued carefully, and then given away to someone in the house staff, although the steward took nothing whatsoever for himself.

Mitsuhiro returned to Kyoto and after three or four days had passed still seemed to notice nothing unusual, so the steward asked him if the garden space didn't look different in some way. It did seem more spacious, Mitsuhiro thought—and then asked what had become of the storehouse that used to be there.

"I thought that you would have become so used to having space in Edo that I felt the storehouse would feel oppressive, so I tore it down," the steward replied.

"But what did you do with the things in it?" Mitsuhiro then asked, to which the steward answered that he had given them to people in the house, high and low.

"Well done, then," Mitsuhiro said. "And what did you take for yourself?"

"For myself—why nothing," was the man's reply.

"Not very smart of you," Mitsuhiro laughed, and didn't waste any more words, it is said.

Someone said that his otherworldliness had its origins in his fondness for the study of Zen Buddhism.

[*MADO NO SUSAMI, BUYA ZOKUDAN, EDO CHŌMONJŪ,* YŪHŌ BUNKO
(TOKYO: YŪHŌDŌ SHOTEN, 1915)]

12

A Miscellany of Stories

MORITA MORIMASA

Morita Morimasa (1667–1732) was the third son of a samurai family in service to the Nakagawa clan, in Kanazawa, a large castle town in Kaga Province on the Japan Sea. He spent most of his life there. After the deaths of his older brothers, he succeeded to the headship of his house. His collection of zuihitsu, Hanashi zuihitsu (A Miscellany of Stories), *is made up mostly of anecdotes concerning unusual events heard from people around him over the course of his lifetime. It was completed in 1727, just a few years before his death at the age of sixty-six. The collection is one of many put together by provincial samurai that have too often been overlooked in surveys of Edo-period literature.*

A man named Shibano Yahei didn't want to use any medicines because as a member of the Ikkō sect[1] he had no fear whatsoever of death. A fine thing, I thought, but Keichō[2] had this to say: "Everyone is mistaken on this count. Medicine—acupuncture, moxibustion, whatever—is not there to save one from dying but to treat illness. Even if you are going to live

---

1. A militant offshoot of the Jōdo Shinshū, or True Pure Land, sect, a sect of Buddhism founded in the late medieval era.
2. A priest of Kamimiya Temple in Kanazawa, a temple of the Jōdo sect affiliated with Nishi Honganji.

only a single day longer, you want to be in the best of health. Why, if medicine could save you from death, it would have to work for people who got their heads cut off or got stabbed in the neck!"

———————

In 1721, the lord secretary Okumura[3] was on duty in Edo. That year, there was an epidemic in the city, and two of his bearers became so seriously ill that they were very near death. Especially because this happened while they were on the road, Okumura felt sorry for them and called a number of doctors in to try various cures, but after trying some cures they said there was no hope. Fully aware of their fate, all the two men could do was wait.

Okumura was so moved by the situation that he said, "Since these two are going to die in any case, let's send them off with some good memories of this life and let them have anything they want to eat." As the men ate gratefully all that they desired—which included not just goose and duck but also rare delicacies—the illness receded, they returned to health, and survived the ordeal.

———————

In the eighth or ninth month of 1695 or 1696, before Abe Sanjūrō[4] had become heir of his house, a serving maid named Yamaji fell ill in an epidemic, and the situation became so serious that she was sent home. Soon news came that medical treatments had failed, and she was dead.

That very evening, however, there Yamaji was at her usual place in the dining room of the house. When a wet nurse, not really thinking, asked her—"Is that you, Yamaji—what are you doing here?"—Yamaji vanished. The wet nurse was so upset over this that she fainted, but after a while they revived her. She said that Yamaji had been such a dedicated servant that her spirit had come back to the house to serve.

———————

I believe it was toward the end of the Kanbun era [1671–1673]. In the Noderamachi area, along the Sai River, a pale woman showed up at eve-

———

3. Okumura Naiki-dono, Okumura Haruyoshi (d. 1736), a high-ranking samurai of the Kaga domain.
4. D. 1722. A middle-ranking samurai of the Kaga domain.

ning for two or three days at a dumpling shop and bought two coppers' worth of white rice cakes. Thinking that there was something unsettling about the woman, the proprietor followed her as far as the area around the gate of Ryūzōji,[5] where she disappeared. He knocked on the door, went inside, and explained to the head priest there what had happened, to which the priest said, "One thought comes to mind. A pregnant woman died recently and was buried here in the temple grounds. Yes, there must be something unusual going on." He told the family, and the next morning they unearthed the coffin and found a baby inside. Around the corpse were five or six of the rice cakes the woman had been buying each day.

Thinking how miraculous all this was, they took the baby home to raise—a boy, who did in fact survive. On the day celebrating the seventeenth anniversary of the mother's death, the boy was among those who went to the temple. A man named Jūhei who was in service to Lord Teranishi Shōbei[6] told this story at Sannomaru Guardhouse[7] in 1687.

It was not too long ago, I think. A retainer to the Maeda house[8] was taking five gold coins to be exchanged; an errand for the lady of the house, it would seem. With the pouch of coins in the breast pocket of his robe, he was on his way to the changing house in Zaimokuchō when he discovered that the money was gone—perhaps dropped in the snow.

The first thing he did was to go home, take off his sash, and shake out his robes, but the money wasn't there. Then he had no choice but to go to the headman and put his own house in pawn, for which he was able to borrow three hundred *monme*[9] in silver and settle the matter with his master.

After this, he began searching through the snow on the street where he had been walking in the area around Shirutani Slope, and there were the coins, still together! Full of gratitude, he went back to his house, feeling that surely he had been blessed by heaven and proceeded to take care of his debt.

5. A temple of the Nichiren sect.
6. D. 1708. The son of a physician named Teranishi Ekian.
7. Located on the eastern side of Kanazawa Castle.
8. The Maeda house ruled the Kaga, Noto, and Etchū domains throughout the Edo period.
9. Thus three hundred *monme* in silver coin would be the equivalent of five *koban*, or gold coins.

All of this took some time, and it was late by the time he prepared to go to bed. As he undid his sash and looked at the folds of his robes, there were the original coins, which had fallen into the cotton padding through a torn seam.

Iwamura Bunpei[10] told me this story.

After giving birth in the Seventh Month of 1726, the wife of Iwakura Hōzaemon (a retainer of Yūbara Kyūzaemon's), who lived in the row houses,[11] was ill for a long time. At about four in the morning on the last day of the Eleventh Month, she was asleep with the newborn babe in her arms when an old nun came to Hōzaemon in his dream, saying, "Your wife is dying; quick—give her some medicine or something!"

Half awake, Hōzaemon thought to himself, "What a strange dream," and went back to sleep, until the same nun came back again and said, "Your wife has just died. Hurry and give her some of that medicine you just happen to have at hand."

Hōzaemon awoke with a start, got up, and found his wife with her teeth clenched and her body cold and dead. He lit a lamp and was about to go to the kitchen to get some medicine when he recalled that the nun had said, "Give her some of that medicine you just happen to have at hand." In the tissue bag nearby, there was a strange medicine that he had asked Kangakuya Taisuke of Ikenohata[12] to make up, so he chewed up two or three of the tablets and put them into her mouth with some water. Suddenly she began breathing again, and came back to life talking about the dreadful dream she had just had.

When Hōzaemon told her the story of his own dream and asked her what it could all mean, she said it must be because of late she had developed a firm faith in Jizō.[13]

---

10. D. 1750. A retainer to Nakagawa Chōkichi.
11. Yūbara Nobuoki (d. 1731). "Row houses" translates *nagaya*, a long house with a single roof beam partitioned into separate units (that is, a tenement).
12. A pharmacist with a shop in the Shitaya area of Edo.
13. A popular Buddhist deity.

In the winter of 1724, a man named Kuzukawa Magoemon[14] was out hunting fowl with a net. Near Tagami,[15] he netted a child of five or six years who appeared to be alive. Surely, a child of five or six who was able to speak quite well and survive in the water when it was so cold out must be a monster of some sort, he thought. So he jumped on the thing, held it down, put his dagger to its chest, and asked, "Just what are you?"

"I am a smallpox god," was the answer. "I have been out taking the lives of children, but there are so many prayers being offered at shrines and temples, so many spells and talismans about, that I had nowhere to go and ended up hiding for a while in this water. Then I got into this fix, caught in your net. Please spare my life," he pleaded, joining his hands in prayer and weeping.

"So, you are a smallpox god," said Magoemon. "Well, I have lots of children, and some of them haven't had smallpox yet. You must agree not to take them, or else I will run you through right now."

The god replied, "I am a very low-ranking god. If an epidemic strikes, no one is immune, but it is up to me whether the case is light or severe. If you will just write your name on the gate of your house, I will see that any case is light."

Magoemon spared him and threw him back in the river, and all his children had only light cases of smallpox. This story was handed down over and over again, and people would write Magoemon on signs over their gates or put it in amulet pouches. A story told by Shichibei the fishmonger.

Ushinosuke, the son of Ichibei of the Asanoya in Yasuigemachi, began smoking tobacco when he was a child. He learned calligraphy from Mudō Sakuhei[16] and showed so much talent that he was also greatly praised by people for his *utai* and *shimai*.[17]

14. Identity unknown.
15. On the Asano River.
16. Identity unknown.
17. *Utai* refers to the chanting of Noh librettos and *shimai* to Noh dancing, both popular hobbies.

In 1681, when he was nine years old, he was smoking his pipe at his master's house when some friends came up behind him and grabbed him to wrestle. As he fell forward, the bowl of his pipe caught in a space between the edges of two tatami mats, and the mouthpiece was jammed back into his mouth. Blood spurted out, and he lost consciousness.

People gathered around and sent word to Ichibei's place, where they hurriedly called for physicians and surgeons. Ichibei himself was away at the time, but servants and bearers began showing up immediately, and they put Ushinosuke in a cart and brought him home. At around the same time, the doctors showed up, among them Hori Sōshū,[18] who said that nothing in particular seemed to be wrong and treated the boy with external and internal medicines that made him well in a few days' time. Inside his mouth, on the right side above his chin, there was a small black mark, but it caused him no pain. His right eye was swollen a bit, the right side of his head was always sweaty, and his voice was gruff, but he had his appetite back and showed no other unusual symptoms.

About five years later, when he was thirteen, he received some *jiōsen*[19] and stick candy as a gift at the time of the Hachiman festival, and after he had eaten a lot of it, he coughed up the mouthpiece. The scar healed well, though, and there were no other ill effects, although he was sickly and died at nineteen, according to Ichibei's wife.

Some samurai were in the house of a certain person in Daishōji[20] in early autumn when the heat was still intense. Going out on the back veranda to cool off, they saw a snake from the mountain behind the house come down and go under the veranda. As they watched, a second snake came, and then a third, a fourth, and on up to twenty and then thirty, until one couldn't count all the snakes that had congregated.

An order was given to try to get at the snakes, first with brooms and rakes and then with poles and sticks of wood and fire hooks, but the snakes just kept coming, all of them entering from under the veranda. Soon they filled every open space in the house—the storerooms, the clos-

18. D. 1703. A physician.
19. A candy made from the roots of *goma no hagusa* (leaves of the sesame plant).
20. The name of a domain and the castle town that was at its center.

ets, the reception rooms, the kitchen, the entry hall, the bedrooms, even the spaces between the pillars and the shelves.

The men and women of the house could do nothing but withdraw to the homes of family or friends and leave the house without human occupants. After three days, however, all the snakes were gone without a trace. When the inhabitants came back to look around, they found snake slime all over the house, from the kitchen and living areas in the back to the reception rooms in the front. And when they opened a box in the closet, they found that the clothing stored in there was also covered with slime and unfit for further use. The pickle barrels, miso barrels, and rice containers were also so slimy that they had to throw everything out.

———————

In the mid-1680s, Lord Nakamura Ihei[21] had a cat he loved dearly but then bought a handsome dog that he also came to treasure. Once when he had settled down on his pillow to go to sleep, he had a dream while he was still half awake in which he saw his dog jumping up as if to get at his throat. This seemed inexplicable, but as he hesitated to react, the dog just kept jumping up and Ihei awoke with a start, only to find his cat there, poised to bite him at the throat—and the dog trying to defend him. In the beginning, the cat had been Ihei's only pet, but now he resented the way his master loved the dog and had decided to commit this evil act—a frightful prospect.

The cat ran off and was nowhere to be found, but after two or three days he sneaked into Ihei's sleeping chamber and Ihei chased him out. Every night, though, he would be skulking around, hiding behind the screens or other furnishings. Needless to say, the people in the house always had to be on their guard. Once they found him hiding in a bucket used for insects and put a board over it to trap him and keep him locked up but couldn't decide how to dispose of him. Someone suggested putting water in the bucket, but since the bucket was designed for insects, it had breathing holes underneath.

An old servant named Kadobei said to leave it up to him and pushed the lid back just enough to let a fire hook in to stab the cat. But when the

21. A middle-ranking samurai.

cat jumped up at him, both the lid and the hook went flying and the cat escaped, leaving Kadobei lamenting and shamefaced.

Another time, they found the cat hiding in the bottom of a kettle in the kitchen and put a slab of wood over the opening and a heavy stone on top of that and then left him there. That night, the cat went berserk and died in the kettle. When they threw him out the next day, they found that he had gouged out holes all over the stone of the kettle with his claws. The steward Ikkenchū[22] told me this story.

Unlike cats, dogs have a deep love for their masters. When I asked about the origins of Dog Temple in Harima, I was told about a man named Baifu, who had been a minister to Soga no Iruka[23] in ancient times. His wife was having a secret affair with a man who was planning to murder Baifu. But when the plotter invited his prey into the mountains to go hunting, planning to kill him there, Baifu brought his two dogs—one of whom jumped up and bit through the assailant's bowstring, while the other got the man by the throat and killed him. Thus they saved their master. Baifu later put the temple up in their honor. This is what is now known as Dog Temple.[24]

Near Komatsu[25] is a village called Gokendō. In the Genroku era [1688–1704], some strange events happened there. Although one could not see it, there was something that spoke and did things. When someone in the village was going to cook, the voice would say, "I'll do that!" and then into the pot would go rice and other grains all of themselves. Or the voice would say, "I'll make that flour for you!" and the stone mortar would go to work on its own and grind the flour. What's more, the invisible helper would light a fire for meals or tea, cook rice, and draw water. In every way, it was such a help to people that they soon got used to it and were

22. Identity unknown.
23. D. 645. A powerful leader of ancient times who usurped the emperor and was eventually assassinated.
24. A slightly different version of this story appears in the early modern Noh play *Inudera* (*The Dog Temple*).
25. A village near Kanazawa.

not afraid. It got so it would do the work of one person, going from house to house in turn.

At the house of a widow lady, the voice said, "What a fine lady you are! Here's some money!" and gave her thirty coppers. The lady was over-joyed, of course, although later she discovered that it was the money she had stored in her yarn box herself. And when a young man went to the Tedori River to catch sculpin,[26] the helper became angry, saying, "Stealing my food—that just won't do!" and proceeded to turn over the miso container and the pickle barrel, doing a lot of damage. That's when people knew that it had to be an otter.

At the time, all ten villages[27] were under censure for evading taxes,[28] and the voice would announce what had been announced by the court—who would be executed, who would be pardoned, always immediately, always accurately. Sometimes the voice read aloud from the Four Books and the Five Sutras,[29] the *Wenxuan*,[30] and Confucian works, or recited from the Buddhist sutras such as the *Sanbu myōden*[31]—never missing a word. At Ikkōdera, it knew to carry a candle aloft, just as if it were walking right down the center of the road. Unheard-of events, all—so said Sakura, a maid of Gokendō who told me the story.

[*HANASHI ZUIHITSU: HONBUN TO SONO KENKYŪ*, ED. SUZUKI MASAKO (TOKYO: KAZAMA SHOBŌ, 1995)]

26. *Gori* (in the dialect of the region), a fish also known as *kajika* (miller's thumb).
27. *Tomura*. A name for the entire area of the Kaga and Toyama domains during the Edo period.
28. *Onden* (literally, "hidden rice paddies"), income from which was not being reported.
29. *Shisho gokyō*. The early Chinese philosophical and historical writings forming the Confucian canon.
30. J. *Monzen*. A large collection of Chinese writings made up of works gleaned from a thousand years of history, beginning with the Zhou dynasty (starting in 1122 B.C.E.).
31. The favored sutras of the Jōdo sect.

13

Chats with Myself

DAZAI SHUNDAI

Born a samurai in Shinano Province, Dazai Shundai (1680-1747) followed his father to Edo as a child and entered the service of a daimyo in his mid-teens. At the age of twenty-one, however, he went up to Kyoto to pursue his interest in life, Confucian learning. In time, he returned to Edo, where he studied under Ogyū Sorai (1666-1728). Although he served as a Confucian scholar in a domain bureaucracy for a brief time, for most of his life he was an independent scholar and teacher.

Shundai is rightfully known primarily for his writings on politics and economy, but in Dokugo *(Chats with Myself)—a series of essays on poetry, tea, music, and drama, written at the end of his life—he shows that he was also a keen observer of the contemporary cultural scene, and one who was not shy about stating his opinions. A pragmatic rationalist, he had little patience with either the haughty traditions of court aristocrats or, as the passage translated here reveals, what he considered to be the overly refined aesthetic of contemporary tea masters.*

I just don't understand the Way of Tea as it is practiced nowadays. In *The Book of Documents* it says, "In vessels, seek not the old but the new."[1]

---

1. *Shu jing*, the earliest Confucian classic, is a compendium of documents from the Xia to the Zhou dynasty (roughly 2060–256 B.C.E.).

Yet today, tea devotees take old teabowls of uncertain age, all soiled and unclean, and usually damaged on top of that, and then fix them up with lacquer and use them. What a filthy business! They seek out some old vessel that was used by Koreans as a spittoon, put green tea in it, and call it a tea container. Again, a filthy practice. They bend a wooden spatula and use it to spoon tea, and call it a tea scoop.

When someone plans to serve tea, first he has people gather in a crowded little one-mat enclosure, and does all the serving himself rather than having food served, also pouring the saké himself—and then washing the things and putting them away with his own hands. Sweets are eaten, then people go outside, rinse their mouths, and go back inside. The host prepares the tea himself and serves it to each guest, giving the prepared tea first to the guest of honor, who passes it to the next person, and so on, all drinking from the same bowl. Whether three people, or five people, or whatever, they all drink one by one, until the last person has imbibed, who then gives the bowl back to the guest of honor. The guest of honor then examines the bowl carefully, praises it as a thing of rare beauty, and passes it down to the others, each of whom also examines it, until it comes to the last person, who returns it to the host. Then the guests, all together, express their thanks and bow their heads to the floor.

After this, all the guests examine the wrapper used to hold the teabowl, the tea container and its wrapper, and the scoop. Even if they are not fine enough to be worthy of such attention, asking to examine them is considered proper etiquette. Even when coals are put in the hearth, all the guests gather round and offer words of praise, and if there is a flower in a vase, they praise that too. In fact, there is nothing the host does that they do not extol. This is puffery at its worst.

Sources say the design of the tea enclosure is calculated to be just a little smaller than the hut of Yuima.[2] As there is only one small window, the inside is dark even at midday, and in the summer the room is terribly hot. The doorway used by guests is like a dog door, which means that participants are obliged to crawl in, a strenuous process that makes breathing difficult. As for the food, on occasion there is something to

2. Vimalakīrti, a rich lay disciple of the historical Buddha who lived in a small hut (*hōjōan* [ten-foot-square hut]) that became the model for later believers and artists.

one's taste, but no matter how thoughtful the host, one is faced with the unpleasantness of eating every last bit of something one doesn't care for. And it is also embarrassing to have to praise as a treasure something that is really not all that special.

Connoisseurs[3] always want a house in which everything from the design to the furnishings is extraordinary, always new and elegant. By contrast, tea devotees use only the most slender of pillars, and even use flimsy ribs in their paper doors. Or they may use a crooked post, with the bark still on it, thinking that will impress their friends. Even when it comes to serving trays, they favor low ones rather than ones with taller legs. In all things, the devotees of tea mimic the look of poverty and emaciation.

As to the origins of tea, records say tea drinking began in China in the period of the Northern and Southern Dynasties, but it was in the Tang dynasty that it reached its apex. For instance, Lu Tong[4] and Lu Yu were extremely fond of it. Lu Tong wrote a poem about tea, and Lu Yu wrote *The Classic of Tea*.[5] In those days, tea was steeped in hot water or boiled. Ground tea was called powdered tea, which was put in boiling water and drunk hot. This is the kind of tea that is still used by tea devotees today. Ground tea made into round cakes was called *tuancha*, and these, too, were steeped in hot water and drunk hot. They used teabowls when serving tea, just as we do today. When Lu Yu prepared tea, whether by steeping or by boiling, he took great care in the choice of water. Details are recorded in *The Classic of Tea*.[6] The way he practiced tea is similar to the way tea devotees do today.

Chang Boxiong, another man of Lu Yu's day, also practiced tea and was an expert in the Way. Once Lord Li Ji, the son of Minister Li Shizhi[7] and an imperial censor, went on an imperial errand to the Jiangnan district, where he stayed at a travelers' inn in Linhuai Xian. While he was there, someone told him that Chang Boxiong was a master of tea, so he asked Boxiong to come and prepare tea for him. On that occasion, Bo-

---

3. Shōtetsu, *Conversations with Shōtetsu* (chap. 3).
4. A poetic disciple of the famous literatus Han Yu (768–824).
5. Ch. *Chajing*, J. *Chakyō* (ca. 760). For a translation, see Lu Yü, *The Classic of Tea: Origins and Rituals*, trans. Francis Ross Carpenter (Hopewell, N.J.: Ecco Press, 1995).
6. Ibid., 105–7.
7. D. 747? A prominent politician.

xiong wore a yellow robe and a black hat of gossamer. He came in with the teabowl in his hand, intoning the name of the tea he was using; prepared everything with the greatest care; and served the tea as if he were performing a religious rite. Those watching wiped the tears from their eyes and were most impressed by the performance. Li Ji had two bowls of tea, and that was all.

After this, Li Ji went to a place called Jiangwai and asked Lu Yu to serve him tea. Clad in shabby robes, Lu Yu placed the tea utensils in front of him, then performed the ritual in exactly the way Boxiong had done. Li Ji drank his tea; however, concluding that Lu Yu must be very poor, he then ordered one of his men to give him thirty coins. This embarrassed Lu Yu so much that from that time on he ceased to practice tea, instead writing the book *An Attack on Tea.*[8]

In our country, it was Zen monks of the Kamakura period [1185–1333] who first brought tea back with them from abroad, but ordinary people didn't drink it that much.[9] The Muromachi shogun Ashikaga Yoshimasa,[10] however, enjoyed it day and night, holding many tea gatherings in his Silver Pavilion[11] in the eastern hills of Kyoto. But since he was by disposition fond of extravagance, when it came to tea he also favored only the most beautiful and fine utensils, in this way being unlike current devotees of tea. To see this, one has only to look at the furnishings of his estate in the eastern hills that have come down to us today.

Among more recent tea masters, most take Rikyū[12] as their father. He was a Zen priest with no family and low social status and therefore practiced tea in a cramped little hut of grass. The rich and powerful of his day, bored with overindulgence in luxuries, emulated Rikyū in his enjoyment of the spare and common, the sere and stringent,[13] leaving their high mansions and lofty towers and building one-mat rooms where they prepared tea with their own hands and enjoyed serving it to friends.

8. *Huichalun.* This story is recorded in the biographical entry on Lu Yü in *Tang shu* (*History of the Tang Dynasty,* 618–907).
9. The monks who first brought tea to Japan in the thirteenth century probably did so because of its medicinal properties. The monk usually credited with bringing tea seeds to Japan is Eisai (1141–1215).
10. 1436–1490. The eighth shogun of the Muromachi period (1392–1573).
11. The temple Jishōin, popularly known as Ginkakuji (Silver Pavilion). The estate was built by Yoshimasa as a retreat in the latter part of his life and later became a temple.
12. Sen no Rikyū (1522–1591), the most famous of all Japanese tea masters.
13. The two Japanese compounds here are *hensen* and *kansan.*

Because they were emulating the ways of a Zen monk with no family obligations who was poor and shabby, they employed nothing new—from the materials used for their cottages to their various tea wares. Even when presenting food, they disdained finer dishes and favored the plain. In other words, the practices of tea devotees all imitate the actions of poor people. Of course, it may make sense for a rich man to mimic the poor for his own amusement; but I don't see what pleasure there would be for a poor man in aping someone even poorer. I really don't understand how rich people can invite poor people to their tea gatherings, just for their own enjoyment.

Now, among the various kinds of objects, it is in the field of music that the oldest things are the best. Since they were created by masters many years ago, the tone of old instruments is elegant and often extraordinary, which is why an instrument of even a little age is regarded as a treasure. But in the case of other objects, outside of musical instruments, the old is no match for the new. Especially when it comes to eating utensils, everyone agrees that they appreciate newer things. When it comes to tea utensils, one should use an old brazier—but that is all. Teabowls should be new, since it can only sully one's enjoyment if the bowl is very old and soiled with the stains of other people's lips. And one must wonder about the sensibility of someone who can use a damaged bowl that has been repaired and not think doing so a dirty practice.

Anciently, a jewel called the Jewel That Illuminates the Night[14] provided light for twelve carriages and was thought of as such a treasure that it was traded for fifteen castles. And the jewel known as Bright Moon[15] lit up the night like a full moon. That objects of such power should be treasured and sold for a high price is understandable. And because ancient paintings or works of calligraphy are appreciated as the finest in the world and show the skill of the artist in such a way as to serve as a model of the art for people even now, persons of wealth seek these, too, and pay any sum for them—not unreasonably. But one cannot say the same for devotees of tea these days, who pay huge sums for unremarkable

14. Mentioned in various ancient Chinese sources, including *Shiji* (*Records of the Historian*), by Sima Qian (145–86 B.C.E.).
15. A jewel that emitted light, mentioned in the Han dynasty (206 B.C.E.–220 C.E.) Daoist classic *Huainanzi* (*The Masters of Huainan*).

porcelains of no excellence whatsoever, and then treat them as if they were matchless treasures. Or they pay a hundred gold pieces for a vase or spatula made of bamboo, which the world then regards as something grand. This is misguided thinking.

Recently, in addition to Rikyū and Sōtan,[16] there are others who have propagated their own Ways of Tea—Katagiri Sadamasa, governor of Iwami,[17] and Kobori Masaichi.[18] Although hardly commoners, these men are not sages either, but just ordinary men. Yet today's devotees of tea mimic them to a fault. One person says he is following the teachings of Rikyū, another the teachings of Enshū, another the teachings of the Seki lineage,[19] and they adhere to these exactly as if they were dealing with the Confucian rites, making great efforts not to deviate in any particular. What a lamentable state of affairs! Even today, if a spirited person who enjoys tea learns from the masters but then comes up with his own practices and attracts colleagues who follow his ways, a new school can come into being. This is because in the Way of Tea there really is no one established Way.

As for myself, I have always enjoyed tea. After a meal at someone's house, if powdered tea of high quality is served, it suits my taste well and I enjoy it very much. But I am speaking of a gathering in a sizable room, after enjoying a fine meal, sharing cups of saké with other guests, and partaking of sweets; and I think tea is best when served in new bowls, with each person drinking from a bowl separately prepared. The manner in which the Way of Tea is practiced these days is disgusting. To store tea, we have appropriate porcelains of our own; lacquerware is also fine, as are things made of silver or copper. To scoop tea, one should use a silver teaspoon. And when it comes to teabowls, it is most satisfying to drink from the newest.

[*MEIKA ZUIHITSU SHŪ*, ED. TAKE RYŪZŌ,
VOL. 1 (TOKYO: YŪHŌDŌ, 1928)]

16. Rikyū's grandson, Sen no Sōtan (1578–1658).
17. 1605–1673. Another samurai warlord well known for his devotion to tea.
18. 1579–1647. More commonly known as Kobori Enshū, a samurai administrator also famous for his accomplishments in poetry, architecture, and garden design.
19. Enshū refers to Kobori Masaichi. Sekishū (here abbreviated as Seki) was the sobriquet of Katagiri Sadamasa.

14

Jeweled Comb Basket

Motoori Norinaga

Motoori Norinaga (1730-1801) is perhaps the best-known literary scholar of the Edo period. Born into a merchant family, he showed an interest in scholarship at a young age and eventually became a physician. Like most young men of the era, he began as a student of the Chinese classics, but his interest in Japanese history and literature was awakened early on, especially through his reading of the poet-monk Keichū (1640-1701). The scholar he acknowledged as his true teacher, however, was Kamo no Mabuchi (1697-1769), one of the early leaders of the National Studies movement. Norinaga is widely recognized as one of the earliest proponents of empiricism in early modern Japan.

In a long career, Norinaga wrote many philological works, essays on literary classics such as The Tale of Genji *and* Man'yōshū *(Collection of Ten Thousand Leaves, ca. 759), ideological expositions, and a large exegetical study of the* Kojiki *(Record of Ancient Matters, 712).* Tamakatsuma *(Jeweled Comb Basket), written between 1793 and 1800, is a compendium of his shorter essays on topics philological, philosophical, religious, and occasionally personal.*

Confucians deem it no shame to say they cannot answer questions about our Land of the Emperors. When asked about China, on the other hand, they are embarrassed to admit ignorance and therefore feign knowledge by making skillful use of words. This all happens because they are so intent on making everything appear to be Chinese that they act as if they were Chinese themselves, treating their native land as if it were a foreign country.

Ultimately, though, these people are not Chinese but men of the Land of the Emperors, and I simply cannot understand how they can justify knowing nothing of their own country, just because they fancy themselves to be Confucians. Speaking to people of our own land, they may get away with acting as if they were Chinese, of course; but what if they were asked something by someone from China? They couldn't very well say then that they know a lot about China but nothing about their own country. For if they were to say something like that, they would surely be greeted with derisive laughter and asked, "How can a Confucian who doesn't know about his own country know about the country of another?"

Reading Chinese books in one's spare time is a good thing. Not to read Chinese books would mean knowing nothing of the evil ways of foreign countries; and since all ancient books are written in Chinese, anyone who cannot read the language of that country will not be able to progress in his studies. Learning that the ways of China are all evil will strengthen one's spirit as a citizen of Japan, and if one remains firmly in place, one's heart will not go astray even if one reads Chinese books day and night. However, there is one thing that one must never forget when reading Chinese books: because the writing style of that country is based on the wisdom of man, and relies on the exhaustive application of reasoning, men of intelligence who read Chinese books will find themselves naturally impressed and therefore be easily led astray.

If you would know the Way through scholarship, you must first of all look carefully at Chinese thought. If you do not, no matter how many old books you read and ponder, you will have trouble understanding the heart of the past; and if you fail to understand the heart of the past, pursuing the Way will prove an impossible task.

In the beginning, scholarship was not how people came to know the Way; rather, the Way resided in the inner heart—meaning the heart people were born with, good or bad. In latter days, however, people have all shifted their attention to Chinese ideas, losing their grip on the inner heart, so that now one cannot pursue knowledge of the Way without scholarship.

———————

Even if it is not in accordance with the Way, one should not be in a rush to abandon something that has been practiced for a long time. Instead, one should eliminate from it any faults, leave be whatever remains, and move on to further research the Way. Forcing everything to fit the standards of the Way is itself not in accordance with the true meaning of the Way. And since all things—their rise and fall, their zenith and nadir—are as they are by the will of the gods, the power of man is not sufficient to move them. Those who would understand the true meaning of the Way should first seek to understand this principle itself.

———————

Administering the Way is the proper work of lords and not men of learning, whose proper task is to think about and analyze the Way. Being of this opinion myself, I too do not seek to administer the Way, but only to think about it and analyze it.

This means that the lord is the one who should administer the Way and seek to enact it everywhere under heaven. For those beneath him to try to alter things at a time when the Way is not being properly administered is a kind of vanity that is contrary to the very meaning of the Way. The place of those below is to follow the policies of those above, for good or for ill. Just because they have understood the Way of ancient times does not mean that they should take it upon themselves to govern.

———————

Suga Naomi[1] said that reading a big book is like going on a long journey. After a while, you get past a lot of the boring places and arrive at bays

———

1. 1742–1776. A disciple of Norinaga's in his hometown of Matsuzaka in Ise Province.

and mountains that delight the eye. Also, a person with strong legs will go fast, while a person with weak legs will go slow—another similarity, he said. An interesting analogy.

Even in childhood, I enjoyed reading books more than anything else. But I just read, not studying properly under a teacher or setting out to be a scholar, without any real goal, without pursuing any particular theme, just taking up whatever was at hand, whatever could be obtained, in Chinese or Japanese, old or new. At the age of seventeen or eighteen, I developed a desire to compose Japanese poems and began trying, although again not studying under the direction of a teacher or showing anyone my compositions, but just working away on my own. I perused various collections, ancient and modern, writing according to established forms in the style of the day.

Then, when I was just over twenty years old, I went up to Kyoto, intent on becoming a scholar. My father had died when I was eleven, and I had been learning the business of the house, which was in Edo, but when that business failed, I resolved to honor my mother's wish that I study to become a physician—which is also why I planned to study Confucian thought, according to the usual pattern. It was when I was in Kyoto that I borrowed a book titled *Hyakunin isshu kaikanshō*[2] and learned of the theories of a man named Keichū and realized the excellence of his work. Beginning with his *Yozaishō*[3] and *Seigo okudan*,[4] I went on to obtain the rest of his writings and learned how to distinguish good from bad among the various approaches to studying poetry. In the process, I learned that the ideas of poets of my day were generally not to my liking and that the style of their poems did not interest me, although I still attended poetry gatherings here and there, composing poems even though I found no friends who shared my feelings. The style of the poems people were composing did not impress me, and because my own way of writing ran

2. 1692. A commentary on *Hyakunin isshu* (*One Hundred Poems by One Hundred Poets*), a collection compiled by Fujiwara no Teika (1162–1241).

3. *Kokin yozaishō*, a study of *Kokinshū* (*Collection of Ancient and Modern Times*, ca. 905), the first imperially commissioned anthology of Japanese poetry.

4. A study of the poem-tale *Ise monogatari* (*Tales of Ise*, mid-tenth century.)

contrary to the thinking of the day, people criticized me, with what must have seemed good reason. I have written about this elsewhere.[5]

Later, when I had returned home, someone showed me a recently published book titled *Kanjikō* and I learned the name of the master of provincial appointments.[6] The first time I glanced over his writings, his ideas were so unexpected and seemed so far afield that I gave them little credence; but later I told myself that there was something there after all. When I read them again, here and there I found lines of thought that seemed convincing to me, and when I read yet again, even more of what he said seemed right. Every time I read him, I believed more, until in the end I came to realize that he was right about the ideas and words of ancient times. Looking back, I see much that is inadequate in Keichū's interpretations of the *Man'yōshū* and realize that the way I had been studying poetry was all too similar.

Now, from the very beginning of my study of the Way, I had read about the gods, in works both ancient and modern, with my interest intensifying around the time I turned twenty. But even then, I had no strong desire to pursue knowledge in that area, and it was only after I went up to Kyoto that I began my studies in earnest. Following Keichū's lead, I concentrated on ancient times in the Land of the Emperors and quickly recognized the folly of the so-called Shinto scholars of my own day. With no teacher to rely on, however, I doubted that I would ever realize my ambition of working out the truths of ancient times. It was just at this time that I acquired a copy of *Kanjikō*, a careful reading of which strengthened my resolve and day by day intensified my belief in that great teacher.

Then, one year the great teacher traveled[7] through the provinces from Ise to Yamato and Yamashiro on the order of Lord Tayasu,[8] and stopped in Matsuzaka for two or three days. Sadly, I didn't know about this visit and was very disappointed when I heard about it only after he had departed. But I was delighted to learn that on his return trip he would be stopping for one night again. I waited anxiously for that day, and when

5. What Norinaga is referring to here remains unclear.
6. *A Study of Poetic Epithets* (1757), Kamo no Mabuchi's exhaustive study of *makurakotoba* (literally, "pillow words," fixed epithets appearing before certain nouns) appearing in the *Man'yōshū*.
7. Kamo no Mabuchi.
8. Tayasu Munetake (1715–1771), son of the shogun Tokugawa Yoshimune (1684–1751) and a powerful figure in Edo.

the time came, hastily went to where he was staying, where I met him for the first time. In the end, my name was put on his registry, and I was able to receive his teachings.

_____

In explicating ancient texts, I often disagree with the interpretations of my teacher[9] and often analyze the mistakes in his interpretations—something that some people seem to think I ought not to do. But this is what my teacher wanted. He always said that when good ideas came to light in the future, students should not be too reluctant to part ways with their teachers. This is a very praiseworthy teaching and is one of the ways my teacher is among the finest.

When it comes to thinking about the past, the power of only one or two people is not enough to clarify things completely. For among the interpretations of any teacher, no matter how good he may be, how could there be no mistakes at all? Quite to the contrary, a little bad will surely be mixed in with the good. In one's own mind, one may conclude that one has understood everything about the past perfectly and that there will never be any ideas besides one's own; but then, unexpectedly, a different and better idea will come forth from someone else. As time goes on, the ideas of the past pass through many hands, being carefully tested and refined in the process. It follows, then, that one should not be too attached to the interpretations of one's teacher just because they are his. In the Way of Learning, adhering to the old regardless of whether it is good or bad is a useless practice.

Thus it is wise to bring the weaknesses of one's teacher to light. Indeed, if one fails to do so, other scholars may be led into error and be impeded from learning the good. To hide the fact that an interpretation is wrong only because it comes from one's teacher, and to make it appear to be correct, would be showing more respect for one's teacher than for the Way of Learning itself. If my intent is to respect the Way, concentrating my efforts on illuminating the Way and clarifying the meaning of the past, then I cannot be worried about anything lacking in the way I respect my teacher.

9. Probably a reference to Mabuchi.

There may be those who will attack me on this point, of course, but I say, let them attack! I cannot proceed any other way. To try to appear good in their eyes, worried that I might be criticized, and then end up distorting the Way and distorting the truth about the past—that is not my way of doing things. My practice is in accordance with my teacher's wishes and is my own way of showing him respect, come what may.

To all those who study under my direction, I say, "After I am gone, when a good idea comes forth, do not cling to my interpretations. Expose my mistakes, and disseminate my good ideas." What I have always taught people is to illuminate the Way, and that to illuminate the Way in any manner possible is the best use they can make of me. For students to revere me beyond reason, disregarding the Way, is not the desire of my heart.

In *Essays in Idleness*, Kenkō writes, "Should we look at the blossoms only in full bloom, or the moon only when unobscured by clouds?"[10] But I wonder. Many ancient poems in fact *complain* about the wind in the blossoms, or resent the clouds on a moonlit night, or express frustration over having to wait to see the moon appear. And is not the reason such poems are moving that we have an intense desire to quietly view the cherries in full bloom and the moon unclouded, and lament not being able to do so? After all, what poem is there that speaks of wanting the wind to blow through the blossoms, or hoping for clouds to cover the moon? What Kenkō says is thus something contrary to what people actually feel, a sham stylishness concocted in later ages and not the true heart of elegance. There are many others who say words similar to Kenkō's, and they are all the same.

Definitions of elegance that go against people's actual desires are in most cases affectations. Among love poems, for instance, it is true that those written about lovers together are less moving, while those lament-

---

10. An allusion to the first lines of *Tsurezuregusa*, section 137, which articulate the aesthetics of the imperfect, the worn, and the spare. See Yoshida no Kenkō, *Essays in Idleness* (chap. 2).

ing not being able to meet—more numerous, by far—are more impressive. But that is because what people most want is to meet! The human heart doesn't feel happiness all that profoundly but feels deeply the loss of cherished hopes. This is why there are few poems on happiness that truly impress us as much as the many poems of deep feeling that lament frustrated plans. With that in mind, however, one must wonder whether people in their true hearts are likely to seek after elegance based on misery and sadness.

In poems from medieval times onward, one reads that it is most seemly to die before reaching forty.[11] To hope for long life is vulgar, according to this line of thought, while to die young is beautiful. But such attempts to impress everyone by showing strong resolve to cast the world aside are really so much flattery aimed at impressing the Buddha—and in most cases no more than a lie. For while people may say such things in words, who truly *hopes for* such a thing? And even in the case of the few people who sincerely feel that way, it doesn't come from their own true hearts but from the wiles of Buddhist teachings. No one in his true heart wants to die soon, no matter how forlorn his circumstances. Everyone wants life. This is why in poems written up to the time of the *Man'yōshū*, poets would pray for long life, in direct contrast to poems written since medieval times. In all things, this tendency to treat as good something that goes against everyone's feelings comes from the influence of foreign ways and is something we should recognize as a sham imitation of human feeling.

———

To want to eat tasty food, to wear fine clothing, to live in a nice house, to accumulate wealth, to be praised by others, and to live a long life—these are the true feelings of all men. There are many in the world who act as if these things were bad, claiming that it is laudable to ask for nothing, to want nothing, to pretend to have no desires; but that is the usual annoying lie. Learned men looked up to as teachers and monks honored with the title of reverend look at the moon and flowers and pretend to enjoy their beauty, but when they see a good-looking woman, they go on their

11. An allusion to *Tsurezuregusa*, sec. 7. See ibid.

way as if they hadn't even noticed. But that is hard to believe, is it not? If one has the sensitivity to appreciate the moon and blossoms, surely the beauty of a fine woman should impress one's eyes all the more. To say that one appreciates the moon and blossoms and not even notice the beauty of a woman amounts to being wanting in human feeling and is the worst sort of lie. Yet such superficial concerns are the way of the world, so I suppose I should not be condemning such things as lies.

In the *Kokinshū*, there is a poem by Narihira, "written," the headnote says, "when he was ill and failing."

> Upon this path,
> I have long heard others say,
> we set forth at last—
> though I had not thought to go
> so very soon as today.[12]

> *tsui ni yuku / michi to wa kanete / kikishikado / kinō kyō to wa / omowazarishi o*

Keichū said, "This poem expresses the truth of human feeling and is excellent for instruction. I despise the way people of later times write grandiose poems at the point of death, or perhaps claim to have achieved enlightenment in the Way, with no sincerity at all. When dealing with everyday events, they may choose to fill their poems with 'wild words and fancy phrases,'[13] but you would think that at the point of death they might return to the truth of how they actually feel. Narihira dies having expressed the true feeling of a whole lifetime in his poem, while these later people die spouting nothing but lies."[14]

This is not the sort of thing one expects a monk to say, and very laudable. Even though he was a Buddhist monk, Keichū had true Japanese spirit. Would scholars of the Way of the Gods or Japanese poetry who

12. *Kokinshū*, poem 861.
13. *Kyōgen kigo*. A standard Buddhist epithet for literary writing, which was considered by some to be frivolous when compared with the serious writings of the Buddhist canon.
14. Keichū, *Seigo okudan*. See Motoori Norinaga, *Tamakatsuma*, ed. Satake Akihiro et al., Nihon shisō taikei 40 (Tokyo: Iwanami shoten, 1978), 165n.

embrace Chinese feelings say such things? Keichū taught people of the world about the ideal of sincerity, whereas such scholars of the Way of the Gods or Japanese poetry teach lies.

———————————

Above all else, one wants to write a good hand. Poets and scholars who have a bad hand will be thought of as inferior, and while this may not seem anything to worry about, still one feels somehow wanting. My own hand is awful; every time I pick up a brush, I feel disconsolate. When someone asks me for a sample of my writing, I blithely dash off a poem strip and then, looking at it, realize what an ugly thing I have produced and wonder what people will think of it. My breast is so full of shame that I ask myself bitterly why I didn't work harder at my calligraphy in my youth.

———————————

How sad it is that so many old shrines have either vanished altogether or exist only in ruins of uncertain authenticity. Those whose names are recorded on the rolls of the Office of Deities should not be in such a state, but during the warfare of the medieval era the old rites and laws were all in such disarray that many shrines ceased to be. Indeed, it is for such reasons that the events of times of turmoil are so lamentable in every way.

In the current reign, however, the happy fact is that order prevails to a degree seldom known in the past, prosperity abounding everywhere. And as this is a time when the past is being researched, the lost restored, and the rundown rebuilt, it should also be a time when shrines are returned to their former glory. In this connection, what is wanted is to search for the remains of those that have vanished, research those for which some remains exist but about which there is some reason for doubt, and establish the facts about both. Furthermore, in such a fortunate age, one also wants research to be done on the many other places of ancient import—utamakura[15] and the like—whose locations are now unclear, even if no shrines ever stood there.

15. Literally, "poem pillows," sites of historical, legendary, or literary significance where visitors were expected to compose poems.

Even in our age, however, it is no mean task to establish the true locations of shrines, tombs, *utamakura*, and other such places of the distant past that perished during the medieval era. The reason for this is that it is difficult to find such old places merely by searching in ancient writings. No matter how thoroughly one researches in books, when one actually goes to the place to look at things and asks around, there are sure to be many discrepancies. The location of a place that is unclear from afar may be clear in writings and stories passed down in the area itself. So if one fails to go to the trouble of actually going there in person, looking at things, and asking people who know the history of the place, one will not have done a proper job. Nor is going just once enough; rather, one must go once, return home to check things against the books, and then go again. If one doesn't do at least this much, one will not be able to arrive at a firm conclusion.

When one does meet with people in such places, one must keep some things in mind. Many of those who speak with great confidence about things of the past have simply taken at face value some fragment in a book and then arrived at a conclusion based on their own arrogance, which means that one cannot rely on them, as their work is full of errors. Also, when it comes to places of renown, there are many people so bound and determined to place the location in their own province or village—even when in truth the location is somewhere else—that they cling to any little tidbit that looks like evidence in order to argue their case. Approaching things in such a way, they proceed without any doubts. Never looking at a book, they prattle on like country dolts—inconsistent, sloppy, and full of nothing but errors, although since there may be items of interest among the things they say, one must at least stop and pay them some attention. It seems, however, that when country people have heard that such and such a place is the true site because long ago some know-it-all made a determination with only the vaguest evidence, they believe it and pass the story down to their children and grandchildren. In such cases, one should not blithely believe what they say, even if it sounds plausible.

There are also many things to keep in mind when investigating sites for oneself. For instance, one may fix upon a place because it looks venerable, with thick groves of trees around it and a worn look—but even then, one should not be too quick to jump to conclusions. There are old groves of trees in lots of places that are of no significance at all. In the space of two or three hundred years, any grove of trees takes on an ancient appearance, and that alone is not enough to base a judgment on. Therefore one must take special note in one's investigations of the names of villages, mountains, rivers, bays, and beaches. One should even pay attention to the informal names of rice fields and so on. Also, there are numerous temples that have names that have existed since ancient times, even though people often make mistakes concerning those names. And records of temple legends too, however full of the usual lies concocted by monks, may hold rare bits of evidence and should not be cast aside altogether. While in every province there are cases where people were fooled by Buddhist monks in medieval times into believing that an ancient place was a holy site, still one should investigate holy sites, too, but keep that in mind. In old temples, there are old writings that record many ancient events, and since there are times when reliable evidence comes from an unexpected place one had not thought to consider, one must be thorough in one's investigations, thinking of every possibility and exploring every nook and cranny.

Even proceeding in this way, however, there will be times when one has researched thoroughly and yet still should not declare a firm judgment. For when a person of consequence establishes a place that is not the true one as the correct location, it may become accepted as such and go on leading people astray.

All of what has been said here not only is true when investigating famous places but applies broadly to all kinds of research.

My great desire would be to somehow repair all the rundown Shinto shrines and reestablish all the Shinto rites. Generally speaking, the shrines and rites of our own day are in the same state they have been in since they fell into decline during the upheavals of the medieval era, and because that is all people of our day have ever known, they have begun to think that things have always been this way. Not many people read books, and those who do tend to focus on Chinese writings and make their judgments in all things on that basis. As almost no one reads the old writings of the Land of the Emperors with any care, no one realizes the importance that was attached to Shinto shrines and rites in ancient reigns. The sad fact is that although there are a few people who know about such things, they are so distracted by the ways of the present that there is no one left to compare the ways of the past and lament our current state.

The reason people today praise Shinto shrines for being so worn and withered is that they know nothing of the times when the shrines were in their glory days. Seeing these old and venerable buildings in such a state of ill repair, they assume that such venerable structures have always been so—a mistaken notion of Chinese derivation.

The question of man's beginnings before birth and what happens to him after death is one that everyone thinks about and for which we all desire answers. Buddhist writings seem to say a great deal about the meaning of life and death and about how our mortal state is determined, but these ideas are just man-made fictions and nonsense of no value in the end, no matter how enlightened a person may be. The Confucians seem to have come up with a better theory: that after death, the body decays and the spirit, too, vanishes without a trace. But while it may seem a more truthful interpretation, one cannot really depend on this either. For the principles that inform all things are truly boundless: fire is red, but things that have been burned turn black, and when reduced to ash, they are white. As there are so many unexpected facts of this sort, there are bound to be many things that defy our attempts at reasoning.

The state of man after death is therefore not something one can comprehend according to transient principles founded on human wisdom alone. It is something quite outside the bounds of normal thought. In such a light, the stories of our Land of the Emperors, which tell of people going to the Kingdom of Darkness,[16] are also worthy of veneration and

16. Yomi no Kuni, the underworld mentioned in many early mythological texts.

make the supposedly profound and wise theories of the Chinese seem rather shallow.

———

One is going to compose a poem, and an interesting idea comes to mind as one is pondering, but one has trouble putting it into words—so the hours pass, or even days, as one struggles with the same idea, trying it one way and another but in the end making no progress. At such times, the best thing is to make a clean break and begin searching elsewhere, but instead one thinks what a shame it is and just cannot give it up, pushing on although one knows that one does not really know how to proceed—a sorry business, of course, but one that everyone goes through sometimes.

Also, when one has been struggling mentally for a long time in this way, another and completely unrelated idea comes from somewhere else, and one is able to compose a poem very quickly. And since it was only because one had thought so strenuously that the good idea came forth, it turns out that the labor one expended was not in vain after all. Of course, what I've said on this topic may be nonsense, but I jot it down as it occurs to me all the same.

———

Declaring that you have no desire for money is the usual Chinese-style prevarication. People involved in scholarship, for instance, have an intense desire for books, and pretending not to want money for them just makes the lie more apparent. In today's world, it is money that gets you what your heart desires—no matter what it may be; so if you want books, how can you claim not to want money? That being said, those who adopt this false pretense are still vastly superior to the unbridled greed that is the general way of the world.

———

Men of learning in past ages and scholars of our own day all seem to say that they prefer to have their residence in quiet mountain groves, far from cities. But for some reason, I do not feel that way. I like a lively place with many people around and think of a remote place as lonely and depressing. Of course, once in a great while I may go on a journey and find it pleasant to spend a night at an out-of-the-way place, but I never feel that I would like to live there all the time. Of course, people do have differing tastes, and there must in fact be many in the world who truly want to live in the quiet far from other people. But among them there must be those who are just mimicking the usual Chinese-style silliness, saying they like to live that way only in order to appear different from normal people. Or is this kind of skepticism just evidence of my own vulgarity?

When I first came up to live in the capital in 1801, I took up residence in a place facing on Fourth Avenue from the south, just east of Karasuma Street. The house was set back from the street, removed from the city bustle, but when I lingered in front of my gate as I left in the morning or returned home in the evening, I looked out on a broad and open avenue where lots of people were going back and forth, which made for a lively sight that seemed a real change for someone used to living in the countryside. I truly felt as if I had new eyes.

Among the three great cities of the world, Edo and Osaka are just too crowded with throngs of people, while Kyoto is just lively enough. There are scores of shrines and temples, many of ancient provenance that are worthy of attention. And things there are so fine, everything that goes on there is so elegant, that in all the world there is no city in which I would rather live than Kyoto.

Rendering human portraits demands above all that one strive to make one's work resemble human features. The face should resemble the subject's face, it goes without saying; and one should also reproduce other details, down to the figure and even the clothing. Thus a portrait should mirror everything in minute detail.

Nowadays, however, there are some people who, while claiming to be painting portraits, are really more interested in showing off the energy of their brushwork, or in trying to make the portrait appear fashionable—even if it doesn't resemble the subject. Then there are those who do not even demand of themselves that they produce something resembling the subject at all, instead making the display of brushwork and the creation of a stylish painting their prime concern. Using only broad strokes and paying no attention to detail, they dash things off so rapidly that far from resembling the face of the subject, the portrait looks like that of some vulgar mountain rustic and not at all like the face of a man of stature and virtue. A most disagreeable state of affairs.

When making portraits of people of old, one cannot really know what their faces looked like, so one should aim for something appropriate to the person's social rank and eminence. In the case of someone of high rank, one should make all the facial features noble; in the case of a person of great power and influence, one should proceed accordingly. Yet latter-day painters disregard this kind of thinking and instead try only to display the energy of their brushwork, making people of rank and eminence look like mountain rustics or ordinary bumpkins.

People have various abilities from birth. There are those whose minds are able to comprehend all things, from the principles that make things work to the advantages and disadvantages of various approaches to human affairs, but who cannot put their ideas into words. Then there are those who are able put ideas into words but unable to carry things out, and those who can both put ideas into words *and* carry things out. Finally, there are those who are able to put ideas into words but unable to put them into writing, and those who are unable to put ideas into words but able to put them in writing.

Paper is used for many things other than writing. One can wrap things in it, wipe things with it, or stretch it over a box of some kind to use it as a container. One can twist it into cords and use it to tie things up. It also comes in handy in many other ways. However, Chinese paper is good for only writing and not useful in any of these other ways. Paper produced from the many provinces of the Land of the Emperors comes in many varieties—thick and thin, stiff and soft: so many, in fact, that one cannot list them all. But for writing, our paper is inferior to Chinese paper. At least that is how I feel, although I do not know about others.

———————

There are countless ways in which the present is superior to the past. To give one example: in the past, the fruit of the *tachibana* tree[17] was praised as without parallel, but in more recent years we have the *mikan*, which is by comparison vastly superior. Among all other varieties—the *kōji*, the *yu*, the *kunenbō*, and the *daidai*—the flavor of the *mikan* is best; and among all these, it most resembles the orange but is more elegant by far. This one example provides a basis for proper judgment. For again, there are many things that exist now but did not anciently, or were of inferior quality anciently and are superior now. Which means that in the future, many superior things will also come forth. When we think of them now, we conclude that people of old were lacking in many things and must have been dissatisfied, but people of that time probably did not think that way—just as later on, in a world of many new things that are sure to come forth, people will probably think of us and conclude that we felt the same kind of lack.

———————

How annoying it is that the ancient books of China are so given over to commandments. Men do not improve because of commandments. People do not wait to be ordered around, and to be preoccupied with nagging commandments is to fail to realize how wicked schemes and falsehoods are only on the increase. The Duke of Zhou[18] established so many annoying commandments that his era ended in warfare. And all the great heresies of the people in the period of Warring States [403–221 B.C.E.] were taught by the duke himself. In the old writings of the Land of the Emperors, one encounters no such dogmatism. This is a distinction to

17. A general term for any citrus tree that produced edible fruit. See *A Tale of Flowering Fortunes: Annals of Japanese Aristocratic Life in the Heian Period*, trans. William H. McCullough and Helen Craig McCullough (Stanford, Calif.: Stanford University Press), 2:839.
18. A legendary ancient political figure idealized in Confucian texts.

which we should give thought. To conclude that strict commandments are a good thing is so much foolishness.

In China, a teaching called Daoism is widely practiced, so much so that it is on a par with Buddhism. This teaching looks to Laozi as its founder but is in fact quite different from his ideas and has become a frivolous thing of dubious value, which if taken to the extreme ends in worthless nonsense.

Fortunately, this teaching has not come to the Land of the Emperors. Yet how lamentable it is that the hearts of people everywhere *have* been carried away by either Buddhism or Confucianism. Under the wide heavens, one cannot find a single man—high or low, wise or stupid, anywhere, even among woodsmen in the deepest forests—who does not believe in the Buddha. And among these, anyone who can read even a single character puts some Confucian thought into the mix when reasoning on any and all issues. This is why only one or two people out of ten thousand give any thought to the true Way of the Gods. In addition, there are those rare few among those serving in Shinto shrines who revere the Way of the Gods because they recognize it is as the profession of their house. Even among them, however, are many who embrace Buddhist and Confucian beliefs. And as the Way of the Gods is always explained via the distorted ideas of Confucianism and Buddhism, the true Way might as well have died out altogether.

This being the state of things throughout the empire, Buddhist temples thrive in every province, while Shinto shrines fall into disrepair, with no one even to lament their decline. Only to heal illnesses or for various prayers are the gods appealed to, with the result that the Way of the Gods seems to be as of no use to the world, just something passed down since olden times but now cast aside. Not even in my dreams have I ever encountered a person who understands this Way as the way to maintain the world, govern the state, and as the means to establish priority in policy and what must be done to proceed. A most lamentable state of affairs.

[*TAMAKATSUMA*, ED. SATAKE AKIHIRO ET AL., NIHON SHISŌ TAIKEI 40 (TOKYO: IWANAMI SHOTEN, 1978)]

15

Idle Chats Beneath a Northern Window

TACHIBANA NANKEI

Born the fifth son of a samurai in Ise Province, Tachibana Nankei (1753–1805) seemed destined for a career in some sort of academic or administrative field. As a boy, he studied Confucian thought under his father and was later taught by a local scholar. When he was fourteen, however, his father died, leaving him in a very vulnerable position. At nineteen, he went up to Kyoto with the ambition of continuing his Confucian studies but was forced to pursue medicine in order to earn a living. Unlike some other Confucian scholars, he seems to have enjoyed medical work and had a thriving practice, first in Fushimi, south of Kyoto, and later in Kyoto proper. Late in life, he was given court rank and was appointed as an imperial physician, serving in that capacity for ten years.

Nankei retired in 1796 and lived a quiet life in Fushimi, where he wrote several travel records, numerous works on medical subjects, and poetry. Hokusō sadan (Idle Chats Beneath a Northern Window), *published posthumously in 1829, was written mostly between 1789 and 1801. The work resembles* Essays in Idleness *in its blend of philosophical reflections, anecdotes, and pronouncements on matters of taste.*

I like the serene look of blossoms on the grasses after they have turned yellow. Nor am I averse to the white of *yūgao*[1] in dusky light.

---

1. Literally, "evening faces." A gourd flower.

If one looks north from Gokōmachi after all the cherry blossoms have fallen, the grove around the palace of the retired emperor[2] looks venerable, and the new green growth on the trees seems more captivating each time one gazes on them. The view looking west from Anegakōji Street also used to be fine, though since the Tenmei conflagration,[3] things have not been the same.

In Fushimi, there are many places with flowering trees. There is a lotus pond more than fifty blocks square.[4] In the sixth and seventh lunar months, red and white flowers cover the surface of the water, producing color and scent beyond compare. And how cool it feels to pole a skiff through the blossoms under the sky at dawn! I have yet to see anywhere else a place with so many lotuses.

"Should we look at the blossoms only in full bloom, or the moon only when unobscured by clouds?"—so wrote Kenkō, whose dedication to the way of elegance was profound.[5] Reading through his *Essays in Idleness*, one can truly see the extraordinary nature of his sensibility. Ah, to sit across from that monk and have a chat—how fascinating that would be!

On the seventh and eighth days of the Seventh Month, my sliding doors were creaking and moaning. People were all upset, telling one another that it was an earthquake in the eastern hills, but that wasn't it. I said that it must have been an eruption at Tate Mountain in Koshi,[6] and after

2. *Sentō*. Located near the imperial palace compound in northern Kyoto.
3. A huge fire that swept over much of the city of Kyoto in the First Month of 1788. The imperial palace and courtiers' quarter, Nijō Castle, and almost forty thousand homes were destroyed in the blaze.
4. Lake Ogura in Fushimi. The lake no longer exists.
5. A quotation from *Tsurezuregusa*, at the beginning of section 137. See Yoshida no Kenkō, *Essays in Idleness* (chap. 2).
6. Ancient name for the Hokurikudō (Far Northern District), which comprised the provinces of Wakasa, Echizen, Kaga, Noto, Etchū, Echigo, and Sado.

a while I heard that there had indeed been an eruption at the peak of Asama in Shinano.[7] The reason I got it right was that once I had heard someone say that when Sakurajima in Satsuma[8] had erupted several years back, the sliding doors in houses far away had creaked and moaned just as if in an earthquake.

When Tani Sachū[9] was a young man in Kyoto, studying under Yanagawa Sansei, the latter was very friendly with an old man who lived near the Great Buddha.

One day the old man said to Sansei, "I'm getting on in years now and am not likely to live much longer. I have a certain skill that I learned over the years that it would be a shame for the world to lose, so if you have a particularly serious-minded student among your disciples, please send him over and I shall transmit my knowledge to him." Sansei then called Sachū, told him of his conversation with the old man, and asked Sachū to go and find out what the teachings were about.

And so off Sachū went, with a letter of introduction from Sansei in hand. When he got to the place, however, the old man said that since Sachū had chosen him there was no need for such niceties and told him that if he indeed wanted to receive the teachings he should come back on a certain day. In reply, Sachū said that he would be truly honored to receive the transmission but asked what sort of skill it was that the old man had to teach.

"Why, the skill I have acquired is none other than that of elevating my body into the air and flying about, for a few minutes or a full day, going this way and that, covering distances from a few hundred to a few thousand *li*."[10]

Amazed, Sachū said, "Well, this will be no simple matter, then," and left after promising to return.

---

7. Modern-day Nagano Prefecture.

8. An island located in Kagoshima Bay, present-day Kagoshima Province. The volcano erupted in 1779 and 1782.

9. D. 1773. A disciple of the famous Itō Tōgai (1670–1736).

10. A traditional Chinese unit of distance, now standardized at 1,640 feet.

As he was returning home, Sachū thought to himself, "This is a strange business. Without knowing a person's heart, how could one know whether allowing him to learn such a thing would be good or bad?"

He went to Sansei's house and told him what the old man had said and then asked, "Only a sage could handle such power—anyone else would harm himself using such supernatural abilities. So I think I should not proceed. What do you think?"

Sansei was equally taken aback: "I cannot very well encourage you, as we are talking about something only a sage could control. What happens now must therefore be entirely up to you."

Pleading illness, Sachū did not visit the old man again, who before long passed away, and one never heard that he had passed on his teachings on flying to anyone else.

The old man must have been a sage himself. Ōkawa Sōjū[11] related that even after Sachū had grown old, he still found the whole incident very mysterious.

Among senseless practices is that of refraining from killing even the smallest of insects.[12] But it is even more inhuman to destroy a living thing just to amuse oneself.

When it comes to furnishings, things coated with lacquer are very fine. Anything intentionally made to look worn and old is no good. I also wonder about having a lot of Chinese-looking objects around.[13] But it is even worse for a poor household to exceed its station by having too much finery.

When one is not feeling well and has to stay inside, bedridden: that is when one becomes aware of the vicissitudes of the human situation and

11. Mori Senzō identifies this man as Akamatsu Sōjū, in *Edo zuisō shū*, Koten Nihon bungaku zenshū 35 (Tokyo: Chikuma shobō, 1961), 205.
12. Some Buddhist sects took the injunction against taking life to this extreme.
13. Here Nankei shows the influence of Kenkō in *Tsurezuregusa*, sec. 10. See Kenkō, *Essays in Idleness*.

life in this world—when one comes to know the sadness of things.[14] Unless he is very wise, the person who in his whole life has never once been confined to bed, always healthy and robust—such a one will tend to be somewhat overbearing.

A man who sets out on a journey of a hundred *li* will take ten days if he plans for ten *li* a day, and he will see more famous places along the way than other people. But if he wants to arrive quickly, he will go fifteen or eighteen *li* a day. Exactly the same is true in the Way of Learning. Everyone else has hands and feet and five internal organs, and no one has an excess of hands and feet or a different number of organs. If you eat until your belly bursts or go to bed so early that you damage your heart, how can you not be inferior to other men?

When Western barbarians, who light their tobacco by holding a glass to it in the sunlight, learn that we Japanese are too awed by the sun to use it in such a way, they wonder why. Also, when they learn that the Japanese enjoy looking at the moon, they wonder what could be so interesting in so ordinary an orb of light. Of course, if one looks at such things logically, reason seems to be on their side, but that is because the taste of the Japanese is so different from their own—as different as wisdom is from stupidity, or heaven from earth.

Cherry blossoms remain fine even if they bloom a little late, after a few leaves have come out, but if peach blossoms are late in blooming, they end up wet with rain and mixed in with green leaves in ways that are most unpleasant.

14. *Mono no aware.* The deep sadness that adheres universally in all worldly things, which are by their very nature transient.

When I was living in Fushimi, there was a mountain grove of plum trees so close by that I would take an apprentice boy along with me and visit every day. Each year, the trees came into full bloom about midway through the Second Month. Since the moon was full at the same time, it was usually there that I also visited at night. In the moonlight, the plum blossoms are so white that you feel as if you were in a world of silver. The scent of the blossoms at night is also captivating, indeed more so than that of any other flower. Mount Luofu[15] in China must be such a place. There are other places in Japan where there are many plum blossoms, but none more elegant.

Whenever Dutch ships enter the harbor at Nagasaki, they shoot off a series of fire arrows, whose echoes make the mountains quake. Everyone, Chinese or Japanese, comes out to watch. I once asked a Chinese friend of mine through an interpreter what sort of sound the fire arrows made, and he answered, "bii—n." Japanese people say it sounds like "doh—n." I find it puzzling that there should be so marked a difference in the ways different people describe the same sound.

In Hyūga, next to Miyako Castle[16] is a deep well that goes down about 120 feet. When you are down that deep, people say that from the bottom of the well you can see the stars at midday.

In the city, it is only after midnight that one can find peace. Take midsummer, for instance: after everyone in the house has settled down to sleep and things have quieted down in the neighborhood, I am unable to sleep, and so I sit out beneath the eaves, looking at the moon as it is

15. Located in modern-day Guangdong Province, it is famous for its many Daoist temples.
16. Located in the Kitamorokata area of present-day Miyazaki Prefecture.

about to set, thinking about the words of Saigyō[17] and Kenkō. Thus even one living amid the dust of the world can get a moment of calm.

———————

Ever since I was ten or so, I have always thought how happy I would be if I could have a level lot of ground about a block square, planted everywhere with deciduous trees, where I could build a hut to live in. Even now my feelings have not changed.

———————

When I was a child, bamboos grew on the back east side of my house, so that in the moonlight their shapes were cast onto my window, just as if someone had painted them there. I found this so captivating that I decided that wherever I lived, I would always plant bamboos outside my east window. As I grew up, however, I had to make my way in the world and was unable to realize my wishes. Occasionally, I remember this and wish I could escape the world and its troubles.

———————

Among flowers, it seems to me that nothing is more appealing than mountain cherry blossoms. Since the Chinese have never seen them before, they can't be blamed; but when people of this country transfer their allegiance to peonies for their color or to chrysanthemums for their fragrance, one can only say that they are lacking in proper feeling.

———————

Food fulfills its purpose if it fills your belly. A house should be appropriate to one's station and as roomy as possible, in order to give the heart space to relax. It is no good if it is too cleverly constructed and cramped.[18]

Silks appear elegant even on someone seen only from a distance.

These days among the lower classes, women don't take much care with their hair or appearance, but to me this seems disappointing.

17. 1118–1190. One of the most highly renowned of Japanese poet-monks.
18. Kenkō, *Essays in Idleness*, secs. 10, 55.

Saké leads to all sorts of misfortunes. It frustrates your plans; it mars your actions. How much trouble it gives rise to! I believe one should not imbibe at all until about the age of thirty.

Yet on a moonlit evening or a flowery dawn, it is saké that one wants. And nothing else will do when one is having a quiet chat with a close friend.[19]

In one's heart one always wants to triumph over others, of course; but it won't do to be too competitive when mixing with people. If you excel in learning and the arts, won't people envy you even if you don't show off?

One can understand why a man whose wife and children have died continues to talk about things they did and praise them to everyone he meets, but it does put people off. It is more impressive to be a bit disheveled and to go on mourning.

I hate it when monks, mountain ascetics, physicians, and shrine priests attending festivals or plays put on a pompous face. I also hate it when women boast about following the Way of the Sages. If they have confidence within themselves, that ought to be enough.

To settle down in a hut surrounded by beautiful mountains and streams and leave the world behind would be a pleasure, no doubt; yet one does hesitate to be separated so far from one's friends that visits either way are infrequent.

19. Similar to what Kenkō says in *Tsurezuregusa*, sec. 175.

Dazai Shundai[20] is severe in his condemnation of haikai poetry as something entirely out of keeping with Chinese poetry or *waka*, but that must be because he knows nothing about it. Many haikai poems show a thorough understanding of human emotion and succeed in expressing in one phrase what all of us feel.[21]

Among the works of Kikaku[22] is this one:

Lightning strikes:
yesterday in the east,
today in the west.[23]

inazuma ya / kinō wa higashi / kyō wa nishi

One could do without that last line, I think. The verse is much inferior to this one by Otoyoshi:[24]

Floating grasses:
today blooming over there
on the other bank.[25]

ukikusa ya / kyō wa achira no / kishi ni saku

This verse says all that can be said about the transience of life in the world. You can sense the depth of the author's feelings.

20. 1680–1747. In *Dokugo* (mid-Edo period), Shundai attacks haikai, along with many other contemporary arts. See Dazai Shundai, *Chats with Myself* (chap. 13).

21. The Japanese expression is *isshō santan* and refers to an early Chinese practice in which one person would sing a line, following which three others would repeat it in unison—showing unanimity of feeling.

22. Takarai Kikaku (1661–1707), a haikai poet.

23. One of Kikaku's most famous poems. See Asō Isoji et al., eds., *Haiku taikan* (Tokyo: Meiji shoin, 1971), 144.

24. A variant reading of the haikai sobriquet of Otsuyū (d. 1739), a rich merchant from the town of Kawasaki in Ise who was a disciple of Matsuo Bashō's. Nankei probably judges Kikaku's verse to be inferior because it relies on explicit reference (to both east and west) rather than suggestion (of the other bank).

25. Asō et al., *Haiku taikan*, 211.

Midway through the autumn of 1783, when I was on an errand to Fushimi, the skies darkened, just like a misty day in springtime, but even more thickly. A rainstorm must be approaching, I thought, but there were no clouds. Even the three peaks of Mount Otowa[26] were lost to sight. The ridgepole of the Buddha Hall receded into the distance, and the tops of nearby trees grew so dark that one couldn't tell a pine from a cedar. Wondering what could be going on, I raised the blinds of my palanquin and saw that people on the road were also perplexed, saying, "It's raining dirt"—and when I thought about it, they seemed to be right. The situation continued the next day, and the one after that, the rays of the sun so feeble that it was as if one were looking at the moon instead. Something like ash accumulated on the floors, which we had swept up. And when one asked people about it, they just said it was raining dirt. After three days, the skies cleared.

For hiking in the hills, an autumn day is best. Mists trail along; grasses grow at the foot of crags; a boat emerges from the shade of willows—all inspiring a most exquisite feeling. From the heights to the depths, there is no smoke and the skies are clear. "Over there is the province where so-and-so lives," someone points out, or, "That over there is so-and-so's village"—most amusing.

People call it *the doldrums*: a person isn't bedridden, but just feels unhappy. The face is pale; the person has no energy and is losing weight. If a young person doesn't suffer from this at all, you know that he'll turn out to be a dolt. But to die of such an illness is also stupid. It's not easy, but the best thing is just to hang on and get through it—that's what Asayama Teihaku[27] said, and I think he is right.

---

26. Located between the Yamashina area of Kyoto and the city of Ōtsu.
27. A close friend of the author's whose identity is otherwise unknown.

There is nothing more discouraging than calling out to a ferryman who won't come. One even considers trying to cross on foot.

In 1786, Ozawa Roan[28] came into possession of a fine koto, but when he tried playing it, it didn't sound as good as it looked. When a musician he asked to examine it plucked a few strings, the sound was still no good. The musician brought it back, saying, "This is a fine instrument, very old and finely carved, the sort of thing you don't often find these days, but if it doesn't sound any better than this, what can you do with it?"

"It's such a fine thing—surely it will sound better with a little repairing," Roan thought, not willing to give up. And so he took five gold pieces, found a poor household, and distributed the money, paying them to use whetstones to file at the openings on the bottom and top of the body. At all times, night and day, even when they were talking together, they never rested but just kept on filing for many days.

Finally, when the strings were attached again and Roan tried playing it, a marvelous sound came forth and the instrument went on to become famous—so much so that people began to envy Roan.

One day, Nakajima Dōkan[29] came to visit, and Roan let him play the koto, which Dōkan praised, saying, "My, but I envy you having so fine an instrument."

"Really?" said Roan. "Doesn't it disappoint you in any way?"

"Would I lie to you?" Dōkan replied.

"In that case, I will send it home with you," Roan said. "Forgive my saying so, but for one as skilled on the koto as yourself not to have a single instrument is regrettable. So I give it to you."

Dōkan was taken aback and tried to refuse the gift several times, but Roan was so sincere that in the end Dōkan happily carried it home with him that very day.

28. 1723–1801. A prominent samurai-poet who studied under the courtly Reizei house initially, later establishing an independent school of his own that was noted for its encouragement of the use of everyday language (*tadagoto*).
29. Identity unknown.

A certain prince[30] had long heard about Ozawa Roan's excellence as a poet, but whenever he sent messengers to invite him for a visit, Roan begged off.

"He is a recluse, and old. It *is* rather rude of him to fail to come visit me and talk of literary matters. Still, I can understand why he hasn't come. So I guess I'll just go myself."

At the time, Roan had lost his house in the Tenmei fire and was living in borrowed quarters near a Jizō shrine in Uzumasa.[31] When the prince showed up at his hut, Roan received him—for the first time, of course—with gratitude. The next day, he called at the prince's residence, and thereafter visited often.

The way Roan rose above the ranks of other commoners of his day and attended on the powerful and rich was remarkable, making him an unusual case in modern days. And the way the prince humbled himself for the sake of art, traveling nearly three *li* to pay a visit to a commoner, made him, too, seem like a man of old, and one of most commendable character.

In 1792, Ozawa Roan took to bed with a serious ailment and was down a long time. During that period, a certain rich man who had been his poetry disciple did not come to visit even once, and so when he had recovered, Roan resented this and remained angry. "This disciple is a well-known and wealthy man, and when he hears that the teacher he has long studied under is suffering from a grave illness, he should visit him himself and leave a few of his many servant women as nurses," Roan said. "Not to visit even once shows a lack of human feeling." He sent the man a letter expressing his anger and cut off all contact. At the end of the letter was appended this poem:

In this world of men,
riches are so many dewdrops

30. Probably Myōhōin no Miya Masahito, the elder brother of Emperor Kōkaku (1771–1840; r. 1779–1817).
31. See note 3. Uzumasa is located just West of Kyoto.

on the grasses—
light shining but a moment
while we wait for the wind.[32]

hito no yo no / tomi wa kusaba ni / oku tsuyu no / kaze o matsu ma no / hikari narikeri

Perhaps this sounds a little ill-tempered and harsh, but his anger was not without cause.

———————

Till nearly daybreak, I was chatting with a friend at his house. As I made my way home, the moon was descending on the western mountains, and the stars were all beginning to fade a little. So chilly was the morning wind that I felt as I had when last year I was about to leave on a far journey, rising just as early in the morning, and feeling forlorn as I said my farewells. So similar was the feeling that I shed a few tears.

———————

People who write are devoted in their love for brushes and inkstones; people who read a lot don't mistreat books. And the way Buddhist monks truly revere the sutras is apparent from how even lowly acolytes, when they are going to read, first hold the book up in reverence and then place it on the desk. Following their example, even wives and old ladies have proper respect for the scriptures. What can they be thinking, those students who these days read the holy books while lying down, or use the words of the sages to wipe their feet?

———————

Observing those who grow orchids as a hobby, I have noticed that they plant them in pots in order to save them from the cold and put fertilizer around their roots, never pausing in their efforts, until the time comes for the plants to bud—when they pluck off the flowers to keep them from fully blooming.

32. Ozawa Roan, *Rokujō eisō* (*Six Notebooks of Poems*), Shinpen kokka taikan 9 (Tokyo: Kadokawa shoten, 1991), poem 1608.

The reason they pluck off the blossoms is because they treasure their scent. When I ask if nurturing the plants continually in this way seems like something other than cultivation, they answer that if one allows too many flowers to blossom, the scent fades and loses its power. The reasoning is thus that those who truly love the scent do not allow the flowers to blossom.

When I heard this, I realized how poor I am. For it would seem that those who truly love money and want to be wealthy must never waste their coins on beautiful clothing, or on running a household, or on fine food. This is how they become wealthy in the end. The reason I seek wealth, however, is so that I can use my money to have the freedom to obtain whatever I desire. If my desires are to go unrealized and I am to remain fettered in any case, I would just as soon not be bothered by money in the first place.

Isn't there a comparison here to made with growing orchids but never seeing their blossoms?

In these latter days, more and more routes have opened up between countries, and commerce in products and wares has increased apace. Someone told me that tobacco seeds first came from Southeast Asia in 1605, arriving in China at about the same time. At first, our government prohibited the use of tobacco out of fear of fires, but the law was abandoned and now it's almost as important as food and drink. In China, too, it was banned, but the law didn't hold, I hear. Its taste is nothing very fine, nor does it make you feel intoxicated, or fill your stomach. I find it hard to understand how something so worthless is so well liked.

Peppers also came in about 1605, and watermelon in the Kan'ei era [1624–1644], from the Ryūkyū Islands.[33] Quince came from Portugal in the Kan'ei era, too. The samisen came in the Eiroku era [1558–1570], and by the Keichō era [1596–1615] a blind man named Takkaku had gained great fame on the instrument. The musket came from Southeast Asia in 1555. The lance has its origins in the time of Kusunoki Masashige.[34] The

---

33. The ancient name for Okinawa.
34. 1294–1336. A famous medieval warrior affiliated with the so-called Southern Court of the late fourteenth century.

carrying case began to be used in the era of Nobunaga,[35] the umbrella in the Tenshō era [1574–1592], the candle in the Bunroku era [1592–1596], and aloe oil in the Shōhō and Keian eras [1644–1648; 1648–1652]. The palanquin originated in the time of Lord Higashiyama,[36] it is said.

The seaside is the best place for looking at the moon. Vapors rising around lakes make the views there inferior to ocean views.

In spring or autumn, of course, but also in summer, one can forget all about the heat by soaking one's feet in a shallow stream running in mountain shade. And there is really nothing to compare with hearing the sound of a crane calling when one is lying awake late on a winter night.

A person of great physical beauty will also have lots of troubles. And this is true not only with people. Spirits and demons hate a grand house, winds break a tree that stands out above the rest in a grove, and waters bring down any earth that protrudes from their banks.

In the Osaka fire of 1792, the home of a certain man of the Kōnoike house[37] burned down, and before rebuilding it, he ordered that the first three feet[38] of earth beneath the structure be dug up and replaced with new soil. His head clerk, however, would not hear of it.

"Putting in three feet of soil is not such a great expense," the master said. "The ground is filthy with the remains of dead cats and mice, and I want to make the house as clean as possible for my descendants. You needn't be concerned over such a trivial expense."

But even after hearing the master's argument several times, the clerk would not have it. "For people of our class to replace three feet of soil

35. Oda Nobunaga (1534–1582), one of the great unifiers.
36. Yoshimasa (1436–1490), the eighth Ashikaga shogun.
37. A prominent merchant house in Osaka.
38. The Japanese measure mentioned here is *shaku*; one *shaku* is close to one foot.

may seem a trivial expense, but replacing soil is something the nobility do, not merchants. Displaying such arrogance before one's descendants will bring worse luck than passing on a defilement.[39] No, as long as I am here, I simply won't agree to it," he said.

At this, the master became angry and reprimanded the clerk, saying, "You're only a retainer, you know. How can you defy your master's wishes in such a way?"

Still the clerk would not listen. So after being reprimanded again, he returned to his own house—and promptly did himself in.

When the master heard this news, he was sorry and gave up the idea of replacing the soil.

Even in the house of a petty merchant there are those who gain fame and wealth and employ such loyal retainers. Such a man would not bring shame even to a great house boasting an income of many thousands of *koku*.[40]

———————

I had my first male child when I was just a year shy of forty. Before that, they had all been girls, and since he was my first boy, I found myself hoping that he would grow up quickly and thinking about what I would teach him, what he would become. Then I realized how foolishly I was behaving to imagine things off in the distant future and had to laugh at myself:

> How stupid of me!
> —to forget that I too
> grow ever older,
> as I wait impatiently
> for my boy to be a man.

ono ga mi no / oiyuku koto wa / wasurarete / hito to naru ko no / sue zo mataruru

I wonder if this is the way other people feel about their children.

39. Contact with anything dead or dying was considered a defilement that demanded a period of isolation from society.
40. Samurai stipends from the government were calculated in measures of rice (*koku*). Merchants gained wealth through trade and were considered below samurai, farmers, and artisans on the official social scale.

During the An'ei era [1772–1781], there was a blind musician named Fujimura Kengyō[41] living in Kyoto. This is what he always said: "When playing the lute in front of people, it is a mistake to try to win praise by pleasing them, because among the listeners will be different people with different tastes; you may appeal to that person over there but not the one over here. So no matter when or where I am performing, I play to the best of my ability and don't even think about pleasing the people seated before me. In my mind, I just think of my playing as an offering to the gods."

How wonderful was the attitude of this worthy blind man, whose reputation as a master was not without foundation. No matter what the art, one should understand it this way. As the sage said, "Examine yourself and you will have no regrets."[42] And, again, there is the phrase "Watch yourself first,"[43] which is the same idea.

At sundown, if the clouds are purple and black, with countless bands of red mist crisscrossing one another inside them, there is sure to be a huge thunderstorm the next day. The sky was full of such clouds when that great thunderstorm hit Kyoto sixty or seventy years ago, I hear.

If the sky at dusk turns red, like the color of blood, and the light shining into the house turns the faces of the people there red as well, it is a sure sign that there will be a flood.

When there are lots of blossoms on the loquat tree, there will be a bounteous harvest of wheat that year.

41. The title *kengyō* was given to officials in the Mōkan (Bureau of the Blind), a government office for blind musicians, masseurs, and acupuncturists.

42. A quotation from *The Doctrine of the Mean* (*Zhong yong*), a classic philosophical text attributed to Zisi, the grandson of Confucius. See *Confucius: Confucian Analects, The Great Learning, and The Doctrine of the Mean*, trans. James Legge (New York: Dover, 1971), 431.

43. Ibid., 384.

Whenever I am staying in the capital, I tire of the dusty world and long for a hut in the mountains; but after I arrive in some remote place far from the capital, it is just those skies over the capital that I miss most of all. If you have never been out on a long journey, you will not know what I mean. Those who live in the capital all the time can no more comprehend this than can a person who has never been sick understand what it means to be well. After one has been ill—that is when one comes to understand the meaning of being free of illness.

In the An'ei era, when I was living in Fushimi, there was a fearsome thunderstorm during which lightning struck a number of places. South of Bingo Bridge, ten people of a farm household who were out in the paddies harvesting rice all ran into a little hut for protection from the storm. Unfortunately, though, lightning struck the hut and passed right down through the group. Several of the people suffered broken limbs or were disemboweled and died on the spot; others swooned and collapsed. Those who had not been hurt at all carried the unconscious ones home, gave them medicine, and tried to nurse them back to health; but after two months or so, the injured were suddenly taken with fevers and chills, and in a day or two all of them were dead. It appears that they had been poisoned by the lightning. The illness resembled mad-dog disease in the way the poison killed them only after some days had passed. A most unusual occurrence.

When someone has been pierced by an arrow, you should remove the feathers and gently push the arrow through in the direction it entered and not pull it out the opposite direction. Furthermore, one should beware of pulling it out too quickly, as the person will surely die if one does so. Instead, one should pull the arrow out carefully and then quickly cover the entry wound with one's fingers. Otherwise, energy will leak from the wound and the person will expire immediately. After covering the wound with one's fingers for a while, one should proceed to sew it up. That is what I was taught.

In the old days, no one was stinting in praise for the prose of *The Tale of Genji*, but many maligned the poems of the tale as being quite clumsy affairs. My own opinion is that the poems in the tale have a style of their own, one that stresses simplicity and straightforwardness and is still elegant in mood and replete with overtones. As so many of the poems are presented as if occasional in nature and written extemporaneously, this is only to be expected.[44] To critique the poems of the tale in the same terms as poems from the various collections[45] is merely to show ignorance of the category to which they belong.

Late into the night, when all is quiet, I sit looking at the moon through my window, remembering the happy things, the sad things, all the things that have happened to me over the years. Rich people have so many people about them all the time, I think, that to them such moments must remain unknown.

Among writers of Chinese poetry in this country since the Kyōho era [1716–1736], many surpass those of olden times. No one knows what the future will bring, but I believe that at present we are seeing the first great flourishing of the form. Akiyama Gyokuzan[46] praised himself, saying, "I myself am the founder of the five-character poem in Japan!" and even someone viewing things from the outside would admit that he was not overstating his case. Just now, *waka* is especially popular—indeed, flourishing at all social ranks—but what is being produced does not compare with the work of the ancients; and even if things change greatly, *waka* poets nowadays are still far from achieving true excellence in their Way. Likewise, haikai

44. On formal occasions, poems were written on prescribed topics (*dai*). In *Genji*, however, virtually no such poems are recorded, probably because the tale concentrates mainly on life behind the scenes. More than seven hundred poems are included in the tale, almost all arising from dramatic situations.

45. *Senshū*. The imperial and other collections, which brought together mostly poems composed for formal court contests and poetic gatherings rather than occasional poems of the sort featured in *The Tale of Genji*.

46. 1702–1763. A Confucian scholar in service in the Kumamoto domain in Kyushu who was renowned also as a poet writing in Chinese (*kanshi*).

flourished in Bashō's time, reaching its zenith then. It seems unlikely that hereafter haikai will ever go beyond what has already been achieved.

A man should do something of use to heaven and earth. In the world today, anyone with a little learning disdains the practice of medicine, but for one of humble station born into this age of peace, what better way is there to relieve human suffering?

Among the physicians of Izumi Sakai was a man named Nakarai Sōshu.[47] About three generations back, Sōshu had gained great fame as a fine physician. One night, an old lady came calling from a nearby village.

"I have come because my son is ill," she said, so Sōshu had her invited in to see him and asked just what sort of illness it was.

The old lady lowered her voice and said, "My son has become a thief, and I am very distressed. I plead with you, sir, please take pity and give me some kind of medicine to cure him."

For a moment, Sōshu thought about this desperate request. Then he said, "I understand," and gave her a number of medicines.

Afterward, the doctor's disciples were all mystified and asked him why he gave medicine to someone who was not ill.

"I gave her the medicines because I came up with a plan of treatment," the doctor answered. "Just for the sake of practice, why don't you think of one, too?" But of course they couldn't come up with anything.

When they kept hounding him for an answer, he finally said, "All right, all right. What I gave him was a medicine that will dry out his throat and lungs. If he's coughing all the time, he can't carry on as a thief, now, can he?" A very quick-witted response.

Chinese physicians are very learned but lack quality, while Japanese physicians have quality but lack learning.

47. Precise dates unknown. Men of the Nakarai lineage had practiced medicine in Izumi Sakai (modern-day Osaka) from at least the fifteenth century.

During the Hōei era [1704–1711], there was a certain major counselor who was an expert on stringed instruments, especially the lute. In a house of equal standing was a famed lute named Boulder that had been passed down since long ago in Engi times [901–923], and the counselor was so impressed by it that he went to the house often and asked if he might be allowed to play it. This they allowed him, which made him desire it all the more, inspiring him to ask if he could borrow the instrument, even if for only a short time. The head of the house, however, was not that generous and turned the counselor away. The instrument was a treasure, he said—something passed down in the house since long ago that was never allowed out.

Crestfallen, the counselor went home but still could not put the fine lute from his mind, and so he went to Kitano Shrine[48] on foot every day, praying there that he might be able to borrow the instrument as he wished. On windy days, on rainy days, he went without fail, until the people in town, seeing a man of high rank, attendants and all, going on foot to the shrine every day for months, concluded that he must be out of his mind.

When the owner of the lute heard about this he didn't believe it, but later he was very moved and deeply impressed. "How can I not give in to someone with such devotion?" he thought, and invited the counselor over so that he could hear the whole story.

"I am so impressed by your dedication that I will let you borrow the lute," the man said. "Send someone over to pick it up—as soon as tomorrow, if you like."

The counselor was overjoyed, but said that he couldn't wait till the next day and asked if he might be allowed to take the instrument now. He then wrapped it in the sleeve of his own robe and, holding it tight, returned home.

In exchange, the counselor sent the other man a prized koto to keep for a while. In the Hōei fire, the earthen storehouse of the man was destroyed, the koto along with it. And since the koto he had sent in ex-

48. One of the most prominent Shinto shrines in Kyoto, located on the western border of the city.

change had been lost, the counselor let the years go by without ever returning the lute—which is how Boulder remained in the possession of the counselor's house. He loved the instrument so much that he always kept it nearby, and indeed carried it to safety himself in the event of fire. The treasured instrument thus exists to this day. The counselor was a true connoisseur of old-fashioned taste, worthy of the fame he gained as a master.

In the area of Karasu Mountain, Shinano Province,[49] there is an animal called a thunder beast that looks like a mouse and is a little bigger than a weasel in size. The claws on its four paws are extremely sharp. In summertime, holes open up spontaneously in the ground all over the mountains, and when the thunder beasts poke their heads out of the holes and look up at the sky, clouds of evening showers form. The thunder beasts can tell which clouds will be hard to ride on and which not. When a promising cloud comes by, they fly up into it. This doesn't mean that thunder will always follow, but that the legends tell only of times when thunder did occur.

In spring, people of the area go out into the snow to hunt the thunder beasts. There is so much snow there in the winter that the farmers can't put in winter crops, so they hate the beasts for the way they dig out and eat up the seeds of the taro that they plant in spring.

In Chinese books, the same animal is called a thunder rat, according to Tōu.[50]

An Osaka samurai named Yamadera so-and-so was passing through the Sanadayama area[51] on the last day of the Tenth Month of 1774 when he heard loud voices speaking just behind him. When he turned around, however, there was no one there. As he proceeded, he heard the voices again, and again turned around to find no one there. This went on for a while, leaving him so mystified that he stood for some time staring into the

49. Located in the Nasu district of modern-day Tochigi Prefecture.
50. D. 1782. A haikai poet, also known by his sobriquet Yūmuan.
51. Located in present-day Tennōji Ward, Osaka.

distance behind him. About half a block away, he saw a merchant wearing a short coat and a mendicant Zen priest with a *tengai* hat[52] hanging down his back walking along, conversing with each other. Looking carefully at the priest's face, he saw that it looked like it was made of tissue paper.

As Yamadera set out walking again, wondering about what he had seen, he heard the voices even more frequently. "That priest must be a monster of some sort," he thought, but walked blithely ahead, all the while making ready to cut him down with one blow of his sword. But when the men had come up directly behind him, he turned, pounced with a shout, and wrestled one of the men down—who turned out to be the merchant. When he asked him who the priest had been, the merchant said, "Something frightening has happened. That Zen priest I was walking with, when he came right up behind you—he just vanished! I was so frightened that I was completely taken aback."

When Yamadera asked the merchant what the two men had been talking about, the merchant said that he was a stranger to the area and didn't know his way around, so he had asked the priest where he might find an inn. The priest had just replied that he happened to live in Nagamachi[53] and was now out on business but would be happy to suggest a place for lodging, when all this happened.

The thing fled because Yamadera had sensed that it was a monster.

On the twenty-third day of the Sixth Month of 1774, a typhoon sent roof tiles flying like leaves from the trees. A huge wave hit the Osaka area, and it's said that tens of thousands of people drowned. The very next night, a wild rumor spread through the city warning that another tidal wave was going to hit Osaka and put sections of the city underwater. Men and women, old and young, all began running to the east, some carrying money, others food, and making a huge commotion. This was true all over Osaka; no area of the city was spared the confusion. No one knows who started the rumors.

52. A canopy hat that entirely conceals the wearer's face.
53. An area of what is now Chūō Ward, Osaka.

A strange business. I stayed in my house, looking after my mother. Around daybreak, things finally settled down.

———————

A man named Naitō of a certain household in Fukuyama, Bingo Province, went out into his garden one day and spied a black snake. Using a walking stick, he struck the snake, which hurried off into the grass. Then Naitō began beating the grass, trying to scare it out, but to no avail—he couldn't see where it had gone.

After a while, a servant found the snake and told Naitō that it was lying dead in the grass, so Naitō went out to dispose of it. But when he did so, the snake raised its head and spat out something like tobacco smoke, which struck him in the left eye. After this, the snake fell over dead.

Suddenly Naitō's eye began to hurt and swell up; soon he was having fevers and chills and was suffering terribly. It looked as if he was sure to die. But then Naitō remembered that tobacco tar was poisonous to snakes and took some tar from his pipe and put it into his eye, after which the swelling went down, the pain eased off, and after a day or so the illness abated, leaving him with only a red eye. Every day, he would put tobacco tar in the eye, and after five or six days he was completely healed.

At around the same time the next year, Naitō's eye began to hurt again, and he went to various doctors for treatment but got no better. But when he again remembered the snake poison and put tobacco tar in his eye, he was healed right away. For two or three years thereafter, his eye would begin to hurt around the same season, and he would always cure the problem with tobacco tar.

I heard this story from Murakami Kenshun.[54] He said that it was a man named Jōzaemon who hit the snake but that it was Naitō whom the poison hit when he went out into the garden.

———————

In reward for his valor on the battlefield, Kusunoki Masatsura[55] was presented with a palace lady but declined the gift:

54. Identity unknown.
55. 1326–1348. Eldest son of Kusunoki Masashige (1294–1336), a hero of the Southern Court. Like his father, he died valiantly in battle.

Knowing I am one
not destined to live long
in this world of ours,
how could I pledge myself
to a bond I cannot keep?

totemo yo ni / nagarau beku mo / aranu mi no / kari no chigiri o / ikade musuban

A true son of Lord Masashige! Reading his words a thousand years from now, people will still have to choke back tears.

———————

Once Miyoshi Chōkei[56] was participating in a linked-verse gathering in the chambers of a certain Kyoto lord. Just when those assembled were puzzling over how to provide a link for the following difficult verse—

Among the miscanthus,
a single clump of reeds.

susuki ni majiru / ashi no hitomoto

—a messenger came in with an urgent message and handed it to Chōkei. He swiftly read the message, put it down, and then picked up the paper with the verse written on it and folded it.

"I will take care of this," he said, and after thinking for a minute produced this:

On the shallow edge
of an old stretch of marshland—
a meadow takes over.

furunuma no / asaki kata yori / no to narite

"A masterful response!" everyone thought, and expressed their admiration.

56. 1522–1564. Another famous warlord who was also known as a skilled poet.

Then Chōkei turned to face the group and said, "As you have seen, a messenger has just brought me news. My younger brother Jikkyū has just died in battle in Izumi.[57] It appears that my comrades are going down in defeat. I must leave for the battlefield at once. Since this may be the last time I see you, I composed this verse as a farewell."

After saying this, he left immediately for battle, it is said.[58]

———————

Once when I was living in Fushimi, at the beginning of the Kansei era [1789–1801], I was bedridden for a long time with a bout of dysentery. After nearly a hundred attacks, I was unable to eat or drink for some days, and the people looking after me thought that my life was in peril. In my heart, I felt no tension at all but only a great physical fatigue, and after many days without eating, I couldn't even move my hands and legs. While I was doing nothing more than lying there on my pallet, however, my ears and nose became very sensitive. Although the kitchen was two or three rooms away, I was able to tell by the aroma very specifically what was being boiled and what prepared, even down to whether it was potatoes or radishes. I could even detect things that normally have no scent at all. Sometimes the smells seemed to bore right into my nostrils, they were so intense. Furthermore, when I had someone play the koto some rooms away, I was able to distinguish things just like a blind musician—noting that one number was a little sharp or another a little flat, and so on.

I thought to myself that the explanation must be that I was just lying there ill, with nothing to occupy my mind; and sure enough, when after some days the attacks had ceased and I was back to eating and drinking as usual, my nose returned to normal and I was no longer able to pick out sounds as well as a blind musician. The reason must be that after many days without food, the veins and vessels are empty and the blood and fluids pure, so that the spirit can circulate easily, reaching all the way to the nose and ears. Come to think of it, it also makes sense that the spirit

57. Miyoshi Yoshikata (1527–1562), also known as Jikkyū, who died in the Third Month of 1562 at the Battle of Kumeda, in Izumi Province (present-day Osaka Prefecture).
58. This anecdote appears in a number of sources. See Kidō Saizō, *Rengashi ronkō* (Tokyo: Meiji shoin, 1973), 2:705.

flows so impressively in sages and Daoist masters who avoid grains and eat only roots and tree bark, thus purifying their blood and fluids in the same way.

———————————

Hidden away now
is the house I came to visit—
amid spring mists.
In the valley, a warbler calls
one solitary time.[59]

tazunenuru / yado wa kasumi ni / uzumorete / tani no uguisu / hitokoe zo suru

Master Norinaga praised this poem as the only poem of excellence he ever wrote, but at the time no one was all that impressed. Only later did Master Kiyosuke[60] record that he thought he understood what the poet was saying. I would say that the word "solitary" is out of the ordinary, but it surely is not the sort of poem that easily gains renown as a work of excellence. That it didn't receive any particular praise in its own time may be because reading a poem is more difficult than writing one.

———————————

Every time I visit Uji,[61] I tell people I meet how impressed I am with the excellence of the calligraphy that was done by the Zen master Kōsen[62] for the plaque over the gate of Ōbaku Temple[63] there, which says, "The First Great Truth."[64] Hearing that I was so impressed, the monk Shōka[65] told me this story:

59. A poem by Fujiwara Norinaga (precise dates unknown) that appears in *Goshūishū* (*Later Collection of Gleanings*, 1086), poem 23, with the headnote "Written on the idea of visiting someone in a mountain village in spring, at the home of Lord Toshitsuna."
60. Fujiwara no Kiyosuke (1104–1177), a prominent poet and scholar.
61. Located south of the capital.
62. Kōsen Shōton (1633–1695), the fifth abbot of Manpukuji, chief temple of the Ōbaku Zen sect, which was established by Chinese emigrés in Japan in the mid-seventeenth century.
63. A reference to Manpukuji.
64. *Daiichigi*. The plaque remains over the main gate of the temple to this day.
65. Identity unknown.

When Reverend Kōsen was writing out the inscription, his disciple Ōsui[66] was at his side, and eighty-four times Ōsui said, "No, that's no good, that won't do." Then Ōsui went out to the latrine for a moment, and Kōsen, a little out of sorts, decided to shock him a bit by really letting his brush go. Just as he finished, Ōsui came in, looked at the writing, and praised it greatly. "Now *this* will surely protect the temple!" he said, and clapped his hands for joy. It was only on the eighty-fifth attempt that Reverend Kōsen succeeded. Shōka said that this story is recorded in a stone inscription near the temple.

One night when I was seven or eight years old, I was sitting with my father and mother. Seeing that my father was reading *Mencius*, I asked him what was so special about the book.

"Well, let me read it to you," he said, and he read aloud the chapter on using a lamb in place of an ox.[67] It was so moving that I couldn't keep from weeping, and seeing me, my father shed tears as well. Thereafter, I asked my father to read *Mencius* to me often, and then we went on to the *Analects*, and I set my mind on scholarship. These days, when I hear my disciples reading that chapter, I remember that time thirty-five years ago as though it were yesterday and realize what a debt of gratitude I owe my parents.

As a young man, when Kagawa Tachū[68] was bustling around treating people as a physician, he would never stop to relieve himself along the way. When a student asked him why, he answered, "If I do my business in the privy after I return home, it can be put to good use as fertilizer by farmers. How could I just waste my urine on the roadside?"

By nature, Tachū was of a manly disposition, and his desires were kind and praiseworthy.

66. Ōsui Genki, Kōsen's chief heir (*hassu*).
67. *Mencius*, trans. D. C. Lau (New York: Penguin, 1970), 55.
68. Identity unknown.

Japanese sliding doors and tatami floors are superior to those of all other countries and do their jobs exceedingly well. During the An'ei and Tenmei [1781–1789] eras, there lived in Nagasaki a Dutch ship's captain by the name of Isaac Titsingh.[69] After the fashion of his own country, he built a captain's room, but did it in Japanese style, and lived there, it is said. At around the same time, a man named Yoshio Kōzaemon,[70] who was serving as chief Dutch interpreter, studied Dutch architecture and built one room complete with a tiled floor, a floor of wood planks on the second level, and stairways and handrails painted with green lacquer. I myself visited the Yoshio place and found it to be just as if one had gone into a Dutch house. However, since there were no tatami and all the guests were seated on chairs, exchanging cups of saké and tea—or any kind of food or drink—presented great difficulties.

In its time, the house of Sano Eian[71] was known as one of the most wealthy in Kyoto. But his heir[72] loved saké and high living and spent day and night becoming an expert in the ways of Shimabara and Gion,[73] neglecting the family business altogether. His family expressed their displeasure continually, and before long they were ready to disinherit him.

Around this time, his father, Eian, was on a trip to worship at Kitano Shrine and happened to run into an evening thunderstorm along the way. For shelter from the rain, he ducked under the eaves of a house, but when the rain didn't let up, a beautiful young woman of perhaps twelve or thirteen came out. "These eaves are rather shallow, and the rain just keeps coming down, so please feel free to step in for a moment and wait

69. 1745–1812. The senior official of the Dutch East India Company in Nagasaki who also was posted to Indonesia and China.
70. Yoshio Kōgyū (1724–1800), a physician who was born in Nagasaki and began studying to be an interpreter at a young age, eventually becoming a master interpreter in 1748.
71. Sano Shōyū (d. 1622), also known as Haiya Shōyū. A rich Kyoto merchant, he was a connoisseur of the arts.
72. Sano Shōeki (d. 1691), son of a nephew of the artist Hon'ami Kōetsu (1558–1637) who was adopted by Sano Shōyū as his heir. He studied poetry under the courtier-poet Karasumaru Mitsuhiro (1579–1638) and haikai under Matsunaga Teitoku (1571–1653), and was a connoisseur of tea, calligraphy, and the courtly sport of kickball (kemari).
73. The most prominent pleasure quarters of Kyoto.

for it to pass," she said, opening the door and guiding him inside, where she put out a round mat for him to sit on and a tobacco tray. Eian sat down and enjoyed a pipe, looking out on the garden, where the placement of paper lanterns and stones and the plantings made for a very natural effect, peaceful and alluring. As he sat wondering who the owner of the place might be, thinking very highly of his taste, the young woman came in and said, "We are only women here, so I have been reluctant to intrude. But it appears that the rain won't be letting up, and since the cauldron is already heated up in the tea house, I wonder if you might not be averse to having some weak tea."[74] Being quite a devotee of the Way of Tea, and wanting to see more of the garden, he said he would be delighted and went inside.

Everything from the scroll hanging in the alcove to the kettle and the hearth seemed elegantly done. As he sat waiting, the lady of the house came in to offer her greetings. Needless to say, she was very attractive, and her speech was very refined, although not at all haughty. Eian was thinking to himself, "It's hard to believe that there really are such women in the world." She prepared the tea herself, and her technique was very skilled. The tea was very delicious as he drank it down.

The rain having finally stopped, he said his thanks and left. Even after he got home, however, he kept wondering about what he had just experienced, feeling as if he had just enjoyed himself in the house of some wizard. "How could there be a tea devotee of that sort without my hearing of him?" he mused, thinking that he must have been taken in by a fox. His heart simply could not rest easy.

Eian asked his stewards and servants repeatedly to go and check out the house and find out the name of the woman, until they finally had to give in and confess that the lady was his own son's mistress. Her name was Yoshino Tayū of the Yoshiwara quarter. His son had recently bought out her contract and set her up in that house.

Eian was amazed to hear this and could understand why his son had been so captivated. "Why, I'm enticed myself!" he thought, and told his son that he should not be ashamed to take such a woman as his wife. Before long, the house took her in formally as the wife of the heir. The

74. *Usucha*, as opposed to strong tea.

Sano house lost its place in the world, but one hears that descendants of the lineage continue to this day.

———————————

People who dwell in the mountains are long-lived, while people who live by the sea die young. It seems to me that those who eat a lot of meat will not achieve long life because they use up their years quickly, just as someone who turns the wick of his lamp up high will have bright light for a time but then exhaust his store of oil. Looking at the world around me, I see that barbarians have short lives, dying at about fifty years of age, while Japanese have long lives, living until they are seventy or eighty.

———————————

In Satsuma, a young child of two or three years, or perhaps four or five, may suddenly begin to cry for no reason—from what appears to be a bellyache. No one can figure out why. Every child stricken with the illness cries night and day, for as long as two or three days, and then dies. If the problem develops during infancy without abating, death is certain. Many in that region suffer from this malady. It is the most serious of all illnesses among infants there but doesn't exist outside the province. I thought about the matter for a while and took them my idea for a treatment but then left. I wonder what happened thereafter.

———————————

Among the paintings in my storehouse are many that I didn't think of as particularly well done when I got them, but later, when I looked at them after some time had passed, so impressed me that I now treasure them greatly. I was at first very disappointed with the landscapes of Baisō,[75] but in fact I have learned that when it comes to highly valued paintings one should put several of them up on the wall for some days and try to appreciate them before making any judgments. Thus a person should understand that it is difficult to identify the good points of paintings when one sees them at a large exhibit, or at the summer airing of a temple collection or a seasonal unveiling. And the same is true not only for paint-

75. A late Edo-period haikai poet and painter.

ings but also for poems. The things that strike you as interesting at first sight, seeming new to the eye or ear, are not truly excellent.

First one must be upright, then others will obey one's command; first one must obey, then others will follow; first one must believe, then others will believe as well. Everyone spews out grand, vain statements at times, but one who has not accumulated merit through quiet self-reflection will not have true confidence. To understand this, one need only look at the great teachers of the various Buddhist sects, all of whom had confidence in themselves because they had spared no effort in their devotions. That is why they were able to establish sects and save people.

For more than twenty years, I have been studying medicine, and secretly I am sure that I yield in my medical knowledge to no one, whether in China or Japan, whether of old or in the present. From my youth, I have also pursued other arts of all sorts but never arrived at competence in any of them, because I did not put enough time and effort into training.[76] If one receives praise when from time to time one succeeds in an art that one has not yet mastered, one feels pleased even knowing that it isn't warranted, while of course being chastened never feels good. However, when it comes to my work in medicine, I am neither pleased by praise nor angered in the least by criticism, for the reason that I have reached a state of security within myself. When one has achieved a position of such moral conviction, I think one's heart cannot be disturbed—not by praise or insult, not by honor or shame, not by fame or fortune. This is how it was with the sages of the past.

The death of Sen no Rikyū[77] has been elegantly described by Muro Kyūsō,[78] but Rikyū was a man who was not impressive only in his death. Nor is he someone who can be judged only as a great tea master.

76. *Shugyō.* A word connoting both study and hands-on practice.
77. 1522–1591. The greatest of early tea masters.
78. 1658–1734. A Confucian scholar in service to the shogun Tokugawa Yoshimune (1684–1751). He describes Rikyū in *Sundai zatsuwa* (*Chats at Surugadai*, 1732).

Rikyū's daughter had already gone as wife to Mozuya Sōan when the Taikō[79] heard of her beauty and asked for her. This Rikyū could not condone, saying that once she had gone to another house as wife she could not go to someone else, no matter on whose order, and that he could not tolerate being told that a merchant should change his mind just because of the Taikō's intimidation. The way he paid no heed to the influence of wealth and power standing right in front of him but only to what was right shows how strong Rikyū was as a person.

——————————

Hosokawa Yūsai[80] was known for his fine taste. For two successive generations, his house was of the first rank in everything, including even the tea ceremony.

Once Gamō Ujisato[81] heard that the Hosokawa had a rich collection of tea utensils. "I would like to see your utensils," he said, and made an appointment to come on a certain day. When he arrived, however, Yūsai had put on display all the martial treasures of the house—swords, suits of armor, even lances.

Surprised, Ujisato said that it was the *tea* utensils of the house that he had wanted to see.

Hosokawa replied, "When you said 'utensils,' I assumed you meant our utensils of war. But I can easily show my tea utensils as well," and had various tea things brought out for the man to view.

This is a story that is frequently told, but I think it is near in spirit to the phrases "Not forgetting your primary duty" and "Enjoying, but never to excess."[82] The tea connoisseurs of that day were generally great men, very different from the worldly tea masters of our own day. I am somewhat skeptical, however, about the Zen masters of that time who indulged in tea with the justification that tea and Zen were the same thing.

79. Toyotomi Hideyoshi (1536–1598). The precise reason why Hideyoshi ordered Rikyū's execution is a matter of debate. Here Nankei is giving one of many possible motives.
80. 1534–1610. A warrior-poet.
81. 1556–1595. A warrior who served both Nobunaga and Hideyoshi.
82. A quote from the *Analects*, where Confucius offers his interpretation of the first ode in the *Book of Odes*. See Confucius, *The Analects*, trans. D. C. Lau (New York: Penguin, 1979), 70.

Among those of recent times, Buson's[83] talent in haikai was extraordinary, and he has received more than the usual praise for his work. This is not something one can arrive at through study but rather a talent that is inborn. His paintings, too, are very fine, and among his landscapes are some that show a skill unrivaled by anyone in recent history. That his paintings did not gain much fame while he was still alive is because they were overshadowed by his haikai and because there was no one around who had the right eye to appreciate their essence.

Chōgetsu[84] was born in Bitchū Province. He took the tonsure in his youth and became the disciple of the Tendai monk Taichi of the same place.

One time when the young monks were being lazy, the chief priest lost his temper and scolded them: "Here you are, all of a goodly age, and yet you neglect your devotions and appear to be of no use at all. Just look at Chōgetsu. He's only thirteen, but he's up early in the morning and stays up late into the night, reciting sutras, studying, and practicing calligraphy with great diligence. What's more, he does cleaning around the temple and even kitchen chores, always most dutifully. One day, it will be someone like Chōgetsu who becomes chief priest of this temple. I doubt whether the likes of you will even be granted a small hut in its precincts."

Hearing this, Chōgetsu said to the chief priest, "Pardon me, but I don't quite understand what you just said. To rise early and stay up all night without sleep, dedicating oneself to one's studies—that is only what is considered virtuous behavior. And as for my efforts—they have been aimed at gaining salvation for all living things. My intent has never been to become chief priest at a little temple like this one."

This surprised the chief priest, who laughed and said, "Well then, you're an idiot."

This made Chōgetsu think: "I will never realize my ambitions if I study under a monk like this one. On Mount Hiei, the central temple of the

---

83. Yosa Buson (1716–1783), a haikai poet and painter.
84. Nishiyama Chōgetsu (1714–1798), who ended up studying poetry under the courtier Mushanokōji Saneoka (1721–1760) and gaining fame as one of the finest commoner poets of his day.

Tendai sect, there are sure to be many monks of great learning and high virtue." So he left the temple at Tamajima and went to Mount Hiei.[85]

It was at the beginning of his thirteenth year that he went up Mount Hiei. He had no money for travel and suffered greatly, and since he knew no one there, he was without anyone to offer him assistance. When he arrived, none of the temples on the mountain would even give him lodging for even the night. Telling him that he should get help from his teacher or relatives back home, they chased him off, and he had nowhere to go. By this time, it was already getting dark, and he was in dire straits. Fortunately, however, there was a manservant who couldn't bear to watch this and who gave him a place for the night, in secret. After some time, Chōgetsu was finally accepted by a temple the servant knew well, and he was able to stay on the mountain after all.

Chōgetsu then set himself to seeking monks of great learning and high virtue, but he did not find as many as he had hoped for. Lamenting the decline of the temple and the sad fate of the sect, it is said that he finally turned to the Way of Elegance and became a poet.

The saying goes, "On underlings, use a hammer." Truly, one must be careful to follow all the rules when using people of the lower classes and stay on the right path. If you show them even a little kindness, they will be sure to take unfair advantage and end up committing crimes. The least show of gratitude will in the end be in vain. Those at the top must understand this and see that people of the lower classes do not fall into error. The same is true of the way the state should govern the barbarians.

In China, they divide commercial wares into three ranks. Those of the highest rank are called Western wares. These go to countries west of China such as India, England, Isuhanya,[86] Holland, and so on, because people there are fond of anything of value and high quality. Wares of the

---

85. Located northeast of the capital, the site of Enryakuji, the largest and most prestigious of the Tendai temples.
86. Isfahan. Probably meant as a reference to Persia (Iran) rather than to just the city itself.

middle rank are sold in China itself, while wares of the lowest rank are called Eastern Wares and go to Japan—because, it is said, the Japanese are fond of anything cheap.

In the household of a certain Lord Kobori was a man named Hisabei. During the worst of the summer heat, he went into his office to work. After long hours of labor on a very hot day, he was exhausted and feeling rather poorly. He finally went home, in the evening. As he sat down to rest and recover from his fatigue, however, he saw that his wife's face looked like the face of a cow. This amazed him so much that he was about to draw his sword and cut her down, but then he saw that the servant girl next to him had the face of a red horse and his son the face of a demon—that, indeed, there was not a single person in his house who had not been transformed, and that these were no ordinary monsters. He knew that if he did the wrong thing now, he might be subjected to ridicule as a samurai, so he got up, went into another room at the back of the house, pulled shut the sliding door, lay himself down, closed his eyes, and stayed calm.

His wife, wondering what was going on, saw that his expression was troubled and that he had lain down without saying a word, so she went over to him and asked if he was all right, but he ordered her away without even opening his eyes and remained quiet for several hours.

When he opened his eyes again, the faces of the people in his house had returned to normal and no vestige of the strange occurrence remained. The monsters he had seen before he now assumed must have been the result of a fevered mind, oppressed by a long day of labor and heat. Had he cut his wife down, he would have been deemed a madman, so his decision not to act had been fortunate. Later, Hisabei told people that certainly the same thing must happen to others and that they should always act with caution.

Lately there are many unworthy priests. Despite the harsh punishments administered by the government, the situation continues. This is because people believe that if a child takes the tonsure, then the whole family will be reborn in heaven. Wanting to be reborn in heaven themselves, parents force a son who feels no calling as yet and no real belief in the Buddhist law to leave the world and enter orders, which means that after he has grown, he is obliged to put on Buddhist robes and take up residence in a temple. Since from the beginning there is no conviction behind his tonsure, he finds it difficult to refrain from women and other fleshly pleasures and ends up secretly keeping a mistress and eating fish and meat. But it is the parents who first forced their will on the man and who in the end make him suffer punishment by the government and lead him to sin against the Buddhist law. A lamentable and pitiable state of affairs; truly regrettable.

———————

People are prone to change to another occupation after working for a time in their own. A man with a little talent develops ambitions beyond his place and fails to adhere to his own way; someone with intelligence gets distracted by a side current and forgets about his primary occupation. In this way, even though they may be prodigies or men of great ability, they lose their talents and never make anything of themselves. They are of no use to the world.

Since all men have their places, each should work hard to achieve success in his own occupation first of all, and only then go on to other things. Anyone who doesn't care for his occupation should change quickly, for there is no use wasting time in something you don't like. But to be changing one's occupation all the time is sure to lead to confusion.

———————

Confucian scholars disdain the Way of Poetry as of little use, but one who has no aesthetic sense at all will be overbearing and lacking in refinement—an unfortunate situation. When a person of noble birth commits a mistake, it is not easy to criticize him directly, but in a Chinese poem one can express things that are difficult to say in a restrained manner. Likewise, when relations between parents and children are strained, or when feelings between man and woman are strained, a poem in Japanese will get by the barriers. Also, when one is feeling forlorn on a journey, offering up a poem will comfort those emotions, just as on a long night when one is sad or angry or melancholy or full of pain, composing a poem will dry the tears on one's sleeves. In both China and Japan, many men of valor, nobles, warriors, and heroes have left behind poems. The best thing, then, is for a Confucian scholar to take scholarship as his foundation but to augment it with poetry.

———————

A Zen priest in the Kantō solicited a small sum of money from his master to go up to Kyoto to be ordained. On the way there, however, he ran into thieves, who took all his money. Not knowing how to explain things back home, he couldn't very well return, so he went on up to Kyoto, where he simply whiled away his time. When people in Kyoto asked him why he was staying so long in the city, the monk explained his situation. He also composed a poem, saying that that was his only comfort, having accomplished nothing that would allow him to return to his hometown with pride and being without the means to stay on in the capital. This is the poem:

> I made my way
> across a sea of troubles—
> my ink-black sleeves
> assaulted by rough breakers[87]
> rising white upon the sea.

kurushimi no / umi o watareba / sumizome no / sode ni mo kakaru / okitsu shiranami

The same people of Kyoto were moved enough by this poem that they told the man's story to some kind people, who were in turn so impressed that they got together and raised the money required for the man to get his ordination right there in Kyoto. After being ordained, the man returned home. The person who told me this story said that it happened not long ago, but I have forgotten the name of the monk.

———————

From my youth up, I have been intensely fond of *Laozi*, which I have read dozens of times and about which I have even written a commentary. Since

87. *Shiranami* (whitecaps), a metaphorical reference to the thieves.

ancient days, it has always been thought of as a companion to *Zhuangzi*,[88] but the final meaning of that book is quite different and I don't care for it. Of course, one reads the book as part of one's scholarly training, and so it seems to have some value, but the outlook of the text is in the final analysis morbid and does no one any good. *Laozi* espouses variety, and it seems to me that its basic import is the same as the Way of the Sages and the teachings of the Buddha. Among these, *Laozi* is in fact the most approachable text, easy to put into practice, easy to comprehend, and easy to remain true to. The one thing that I have found to be of most value in understanding how to comport myself in life is this line from *Laozi*:

Serving, yet asking no gratitude;
Engendering, yet not claiming ownership.[89]

If one abides by this counsel, one will not glory in one's accomplishments,[90] and if one refrains from glorying in one's accomplishments, one will not invite resentment from others but instead realize one's hopes naturally and never tire in one's labors. The efficacy of that phrase is considerable. In later times, if there is anyone who shares my feelings, I invite him to test the matter.

———————————

At the age of nineteen, I left home and began my struggle to keep body and soul together. Before that, I had been caring for my mother but feared that I was only adding to her anxieties. My house was so poor that I couldn't buy books or seek instruction from a master. So I ended up making a circuit of the country about four times, which took me over five years. After that, I did return to Kyoto, but had to spend my energy treating patients and wore myself out with teaching. I had no time for scholarship and accumulated no merit from my writings. Furthermore, since my youth I've been sickly. I'm skinny as a stray dog, four times I have suffered from nearly fatal bouts of dysentery and a bout of influenza and another

88. A Daoist classic, attributed to Zhuang Zhou (369?–286? B.C.E.).
89. *Daodejing*, sec. 2. See Lao Tzu, *Tao Te Ching*, trans. D. C. Lau (New York: Addison Wesley, 1964), 58. Nankei has reversed the order of the statements.
90. The next line in the *Daodejing* reads, "Achieving merit, but not claiming it."

of the shivers, and I've never made it through a single year without being down in bed for a month or two with ailments less serious. Since the age of thirty-eight, I've been stricken with asthma, which put an end to my writing and reading. Because of my asthma, in fact, I have been unable to realize either my ambitions in scholarship or the possibility of worldly success, having instead to withdraw from worldly affairs and be satisfied with just nursing myself along. Life doesn't last for even a hundred years, and still nothing goes how one would like.

The upheavals attendant upon the Great Kyoto Fire of the Tenmei era[91] cured some people who had been suffering from madness. Of course, there were also lots of other people who *went* mad because of the disturbance. That some were cured, however, is extraordinary. In all things, what does great harm also does great good.

[*HOKUSŌ SADAN*, ED. MIURA OSAMU, NIHON ZUIHITSU ZENSHŪ 4 (TOKYO: KOKUMIN TOSHO, 1927). I HAVE ALSO CONSULTED THE MODERN JAPANESE TRANSLATION OF PORTIONS OF THE TEXT BY MORI SENZŌ, IN *EDO ZUISŌ SHŪ*, KOTEN NIHON BUNGAKU ZENSHŪ 35 (TOKYO: CHIKUMA SHOBŌ, 1961)]

91. See note 3.

16

Blossoms and the Moon

MATSUDAIRA SADANOBU

Matsudaira Sadanobu (1758-1829) was a high-ranking official in the Tokugawa government. He is known primarily as the man responsible for the Kansei Reforms of the late eighteenth century, which aimed at restoring stability to the government, fiscally and institutionally. After suffering political reversals, however, Sadanobu resigned from government service in 1793 and dedicated much of the rest of his life to scholarly and artistic pursuits.

In addition to treatises on politics and economics, he wrote a short work of fiction (published anonymously) and the miscellany Kagetsu sōshi (Blossoms and the Moon). *The essays that make up this work were written between 1796 and 1803. Often cautionary in tone, his essays are considered models of* gabuntai, *a kind of neoclassical style reminiscent of the great works of the court tradition.*

Once there was an old man who had lived a long time in a village by the sea.[1] During interludes when he rested from cutting seaweed and burning it down for salt, he collected useless scraps of paper and stuck them in the outer hinge of his window, where an idler happening by made off with them. When the idler went back the next year, he found that

---

1. A thinly veiled reference to the author.

more scraps had been left there, most casually; and so, like white-capped waves[2] breaking on the shore, he came back again and again, until he had such a pile of papers that he made them into this book. It was the idler who gave the book its title, having in mind the way the first of the scraps goes on about blossoms and the moon. "No more than the chirping of fisherfolk," someone from the village was heard to say.

———————

Speaking against what you are told, saying yes when others say no, calling good what others call bad—such things are perverse indeed. Nevertheless, despite knowing that the cherry blossom was supposedly peculiar to our country, still I thought that it must exist in China as well and did a good deal of searching, in the end finding not one Chinese painting of cherry blossoms and not a single poem that seemed to refer to that plant. Thus I must conclude that cherry blossoms indeed do not exist in China.

Now then: call them just blossoms or call them cherry blossoms, no one will mistake the cherry for any other tree.[3] It would be vain to mention only the sight of blossoms so grand on a mountain ridge in the first light of dawn that one thinks they might be clouds or snow, or so bright on a hazy evening that a faint view of them seems to reveal one place where the day has not yet ended. And all the more haughty would it seem to say that the loose calyx of the blossoms makes them less excellent when seen up close. Whether tossed on wind or drenched by rain, viewed on far-off mountains or close-up near the eaves of one's house, at dawn or in evening light—in all these situations, one cannot take one's eyes off them, not even for the moment it takes dew to fade away. Moreover, the plant seems especially suited to the ways of our country, with branches so fine, flowers so delicate in shape, and hues so simple that the ultimate effect is perfect beyond belief. And yet it is true that they are found everywhere, and to multiply words insisting that they are more alluring at dawn or at dusk would reveal only that one has not yet considered the matter deeply. Only those of shallow feeling would think that such things could be explained by an abundance of words.

2. *Shiranami.* A metaphor for thieves.
3. Unless otherwise qualified, in classical texts the word *hana* ("blossom" or "flower") usually refers to the cherry blossom.

The rising of the moon calls to mind the sky at dawn. Off where clouds trail along the horizon, the moon begins to shine, only to hesitate among the treetops on far mountains, still out of sight, before it finally rises into view. Just when you think the gloom above the treetops has lifted, however, a single cloud appears, drawing near to the moon at the same time that the moon, unfortunately, moves also into it. For a while you watch, wondering what will come next, as the cloud brightens on one edge. But then again, just when you think the light has emerged completely, another white cloud appears, as if lying in wait. And so in consternation you gaze up, with the light issuing forth from the first cloud seeming so new, so bright, that it is painful indeed to see that waiting cloud. Once the moon has gone inside it, though, the cloud is not so inconsiderate, for here and there you can catch glimpses of light, and as you watch, not so resentful now, the sleeves of your robe grow more and more damp, and both dew and insects flourish. There, gazing so intently at the moon, you think to yourself, "Here the heart has no limits."

———————

"I will leave it up to the distant skies, and not depend on my own puny talents," so the saying goes. Yet one should ponder carefully before leaving things up to heaven. For even when you can see starlight, a rough wind may come up offshore. Thus to get on a boat only after learning beforehand that the winds will blow here around noon tomorrow—that is what "leaving things up to heaven" should mean; while rowing out without even asking whether the wind is blowing offshore, all because the waves are calm where you are at the moment—this is not the same thing. The same is true even of eating: only after taking the greatest care and doing all one can to nurture one's body should one leave one's fate up to heaven—although I suppose there are those who say that they are leaving everything up to heaven by giving no attention to nourishment and just following their desires.

———————

Snow had fallen, and since it seemed a shame to have the blinds down, the empress said, "How is the snow on that high peak?"

How fine it was of the lady to merely smile and, without arising herself but also without desisting, say quietly to the maids, "Put the blinds up."[4]

Someone praises a man who has spent years by his window, gathering snow and fireflies for light, using all his energy in reading books and remaining removed from things of the world—proclaiming him one who truly pursues the Way of Learning. But what is it that truly constitutes the Way of Learning if not beginning with the Five Ways[5] and learning to govern others and oneself? We should praise as pursuer of the Way of Learning only the person who not just knows about his own world in the present but also is enlightened on everything else—things of a thousand years past, unseen things of China now or long ago, the signs of prosperity and decline, the thoughts of people's hearts—indeed, everything down to the details of how to serve one's lord. Someone once said, "How can one call a man who is ignorant of the world around him one who truly pursues the Way of Learning?"

In a time of drought, the east wind blows your way, clouds form, and you think, "Ah, today it will rain." Then the wind suddenly dies, the clouds break up, and the sunlight begins to beam down once more. Or, again, after the rains have continued for some time and you hear the wind sounding strong in the pines, you feel sure the skies will soon clear. As you watch the way clumps of cloud turn green over here and deep red over where the sun is going down, you think, "Ah, the moon will shine brightly tonight!" But then, when the moon does come out, clouds form and you hear the sound of raindrops. I hear it said that this is the way also with times of unrest and times of order, and with the state of our hearts.

---

4. An allusion to a famous anecdote in Sei Shōnagon's *Pillow Book*. See Sei Shōnagon, *The Pillow Book*, sec. 280 (chap. 1). Sei's order to the maids showed that she was able to identify a poem by Bo Juyi (772–846) to which the empress was alluding and respond according to the model of the poem, in which the narrator, in bed on a chilly morning, pushes the blinds up to get a glimpse of snow on nearby Xianglu Peak.

5. A Confucian term referring to the qualities of benevolence, righteousness, ceremony, knowledge, and trustworthiness.

A doctor told someone, "Come autumn, you are sure to be stricken with some illness." But the man only replied testily, "How can that be?" He was fine until autumn arrived, when he did indeed take ill. Too embarrassed to face the first doctor, he called for another one instead, and that doctor tried various medicines, none of which worked. At first, the latter doctor thought the problem must be in the abdomen, so he tried medicine for the stomach, but this gave the man chest pains and he lost interest in food, so the doctor desisted. Then the doctor tried sweat treatments, but those didn't work either, and when he tried laxatives, it made the pain in the man's belly even worse. At wit's end, the doctor prepared yet another medicine, just to see if it might help, and as soon as the man drank it down, his chest did indeed feel better, and before long he was cured. Realizing that he owed the doctor his life, the man would have done nearly anything to reward him, even up to giving him all his wealth.

In another case, a doctor told a man that in autumn he was sure to suffer a certain ailment and should begin taking the prescribed medicine right away. "How can that be?" the man said. But then he thought, "After what he said, I guess I should go ahead and take it," and took the medicine, though without much enthusiasm. Then later, when he did not take ill, he said, "Just as I thought—I would have been just fine even without the medicine."

———————

Said a man who was good at remembering things that he had stored away in his mind, "Long ago in a certain place, I climbed into the mountains, where I found on one peak a number of pines, one of them with limbs drooping thus and so around a single tree that towered above the rest. Next to it was a large black pine, which had grown outward horizontally, with green vines hanging on it."

At this, someone said, "My, what a memory for details! Did you perchance model your own garden on that mountain? I remember seeing a black pine there amid other pine trees; but just how was everything laid out?"

The man then said, "Was there a black pine in my garden? I see it so often that I have quite forgotten."

————————

I gave some rice to an Ainu man, and he took it happily but then spilled a lot of it in the process of eating.

"Hey you," I said, "don't you know that rice is what sustains life? How can you waste it so?"

"Oh, but we don't depend on rice for life," he said. "No, we rely on a fish called salmon."

So I said, "If that's so—if you do sustain life by eating salmon—then you should respect salmon, right? But aren't those things on your feet made of salmon skin?"

The man cocked his head a moment and then said, "But those sandals you're wearing—aren't they made of grass from the rice plant?"

We shouldn't ridicule the Ainu, someone said. Since people of our country know little of outsiders, there are many of us who think that just because they don't look like us the Ainu are all stupid and ignorant. This is why there are those who laugh out loud when they see someone who looks unusual, or when they hear words that they cannot understand, whether from a Chinese person or an Ainu. This is because such people are narrow-minded and have not seen the outside world.

————————

"On a moonlit night, no worries trouble one's thoughts and one's heart is clear down to the very depths," someone says. "Yet I feel that a dark night, when the sky is free of clouds and the stars are shining bright, with the wind coursing high above—that is somehow superior."

To this, another replies, "But a rainy night is even better."

"How so?" comes the rejoinder.

"Well, consider the rain in a time of drought—that goes without saying. Then, too, the flowers that bloom on grasses and trees are a result of the blessing of the rain, are they not? And, to speak of the profoundest of feelings, just think of the first day of the year when the rain comes softly down, creating a mist all around that makes one feel that spring has truly arrived. Or think how intrigued one is by the gentle rain on the last day of the old year that seems to be anxious for spring to begin.

"The rains of spring are always mild. Out by the eaves spreads a mist so fine that though one's robes become damp, no rain seems to be falling at all. Everything about the scene is mild—the way an abandoned spider's web on the eaves is strung with beads of water, where the sound of raindrops seems far away; the way green growth begins to show itself low on the withered grasses of the garden; the way raindrops accumulate on willow branches still unmoved by wind. One lights a lamp, and its light seems moist, as the faint tolling of the evening bell clears the heart. The damp scent of plum blossoms spreading abroad in the depths of night, and even one's complaints against the rain on behalf of the blossoms—these, too, are most touching. And when spring grows old, how attractive are the gathering voices of frogs, claiming the season as their own.

"Wondering when the first cuckoo will call, one may hear the pitter-patter of raindrops coming down. Or one may be spending all one's hours leafing through books as the rains of the Fifth Month persist, leaving one feeling more and more distant from the ways of the world as time goes on. Or, just when the heat seems most unbearable, the clouds above may roil with rain, the winds descend in a rush, and the leaves and the willows and lotus plants appear to turn white—a most cooling scene. Then, when the big raindrops that had seemed so far away finally come, falling so hard now that one can hear nothing else, one may catch the scent of wet earth and feel renewed. A curtain of raindrops hangs from the eaves, and the constant downpour makes the garden into a lake, here a waterfall, there a running stream, with people—most amusingly—just watching it all in silence. Then the clouds thin out, with a few raindrops still splashing here and there on the pond, as the birds prance about in the garden searching for food. Off where the clouds first arose, the sky is showing blue, as a rainbow appears. And how cool one feels looking at the reflections of trees in the puddles in the garden!

"Startled by the thunder, an old woman crawls out and says, 'How nicely the sky has cleared, just like when I was young; these days it rarely clears up so well,' and babbles on while the people around laugh at her for making such a fuss. 'There won't be many mosquitoes today, with the thunder sounding so faintly; I can almost forget how hot it's been,' someone says, going out onto the veranda to enjoy the captivating sight of light from the evening moon shining everywhere, making waterdrops on the bushes shine like jewels, while fat frogs, gazing up into the sky as if waiting for something, call out in clumsy voices.

"The rain of autumn seems different from what it was just a few days before, and sadder, somehow. The wind blowing over the reeds, the call of a deer crying in the foothills—these seem to strike more deeply into the heart than even the moonlight. The sound of the bamboo water pipe that one is so used to hearing seems even more moving.

"Also captivating are rain showers passing in front of the moon. And more moving still is the sound of crickets in the chill of night, their voices hoarse from wear, calling out feebly near one's pillow during a short break in the rain. 'Surely this rain will be dyeing the leaves,' one thinks, only to hear a different reaction from one's children, who, crowded around a lamp, chatter forlornly about how the bamboo shoots will be coming up and the chestnuts will be falling.

"A bell ringing out late at night always sounds damp, but in autumn the sound takes on a special chill, calling to mind nights spent waiting for someone or times of parting, so much so that one's feelings grow even deeper, reaching out in sympathy to the one who strikes the bell. The rich colors of the autumn leaves, the final flourishing of faded chrysanthemums in the moment before they die, the resentful look of gentian in bloom while the eulalia bends under heavy dew—all seem somehow appropriate to the season. And how moving it is that the morning glories, blooming in bright purple amid the general withering, should stave off their decline until after noon.

"Monsoon winds are a fearsome thing, and the rain they bring is no less fierce than the rain of a summer thunderstorm, so the lonely feeling they inspire can be attributed only to autumn's melancholy. Suddenly one hears the sound of showers falling whitely in the evening sunlight—a yet different sound and very alluring.

"So, don't you agree, then?" the man says. "Isn't a rainy night more moving than a moonlit night, or a night of darkness?"

I answer to myself, "After running through all those examples, I am quite ready to agree, but listening to you go through them makes me feel like I've just been through a whole year of rain. And this rain we're having now started only the day before yesterday, and already I'm tired of it—and that hasn't changed!"

Principle[6] of course dictates that in summer one wear robes of hemp and in winter, robes of cotton. But when it is overcast, one may also wear cotton robes in summer; and when an odd warm spell comes in winter, one may wear a single thin set of robes. Those who insist on doing precisely as principle dictates in such cases will become ill. The same will happen to anyone who in our time tries to pacify the country and the people with principle alone.

It is said that a person can see the unseen and hear the unheard, having penetrated to the truth, but this is true only of those who have truly arrived.[7] Did not Confucius himself say that he could follow his own ears only at age sixty?[8] Anyone troubled by even the slightest desire, not to mention those steeped in love or in thrall to the senses, will be alienated from the truth and never arrive. A person who excels in the way of the bow, gaining the deepest secrets of that Way, has of course gained the ultimate truths of the bow; but would he think to use that knowledge to ride a horse?

"It is because they in truth know nothing of a certain Way that some speak of what is difficult as being easy," someone once said.

It is written that the Komatsu Palace Minister[9] prayed, "I would rather leave this world behind now than live to see the end of the Heike clan," but that can't be true. If he ever did say such a thing, then he must have been fainthearted. His duty was to live on to see the future of the clan,

---

6. Ch. *li*, J. *kotowari*. Here Sadanobu uses the term to mean "logic" or "established convention."

7. *Sakai ni itaru.* To arrive after patient effort and study.

8. An allusion to a statement in the *Analects*. See Confucius, *The Analects*, trans. D. C. Lau (New York: Penguin, 1979), 63. The phrase "follow his own ears" means to act immediately without rational analysis, "principle" having been so completely ingrained over time that acting accordingly seems natural.

9. Taira no Shigemori (1138–1179), one of the leaders of the Taira coalition, which eventually lost to Minamoto Yoritomo's forces during the Genpei Wars.

doing all in his power to correct their mistakes and encourage them. Praying to leave this world before facing up to that duty would be evidence of a weak will. I believe that the statement must have been attributed to him later by some Buddhist priest.

Comments made by bystanders often turn out to be true. Someone says, "My, how that fellow has aged," even though the man himself doesn't see it when he looks in the mirror. Or someone says, "Now he acts this way, but later he will regret it," whereas the one referred to is oblivious. If not for our self-centeredness, we might see what those next to us see.

In *An Outline for Composing Poetry*, Teika[10] says, "In feeling, seek the new,"[11] and so on, but this means something along the lines of "Every day is a new day," just as water flowing by is "new." To substitute bad for good, or good for bad, is modish, but I would not call it new. To see blossoms as clouds, or snow as blossoms—no matter how many times one says such things, they are new if they come from within your heart. Something that stands out just for the sake of standing out is not "new."[12]

When the blossoms are out, rain begins to fall, and a breeze comes along with it.

I heard someone say, "At blossom time, spring rain and wind always come, too, as if to show us that in this world the time of parting must come. Still, how one hates the rain, how one despises the wind!"

But another person said, "True, the rain may fall, but it's not like the summer rains; however intense, it doesn't come down like a thunder shower in summer. And the wind may blow, but not like the typhoons of late autumn or the storm winds of winter. If you resent the fate of the blossoms, you must want a world with no rain or wind at all."

10. Fujiwara no Teika (1162–1241), one of the chief poets of the early medieval era. Later generations looked to him as the founding figure of their tradition.
11. A quotation from *Eiga taigai* (*Essentials of Composition*, after 1221). See Hisamatsu Sen'ichi, *Chūsei karonshū* (Tokyo: Iwanami bunko, 1934), 188.
12. A fundamental tenet of the orthodox Nijō school of poetry.

For three or four years, a certain man never went out his gate, but spent all his time reading, without even sleeping, until at last he fell ill. At this, someone said, "Reading makes you sick; I won't do it." Another person replied, "If you saw someone spend all his time drinking saké and then fall ill, would you stop drinking?"

———

He would not exchange him for anything, this child crawling about. "This child of mine is sure to do well in the future. Show him a breast, and he crawls after it. Go against his desires, and he'll pick up whatever is to hand and strike out. Just take a look at the scratch on my forehead. That's where he hit me with my own pipe! Even when it's his own parent, he does things like that—and that shows real self-confidence. He's strong beyond his years, that's what this scratch shows." So the parent exults, rubbing his wound all the while.

A fool laughs, but the parent is at least smarter than that.

———

There is a river in Settsu Province. On its banks stands a brewery that uses the river water to make saké known as the finest saké under all of heaven.

Upriver from the brewery lived a tanner who put stakes in the river and used the place to soak animal skins. One year, someone complained about this. "We offer saké to the gods and the Buddhas. I wonder whether it's right to use water from a river where skins are soaked.[13] Let's have the tanner move downriver," and it was done as he requested.

From that time onward, the saké they made there just wasn't the same, no matter what they did. Now it appears that they are secretly using water downriver from where the skins are soaked to make their saké.

———

Someone asked an old man, "That fellow—what sort of person is he?"

13. Anything tainted with blood was considered unclean.

"A good man," was his answer.

Then someone asked, "And what about that fellow over there?"

"A good man," he said.

The person asking the questions then chose a person he himself would surely say was bad and queried the old man again, but got the same answer—"A good man."

"How so?" the inquirer asked.

"When looking at people, I judge a man to be good if he has five good qualities out of ten. And if a person who has one or two good qualities out of ten, I also see him as a good man. So: I wouldn't call a man bad unless he is bad on all ten points."

This is how he judged other people—it would not work as a way to judge oneself. In judging good and bad, it is always a question of degrees.

Nothing is more delightful than the scenery of the four seasons as they change, but oh how it pains the heart as we yearn for flowers before their season or worry about their demise while they are still in their prime! Yet it is because they perish that they will bloom again in a year. And no matter how much we may fret, it is senseless to expect the lotus to bloom when the frost is shining white and the pond is frozen solid.

Yet still the Way is to wait anxiously for the flowers to appear and to resent their falling. Only someone who does not understand the Way would remain aloof and put all thoughts of their passing aside.

A lowly man stopped eating the rice that he would normally eat and sold it for gold, which he put in a pouch and carried around with him, thinking that he would not trade it even for his very life. At the end of autumn, a flood came, and he hung his pouch around his neck and made off for high ground; but the water rose so fast that he had no choice but to scramble up a tree, though he knew that he would face starvation.

Just then, he saw a man swimming by with a little bundle of rice on his back. Showing him his pouch of money, the man said, "I'll give you this—just share a little of the rice you're carrying."

The other man said angrily, "What a stupid thing to say! What good is gold at a time like this?" and swam away.

———————

Once there was a most elegant man who lived above the clouds.[14] He was sitting with his son when the wind blowing from outside made the flame of the lamp flicker, upon which the young man summoned a servant, saying, "The wind's blowing—get a screen up so it doesn't put the lamp out." Hearing this, the father became quite out of sorts and upbraided his son, saying, "How can anyone who uses words in such a way expect to compose poetry?" At this, the young man became fearful and withdrew. Wondering what lesson the father had intended, those in the room inquired. The father said, "One should not put everything into words."

———————

A certain nobleman said, "When you're on the road, you should go to bed early and rest thoroughly, and then you won't suffer at all. The best thing is to leave one's inn early and arrive at the next one early, too. This should please the servants, since it will be to their benefit."

So the man would arrive early at an inn, shut his windows, light the lanterns, and go to bed about two in the afternoon. His servants, however, could not simply do just as they wished, since it was not the time when most people retire. Afternoons are busy, with travelers always going by, and one couldn't very well say to people, "It's nighttime." By the time they did get to bed, their lord would be getting up, in the middle of the night, and gathering everyone together to leave.

The man thought that he was being considerate of those below him, but he was not really being considerate at all. When you think that you are being kind but don't really know anything about the lives of those beneath you, this is what happens.

———————

A certain doctor put his whole heart into treating anyone who was ill, whether high or low.

14. A metaphor for the imperial court.

Once a very poor person was terribly sick. The doctor had opened his medicine box and begun mixing up a treatment when an old woman—the patient's mother—who had been watching him most intently crept forward on her knees and said, "I hesitate to impose, but I would like to make a request of you . . ."

When she seemed unable to finish what she had to say, the doctor said, "Please just tell me what you are thinking, whatever it is."

In reply the woman, with great deference and in a quivering voice, said, "Might we also have some of the medicine that you have placed in the bottom of your box?"

Although taken aback, the doctor smiled and said, "Why of course!" Then he took out two or three harmless medicines, prepared them, and told the woman, "These should work nicely."

Even if he had tried to talk seriously with such an ignorant person—explaining that this particular illness called for such and such a treatment, using this medicine and that, which he had taken from the top of the box only because they just happened to be there; and explaining that just because a particular medicine came from the bottom of the box didn't mean that it was of lesser value—she would not have understood. The way he let her have her way as long as it would do no harm was very impressive.

———————

Once there was a man who would always give food to a fox that came by every night. Since the fox was one of the most intelligent of beasts, he thought it would someday repay him for his generosity. So every day, without fail, he left some food, until the fox became accustomed to it. Then on a certain day, the man's horse foaled, and he was so busy that for two days he forgot to put food out, at which the fox—out of resentment, perhaps—ate the foal.

———————

In one's personal conduct, in one's relations with other people, or in one's government responsibilities—in everything, one must not forget the word "new." Indeed, in all matters one must always be inclined each day toward what is new. Too many people continue on in what they learned yesterday, even if it was mistaken, and make blunders because they blithely assume they must have been right. The reason even the wise are led astray by women or deceived by foolish men is that they do not always stop to consider things anew. I have also heard of cases where people went astray because they finally got accustomed to something hateful to them or tired of something that had formerly been a source of pleasure. An old man once said that the importance of starting afresh each day in all things was a tenet one should hold to all one's life.

In those who have grown old and had their teeth out, the workings of the spleen and stomach will also go bad, so that, unlike when they were young, they must eat soft things. If they insist on eating hard things, they will suffer in the end. Also, since those who have become hard of hearing cannot hear what is going on, it is only natural that they should become withdrawn and not be involved in things. If they do mix with people, they will not know when they are being scoffed or laughed at. Someone said that such things happen when we go against the way of things, even in the smallest of matters.

Warts began to appear on the neck of a certain woman, growing to great numbers in the space of a single night; then another woman got warts on her forehead, which came to look like the skin of a shark, covered with warts more numerous than the stars on a warrior's helmet. Being a woman, the first victim noised her grief about and learned that in Meguro[15] there was a temple to Takoyakushi, the Octopus Healer, in whom she proceeded to invest all her faith, pledging not to eat any octopus and then putting her heart into prayers for a whole night. When the new day dawned and she washed her hands and face as usual, the warts began to fall off, two or three at a time. This made her so happy that she put her heart even more fully into the task, with the result that all the warts fell off within two or three days. The woman with warts on her

15. An area of Edo.

forehead learned from this example, and her warts dried up just as red pox do, then became flaky like frost and disappeared.

Someone said, "If only people with these spiritual gifts were more earnest, what troubles would they have?"

———————

There once was a man who was in a very sorry state because his legs were afflicted and he could not walk. Three years had passed, and he was not even a little better.

A doctor said to the man, "Here—I'm giving you this medicine. Take it for three years, and you'll get better."

"I shall drink it, then," the man replied.

Someone standing nearby said, "Three more years? Why, that's six years in all that he'll have to suffer."

"Not true," said the doctor. "As he takes the medicine over the three years in order to attain full recovery, he will show some improvement after the first year and be even better by the end of the second. In this way, he will have completely recovered in three years. After being like this for three years already, how can one expect him to recover immediately? If it means improving a little each year from now on, he should take the medicine for ten years, let alone three."

———————

A man who was fond of gardens said, "Here we will raise a mountain, plant these trees there, build a pond, and put trees of various kinds on its banks."

When someone asked, "When will you build?" the man said, "First off, we will move these trees over there—because they are beautiful in spring—while these others we will move in the autumn. After we have finished the work of transplanting, we will dig the pond and use the dirt to raise our mountain."

Then someone said, "But you are usually so quick to get things done, and what you said will take a long time. Why, even in several years' time the place will not look like a garden."

The man replied, "If I plant these trees now, they are sure to wither and die; so I have not the least desire to plant them now. No, these I will plant at the beginning of winter and those over there at the beginning of summer, whereas these grasses I will plant after the new growth has come out. If I were to plant on the mountain big trees that are impressive to look at now, their branches would only wither and destroy the view; so I will plant small trees five or six feet in height that will grow naturally on the mountain and create a view of truly great beauty. How could such a thing be accomplished in two or three years? I will have to wait perhaps ten years for the view to be interesting. Since I know that this is not something to do hastily, I have not the least desire to begin in a rush. That you want results quickly shows that you don't truly know about planting trees."

He also said to someone, "To know may seem simply to know; but to not know for certain—one cannot call that knowing at all. That man who dangled his fishing line long ago, now he was one who truly knew his time."[16]

———————————

There once was a man who predicted the weather. "Tomorrow it will snow," he said, but on that day it didn't snow. "Strong winds are going to come up," he said, but on that day no wind blew.

When people asked him to account for this, he said, "It didn't snow here, but it snowed somewhere. And the wind didn't blow here, but it did blow somewhere else." This, of course, made people laugh.

Later, it turned out that snow had indeed fallen on the day in question at Hakone, and that the wind had blown in Musashi. But if your forecast isn't correct for the place where you make it, you can't avoid being laughed at. It would be better not to say anything at all.

———————————

"From birth to old age, if one works hard, never slacking, one is sure to excel at whatever one does," someone said.

In reply, another person said, "But if you don't take care in what you do, you will never succeed, no matter how many times you try. For in-

16. Taigong Wang, founder of the state of Qi in ancient times, was an adviser to two kings during the early Zhou dynasty (1046–256 B.C.E.). He had removed himself from worldly affairs when, while out fishing, he was approached about serving.

stance: from the time you first become aware of things, you eat rice and slurp broth three times every day; but if you put no thought into it, you will not become skillful at eating but will instead only spill your food all over the place and end up choking on fish bones. To succeed in anything, one must first have that single aspiration—to do it well."

A woman named Imamairi was still young when she came up from the countryside to go into service, so people were always playing tricks on her. At dusk one day, she went out on an errand.

"It won't be completely dark when she gets back. Let's give her a scare," the women thought, and put a white silk robe just inside the gate, where the willows grew very thick, making it up to look like a woman with her hair in disarray.

When Imamairi returned, it was just dark enough that it was getting hard to make things out. As she passed the willows, all the women peeked out, stifling their excitement as they waited for her to scream and come running in. But she came right inside without so much as a word.

"We've heard that of late there's been a demon of some sort around those willows," they said. "Did you see anything?"

"Yes," she replied, showing no surprise, "I did see a woman in a white robe standing by the willows."

"How is it that you weren't frightened, then?" they asked.

"When I left for the city," she said, "my mother gave me amulets—of Lady Kannon[17] and the God of Kitano[18]—and told me never to be without them. 'If you encounter a demon, they will be there; if someone tries to kill you, they will protect you. There wouldn't be any demons at all if there were no gods and Buddhas.'"

On understanding people: it is only from an unbiased position that one can see clearly. Something leaning one way is no longer straight. If your own heart is clouded, how can you shine light on that of another? You

17. A Buddhist bodhisattva, sometimes called the Goddess of Mercy.
18. Kitano Tenjin, the deity of Kitano Shrine.

may try to use your knowledge and wits, but at times you will yourself be in the dark. How, then, can you illuminate others?

Someone compared governing to flying a kite, in terms of making use of opportunity, energy, and elevation.

"If we are speaking of Edo, grasping opportunity would be like waiting for springtime. For wind, you would use your own vitality, and gaining elevation would mean attaining high position so that you could release your kite at a place above the tops of all the trees. For string and the other things you need for kites, you have people. Then you must gain the skill to gauge the wind and deal with the tail and the string as you reel it in, let it out, and so forth. By skill, I mean nothing more than getting the kite up: it is not something that requires much cleverness. One who desires to save the people—who are benighted and foolish—cannot very well go door to door explaining things to each of them, so one simply adopts a strategy and tries to stay on the path.

"If you get no results even when your ideas are good, it's because you haven't given sufficient consideration to those three things," he said.

A man said, "Anyone who hates the cold stays away from cold; anyone who hates the heat avoids exposure to it. It is the man who says he's in the best of health and never tires even when walking a long distance who often develops an ailment of the legs. The man who says his eyesight is so good that he can see anything, whether far off or up close, is sure to come down with an ailment of the eyes. Yet someone who complains every day, today a headache, yesterday congestion in the chest, and so on—such a person rarely gets gravely ill. And someone who says, 'Since my youth, I've never taken much medicine, and I'm never sick,' will soon catch a serious disease."

A man of noble stature heard this and nodded his head in agreement, it is said.

A man and wife are on the way to divorce if they forget the feelings they had when they got up after spending their first night together, someone said.

There was a kind of bug that lived in the feathers of a hawk. When the hawk flew high into the sky, looking down on the houses of men far below, he thought to himself, "I am truly without peer, for without moving my wings I can sail over a thousand *li*,[19] rising even beyond the clouds; and I send other birds fleeing in fright, for there is none that can best me."

Yet in the same hawk's feathers lived bugs that pierced his flesh and sucked his blood until—because they became so numerous—the hawk collapsed. In response, the bugs first tried to fly away themselves but could not succeed in getting off the ground, and then tried to run but could not get up any speed. With the hawk's blood all gone and his flesh dried up, the bugs had no way to sustain life, and so they left. Just as they had succeeded in making their way out from among the hawk's feathers, a baby sparrow showed up. "Certainly he will fear us," the bugs thought, but the baby sparrow was unimpressed; and when they crawled over toward the bird, thinking that he could not fail to see what they were, the bird suddenly became happy, stuck out his beak, and began to peck at them. So amazed were the bugs that they became frightened and hid themselves—so said the friend who told me this story.

[*KAGETSU SŌSHI*, ED. MATSUDAIRA SADAMITSU AND NISHIO MINORU (TOKYO: IWANAMI BUNKO, 1939)]

19. A traditional Chinese unit of distance, now standardized at 1,640 feet.

17

Year by Year: A Miscellany

ISHIWARA MASAAKIRA

Although born into a farm family, Ishiwara Masaakira (d. 1821) displayed bookish tendencies from an early age and lived at a time when even someone from the provinces—he came from Owari, east of Kyoto on the Tōkai Road—could attach himself to a teacher and hope for a place in the scholarly world. Going up to Nagoya, he at first studied ancient ceremonial and traditional legal codes, eventually enrolling as a disciple of Motoori Norinaga's. Seeking some kind of government position, he went up to Edo in 1801, but, lacking political skills and experience, failed to find a place for himself. Fortunately, however, he soon became known to the textual scholar Hanawa Hokinoichi.[1] Under the latter's direction, Masaakira played a major part in the compilation and editing of Gunsho ruijū (Classified Collection of Books, 1793–1819), *one of the first large collections of Japanese literature ever produced in Japan. While in Edo, he lived first in Shinagawa and later in Ichigaya. In addition to his work as an editor, he was active as a* waka *poet and wrote several scholarly treatises and commentaries, as well as the work from which the selections here are taken,* Nennen zuihitsu (Year by Year: A Miscellany), *a four-volume miscellany produced between 1801 and 1805.*

Snow is beautiful wherever it falls, but especially awe-inspiring at seaside. Particularly delightful is the sight of two or three boats moored at

---

1. 1746–1821. Known for his work in literature and medicine.

an inlet, glimpsed through gaps between a few broken reeds, their sedge-topped cabins white with snow.

In a market town, there is usually nothing to attract the eye, but even such a place is a rare delight on a snowy morning. Wherever the snow has fallen, the scene is transformed. The sun rises, everyone gets up, and the streets are so bad that people have trouble walking about—a real vexation, one must admit. But how sad it is to hear them making a fuss, saying, "Come on, shovel it up! Get it out of the way!"

It must have been about four years ago. It was in the Ninth Month of the year when I moved into the house at Shinagawa[2] where I now live. Few leaves were left on the surrounding wild grasses, and the garden had so gone to seed that the place didn't seem fit for human habitation. It was a deserted field, really; except for children passing through, there were no signs of life, not even rabbit trails. Yet here, choked by tangles of weeds, was my little house, standing by itself—my mansion, albeit one without a single samurai in its guardhouse, a place where I lived my days entirely alone.

On the last day of the Tenth Month, the wind was blowing hard, so I snuggled up to my charcoal brazier and gazed out at the evening sky, quite overcome with regrets. Looking out on that blank and colorless scene, I drank two or three cups of saké, and when I got sleepy merely lay down right where I was. When I awoke, the lattice shutters were still up and my lamp had not been lit. Yet while I had slept, the frost-seared field of weeds before me had been covered everywhere with dewdrops that sparkled in the moonlight.

Thus what had been a sorry abode had become a place of indescribable beauty.

2. Located just south of Edo, on Tokyo Bay.

How captivating it is, at the end of the Ninth Month or the beginning of the Tenth, to pass by a mountain ravine that opens itself a little to view. Some leaves are crimson, some golden, some richer in color and some fainter, some with scent and some without, each moving and beautiful in its own way. It's also captivating the way the lower leaves on evergreens of deep green take on other hues. In the Edo area, the best places are Meguro,[3] Sugatami Bridge,[4] and the gardens around me here in Shinagawa.

Ueno[5] always offers fine views, with its thousands of cherry trees mixed in among evergreens, a place as captivating as Arashiyama[6] in its way. In summer, the new growth comes in so thick that it keeps the sunshine at a distance—while through gaps in lower branches, one gazes out on lotus flowers occupying the whole expanse of Shinobazu Pond.[7] A trailing breeze blows coolly by, carrying a faint but delightful scent. When the autumn leaves appear, the scene is also beyond the power of words to describe.

Evening—yes, surely evening is the best time of day. All traces of rain showers vanish, a cool wind blows, and white clouds hover on the mountain rim, where rays from a waning moon seem about to break through here and there.

But, no—surely morning time is best. A half sun rises with a red glow like smoldering fire, set off against the deep green of pine groves on the peak above.

3. Located in southern Edo, not far from Shinagawa.
4. Located in northwestern Edo, near the Takata Riding Grounds.
5. Located just north of Kanda, in central Edo. A favorite spot for picnics, blossom viewing, and other outings, it is now the site of a large garden and museum.
6. An area just west of Kyoto famous for its seasonal delights.
7. A large pond, now located within the confines of Ueno Park.

How fine a thing is dawn! Although I live in a place quite cut off from the world, there are always things to distract me in the daytime; and in the evening, fatigue from the day's exertions builds up until I grow sleepy. At around two in the morning, however, when I get up and sit down at my desk to read, there is not a sound to be heard from any quarter and my heart is clear and calm. In the winter, when the cold wind blowing in through cracks in my walls has me stirring up the coals in my charcoal brazier, I hear the sound of a bell booming at a distant mountain temple and feel how far removed I am from the affairs of men. In spring, amid a constant drizzle, I hear the patter of raindrops falling on withered oak leaves. In summer, I leave my door of black pine open despite the pesky mosquitoes and let the light of the waning moon shine in through my window. And in autumn, moved by the sound of wild geese and crickets, I feel like weeping with them through the night.

In a *zuihitsu*, one records things that one sees and hears, says and ponders, whether frivolous or serious, just as they come to mind. One may forget something one knows well and say something mistaken about it, with the result that some shallow thinking may enter into the mix. Unable to put things down in language that is elegant and precise, one may produce something lacking in polish or a bit clumsy—an unappealing prospect. Yet precisely because it is not carefully fashioned, one's feelings, talents, and character show through, making for something truly interesting.

In Master Motoori's *Tamakatsuma*,[8] he refers to the word *sayomi*[9] as mentioned in *Azuma kagami*,[10] wondering if it might be what is now called *saimi*. For this, he was scorned among Edo pedants, who pointed out that focusing attention on the term in *Azuma kagami* was laughable since it

8. Motoori Norinaga, *Jeweled Comb Basket* (chap. 14). As noted, Norinaga, one of the chief intellectual figures of the eighteenth century, was Masaakira's teacher.

9. Coarsely woven hempen cloth, also known as *sayumi* and *shinanuno*.

10. *Mirror of the East*, a Sino-Japanese historical chronicle covering the years 1180 to 1266.

had already appeared in *Wamyōshō*.[11] But here, it's the people laughing who are being silly. True enough, the word *sayomi* does appear in texts very early on, but Master Norinaga's statement in *Tamakatsuma* was something that came to him as he was reading *Mirror of the East*—something that he really just noted in passing. Certainly he must have been aware of the passage in *Wamyōshō*, but there was no reason to refer to it. This is the true character of *zuihitsu*. Whenever slight "misstatements" of this sort appear in *Tamakatsuma*, it is because it is a *zuihitsu*.

———————

There is a theory that all the finest *zuihitsu*, ancient or modern, have *The Pillow Book* and the miscellany of Yishan[12] as their foundation. When one considers the time that has passed, however, it is impossible to know whether this is true or not. And how could one ever be sure it is true, after all? Some may say there are definite similarities, but it's like comparing the purplish gold of the Buddha's body[13] with jaundice. The colors may be similar, but how can the fine and the base be compared? No doubt, Chinese people like Yishan's work. There are a number of volumes—four in all, each more base than the last.

———————

In all things, people crave not the bland but things with an edge to them. This is the reason Prince Hotaru harbors no ill feelings against Makibashira even after she has caused him such distress.[14] For people to like spicy things seems improbable, but for that very reason, even if it means facing pain, there are those who relish horseradish, ground pepper, and hot peppers, favoring more intense tastes over the usual sweet and mild fare. One example of this is what one reads of the nobility in olden

11. *A Dictionary of Japanese Words*. An abbreviated form of the title *Wamyō ruijushō* (931–938), an encyclopedia compiled by Minamoto no Shitagō (911–983).

12. *Zazuan*, a book of lists written by the Chinese literatus Li Shangyin (813–858). For a translation, see "Li Shang-yin's Miscellany," in *The Columbia Anthology of Traditional Chinese Literature*, ed. Victor Mair (New York: Columbia University Press, 1994), 631–44. For a consideration of the relationship between *The Pillow Book* and *Yishan zazuan*, see Mark Morris, "Sei Shōnagon's Poetic Catalogues," *Harvard Journal of Asiatic Studies* 40, no. 1 (1980): 5–54.

13. The skin of the Buddha was described as *shimagonjiki* (gold of a purplish tint).

14. A reference to the "New Herbs" chapter of *The Tale of Genji*, in which Prince Hotaru continues to consider Makibashira his wife despite rumored criticisms from the girl's grandmother.

times—how despite having an abundance of fine people around them, they carried on with Buddhist monks. Those are the sort who love hot peppers.

That poem that says it is a blessing that blossoms scatter makes sense.[15] For however disappointed we may feel that cherry blossoms are in their prime for only two or three days, we also know that our impatient hearts won't have to wait too long for spring to come around again. The leaves of the paulownia have a refreshing look about them, and the flowers of that tree are a delightful color, but because they are in bloom from mid-summer and all the way through autumn, we grow tired of them and end up wishing that they would be done with it and fall.

In ancient times, poems seldom praised the cuckoo—only occasionally, in fact, and not with the universal acclaim of later times, when from a certain point on everyone seems to have begun admiring it.

The reason behind this admiration is that the cuckoo is so rarely heard in the Kyoto area. In Edo, one may be impressed on the day one hears the first song of the season, but as the days go by and the bird spends more time around one's house, one tires of hearing it. In Yotsuya and Ichigaya,[16] from about the middle of the Seventh Month, it's almost cruel how the singing never ceases.

One year, during an intercalary Fourth Month,[17] I made a trip with two or three friends to Akagi Grove,[18] thinking to enjoy the cool beneath the trees. The green growth was dense all around, and the scenery near and far was so fine that we stood there for some time, until two or three cuckoos, as if to claim the place as their own, gathered in a zelkova tree and

15. A reference to an anonymous poem on an unknown topic, in *Kokinshū* (*Collection of Ancient and Modern Times*, ca. 905), poem 71: "What a blessing it is / that cherry blossoms scatter / —without a trace. / For in this world, things that last / are things we tire of in the end" (*nokori naku / chiru zo mede-taki / sakurabana / arite yo no naka / hate no ukereba*).

16. Areas of western Edo located just outside the central moat surrounding the government districts.

17. Because the lunar calendar came up short in total days, an extra month had to be inserted into the calendar periodically.

18. In Ushigome, located in modern-day Shinjuku.

proceeded trying to outdo one another in song. It was most unpleasant, of course, and while we knew that their calls would have seemed alluring off in the distance, hearing them so close, we were annoyed beyond words, as I explained in a rather gloomy poem:

Such a racket!
We're only in the Fourth Month,
and already
I think I've had enough
of the cuckoo's endless songs.

urusashi yo / kiku mo utsuki no / kotoshi mata / amari aru made / naku hototogisu

Having said this, however, I do still get excited every year at the beginning of the Fourth Month, anticipating the bird's first song. A sign of weakness, I suppose. When I learn that it was heard yesterday in Higurashi, or the day before that in Koishikawa,[19] for some reason my interest is aroused.

———————

The reason Buddhists have the practice of "summer devotions" is because India is a very hot country where the summer heat is so hard to bear that people usually do nothing during that season, which means that those who can bear up in pursuing their devotions make progress in their faith. The way people in various arts and disciplines nowadays do "cold training" in the chill of winter, getting up early in the morning and going out to undergo rigors, is the same kind of thing. Since the reason people do cold training in Japan is because between the heat and the cold it is harder to bear the cold, perhaps it would be better for monks here to do winter devotions.

———————

As the Chinese say, people are born with appetites for food and sexual pleasure.[20] While there are many stories about lovers moved by various

19. Places well north of the author's home in Shinagawa. The birds generally appear in the north first, which may be one reason that people in Edo—north of Kyoto—tired of their call.
20. *Mencius*, trans. D. C. Lau (New York: Penguin, 1970), 161.

emotions—even in relation to blossoms and autumn leaves—it seems that food is given short shrift, with few references to it in those sources. Yet it is food that arouses feelings more than anything else, and there are not a few examples where the state went down to destruction for that reason, as in the story of the mutton soup.[21] After all, the first thing one thinks of when getting hold of something tasty is to invite someone over to enjoy it with some saké.

———————

Robbing old graves has gone on in China since olden times. Needless to say, people did this only to survive, much like bandits or pirates. In our imperial land, such things did not happen until recently. Of late, however, jeweled swords and mirrors and old objects of all sorts have become so popular with connoisseurs that one hears of graves being robbed by people wanting to get their hands on them.

This is an alarming situation, truly lamentable. For who knows if a grave may hold the body of a noble person of long ago? Likewise, how can one know if the body might be that of one's own ancestor of generations past, or someone of the same clan or lineage? Even if the person is no relation at all, the idea of rummaging through someone's dried bones and perhaps stirring up resentment over such a travesty in the land of the dead makes my hair stand on end and gives me the shivers. Trying to excuse their stupidity, such people as these may make a pretense of scholarly interest and claim that they simply want to learn about the past. But if they can't learn about the past without engaging in such evil acts, they would be better off remaining ignorant. If they want to study the past, why not read books? If they don't have the perseverance to read books, they won't come up with any ideas no matter how many graves they dig up or how many ancient objects they acquire. The whole thing is a disgrace.

In the case of the Chinese, they knew from the beginning that such acts were not good, and turned to them only when they had no other way to preserve their lives. In that sense, their acts may be forgiven, but

21. *Zhan guo ce* (*Strategies of the Warring States*, early second century B.C.E.) relates a story in which fighting ensues after the lord of Zhongshan does not offer a visitor from the capital some mutton soup.

to commit such a sin in pursuit of a hobby and try to call it something else—such a thing is unspeakable. Detestable, truly detestable.

The saying "Adding a little more to a heavy burden" is quite old. There is a poem by Emperor Murakami in *Gosenshū*:

> In recompense
> for the bounty of years
> you request for me
> I would add a little more
> to your own firewood pile.[22]

> *toshi no kazu / tsuman to sunaru / omoni ni wa / itodo kozuke o / kori mo soenan*

In recent times, Roan[23] wrote,

> Like adding some
> to the burden on the back
> of a skinny horse,
> and then cracking the whip—
> that is the way of the world.

> *yaseuma ni / omoni ni kozuke / tsukesoete / muchi o ōsuru / yo ni koso arikere*

Roan was always praising the *Kokinshū*, but this is more like the *Sanbokushū*.[24] Puzzling. The poem sounds like a lament by someone who's

---

22. The poem by Emperor Murakami (926–967; r. 946–967) is in the "Felicitations" section of *Gosenshū* (*Collection of Gleanings*, ca. 1006), poem 1381. Masaakira gives the first word of the poem as not *toshi* (years) but *koto* (things). The poem was composed in reply to one by Chancellor Fujiwara no Tadahira (d. 949), with the headnote "Composed when he had firewood cut and sent to the emperor while the latter was residing in the Umetsubo": "This firewood / cut by mountain peasants / I offer up— / in the hope that My Lord's years / will make as high a pile" (*yamabito no / koreru takigi wa / kimi ga tame / ōku no toshi o / tsuman to zo omou*). It was the custom for court officials to send firewood to the imperial palace on the fifteenth day of the First Month as a symbol of their loyalty.

23. Ozawa Roan (1723–1801), a prominent Kyoto poet and scholar.

24. *Kokinshū*, the first imperial anthology of Japanese poetry, was one of the canonical texts of the Japanese poetic tradition. *Sanbokushū* (*A Collection of Worthless Wood*) was the personal anthology of Minamoto no Toshiyori (1055–1129), who was known for his unorthodox poems.

fed up with worldly affairs. But what would a recluse have to be so angry about?

———————

Mornings come; evenings follow; the times and the seasons of the year pass by. Along the way, I find myself moved and attracted most of all by scenes of early spring. There is something remarkable about haze spreading across that first sky.[25] At dawn, a cock crows, in sturdy voice; pine branches adorn each gate, together with stalks of bamboo— and one is left happily waiting for the sound of a spring breeze.

Plum blossoms are a delight, their scent quite beyond description, their hue bringing to mind the gentle and refined scene of the ancient maiden of Luofu standing in the moonlight.[26] Most people reserve their praise for the cherry blossom, which is a true delight, no doubt; surely, though, the flowers of the peach and the crabapple[27] are nearly equal in reputation. And as for the plum blossom: the way its incomparable scent emerges while other trees are still held tight in winter's bonds, the way its flowers stand alone except for whitecaps rising through gaps in the ice—well, it is all so captivating that it makes one's heart melt. Beneath the branches of the plum hides the warbler, whose call is more alluring at first than it is later on, when it has warmed to the season and shares its voice less sparingly. This is equally true of willow branches, which are most attractive when they begin to turn a light shade of green and before they start unraveling in the wind.

One almost detests those stubborn pedants of the past who had scant praise for anything but the flowers in spring, claiming for themselves sole purchase on the beauty of things. True, one hears how courtiers high in the precincts of the clouds[28] enjoy their banquets. But out in the thickets of the countryside, too, people since ages past have always delighted in the gathering of greens and digging up of pine seedlings.

25. *Hatsuzora.* The sky on the first day on which the signs of a season appear.
26. A reference to a poem by Liu Zongyuan (773–819) in which a man meets the spirit of the plum blossoms in a dream in a grove below Mount Luofu, a sacred mountain in Guangdong Province.
27. *Kaidō* or *hanakaidō*.
28. The imperial palace and other dwellings of the aristocracy were commonly referred to as the precincts of the clouds.

The words "moving" and "captivating"[29] may be used of every season, it is true; but how truly apt they are for early spring!

———

Just a year after settling in Shinagawa, I was in my house on the last day of the year. Having no pressing matters to occupy my time, I sat looking out on the barren scene of my garden until well into the night, without even putting down my blinds, musing that I was feeling like the Chinese poet who wrote,

Tonight I think of home—a thousand leagues off;
Day dawns on a New Year, adding frost to my hair.[30]

Death had taken my brother, whom I had relied on over the years even more than my parents, and I felt like a sojourner who must make grass on the roadside his pillow for the night. I had no contact with society, and therefore few cares, yet my life bore so little resemblance to what I had known before that I felt terribly alone. Gazing out at the ice covering my little pond, I wrote,

The pond here
where I make my new home
is bound now by ice:
a mirror showing all has changed—
the way of things in our world.

waga yado to / suminasu ike no / himokagami / utsurikawareri / kore ya yo no naka

Not much of a poem, I suppose, but I had feelings that I could not suppress.

———

Poems like these are the most exemplary:

29. *Aware* and *okashi*, two of the most important terms in Japanese aesthetics. The first is used to describe beautiful scenes of a poignant nature; the second, to describe scenes of more sensory elegance and charm.
30. From the poem "On the Last Day of the Year" by Gao Shi (702–765).

At the old capital
in the mountains of Yoshino
the bloom has passed.
Now it is through bare branches
that spring breezes blow.[31]

yoshinoyama / hana no furusato / ato taete / munashiki eda ni / harukaze zo fuku

Looking far, I see
no cherry blossoms,
no autumn leaves.
A reed-thatched hut on a bay
on an evening in autumn.[32]

miwataseba / hana mo momiji mo / nakarikeri / ura no tomaya no / aki no yūgure

The upper and lower halves of the preceding poems are not directly connected by any words.[33]

In the damp air—
the scent of sweet flags in bloom.
A cuckoo calls
in the Fifth Month,
on an evening of rain.[34]

uchishimeri / ayame zo kaoru / hototogisu / naku ya satsuki no / ame no yūgure

Here "damp air" is associated with "rain." A poem with such subtle connections does not lose status as an exemplary poem.

31. A poem by Gokyōgoku Yoshitsune (1169–1206), in *Shinkokinshū* (*New Collection of Ancient and Modern Times*, ca. 1205), poem 147, with the headnote "On the idea of the end of spring."
32. A poem by Fujiwara no Teika (1162–1241), in *Shinkokinshū*, poem 363, with the headnote "For a hundred-poem sequence requested by Saigyō."
33. In other words, there are no obligatory word associations (*engo*) connecting the upper and lower halves of the poems.
34. A poem by Gokyōgoku Yoshitsune, in *Shinkokinshū*, poem 220, with the headnote "Composed as a summer poem, when people were asked to write five-poem sequences." Yoshitsune alludes to an anonymous love poem in *Kokinshū*, poem 469: "The Fifth Month has come / with its calling cuckoos / and spreading sweet flag— / growing with the same / abandon as my love" (*hototogisu / naku ya satsuki no / ayamegusa / ayame mo shiranu / koi mo suru kana*).

The highest priority in Japanese poetry is poems with overtones[35] and reverberations.[36]

Poems with overtones are of this sort:

The years passed by,
and my prayers ended empty—
null as that bell sound
that signals from Hase's peak
an evening somehow far away.[37]

toshi o hete / inoru shirushi wa / hatsuseyama / onoe no kane no / yoso no yūgure

Wet now from dew
on anise I picked at riverside
in the mountains—
such are my ink-black sleeves
when I arise at dawn.[38]

*shikimi tsumu / yamagawa no tsuyu ni / nurenikeri / akatsukioki no / sumizome
no sode*

In the first poem, the phrase "an evening somehow far away" makes one think of a meeting for someone else and not the speaker; and in the second, the phrase "rise at dawn" makes one think of tears shed on the speaker's sleeves when she parted from a man in her younger days.[39]

35. *Yojō.* A term of praise that was of special importance in the poetics of the Shinkokin era, used of poems judged to have particular evocative power. It was often, but not always, associated with allusion.

36. *Yoin.* A term used in music to refer to notes that linger. It was often used as a synonym of *yojō* and was similar in meaning.

37. A poem by Fujiwara no Teika, in *Shinkokinshū*, poem 1142, with the headnote "On the topic 'Praying for Love,' composed for a hundred-poem contest held at his house." Masaakira slightly misquotes the first and second lines.

38. A poem by Kojijū (fl. ca. 1160–1180), in *Shinkokinshū*, poem 1666, with the headnote "Composed for a hundred-poem sequence on the topic 'The Idea of a Home in the Mountains.'" Anise was offered on Buddhist altars. Masaakira misquotes the second line, which should be *yamaji no tsuyu ni* (dew [on anise] picked at roadside) rather than *yamagawa no* (at riverside).

39. The suggestion being that looking at the dewdrops on her Buddhist robes—fallen from the anise plants that she picked to put on her altar—reminds her of tears that fell on her sleeves upon parting from a lover in her youth.

"Reverberations" refers to the lingering effect that one feels after reading a poem, when it sinks into your mind, as if floating before your eyes, in poems such as these:

I stop my pony
in the green grasses growing
by the roadside—
looking back at my home
once more before I leave.[40]

michinobe no / kusa no aoba ni / koma tomete / nao furusato o / kaerimiru kana

Waving there
in gaps among white clouds—
green willows
blowing in the spring breeze
on Katsuraki's slopes.[41]

shirakumo no / taema ni nabiku / aoyagi no / katsurakiyama ni / harukaze zo fuku

In the first poem, the image of someone stopping his horse and looking back toward home sinks into your heart and remains with you, and the second poem paints a picture that stays on in your eyes without fading away. The way something lingers in your eyes or in your heart—that is the meaning of reverberations. Those who say that this effect is too high to aim for are in the lowest rank of beings.[42] Those who aspire to compose Japanese poems are sure to have the power to achieve this effect. It is a goal one should embrace in full.

[KANDENKŌ HITSU, NENNEN ZUIHITSU, YŪKYŌ MANROKU, KAGETSU SŌSHI, ED. MIURA OSAMU (TOKYO: YŪHŌDŌ, 1915)]

40. A poem by Fujiwara no Shigenori (1135–1187), in *Shinkokinshū*, poem 965, with the headnote "Composed on the road when he was leaving for the Kantō."
41. A poem by Asukai Masatsune (1170–1221), in *Shinkokinshū*, poem 74, with the headnote "A spring poem, from the Poem Contest in Fifteen Hundred Rounds."
42. Skt. *icchantika*. A Buddhist term for the lowest and most spiritually bereft of all types of beings, those who speak derisively of the Law and engage in all kinds of depravity, thus lacking the ability to attain nirvana.

18

Behind the Koto

MURATA HARUMI

Murata Harumi (born Murata Heishirō; 1746–1811) was the younger son of a wealthy Edo merchant. In his youth, he studied poetry under the nationalist scholar Kamo no Mabuchi (1697–1769) and others and was later adopted into the house of a master of linked verse to pursue a literary career, probably with some financial support from his own family. In his thirties, however, his older brother died, and Harumi was called back home to take over the family business. Suited by neither disposition nor education to financial affairs, he pushed the house toward bankruptcy very quickly. Thereafter, he spent the rest of his years as a professional poet. In the beginning, he was in dire financial straits, but over time he developed strong relationships with many powerful literary figures of the day, such as Mabuchi's disciple Katō Chikage (1735–1808), attracting a number of his own disciples. In addition to Japanese poetry, he studied Confucianism and Chinese poetry.

Harumi titled the collection of his major poetic and prose works Kotojirishū (Behind the Koto, 1910) because he was in the habit of storing his writings in a cabinet kept behind his koto. Following are three short essays from that collection: "Chisokuan no ki" (Ample Dwelling), "Yasuda Mitsuru no ie no bundai no ki" (On the Writing Desk Owned by Yasuda Mitsuru), and "Yuki o mezuru ki" (In Praise of Snow).

Ample Dwelling

How vain are the world and its ways![1] Highborn and low are not the same, yet for neither do things often go just as they wish; disappointment is the lot of all. Hoping to enjoy blossoms, one ends up resenting the wind; and who has never waited on moonlight, only to end up frowning at clouds on the peak? "However far back in the wood, the wren has but a spindly branch to rely on, and a mouse seeking water from a stream can drink only what his belly will hold," wrote a man of the past.[2] Those who comprehend the principle that nothing can endure will expect little more of the world.

But here we have Nakamura,[3] living quite apart from the dusty world, beneath a thatched roof and behind a door of pine, his heart pure as moonlight. At evening, he picks flowers; at dawn, he puts water on the altar. When he does pause from his Buddhist devotions for a little relaxation, it is only to break up ice or heat snow for some water to brew tea in remembrance of long-ago events in Togano'o.[4] Worldly desires he has put aside; no longer does he trouble himself envying others. And because he is sufficient within himself, he truly lives in accord with the principles that the sage spoke of long ago. Indeed, one can claim he does not live through the same days as those still searching in vain for something enduring in an ephemeral world. How appropriate that he has named his hut Ample Dwelling.

1. "Ample dwelling" (*chisokuan*) is an allusion to a phrase in *Laozi*: "To know sufficiency is to be rich" (Lao Tzu, *Tao Te Ching*, trans. D. C. Lau [Baltimore: Penguin, 1963], 92).
2. An allusion to *Zhuangzi*. See *The Complete Works of Chuang Tzu*, trans. Burton Watson (New York: Columbia University Press, 1968), 32.
3. Identity unknown.
4. In 1191, the monk Eisai (1141–1215) brought back tea seeds that he had acquired in China and gave them to the monk Myōe (1173–1232), who planted them at his home in Togano'o.

On the Writing Desk Owned by Yasuda Mitsuru

When it comes to furnishings, things in old styles are always highly decorative and well turned out but not very practical for everyday life. Things made in our own day, on the other hand, are cruder and less pleasing to the eye but easier to use.

They say the writing desk of Yasuda Mitsuru[5] follows the style of the monk Tōsei,[6] a man known for leaving the world behind to live in a meager hut, for not adhering to old styles but instead following more modern and simpler ways. It is also said that Tōsei made his desk from a cryptomeria limb he found near the mountain road on the way to the Great Shrine.[7] He may not have had such a thing in mind, of course, but one must admit that dressing things up and making them pretty is the way of things in the era of men, whereas keeping things simple and unadorned was the more straightforward way of things in the era of the gods. Tōsei's use of the cryptomeria was therefore not unfitting.

In any situation, a thing ought to be acceptable if it serves its purpose; being too fussy in choosing things may not be the best course in the end. My friend Mitsuru, for instance, is fond of the old, elegant ways, but he does not throw something away merely because it is not in the ancient style—a sign that he truly is a man of sensibility.[8] The leaf of a scrub oak holds rice as well as a celadon bowl,[9] a wickerwork screen makes no less a barrier than a curtain of brocade. In all things, it makes no sense to demean one thing just because you have chosen the other.

In Praise of Snow

Among the feelings we have in connection with the four seasons, three seem to be regarded by the world as peerless in their ability to soothe the heart: our affection for blossoms, our fascination with the moon,

5. 1758–1816. A physician and poet.
6. One of the sobriquets of the haikai poet Matsuo Bashō (1644–1694).
7. Ise Shrine, the most prominent of all Shinto sites.
8. *Kokoro ari.* A term often used in literary criticism to refer to someone who has an educated sensibility.
9. *Hisoku.* A highly valued form of celadon produced in China during the Tang dynasty (618–907) .

and our fondness for snow. In far-off China, as well as here in our land of Yamato, people high and low, without distinction, past and present, have recorded their admiration for these in poetry and in prose. Since the question of which is superior can hardly be resolved by argument, however, the matter must be left to the preference of individual hearts.

On a spring morning, if one sets out to visit blossoms just starting to bloom, going first to a hill in the meadow and then on to a mountain village, braving the dew and trampling over boulders, one will find a worthy place beneath branches that give off a matchless glow. To transplant just one or two trees to the space in front of a ramshackle hut, within a fence overgrown with weeds, however, is sure to injure the blossoms' pride. Likewise, the moon of midautumn shining everywhere on bush clover in full bloom, or seen from a second-story room with the blinds rolled up as one gazes out for a thousand leagues, or reflected in water, bobbing along as if on the river bottom—such sights truly clear the heart of clouds. The moon you gaze at as you squat down in the little garden by your front door in a tract of tiny city homes, however, does no more than illuminate the dirt and grime of the place, making you feel that it might be better for it to stay away. When it comes to blossoms and the moon, then, surroundings have a role in how one feels.

But where does that leave an old beggar like me, a man of lowly station, holed up in a cramped little house, constantly vexed by illness? How can someone like me ever enjoy the view from an upper story or a pleasure boat? Even when it comes to going out to enjoy the fields and hills, I am always too late: the season has passed, and my hopes are dashed.

With snow, however, things are different. Even a house overrun by weeds can change in a single night when rough boards and eaves are coated as if in silver, altering things so completely that the wretchedness of ordinary days and nights is banished from one's mind. What's more, shop streets, too, take on a sudden sheen, reminding one of life in a mountain village and making even the hats and cloaks of tradesmen seem somehow things of beauty. Indeed, in the snow, everything from the lowliest trees and shrubs on up strikes one as fresh and new. It is as if one had entered a different world while never leaving home, as if one had truly gone to another place. At last, one has all one needs; there is nothing on the outside to resent. This is why it is snow that truly pleases my heart, the one pleasure left to an old man in a world where tastes change from place to place and person to person.

[*WABUN WAKA SHŪ*, VOL. 1, NIHON MEICHŌ ZENSHŪ 24 (TOKYO: NIHON MEICHŌ ZENSHŪ KANKŌKAI, 1927). I HAVE ALSO REFERRED TO FUJIKURA KŌICHI, *KAGETSU SŌSHI*, *KOTOJIRISHŪ YŌKAI* (TOKYO: YŪSEIDŌ, 1973)]

19

Shunparō's Jottings

SHIBA KŌKAN

Shiba Kōkan (1747–1818) was a painter and a student of Western science. Born in the Yotsuya area of Edo, he spent most of his life in that city. He began his artistic career as a disciple of the Kanō school, then became a painter of ukiyo-e, and finally moved on to become one of the first Japanese artists to do copper etchings and oil paintings and to attempt to popularize Western art and science. He was also a mapmaker and the author of numerous essays, travel records, and scientific works. Among his acquaintances were the eclectic scholar, dramatist, and fiction writer Hiraga Gennai (1728–1779) and a number of other men known for their work in Dutch Learning—the phrase used to refer to the study of Western science.

In his last years, Kōkan turned away from his earlier interests and lived a solitary life, spending much of his time writing. Shunparō hikki (Shunparō's Jottings) is a collection of short essays written in 1811 under one of his pen names and published posthumously. In it, he shows his broad acquaintance with and critical engagement with Buddhist, Daoist, Confucian, and even Christian thought, as well as his interest in eccentric people and unusual events and his skeptical attitude.

The world has a way of snagging people in traps, as if they were foxes and badgers—with knowledge as bait. Of course, foxes and badgers will say that, unlike people, they know how to change shape—something beyond human understanding. Yet when a mouse gets a whiff of that fried tofu, he risks his life to eat it, knowing all along that he is in danger of being caught in a trap, which shows how wretched the lot of animals truly is.

Come to think of it, though, aren't people just as likely to get caught in traps? If you use something they like as bait, people are all bound to go for it. For instance, lots of people are fond of saké, money, love letters, or food. When it comes to food and saké, they collapse from overeating or drinking too much and end up behaving like madmen, not even caring if they lose their heads in the process. The same is true for those tempted by money: unsatisfied with normal progress, they get caught up in risky ventures and lose so much that they have to turn to thievery. Then there are those seduced by love letters—in other words, by women. Use that as bait, and everyone—rich and poor, high and low, old and young—ends up with his neck in the noose.

Yet the face is human, the heart a beast, I think. So maybe it makes sense that we put our hands together and bow before Inari-sama,[1] all the while knowing that he's a fox.

———————

As I see things, it is through overindulgence that we do ourselves harm. We should not go beyond our limits. To take the middle way is best, inclining neither this way nor that.

Try though you may to lead people in this world toward the good, you will discover that those who do become good were born with inner goodness. No matter how much you try to instruct a bad person, he remains

———

1. The Harvest God. According to old traditions, Inari used the fox as a messenger. So strong was the association that the word *inari* became slang for "fried tofu" (*aburaage*), for which foxes were believed to have a special taste.

bad. In fact, it is only because there are bad people that we recognize good people in the first place. If everyone in the world were good and had been that way since before birth, there would be no strife.

People are born into this world and then gradually grow and become captivated by worldly things, ending up befuddled. In their middle years, they begin to wake up; then in old age, they awaken completely and at that point return to what they were before they were born. To understand the natural state of emptiness and die in peace is the true Way of Humanity.[2] But if you attain this enlightenment too young, you end up like Tenmaya.[3]

If something won't work, accept that it won't work. If you can make money, make money. If you can achieve fame, let it happen. Just know your own capacities and don't attempt to do what you can't do. Always plan well to take care of yourself in all things, and go to no extremes. If things are going well, be satisfied and don't overdo it. Moderation—that's the important thing.

The sages avoided danger. If someone says, "If you step down here, it'll just come up over there[4]—this is too risky!" then there's nothing for it, and it won't do to try to cross by horse or boat either. In the end, it all comes down to knowing yourself.

————————

Ikkyū[5] was a truly unusual priest of prominence in the Kyoto area. Unlike normal priests, he was always gobbling down fish. When he vomited back up the fish he had eaten, they would change into little fish and swim around in the water.

Hearing how people marveled at this, he decided to put on a show for the public and wrote out this announcement, which he tacked up on gates throughout the town:

2. *Jindō*. A rough equivalent of humanism.

3. In the immediately preceding entry (not included here), Kōkan describes a man named Tenmaya Zembei, who after achieving enlightenment was so blasé about the vagaries of existence that he failed to even mourn the loss of his own child.

4. A proverb that means that even if things go well here, they may not go well over there. Seldom do all things go well at the same time.

5. Ikkyū Sōjun (1394–1481), a Zen priest known for his eccentric behavior.

This coming —day, at Sagarimatsu in Murasakino,[6] I shall eat fish and then vomit them back up and make them frolic in the water.

Anyone interested is invited to come and watch.

ZEN MASTER IKKYŪ, VENERABLE STEWARD OF ALL UNDER HEAVEN

Seeing this announcement, people from all over Kyoto gathered on the day in question and went to his temple. In the middle of the courtyard was a large tub filled with water, and next to it a plate piled high with various kinds of fish. As the spectators were waiting anxiously for him to appear, Ikkyū emerged from within and proceeded to eat all the fish on the plate. Then he bent over the tub and tried to throw them back up, but he couldn't do it.

"My stomach has already disposed of them," Ikkyū said, "so they won't be coming out. I guess I'll just make them into shit instead. You can all run along home now."

———————

If one does not think of poverty as poverty or wealth as wealth, the two are the same thing. Yet the world honors the wealthy man who disregards his wealth more than it does the poor man who disregards his poverty. Like Yan Hui,[7] a man may bend his elbow for a pillow and be happy with his lot, but in our estimation we still think it hard to be in such dire straits. A man who suddenly loses his fortune and yet does not bemoan his luck or lose his composure—now *that* is a wealthy man who disregards his own wealth. He, too, ends up with nothing, but the way for him seems easier than the way for the man who was poor to begin with.

———————

From the very first time you meet a person with the same disposition,[8] he's like someone you have known since long ago.

6. The area around modern-day Daitokuji in northern Kyoto.
7. The foremost of Confucius's disciples.
8. Ch. *zhi*. The word is often translated as "intent." Kōkan seems to use the term to refer to the "will" in individuals that provides motivation for their lives.

Even the biggest fool thinks he's smart and is unaware of his own foolishness. To recognize one's own capacities is exceedingly difficult. Some people finally recognize them in old age, but most never do.

When judging someone else, we may be perceptive; but judging ourselves, we're in the dark. The best one can do, then, is to improve oneself by observing the faults of others. For instance: on the street, I hate to see someone chatting with a servant or losing his temper. I also hate to see someone pass by all alone, laughing; or looking back at a woman again and again; or walking along picking his nose.

According to Osada Shundai, a physician of the Mori domain, "When a certain Confucian scholar took ill and died, a cache of coins was found attached to his waist. It made everyone feel let down."

On the fourteenth day of the Fourth Month of 1811, a Zen priest of Fudōdaishōji in Ōsagami, Musashi Province,[9] was eating soba noodles. At first, he poured some broth on the noodles, but then he began to eat them without broth. "Don't you like the broth?" someone asked, and he said, "No—I like it fine," but still didn't take any. After he left, I thought to myself, "It must have been because the broth tasted like fish." An understandable reaction from a priest, I guess.[10]

Once when I was visiting Lord Abe,[11] one of his retainers was in the room next to mine. At the time, I was carrying a pocket watch, the workings of which made a monotonous tick-tock sound. "That thing makes you feel

9. An area encompassing what now includes eastern Tokyo, Saitama Prefecture, and part of Kanagawa Prefecture.
10. Priests were supposed to abstain from eating flesh.
11. The Abe lineage began service as daimyo in Fukuyama, Bingo Province (the eastern part of present-day Hiroshima Prefecture) in 1710 and continued there for ten generations. Exactly which Lord Abe Kōkan is referring to here is not clear.

like your life is shrinking away," he said. Indeed, it does. We usually don't realize that every day death comes a little bit closer.

In this country, we have a way of labeling anything at all unique as a treasure, and then attaching a high price tag to it, which is utter foolishness. Anything there are two of goes down in value. Yet we have nothing but praise for even the most dirty, torn, and obscure old Chinese painting as long as it's by a well-known painter. What good is such a thing, even if it is an original?

When the Way of the Buddha arrived here anciently, no one even considered what purpose would be served by worshipping Buddhist images. Even the imperial family adopted the new faith, lining the streets with temples and lecture halls; and to this day, temples are granted considerable landholdings and useless priests are placed in high offices. In India, Buddhism was created to govern the masses. It was not something for the high ranking to have faith in, but a means of imposing morality on the populace, using ideas like hell and heaven.

On the fifth day of the Sixth Month of 1811, a farmer of about sixty years came from the Kumagai[12] area to visit me.

"Master," he said, "I heard from a relative in the Yoshida clan that you have a map of the stars, and that if one has the map in hand when doing morning prayers, one's house will prosper and be spared misfortunes. So I came to ask for this talisman."

"I do have a star map," I said, "which I will be glad to give you; and you can worship with it if you wish. But our fortunes are not dependent on the stars. Then again, in Dutch the Fire Star *is* called Mars—perhaps the equivalent of our Marishiten, God of War; and in the Shingon sect, all the stars are gods. Praying to them can't do any harm."

"What a rude answer!" he said, and went home.

12. Originally Kumagaya, an area in what is now northern Saitama Prefecture, along the northern banks of the Arakawa River.

I went to Iwakuni and set out to climb Misen Peak.[13] The road—called Dogs Turn Back—was all outcroppings of rocks and boulders and swift streams, perhaps the very place they had in mind when they named the area Iwakuni [Province of Stones]. It is used mostly by farmers and wood-cutters, but after a while it brought me to a village. A little girl of five or six walked by, with a baby of three strapped to her back. The two had lost their parents and had no one to take care of them. Thus far, they had survived by begging leftovers from people in the village. It appeared that they did have a house to live in.

Those without the support of family—widows, orphans, and the like—should be cared for by their rulers. I had heard at the time that the steward of the province was a true sage, a man of learning. It appears that his learning does not go far enough. People often make the mistake of using the word "scholar" in reference to those who merely have elegant ways and a taste for things Chinese.

A certain man wanted to make his son a Buddhist monk and set him to studying. Finding the Buddhist scriptures boring, the young man developed a liking for literature and began to yearn for the ways of men of old, which changed his interests and left him knowing nothing at all about the Way of the Buddha.

What everyone—rich or poor, high or low—should study is the Way of the Sages, reading the *Analects* and *The Great Learning* over and over again. One should not study the teachings of Buddha; they are heretical.

The Eight Sects and the Nine Sects[14] all originated from the Christianity of the West. Shaka[15] built on that foundation. During the Tenshō era

13. The highest point on Itsukushima, an island in Hiroshima harbor. Itsukushima Shrine is located on the shoreline nearby. The city of Iwakuni is south of there, also on the coast.
14. Both terms refer to the various sects of Buddhism.
15. Śākyamuni, the historical Buddha.

[1573–1592], Nobunaga[16] put trust in the Christian faith, established the Nanban Temple[17] in Ōmi, and began to spread its doctrines. According to Christian teachings, in the eons before heaven and earth began, the Lord of Heaven created heaven and earth, the sun and the moon, and then brought forth living things. Out of compassion, the Lord of Heaven leads all those beings who have wandered in suffering and desire because of their selfishness into a world of comfort and ease called paradise. This world of ours is thus a temporary world. While here, we may pass through difficulties and trials, even losing our heads or suffering grievous punishments. Yet we should not despise our lot, for soon we will be born into paradise, where we will receive the pity of the Lord of Heaven and never die, through countless eons.

It was also on this foundation that Shaka erected his Mount Sumeru,[18] employing the "expedient teachings"[19] about hell and heaven. And the foundation of enlightenment in the Zen sect is the same, leading through metaphor and expedient means toward understanding of the ultimate principle: that human beings and the myriad forms emerge from the emptiness of heaven and earth, and then return into that nothingness. These teachings are so heretical that normal people shouldn't study them. Perhaps those who want to learn about enlightenment should study about it after the age of sixty. For people in their prime to study such things would lead the world into degradation.

About fires: Those who start fires are often not punished, with the justification that they made an unintentional mistake. The reason for this is that there are those who have greater need of fire than the wealthy. In wealthy houses, there are many servants and even more menials at the very bottom. It is menials who are careless with fire. Since most of them are in short-term service, they have no homes and no possessions. Their

16. Oda Nobunaga (1534–1582), a great warlord who was sympathetic to Christianity—or, rather, used it for his own purposes.
17. Formally, Eiroku Temple, commonly known as Nanbanji (Temple of the Southern Barbarians). The temple was destroyed in 1588, upon the order of Nobunaga's successor, Toyotomi Hideyoshi (1536–1598).
18. The mountain at the center of the universe, according to Mahayana Buddhist cosmology.
19. J. *hōben*, Skt. *upāya*. Any rhetorical means used to guide people toward enlightenment, including ruses.

robes are so thin that in the winter months they rely on fire to cope with the cold, so much so that they have no fear of it and feel fortunate when there is a fire. Carpenters, roofers, and those who work for them, on the other hand, wait for fires as if they were praying for good fortune.

Long ago, when Edo became the capital, there were 808 wards in the city; now there are 1,808 wards. This means that there are many thousands of cooking hearths in the city, explaining why there are lots of fires in the winter months. Year after year, the fires come, with losses occurring in warrior and merchant homes alike.

According to a story I heard, an official named Tomi and four or five underlings went to the country and visited the home of the village headman, where they had lunch. After eating, they all died. Upon looking into what happened, it was discovered that there was lizard meat in their food. It appeared that it had fallen into a container when the food was being prepared. The girl who had cooked the food was only seventeen or eighteen, but because she had killed five high officials, she was put to death even though she had committed no crime.

In my opinion, you can't dismiss putting poison into someone's food as an unintentional mistake. The act was utterly careless. The fire in Shiba Ward was started by someone smoking a pipe, and the fire in Tani Ward broke out when someone lit a fire and then went next door. To not be wary of fire when a steady wind is blowing is more than a lapse of attention. Unlike the people of Kyoto, Edo people are not very careful. Furthermore, lots of people from nearby provinces come to the city as servants, and they are the ones who are really not properly wary of fire. When it comes down to it, though, it's always one person who starts a fire. If it is treated as a serious offense, the number of fires should decline.

This is why there are fires in the winter months but not in the summer months: In summer, the chi[20] of heaven strikes the earth with great force, which excites the chi of earth into rising, making things so damp that they won't catch fire. In the winter months, the chi of heaven is weak, which means that the chi of earth fails to rise and everything dries out, making it so that even a little flame spreads quickly.

20. Ch. "chi" or "qi," J. *ki*. The vital force that informs all things, according to neo-Confucian cosmology.

Two *li*[21] past Okayama in Bizen is a place called Miyauchi.[22] There is a teahouse there, and some prostitutes. About two *li* from there, on the right, you come to Ashimori. This area is in the domain of Lord Kinoshita.[23]

I was visiting there for some days and said that I would like to drink some fresh deer blood. The lord immediately went hunting and got a deer. I pulled out my dagger and, while it was still alive, slit the skin open at the base of one of its ears and sucked the blood out, to the amazement of the people around me. Being of a frail constitution, I had heard that fresh deer blood was a potent medicine for building good health but, of course, had had little opportunity to obtain any. While I was there, I also said that I would like to eat some venison and asked the cook to prepare it, but it stunk so badly that I couldn't eat it. When I asked what had gone wrong, I discovered that the Kibitsu Shrine[24] was nearby, and that among the clans affiliated with the shrine, wild animals were proscribed as unclean. So they had made a fire outside and cooked the meat on a long pole to avoid inhaling its vapors and thereby ruined it in the process.

I guess it's understandable that the people there who heard I had drunk the fresh blood thought that I was some kind of demon.

———————

In my middle years, I had only my aged mother. I had lost my father at age fourteen and have never married. My mother was very honest by nature and exceedingly virtuous, like the mother of Mencius.[25] So even after turning thirty, I still hadn't taken a wife. At a certain point, I considered the example of a man who never sought a wife and after his mother died traveled all over Japan, in the end taking up residence in a place between Kyoto and Settsu, calling himself Tantan[26] the haikai master, and still with no wife. He always had a bunch of twelve- or thirteen-year-

21. A traditional Chinese unit of distance, now standardized at 1,640 feet.
22. Located in modern-day Okayama Prefecture.
23. The Kinoshitas had been daimyo of the Ashimori domain since the beginning of the Edo period.
24. Probably a reference not to the main shrine, located in Yamaguchi, but to one of its offshoots, located in the Ashina district.
25. According to tradition, Mencius's mother moved the family dwelling several times in order to provide a better environment for her son and in general was a paragon of motherly virtue.
26. Matsuki Tantan (1674–1761), a disciple of the haikai master Kikaku (1661–1707).

old girls around to get things for him. For this reason, few people have anything written in his own hand, since he always had the girls write for him. When my mother died at age seventy-three, I decided to follow the example of this Tantan and planned to leave my house and travel to see the famous mountains of the various provinces, all by myself. However, my relatives stopped me, calling on the teachings of the sages to convince me that the Way of Humanity was to have a wife and children, and then grandchildren, and that to do anything else was against the Way. So I gave up my plans—another mistake in judgment.

———————

People who don't have children don't understand *mono no aware*.[27] For it is through love of your own children that your love extends to the children of others. This affection is something that can't be explained in words.

After a child starts to grow up, though, he reveals his own disposition, which is inevitably different from his parents'. Few children realize that they owe their existence to their parents. Not many are filial, and most don't even treat their parents as parents. To a parent, however, one's child is ever one's child, for whom one has deep affection, seeing as how the child is after all a product of one's own body. Thinking about it now, then, I realize that the best thing is never to have children at all.

———————

People are easily diverted. Read poems, and you want to write a poem yourself. Look at a book, and you want to make one. Hear talk of travel, and you want to depart and see far-off places. Yet most ordinary people don't read but rather find their diversions only in pleasures of the flesh and in food and drink.

———————

Even a man who lives to a hundred years doesn't lose his passions. Old people may be too embarrassed to admit it, but passions are synonymous with the nervous system, the spirit: as long as we are alive and moving,

27. Deriving ultimately from Buddhist writings, the term became prominent in the aesthetics of medieval court poetry and later in the writings of nationalist scholars such as Motoori Norinaga (1730–1801).

desires will remain. Even an old monk leaning on his staff has these at the core of his being. Birds chirp and call because of overflowing passion; bugs beat their wings or make noises for the same reason. When autumn draws to an end and the west wind blows leaves from the trees, the voices of insects in the grasses wither. But the reason they continue to sing right up until death is because of their passions. All living things in heaven and earth are moved by this strange mechanism. In every case, this is the fire of heaven[28] at work.

One true wonder of our country is Mount Fuji. Because it protrudes slightly into the chilly regions of the sky, snow remains on its peak in all four seasons. In summer, snow melts everywhere but on the peak and is barely visible. The scene after the first snow of winter has fallen is truly a marvelous sight.

The view of Fuji from Suruga Province is no good; the mountain looks higher when seen from a distance of perhaps twenty or thirty *li*. There is no charm in the view from low ground. The shape of this mountain is unique in all the world.

Motoichiba[29] is a place where they sell white saké. Here they have engraved pictures of Fuji on plates, which they press out as occasion demands. When Hollanders pass by, they always want a bunch.

This mountain burst forth before the age of the gods, spouting out sand on all four sides for thousands of years until it gained its current shape. Until my middle years, there was always smoke rising from the summit, though there isn't any now.

The peak, which has existed since before the beginning of the world, is in the shape of a billow.

This Fuji stands all alone. One should view it from a distance. One should not climb the mountain. We should praise Fuji above such useless things as Ama no Sakaboko.[30] This is why I have painted this mountain

28. In his later writings, especially, Kōkan argues that all things in the universe are made up of the two basic elements of fire and water, a variation on the ancient Daoist idea of yin and yang.
29. A town at the foot of Mount Fuji.
30. The name of the heavenly spear that Izanagi and Izanami are said to have used to create the Japanese islands. Kōkan's point is that actual mountains should count far more than fanciful ones.

many times myself. Because I use Dutch oil paints for the colors, the effect is quite realistic, showing the various valleys, places where the snow has not yet melted, or again the clouds spewing forth from the peak or the sunlight illuminating the snow, looking a little like silver.

In our country, there are houses that specialize in painting: the Tosa House,[31] the Kanō House,[32] and more recently the houses of Chinese-style painters. They don't know the first thing about painting Mount Fuji. Tan'yū[33] has made many paintings of Fuji, but they bear no resemblance to it at all. He merely paints according to proper attitude and brush style. Nor are so-called Chinese painters able to render Japan's famous mountains and sights. They paint nameless mountains and call their work landscapes. Rather than painting a particular scene or famous mountain in China, they simply let the brush do its work, creating mountains and water according to their fancy. It's the same thing as painting a dream, as if neither the viewer nor the artist had any grasp of principles.[34]

The time we spend living in this world of ours, from youth to old age, is truly meaningless:

Life in this world
is a day of fuss and flurry
in a market stall—
where beneath the evening sky
not a single soul remains.

yo no naka wa / ichi no kariya no / hitosawagi / tare mo nokoranu / yūgata no sora

31. Tosa-ke. A lineage of Japanese-style painters prominent in the medieval and Edo periods. Members of this lineage dominated the Bureau of Painting at the imperial court.
32. Kanō-ke. The most prominent professional practitioners of Chinese painting (*kanga*) in Japan from the late medieval period and throughout the Edo period. Just as the Tosa school was patronized by the imperial court, the Kanō were patronized by the shogunal government and other high-ranking samurai. Kōkan studied under a Kanō master in his youth.
33. Kanō Tan'yū (1602–1674).
34. *Wake*, a synonym of *kotowari*. A term used in Confucian thought to refer to the ordering principles that inform all phenomena.

This is a poem written by someone recently. It is a Buddhist poem.

———————

According to *Kijinden*, there is a tea master named Mine Genchi in Izumo.[35] He is a devotee of Japanese poetry. One day, he went outside town to where the plum trees were in full bloom, asked who the owner of one tree was, and tried to buy it. When the owner wouldn't go along, he increased his offer and pushed until the owner finally agreed.

The next day, he brought saké and fish and proceeded to enjoy himself beneath the tree. The farmer said, "I'll dig out the tree carefully so there's no damage to the roots and deliver it tomorrow."

Genchi replied, "No—no, that's not what I want. Just leave it where it is."

"What should I do with the fruit when it appears?" the man asked.

"I have no use for it. I just wanted to look at the blossoms, but it wasn't any fun unless I could make them mine," Genchi said.

A single branch
I now make mine alone—
blossoms of plum.

hitoeda o / waga mono ni shite / ume no hana

———————

Since ancient times, there have been many masters of the Way. Those with worldly fame are not true masters of the Way. Shaka of India was of a princely family but cast his privileges aside and lived the life of a beggar. Confucius attempted to spread the Way of Benevolence and Righteousness, but when people rejected him, he went back to his home town, wrote *Chunqiu*,[36] and gained fame only after his death. True masters of the Way are unfettered, without fame or reputation.

35. *Kijinden* (*Unusual People of the Modern Era*, 1790), a collection of tales and vignettes by the poet Ban Kōkei (1733–1806). In fact, the man's name was Kishi Genchi, and he is mentioned in a sequel that appeared in 1798. See Ban Kōkei, *Kinsei kijinden, Zoku Kinsei kijinden*, ed. Munemasa Isoo, Tōyō bunko 202 (Tokyo: Heibonsha, 1972), 448–50. See also Ban Kōkei, *Unusual People of the Modern Age* and *Kanden's Crop of Jottings* (chap. 20).

36. *Spring and Autumn Annals*, a chronicle of the Chinese state of Lu that covers the years 722 to 481 B.C.E.

What do we mean by "the gods"? What do we mean by "the Buddhas"? Well, "the gods" refers to the spirits [*rei*] of those whom we worship as the ancestors of our country. And what do we mean by spirits? Ghosts.[37] And what do we mean by ghosts? Vital force,[38] the substance that fills the space of heaven and earth. We assume that space is empty, but this is not so. The earth is a sphere suspended in the heavens, without top or bottom, supported by the surrounding chi. This chi fills the universe, with no lacunae: if you excavate one yard of earth, you add one yard to heaven. Fish frolic in the water, not knowing that they are in the water; men dwell in chi, but cannot see it. The chi of heaven feels like the chi of earth and is responsible for wonders and marvels; everything in the universe comes into existence because of this chi. Men, beasts, and everything down to the grasses and trees are the instruments of heaven and earth, responsible for all movements, all changes. Is this not awe-inspiring? Thus the gods are chi, which we proclaim to be deities. Men and all the myriad phenomena come forth from chi and return to chi.[39]

The source of chi is the sun. This is where the Sun Goddess gets her name. Shinto writings use metaphors rather than speaking the truth directly. Those who read them should be aware of this.

———

The word "buddha" was created by Shaka, and it refers to the great vital force of heaven. People call this nothingness and declare it buddha; the sun they refer to as Amida and make images in the form of human beings. "Brightness illuminates all the ten worlds,"[40] shedding light in all four directions—so the doctrine goes—and images are made to represent this figuratively. Emptiness unites in one world the teachings of the three worlds. The vital force of heaven permeates the earth, engendering all

37. *Oni*. The word is usually translated as "demon," but Kōkan seems to hark back to an earlier, Chinese sense of the term meaning "invisible spirit."

38. See note 20.

39. Kōkan's thinking here shows the influence of the neo-Confucian conceptions of the Chinese philosopher Zhu Xi (1130–1200).

40. A quotation from the Great Compassion Mantra (Skt. Mahā Karuṇā Dhāraṇī).

living things—what we refer to as This World. Everything that lives must decline and perish, returning to chi. This is what is meant by becoming a Buddha, by being born again into paradise.

In the ultimate sense, gods and Buddhas are the same. In these latter days, Buddhist monks have mixed the gods and Buddhas—Fudō, Aizen, Dainichi, Yakushi, and so on[41]—all up together, giving each a human form as an expedient means that ends up deceiving the ignorant. These are all figures for the sun. This is why all the statues have the sun at their back or have halos. People should understand this.

———————

The way bats hanging upside down from the eaves look askance at human beings walking by is just like the way an evil man looks at a good man because he is different from himself. Yet when they fly or eat, or when they drop their dung, bats remain upright. It is only when they intend to rest that they hang upside down, in the same way that we ourselves lie down.

———————

In my house, there is a man from Kazusa Province.[42] According to him, one day seven or eight bonito boats were out in Higashiura fishing when something that looked like a chest floated by. When they fished it out and looked inside, there were a bunch of coins in it, which they divvied up and went home. Although they said nothing to their neighbors, the word got out in the end because they neglected their fishing and were always getting together to drink saké.

———————

Once something washed up on the beach. Inside it were a number of things that looked like rice cakes. Looking closer, it was discovered that they were candles. Probably they had drifted there from a ship broken up in a storm. A European, remarking on how little the people of our coun-

41. All Buddhist deities.
42. The central part of modern-day Chiba Prefecture.

try—seabound, or not—know about navigation techniques, once said, "The Chinese steer blind; the Japanese, with only one eye."

———————————

Lord Seki[43]—now retired—told me this story in the fall of 1803, in the Eighth Month. That summer, rain had not fallen in Niimi, his place of residence, for sixty days. In a village called Kusama, all the paddies were mountain paddies and had no direct access to water. The women of the place had to rely on drawing water from the river, which was one *li* away over mountain paths. The women would carry the water buckets on their heads while twining hemp with both hands.

In the village was a temple. The priest there fasted for seven days and prayed for rain. And—wouldn't you know it—on the seventh day, a great rain drenched the paddies and fields. The lord of the estate sent the priest money and grain as a reward, but the priest wouldn't take it. Then other villages that had also shared in the blessing sent rice and money to the temple, which he finally had to accept. This was not a case in which heaven was responding to his prayers; it was just that this priest, so honest and innocent, was truly saddened by the distress of the farmers and very unselfish and straightforward, and so fortunately the rain fell. This is what we refer to as virtue.[44]

———————————

In Kamakura, there is a little shrine called Anywhere Jizō.[45] Once, the priest in charge of the place decided that rather than watching over a shrine that was never visited by pilgrims, he would go somewhere—anywhere. That night, he had a dream in which Jizō said to him, "Anywhere, anywhere." When the old monk awakened, he thought to himself, "This must mean that anywhere you go, it's the same." He lived out the rest of his life at that shrine.

43. The Sekis had been lords of the Niimi domain (in what is now northern Okayama Prefecture) since the early Edo period.
44. *Toku*, sometimes translated as "power" or, in some contexts, "profit."
45. A bodhisattva revered as the guardian deity of children in particular.

Someone told me this story. "I was born in Suruga,[46] and every year I go on pilgrimage to Akihasan Shrine in Tōtōmi.[47] At the Shinto festival on the seventeenth day of the Ninth Month, they perform a fire dance, in which torches are tossed around in front of the shrine. The miracle is that no matter where the flames alight, nothing ever catches fire. The god protects against fire." But I wonder. Fire is everywhere in heaven and earth as the source of creation; it can penetrate anything. This is obvious to anyone. But when water vapor prevails, things don't catch fire. Up on a mountain, misty shadows predominate, and everything is shrouded in dampness. Trees and bushes proliferate, and earth vapors rise to create clouds and mist, with the fire potential thus declining so that nothing catches fire. This is why there are few fires in the summer months and many in winter. It is not the god that is protecting against fire.

Last year, I visited Kamakura in the Tenth Month, going to Kōmyōji.[48] The worship hall was filled with people old and young, male and female, all reciting the *nembutsu*.[49] Looking at the veranda outside the hall, I saw several dozen people, all wearing rough clothing. It was a cold and windy night. When I asked why they were out there, I was told that such lowly peasants were not allowed inside. They believed that they could achieve buddhahood just by listening to the scriptures.

Looking at a map of Edo in the Eiroku era [1558–1570], I notice that on the south are Kanasugi and Shiroganedai; on the west are Azabu, Iikura, and Imaimura—the area that is now called Edomizaka. What is now Kasumigaseki was then Sakuradamura. On the north are the Kanda River,

46. Located in what is now the central part of Shizuoka Prefecture.
47. Tōtōmi comprised what is now the western part of Shizuoka Prefecture. The shrine was located in the Shuchi district.
48. A Jōdō-sect temple located in the Zaimokuza area of the city.
49. A formulaic prayer, "Hail Amida Buddha!" recited as a devotional act by adherents of the Pure Land sect.

Yūjima, and Shinobigaoka—what is now Ueno. There is a river flowing from Shinobazu Pond toward Shitaya. Also, what is now Senjugawa was Arakawa, and Asakusa Kannon was like an island. In addition, Shibadōri and the wards around Nihonbashi such as Ogawamachi, Shitaya, Honjo, and Fukagawa were all in shallow water, like ponds. This explains the term "Asakusa laver." From all this we learn that the ocean is gradually becoming land. Ten billion years from now, our Japan will be butting right up against America.

In my old age, I have lost interest in the pleasures of people in the floating world. When I remember something, I simply let my brush have its way and write it down. If there is someone of a disposition similar to mine in a later age, I say, "Enjoy!"

As I have said many times, those who love literature want to write in Chinese, but fortunately I never learned Chinese properly, so I write in Japanese. I am conversant in both Ways. Yet I find it difficult to express my thoughts in Chinese, while interpreting what I have written must surely be difficult for those trying to read it. Anciently (at the time of Empress Suiko[50] and Prince Shōtoku),[51] our country used kana.[52] Later (in Kojiki[53] and Kujiki),[54] Chinese was highly admired, but then the country descended into turmoil, the military houses took control, and Chinese learning declined. At present, the country is at peace and there are many even among commoners who enjoy literature, but not as at the time of the Kan minister[55] or Ono no Takamura.[56] The nation is now ruled by military power. Also, this may be because our country did not follow China, instead establishing itself as an independent country.

50. 554–628; r. 593–628. The thirty-third sovereign of Japan.
51. 574–622. Empress Suiko's regent.
52. The native phonetic syllabary.
53. *The Record of Ancient Matters* (712), a mythological account of the origins of Japan.
54. A work of the ninth century that covers the history of Japan through the reign of Empress Suiko.
55. Sugawara no Michizane (845–903), a scholar-bureaucrat later apotheosized as Tenjin, the god of scholarship.
56. 802–852. A prominent government official and poet.

About fifty blocks north of Atami in Izu[57] are the Higane Mountains, the highest peak of which is called Maruyama. In the Ninth Month of 1811, I climbed to the peak and gazed out at the ten provinces and five islands, the mountains all in a row, going down to the sea. To me, it seemed that wherever the water had dried up, wrinkles had formed in the mountains. Only Mount Fuji truly stands out. For thousands of years, beginning in ancient times, it has erupted, its gravel then congealing and hardening into stone. The earth is transformed into boulders, and after years becomes stone. Water is transformed into quartz and crystal. All this happened before the creation.

"Whatever is full will be emptied" is a common cautionary teaching these days. The full moon wanes; fill a bowl of water to its brim, and it overflows; a tranquil country descends into disorder; a tree full of leaves withers; a man full of years dies. That anything with a beginning must also end is obvious: drink lots of saké, and you end up lying down, drunk. The gentleman is the one who knows when he is at the mean.

The proper age for marriage is thirty for a man, twenty for a woman. Generally, this is the accepted standard in both China and Holland. In recent years in Japan, men not yet in their twenties have been getting married. When neither the man nor the woman is in their twenties, the children are always dolts. The children of couples in their middle age are talented. The life force is what we call nerves—the spirit. It's the same as with fruits, which are either ripe or unripe.

In some places in Chikuzen and Chikugo,[58] they don't want many children. Out of every five children, two are put to death. People have been

57. The Izu Peninsula. Atami is located at its northeastern corner.
58. The northeastern and southern parts, respectively, of present-day Fukuoka Prefecture

taught that this is the usual thing, so no one balks at it. But should people be treated like beasts? Jia Biao of the Later Han,[59] lord of Xinxi,[60] outlawed this practice and made it a crime equivalent to murder. During the years that followed, a thousand or so of these children grew to adulthood, and it was said of them, "It was Father Jia who gave them birth."

———————

I, Kōkan, say this:[61] It's not only in the provinces of Chikuzen and Chikugo where people don't want lots of children. In Buzen, Bungo, and Hyūga, and even in Hitachi, Dewa,[62] and the far north, farmers take wives very young and have ten children or more, many of whom they put to death. Our country has little land and is crowded. In the various countries of the Western world, people just move on into neighboring countries, and therefore lament not having more people. This is why the practice doesn't exist there.

———————

I, Kōkan, say this: No one becomes a monk after extinguishing desire. Rather it is because of desire that people take the tonsure. Also, the practice of "following one's lord in death" refers to a custom of the Warring States period,[63] when a lord's retainers would follow their lord in death because his army had lost or his castle fallen, leaving them no way out. Anciently, there were also cases when a lord's close retainers would follow him in death when he died of illness. This is because in those times people were ignorant of the Way of Humanity. Perhaps they were deceived by the teachings of the Buddha, as if there really were a place for them to go after death. What stupidity! Also: to refer to someone who dies of illness as having "followed his lord in death" is fallacious. How can one lie and call it giving one's life?

59. The Later Han lasted from 25 to 220.
60. Modern-day Henan Province.
61. Kōkan begins this and several subsequent sections in this strident way to make a clear distinction between himself and other people he quotes in these last sections of his *zuihitsu*.
62. All provinces in the far south or far north of the Japanese islands.
63. Sengoku Jidai. The period between the effective collapse of the Ashikaga shogunate in the late fifteenth century and the establishment of the Tokugawa regime in 1603.

I, Kōkan, say this: Shōtoku Taishi connived with the empress [Suiko] to make people believe in Buddhist images. What was he doing? Moriya[64] said, "Our country follows the Way of the Gods and has no business adopting the ways of foreign realms," and threw the images into the cove at Naniwa.[65] Taishi appealed to the empress and destroyed Moriya. Which was correct? Buddhism has so thoroughly infiltrated everything that nothing can be done about it now. Thus Taishi is the founder who spread abroad a worthless way.

During the Kan'ei era [1624–1644], Inoue[66] made Lord Doi[67] steward of the Inoue clan and said to him, "When you make judicial decisions as an official, you are never wrong. I am very impressed with your knowledge."

Lord Doi replied, "It's not knowledge; I have a method."

"What is it, then?"

"Whenever we convene, I am seated above everyone else. I always have those seated below me state their opinions, and among them is always something I would not have thought of myself. So I collect their words, embellish them a bit, and make them my own. This is why I make few mistakes."

This impressed Inoue all the more.

Although Lord Doi had not studied legal affairs, his words were close to those of the sages.

Someone asked, "My wife died and left a child behind. Should I remarry or not?"

I said, "Not even Sage Zeng[68] took another wife. Still less should an ordinary man."

64. Mononobe Moriya (d. 587), who was assassinated on the order of Prince Shōtoku.
65. Modern-day Osaka.
66. Identity unknown.
67. Identity unknown.
68. Zeng Shen, one of the youngest disciples of Confucius, second only to Yan Hui in his reputation for courage and virtue.

Someone nearby said, "I notice that children raised by stepmothers are very talented, generally surpassing their real mothers. It's not true that they are not good for children."

His words made sense.

I, Kōkan say this: There are people who always suffer from cold when they are in a weak state. The more they cover up and take care of themselves, the colder they feel. If they brace themselves, however, they don't get worse. Few people get sick while traveling, because their spirits are up.

Also: After the age of forty, one should not take a wife. After forty, people start to lose their vitality, and it becomes difficult to raise girls and little children.

[*MEIKA ZUIHITSU SHŪ*, ED. TAKE RYŪZŌ, VOL. 2 (TOKYO: YŪHŌDŌ, 1928)]

20

Unusual People of the Modern Age and Kanden's Crop of Jottings

BAN KŌKEI

Ban Kōkei (1733-1806) began life in a Kyoto merchant household that produced umbrellas, mosquito nets, and tatami mats for the domestic market. Adopted into another branch of the family at the age of eight, he succeeded to the headship of that household in 1750 and for the next twenty years ran a very successful business, opening new branches in both Edo and Osaka. At the age of thirty-six, however, he turned business affairs over to his heir and settled into retirement in the eastern hills of Kyoto. Despite fragile health, he lived into his seventies, in time gaining great fame as a poet. In addition to much poetry, he penned a number of zuihitsu, including Kinsei kijinden *(Unusual People of the Modern Age, 1790), from which the first nine essays are taken. A sequel to that work,* Zoku kinsei kijinden *(Unusual People of the Modern Age, Continued, 1798), is the source of the next two pieces. It was initially written by Mikuma Katen, who had been the illustrator of the first book, but was evidently edited substantially by Kōkei after Katen died in 1794. Another miscellany,* Kandenkō hitsu *(Kanden's Crop of Jottings, 1811), contains humorous or instructive anecdotes about history, people, and events—as seen in the final four selections.*

Kuriko of Kai

Kuriko was the wife of a farmer in the Yamanashi district of Kai Province. She was renowned for her filial piety toward her parents-in-law. After both her husband and his parents had passed away, she was caught in a mountain torrent (which refers to an event in which a river overflows its banks, causing a flood that destroys villages and kills people) and drowned. When they dug up her body afterward, she had her twelve-year-old foster child on her back and her own eight-year-old by the hand. The reason she had put the older child on her back rather than the younger one was that as she was attempting to flee she felt a heavier obligation to save the foster child.[1]

From a woman—and a woman born in the countryside, at that—one doesn't expect to learn anything, but surely examples of such a beautiful character are a rare thing in this world. It is sad when a person is unable to die a good death because he is taken by misfortune unprepared. Through this tragedy, this woman's virtue became even more apparent. For this reason, the people of the place erected a stone tablet that tells her story.

Tsunako of Wakasa

A mad wolf was terrorizing the area around Obama in Wakasa Province. In the house of a certain samurai was a serving girl, fourteen or fifteen years old, named Tsuna. One day, she put her master's infant on her back and took him off to play, and the wolf appeared and came running after them. She quickly hitched up her skirts, clutched the child to her breast, and went down on her face to protect him as the wolf began to bite her in the buttocks.

---

1. An independent source alludes to the wife of a farmer in that area who died in 1729, at the age of thirty-eight.

When the people around heard the ruckus and gathered around, the wolf ran off. As they put the girl on something to carry her away, she was still able to talk and asked if the master's child was safe, but then she stopped breathing. When they arrived at the home of Tsuna's parents, the master's wife came running up. Tsuna's mother gave her the infant. "He is all covered with blood, but I am happy to say that he sustained no wounds at all, not a scratch." The mother, too, was no ordinary woman.

Hearing about this incident, the governor of the province called the mother before him and was very moved. He had a stone pillar put up, and had it inscribed "The Grave of Tsunako the Loyal" by one of his Confucian scholars, Ono Chūjirō. I hear that a three-day Buddhist service was held and people attended from far and wide, many offering up poems in Tsuna's honor.

The Wife of the Woodcutter Shichibei and the Wife of Hisabei

One day, a woodcutter, Shichibei, of Keage in the eastern hills of the capital, went into the mountains and was very late in coming back, so his wife went to look for him. Beneath an embankment, she found a load of greens attached to his staff, but no sign of Shichibei.

Looking up, she saw a large snake, its head dangling from a tree branch and its belly bulging. She was a smart woman, so she realized that the snake must have swallowed her husband. Quickly, she picked up the scythe that was also attached to the load of greens and confronted the snake—which opened its mouth and swallowed her, too. While being swallowed, however, she slit the thing open from its mouth to its belly so that both she and her husband, who was indeed inside there, fell out onto the ground. Then she took her husband on her shoulders and carried him home, where after receiving care for ten days or so, he recovered. Thereafter, he had no hair on his head at all. People of the area took to calling him by the name Teakettle Shichibei.[2] He spent a hard life in the moun-

2. An interlinear note here reads, "In common speech, men with bald, red pates are referred to as 'teakettle.'"

tains, selling produce. Someone I know told me that he was an old man of over sixty years, about forty years ago. In courage and knowledge, he was not inferior to Feng Yuan, who took on a bear for the first emperor of the Han dynasty.[3]

Another story of the same sort took place on the twenty-eighth day of the Eleventh Month of 1718, in the district of Funai, Tamba Province. A wounded wild boar was on the rampage, running from Yagi Village to South Hirose Village. Going around the foot of the mountain, it was headed straight for Yamamuro Village through Toba Village. There it gored a solitary man working in the paddies, going more and more berserk. Then a woodcutter named Hisabei, aged sixty-four, carrying a load of firewood on his back, ended up right in the beast's path, with no place to escape. He scrambled up a tree, but it was only about ten feet off the ground, and the boar grasped some of the lower branches in its teeth and pulled it down, so he had to grapple with it, until they both fell down an embankment. More furious than ever, the boar bit into the man, tearing him up in numerous places, and when he called for help, there was no one to reply. His wife, however, who was a woman of fifty-four years, heard him and came running. She covered the boar's head with the sleeve of her robe, straddling his neck with her legs, and managed to subdue it. When the boar couldn't move anymore, she called out for someone to save her. Finally two men from the village came out together and stabbed the boar with a dagger, and another man came and hacked at the animal's legs with an axe. By this time, a number of people had gathered, and they weakened the boar to the point that they were able to bring it down.

In the end, the woodcutter survived, and after some months was restored to complete health. According to Tōgai,[4] the area was in the Kameyama fief, which recognized the wife for her valor with a gift of grain.

---

3. In 38 B.C.E., while Emperor Yuan (75–33 B.C.E.; r. 48–33 B.C.E.) was, as entertainment, watching animals fight, a bear broke free and attempted to get out of the cage. One of the emperor's consorts, Feng Yuan, stepped forward to shield the emperor from attack.
4. Itō Tōgai (1670–1736), a Confucian scholar associated with the Ancient Studies (Kogaku) movement.

Yoemon the Rice Merchant

In Settsu Province, in the village of Imazu, there lived a rice merchant named Yoemon who was expert in Confucian thought and lived frugally. Although well off, he got right down and worked with his servants, producing his own saké, and was so unstinting in his work that his wealth only grew.

But the more wealth he accumulated, the more Yoemon engaged in secret acts of kindness. When the servant of one of his relations lost a hundred *ryō*[5] of his master's money and disappeared, Yoemon asked around and found him out, but after chastising him severely, gave the man an equal sum of money and sent him back to his master. When he saw a place in the village where the road was very narrow, he worried that it would pose an obstacle if people had to flee from a fire, so he bought the tract and widened it. Where he thought a plank bridge would be too dangerous in a fire, he rebuilt it in stone. And, of course, he made it his habit to give to the poor.

When Yoemon died, men and women came from near and far and wailed out loud in sadness—bringing to mind, as someone who witnessed it said, the demise of the Buddha himself. Amusingly, among those mourning his loss was an ignorant old woman who said, "A scholar he was, and still such a good man. Why, had he not been a scholar, just think what a good man he would have been!"

Thus with a single statement, she stuck all the scholars under heaven to the wall!

A Servant of the Ōishi Clan

When Ōishi Yoshio[6] retired from Akō Castle,[7] he stayed in the castle town for a while taking care of things. As he prepared to leave for

5. One hundred *koban*, or middle-size coins. One *ryō* was defined as the equivalent of one *koku* of rice—the amount necessary to support one person for one year.
6. 1659–1703. A samurai in service to Asano Naganori (1665–1701), a daimyo who was forced by the central government to commit ritual suicide in 1701 after an altercation with another samurai at the shogunal palace in Edo. Two years later, Ōishi and his comrades assassinated Kira Yoshinaka (1641–1703), the man they held responsible for their lord's death. This became the basis of the famous story of the Forty-seven Rōnin.
7. Located in western Honshu on the Inland Sea.

Kyoto, a servant named Hachisuke, who was still living in town, came to visit him.

"I, too, would like to accompany you to Kyoto, but I am old and cannot do as I please. How sad I am to think that this will be the last time I will have the privilege of seeing you. If you have something—anything, really—that I could have as a memento, I would treasure it in the years that remain to me."

Yoshio nodded and said, "Yes, of course," and looked around for something to offer, but the better part of his furnishings had been sent to Kyoto and what remained was already packed up. Then he opened a box that had an inkstone in it and found twenty gold coins.

When he said, "Here, at least take these," however, Hachisuke became furious and threw down the coins.

"What kind of memento is that?" he said. "I may be of low station, but do you think my feelings could be so common? When the lord died unexpectedly, even we people of mean rank were overcome with sadness. How could such a memento be worthy of the feelings we had as we vacated the castle, crawling away in disgrace? No—now I think I don't want a memento at all!" With that, he made to storm off.

But being the kind of man he was, Yoshio stopped him and said, "I understand, of course; my mistake entirely. It was just that I didn't have much around to give you. But now that I think about it, there is something."

He began to grind some ink, pulled out some paper that happened to be nearby, and sketched out a samurai wearing a braided rain hat standing on an embankment, with a servant next to him.

"Do you remember?" he asked. "This is the path we used to travel when I would take you along to the Yoshiwara Quarter[8] as a young man in Edo. Perhaps this may serve as a memento."

Hachisuke was overjoyed. "Yes, there could be no better memento than this," he said. Then they talked about this time and that in the past, until the two parted tearfully and Hachisuke went home.

The sketch was passed down to the servant's daughter, and it was treasured in the family of the physicians who were in service to the lord of

8. A licensed prostitution quarter.

that castle, according to someone from that province. One must hold in highest regard such stories that tell of servants who are so straightforward and true, so honest and unselfish toward righteous masters.

Oka, Governor of Suō

A certain Oka, governor of Suō,[9] was a Shinto priest at Sakaori Shrine[10] in the province of Bizen who was renowned for his scholarship on the gods and was a truly unusual man.

Once he bought a sword and was out on the street with it strapped to his waist when someone said something offensive to him that made him angry. Then later, when he went out wearing the sword somewhere else, he felt angry again, so he concluded that the sword must not suit him and simply gave it to a fishmonger he knew who happened to be passing by on the street.

Another time, he lost his way in the mountains, and to make matters worse, rain began to fall. Although he was able to make it to a nearby roadside chapel for shelter, and the rain had finally stopped, by then it was night and he couldn't very well go on. He and the one servant he had with him went out to gather fallen leaves to make a fire, but the leaves were so wet from the rain that they wouldn't burn. Just as they heard a wolf howl several times and began to be really frightened, however, flames suddenly burst out from down among the wet leaves. With the flames as their light, they were able to gather wood and make a fire that kept burning all night long—a miraculous turn of events, indeed.

On another occasion, he developed a carbuncle on his back against which the treatments of various doctors had no effect. When he thought that he was going to die, he said, "Take me to the shrine, and I shall take my leave there." His physician and relatives tried to restrain him, warning that it would not be good for him to try to move, but he would have none of it. "If I die on the way, so be it—I must go!" So they carried him off on his pallet to the shrine hall. Many people were there watching over

9. A vassal of Matsunaga Hisahide's (1510–1577), who was in turn a vassal of Miyoshi Chōkei's (1522–1564).
10. Now known as Okayama Shrine, located in the city of that name.

him, but in the middle of the night, he and all those around him were so fast asleep that no one even noticed that the lamp had gone out. A voice said, "Governor, Governor," and he awoke feeling that a strange hand had reached out to rub his back. Waking up his guards, he asked them what was going on, but no one could say. When he lit a lamp and had them examine his back, however, the carbuncle was gone—completely healed!

The story goes that he lived on for more than twenty years. Acquaintances have told me that such things happen all the time. The gods be praised, for it all must be in accordance with their will.

Muromachi Sōho

Sōho was a rich merchant who lived near the intersection of Muromachi and Fourth Avenues in Kyoto. His two sons were both good-for-nothings, so he disinherited them. After this, the world thought very highly of him, but he knew that he would be unhappy if he were to take in a foster son only to have the two real sons come back to make trouble, so he sold everything, beginning with his house, which yielded him twenty thousand gold pieces altogether. Then he holed up in a secluded place, kept to himself, and used his money to assist poor people.

Occasionally someone would say, "So-and-so is in a very sad state. Why don't you give him some money?" Then he would reply that he was poor himself but would secretly toss five pieces of gold into the person's house. When that person would later come to him, guessing that it must have been him he should thank, he would merely say, "No, it wasn't me!" Surprisingly, he always gave the same sum of five gold pieces.

If he heard that a poor person was selling a house, he would buy it for a high price, making up for his losses; and if he saw that the person was having to move, he would let him have the house cheaply. In this way, through acts of secret kindness, he used up all his twenty thousand gold pieces.

There was one funny thing about him. While he was still in the commercial world, he loved blowfish but was afraid to eat it.[11] But now that

11. If not prepared properly, the poisonous blowfish can be fatal to those who eat it.

no one depended on him anymore, he ate it day and night. After he became poor, that was his only luxury.

He was wearing plain cotton clothing of gray and black when he took ill and was about to die and had only three hundred *mon*[12] and two measures of rice. Yet those who had benefited from his generosity, hearing that he was dying, came and nursed him through till the end and eased his passing. He had lived as he wished for more than twenty years, it is said, and was over seventy years old.

Entsū of Kaga

He was the dharma heir of the Zen master Dokutan of the Ōbaku sect.[13] His devotion to the bodhisattva Kannon far exceeded that of most people, which may be why he was called He Who Is Already Fully Knowing.[14]

He was rather an otherworldly sort. Once he was asked to write an afterword for a book, and he wrote it out himself, but because he wrote it in draft script just as the impulse took him, there were lots of places that were unreadable. When it was brought back to him, he looked it over for a while and then said, "I can't read it either, but one of my disciples reads well—have him look at it for you."

Another time he forgot the name of a house he was supposed to visit in Kyoto, so he walked around the area asking people, "The place that Entsū of Kaga is supposed to come visit—is it this one, or maybe that one over there?" This amused people very much.

A Recluse of Mino

In the mountains of Mino Province,[15] there was a recluse who never left the place. His name was Reverend Reigan. A devotee of the Pure Land

12. *Mon* were copper coins. One *ryō* was the equivalent of four thousand *mon*.
13. Ōbaku was an offshoot of the Rinzai sect. Dokutan Shōkei (1628–1706) was a Chinese priest who became fourth abbot of Manpukuji, headquarters of the Ōbaku sect.
14. Sunawachi Entsū. Fully Knowing is one of Kannon's names.
15. An interlinear note here reads, "The name of the place has been forgotten."

sect, he had lived in a cloister attached to Chion'in Temple[16] in Kyoto, but because the place in the mountains was not far from his hometown, he made a vow never to leave the mountains after returning there. At first, he found himself yearning for contact with the world and even climbed up a pine tree once because he couldn't stand the loneliness, but he couldn't see anything different from up there. Even after that, he still suffered inwardly, and this went on for a while, but after a year living there, he is reported to have said those feelings faded away.

He was always reading the eighty chapters of the *Flower Garland Sutra*. Perhaps because he would always begin right away after finishing each time, he would finish the sutra every two days, reading forty chapters a day. Even at night, he would sit up, never sleeping, reciting the *nembutsu*[17] in a faint voice.

The monk Sekkyū of the Ōbaku sect went to visit him at his hut, thinking that he might get some guidance. He spent a year there, along with one of the reverend monk's young relations, who served as a helper, and the two rarely exchanged any words at all. Other than eating their meals together twice a day, they had no interaction, and no visitors ever came by. The monks just did as they pleased, either reciting sutras, or reading books, or saying the *nembutsu*, or sitting in meditation, with nothing to disturb their peace.

Then one day the reverend monk ordered his helper to go to his hometown and get his nephew. It was two *li*[18] away, but the nephew came immediately because it seemed urgent.

"It's just that tomorrow this old monk[19] will be dying," the reverend monk said. Then he explained that since he would not be coming back, he wanted some of the money he had received as an allowance to go to the mortuary chapel of a certain temple, and some more of it to go to two monks he named—but that not a cent should go to anyone in the lay world, because it was all money dedicated to the propounding of the Law.

---

16. Located in Higashiyama.

17. A formulaic prayer, "Hail Amida Buddha!" recited as a devotional act by adherents of the Pure Land sect.

18. A traditional Chinese unit of distance, now standardized at 1,640 feet.

19. Reigan here refers to himself in the third person, underscoring his attitude of indifference toward his own demise.

His nephew was surprised, of course, and said, "You don't seem a bit ill today—why would you say such a thing? If indeed you are going to die, though, my wife and children should certainly come and say their farewells."

The monk shook his head and said, "No, it won't do to have people thronging about. And you don't need to stay around here either, as I have nothing left to say." Then he insisted that the nephew be on his way.

The monk bathed, shaved his head, and told his helper to put him in his coffin just as he was, and to do nothing special with his remains. Then he spent that day as he had every other. When the next morning came, he ate his morning gruel and his breakfast meal, and at about noon, sitting erect in lecture posture, he passed on, as if going to sleep. He was seventy-two or seventy-three, it is said.

Sekkyū was a monk who had spent one summer working at Shōshūji, an Ōbaku Zen temple located in Ōmi Hachiman. After studying under the reverend monk in Mino, he returned to that temple and told the story to Reverend Kokei.[20] These events happened about forty years ago now, which would mean the Kan'en era [1748–1751].

Lady Kita

In Okayama, Bizen Province, there lived a very wealthy samurai who wanted to begin cultivating a new rice field bordered on one side by the sea and on the other by mountains. He calculated that if he put up a stone embankment on the seaside, he could get 100,000 bales of rice from the plot. In order to start, however, he believed that he had to offer one person—man or woman—to the dragon god as a sacrifice or the venture would not succeed. But tradition said that a criminal could not be used, nor could someone who had fallen into the sea accidentally. So he gave up the idea—until a widow named Kita heard about it and said that if her life were not unacceptable, she would offer it.

When he summoned her, she said that she was not under any duress, but felt that since her life was of no use now she might as well benefit

20. Identity unknown.

the world with her death. She seemed entirely earnest and unshaken in her resolve.

The man told her that after her death, she would be honored as the god of the new fields. After purifying herself in mind and body, she bravely threw herself into the sea. Even now, there is a shrine there dedicated to her as the god of the place, and she is called O-Kita Myōjin.[21]

Kaga Chiyojo

Chiyojo[22] was from Mattō in Kaga. From childhood, she was devoted to the elegant arts and loved haikai, but was not able to secure a teacher. When she would ask travelers about the matter, they were all alike in recommending Genbō[23] of Mino. She was about to make the trip to see the man herself when it so happened that he came to Mattō on a visit, so she asked for an audience with him at his inn and expressed her desire. Genbō said that he was tired and went off to his room to sleep, but she pursued him, asking for instruction, so he said, "All right. Then write a verse for me."

As it was summertime, he chose the topic "Cuckoo." When she came out with a verse, he saw that it was nothing out of the ordinary and said, "This won't do—anyone could write it."

Then Chiyojo came up with another verse, which he again rejected, just as before.

By this time, Genbō was already falling asleep, but Chiyojo stayed on, trying to come up with a verse. Whenever she saw his eyes open, she would recite another one. In this way, she produced many verses, until dawn came and Genbō got up.

"Have you been here all night?" he said, amazed. "Why, it's light outside."

---

21. Here Kōkei appends a note: "Dōnyū made life and death one through the Buddha; Gikan gave his life for duty. We count them as extraordinary, but the integrity of Lady Kita, who threw herself into the sea for her province, was beyond even the wisdom and courage of those samurai. She was extraordinary among the extraordinary."

22. 1703–1775. Chiyo's father was an artisan specializing in the production of picture scrolls and frames.

23. D. 1747. A disciple of Shikō's (1665–1731), one of the leaders of the Bashō school.

At that moment, Chiyojo produced this verse:

"Cuckoo," you say,
then again, "cuckoo"—
and the day dawns.

hototogisu / hototogisu tote / akenikeri

This time, Genbō offered praise. "That's more like it. If you can just keep that feeling from now on, you will be sure to gain fame under all of heaven," he said, and made her his disciple. And, indeed, she did become one of the most famous poets of that Way, which was unusual for a woman.[24]

This seems to have taken place while she was still a young woman. When she married,[25] she wrote,

Will it be bitter?
Who can know, first trying
a persimmon.[26]

shibukaro ka / shiranedo kaki no / hatsuchigiri

This is truly in the spirit of haikai, and very amusing. When her husband died at twenty-five, she wrote,

I arise, go to bed—
in the empty expanse
of my mosquito net.[27]

okite mitsu / nete mitsu kaya no / hirosa kana

24. Scholars are highly dubious about the historicity of this anecdote, as they are about many of those connected with Chiyojo.

25. She married into the Fukuda family of Kanazawa at age eighteen.

26. This poem does not appear in her personal collection.

27. This poem appears in a collection put together even before Chiyojo's birth, where it is attributed to a "lady of pleasure" named Ukihashi. See Ueno Sachiko, *Josei haiku no sekai* (Tokyo: Iwanami shoten, 1989), 35.

Never marrying again, she made her one male child the heir of her husband's house and later left to live alone as a nun, with the name Soen.

She also studied painting under Goshunmei[28] of Echigo and showed excellent taste. Once when she was asked to do a sketch with an inscription underneath, she sketched in some morning glory vines dangling from far above and wrote,

Morning glories—
wary, it seems, of blooming
on the ground.[29]

asagao ya / chi ni saku koto o / abunagari

Her poems all had a feminine feel and were always delicate:

With the well bucket
taken by morning glories—
I go begging water.[30]

asagao ni / tsurube torarete / moraimizu

This verse was well known and highly praised.

The chief priest of Eiheiji[31] once visited her as he was traveling by and asked for a verse that expressed the idea of *ichinen sanzen* [three thousand in a single thought]:

A thousand seeds—
all from the heart
of a single vine.[32]

sen nari mo / tsuru hitosuji no / kokoro kara

28. Igarashi Shunmei (1700–1781), a Confucian scholar and painter.
29. This poem does not appear in *Chiyo-ni kushū*, her personal anthology.
30. This poem does appear in her personal anthology. See Kaga Chiyojo, *Chiyo-ni kushū*, Nihon haisho taikei 9 (Tokyo: Nihon haisho taikei kankōkai, 1927), 137.
31. A famous Sōtō-sect temple in Echizen Province.
32. In her anthology, the first line reads *hyakunari ya* (a hundred seeds). The original, which Chiyo judged one of her finest poems, bears the headnote *sangai yuishin*, a Buddhist term meaning "the three

This verse also became famous.

She died very old, it is said. Her personal collection of poems has circulated widely.

A samurai of the province of Ueno had in his house twenty treasured saucers. The man let it be known that he would take the life of anyone who broke one of them. So when one day a maidservant made a mistake and broke one, all the people of the household were in a state of shock and grief.

A man outside the house pounding rice with pestle and mortar heard these goings-on and said, "In my house, I have a treasured medicine that glues china back together so well that it leaves no sign of a break. Let me have a look at that saucer."

Thanks to this, the people regained their composure, called the man in, and showed him the saucers. At first, he pretended to examine where they were, all stacked in a pile, until suddenly, using the pestle he was carrying, he smashed them all to bits. Taken by surprise, the people asked him what he was doing. The man laughed and said, "Break one saucer or break twenty, he says he'll have your life either way; so just tell your master that I broke them all. These saucers are made of china, after all, and the time will come when every single one of them will be broken. So I offer my one life for the twenty. What I said about the treasured medicine was just a lie I told so I could do what I've done." Then the man waited for the master to return, with not a sign of wavering.

When the master came home and heard the details of the story, he was so impressed with the man's integrity that he spoke to the lord of the castle, who made him a samurai. In the end, it is said that he became a most honorable government officer.

A destitute samurai was crossing over Ryōgoku Bridge in Edo, with his wife and child in tow, when the child saw a man selling Satsuma yams and wouldn't budge until he got one. The father tried to cajole him, but

realms exist in one heart." The three realms are the different stages of experience: the realm of the passions, the realm of the senses, and the realm beyond the senses. See Ueno, *Josei haiku no sekai*, 43–44.

[328]   THE EDO PERIOD

the boy wouldn't listen, so there was nothing for it but to ask the peddler. "You see how it is," the father said. "I don't have a penny at the moment, but if you'll just let him have one, you can be sure I'll come with the money just as soon as I can." But the peddler wouldn't hear of it. "Give to someone with no prospects? Not a chance!" he said. So the father led the crying boy away and continued across the bridge.

Now, watching all this transpire was an *eta*[33] who made his living repairing thongs for wooden sandals. He called the samurai over to him inconspicuously and said, "I feel so sorry for the boy—please let me give you what I have, ten sen. Then you can get him a yam—and we can just leave the matter of when to pay me back up to you." The father took the money and reverently held it above his head, but then replied, "This is an unexpected show of kindness, but just the thought of such a gesture is too much, I can't possibly accept it," and returned it. The *eta* countered, "Being what I am, I understand why you would say that, but certainly in such a situation . . ." and then tried to insist, but to no effect.

The samurai then appeared to head over to the bridge railing, when suddenly he snatched up the child, threw it in the river, and then grabbed his amazed wife, swept her up, threw her in too, and then jumped in himself. Everyone watching was taken aback; but there was no way to save them. It's said that they drowned almost immediately. Although he was not a man of high ambitions, one can only be impressed and saddened by his sense of honor.

A friend told me this story: One day when a priest from a subtemple of Eigenji was in the Kantō, he met a fierce thunderstorm out in the fields and took refuge in a little shrine. After him, a woman holding a child came running in, and some time passed while they waited for the skies to clear. Since the priest had an urgent matter to attend to, he finally had to brave the rain and move on. After he had gone only a little over a block, however, he heard a thunderbolt behind him, and when he looked back he saw that the little shrine had been set afire by lightning. The monk was quite overwhelmed with pity when he learned that both the woman

33. A man of the outcaste class.

and her infant had been struck dead and said that he wondered why he had been allowed to escape.

And yet here is another story: Recently four or five people were resting in a tea shop in Takeda on Aburanokōji Avenue during a thunderstorm, when two of them said, "Ah, forget it!" and insisted on going out in the rain even when the others tried to stop them. Just a moment later, lightning struck close by, and when the people left behind went on their way to the south after the skies had cleared, they found the two men struck dead right in the middle of the road. In this case, the men insisted on going out and met disaster, whereas the monk in the previous story went out and escaped it. I have also heard in recent years of cases in which lightning strikes and kills a next-door neighbor while leaving those in the house it struck without injury. We can do nothing about our life spans.

Among mountain beasts, it's bears that tame most readily. Once I stopped where a cow path intersects Third Avenue in front of Kazan[34] to look at a bear cub tied on a leash by a woman who had come to peddle fruit. When I bought a piece of fruit and gave it to the beast, the woman said to the bear, "Now, say, 'Mm-mm, good,'" and the bear obeyed her, making a sound very much like "Mm-mm, good."

"I bought him from someone who caught him on Mount Ibuki before he had even been weaned," the woman said, "so that at first I had to feed him things I chewed up for him. Now it's been three years."

The bear was still small. When a passerby said to her, "Once he gets big, you should sell him to a freak show!" she said, "Why would I sell him after raising him this way? No, I'll take care of him all his life. Besides, a lot of people buy things from me because of him." The passerby could say nothing in reply to this. A most admirable answer, I thought then, and have not forgotten it.

[KINSEI KIJINDEN, ZOKU KINSEI KIJINDEN, ED. MUNEMASA ISOO (TOKYO: TŌYŌ BUNKO, 1972); KANDENKŌ HITSU, NIHON ZUIHITSU TAISEI, SER. 1 (TOKYO: YOSHIKAWA KŌBUNKAN 1975); KANDENKŌ HITSU, NENNEN ZUIHITSU, YŪKYŌ MANROKU, KAGETSU SŌSHI, COMP. MIURA OSAMU (TOKYO: YŪHŌDŌ, 1915)]

34. In Kyoto.

21

Hoary Stories

TADANO MAKUZU

Born into a samurai family in Edo, Tadano Ayako (generally known by the pen name Tadano Makuzu; d. 1825) was the oldest daughter of the household. Encouraged by both her father, a physician and a student of Dutch Learning, and her mother, a physician's daughter who had received a classical education herself, Ayako studied classical Japanese literature in her youth and began to compose waka *when she was sixteen. The same year, she went into service in the Edo quarters of the Sendai domain—in which her father had also served—where she stayed for ten years. At age twenty-six, she was married to a much older man, and when that union failed, she waited until thirty-five before marrying again. Her new husband, Tadano Iga, a middle-ranking samurai, stayed in Edo much of the time, but Ayako moved permanently to Sendai. It was only after the deaths of her father, older brother, and husband that she began to write prose works.* Mukashi banashi *(Hoary Stories), from which the following pieces are taken, is a collection of stories dating from 1812.*

There was a man named Kikuta Kidayū who had a very small stipend. When he was still single, he thought to himself, "Nothing leads to more expense than a fondness for good food, so I'll be as thrifty as I can." At first, he used no spices in his broth and only a little miso, but the result was so forlorn that he carved a fish out of wood, put it on a bamboo skewer, coated it with miso, and fried it—licking the miso off and frying it, and licking it off, over and over again. For three years, he went on in this way and, during that time, became wealthy by doing various similar things. When he eventually got married, he cautioned his wife, "People of our status don't eat tasty things," and wouldn't allow fish to be eaten in his house.

Once when she was asked, as a favor, to take care of a financial matter, the wife received a sea bream as a gift, at a time when Kidayū happened not to be at the house. Happily thinking that she would be able to taste some fish, she took it home, but when Kidayū returned and she showed him the fish and told him what had happened, he said, "Whether you were given it or not, we don't eat it!" and then tossed it—head, tail, and all—over the fence into his neighbor's yard.

The wife simply stood there, stunned, until one of the people next door came outside, discovered the fish, and said in a loud voice, "How did this fish get here? There are no teeth marks on it, so it can't be that a dog dropped it." But after a few minutes' looking at it, he then said, "Finding a sea bream is a happy thing, either way—let's eat it!" He then gathered some people together, bought some saké, and put on a feast.

Hearing all of this going on, Kidayū took the occasion to instruct his wife.

"Listen to those fools. They find one sea bream, so they go buy saké, waste some soy sauce, and then invite people over to waste even more on food. Just goes to show you how stupid eating fine food really is."

There are people who think like that.

———————————

Oteru's[1] wet nurse, Gen, tells of a farm family who made their living hunting on the Tama River. The younger brother was adopted into another house, and then the older brother lost his wife—leaving him two children—and then fell sick himself.

Because someone had told the older brother that eating a field rat would cure his illness, he asked his younger brother to get one for him.

1. Teruko, Ayako's younger sister, married a Sendai physician and lived nearby.

But just as he was leaving, along came a big weasel with a field rat in its mouth. "Just what I was praying for," the younger brother thought. He grabbed the weasel and took the rat, which he gave to his brother to eat, so the story goes.

The next day, the younger brother went to his older brother's house to attend to funeral matters regarding the wife, and right there in broad daylight the weasel attacked him, biting at his heels. He struck back at the beast, which ran off somewhere. From that night on, however, the weasel would crouch by the entrance to the older brother's house, glaring at the people inside with an indescribably baleful look in its eyes. One night, after the older brother had fallen asleep, the weasel came in and grabbed his topknot string in its mouth and pulled, in response to which the brother took a swipe at it with his hand, sending it off in the direction of where the children were sleeping, getting bit in the process. The next day, when he went to look at the children, both of them had been bitten also and were crying in agony.

The next evening, the weasel was there at the doorway again; and again when they fell asleep, he attacked. When the man tried to catch the beast, he got bitten on the hand where he had already been bitten before. The children perished first, the father dying in agony about half a month later. In this way, three people lost their lives trying to cure an illness.

Gen lived not far from the place and saw the weasel herself. She was always saying what an awful story it was and how frightened Oteru was of weasels.

Ii Genban no Kami[2] passed away on the tenth day of the Seventh Month. Beginning in the Sixth Month, there had been times when the torches in his hallways and even the lanterns would go out as soon as they were lit, plunging everything into darkness. People thought that maybe the oil they were getting was impure and changed oil dealers, but the problem persisted. Finally, the flames went out so quickly that they were forced to use candles. This must have been an omen of the dire event that was to come.

2. Ayako served the Ii clan in the Hikone domain for five years before her marriage.

It's foxes who eat the scabs off pox sores. To us, it looks like people must be doing it, but in truth it's foxes.

This is a story about a fox following a man that I heard firsthand, so it must really have happened.

A certain village head went to a Buddhist service and was bringing home with him ten slices of very tasty fried tofu when he came to a place where a mischievous fox was thought to live. The night was clear, and the moon was shining bright, but suddenly the sky went black. When he looked carefully, however, he saw that the moonlight was still bright for a yard or so above the ground, but that above that all was darkness.

"That fox wants my tofu,"[3] he thought, and rather than have it taken from him, he sat down at the foot of a tree and began to eat. When he had finished, the sky cleared, just as it had been before. Ten slices of fried tofu is too much to eat after a memorial service. But it wasn't making him sick, so he ate it all.

Hinata Tōan went to enjoy himself at Shinagawa and decided to go see the cherry blossoms at Goten Mountain. He had the big drums brought in and even called in some geisha, ordering food for about thirty people, who began enjoying themselves with saké outside. At the ninth hour, someone said, "Let's go in and eat!" and all of them went inside, only to find that all the food had been devoured, right down to the bone. Everyone was so hungry that they had to order food despite the late hour. Tōan said that the food must have been eaten by foxes.

———

Suzuki Tsunehachi[4] likes true stories. One he told often was about a tool dealer from Honjō.

Once there was a gathering of toolmakers across the river from where the dealer lived. He took the ferry over but found nothing there that he liked, so he put his money inside his jacket breast and headed for home just as daylight was fading, arriving at the river crossing just when the

3. Foxes were thought to have a special liking for fried tofu (*aburaage*).
4. A professional painter and friend of Ayako's father.

ferryboat was moving away from shore. As he was looking around waiting for the boat to return, he spied a young man and woman walking along the top of the stone embankment, talking in whispers. He realized that they must be planning to throw themselves in the river because they were in some kind of trouble.

He walked over toward the couple and said, "When I saw you, you looked as if you were planning to die because you are in need of money. I don't know you, of course, but I couldn't just stand by. Inside my coat here I have ten *ryō*[5] that I will lend to you, so please arrange things so you don't have to kill yourselves."

The couple was so surprised at this development that for a moment they seemed not to comprehend what he was saying, but the boat had arrived, so the dealer quickly tossed them the money and hopped on for the trip across the river. When he arrived home, he was feeling very good about himself, and said that he had made a fine purchase.

One day two years later, the dealer went over to the market as always and was on his way home. On an errand, he ended up on a path he had never used before, where he saw a woman inside her house combing her hair. She hurriedly ran out to greet him, with her hair still down.

"You're the man we met a few years ago—yes, I'm sure it's you," she said. Getting a look at her face, he saw that she was the woman he had given the money to. Soon the man, too, having heard all this, came running out, and they insisted that the dealer come inside. All the while, they showered him with thanks for saving their lives. At that time, he learned, they had been in a bad way. They had so regretted not learning his name and where he lived that they had decided to rent a house near the crossing, thinking that if they lived there they just might see him when he passed that way again. Then, believing that their lives had been spared by the intervention of the Kannon of Asakusa, they visited the shrine daily to pray for a chance to meet their benefactor again.

As they went on and on like this, time was going by and the dealer tried to leave, but they wouldn't hear of it. Out came the cups, and they drank saké together until it was getting quite late.

5. One *ryō* was defined as the equivalent of one *koku* of rice, the amount necessary to support one person for one year.

As he made his way to the crossing, the boat was just returning to shore, and everyone was talking about how a bunch of people had just died in an accident. Had he not been delayed, the dealer would have been on the boat that sank—the one he usually took. Thus he concluded that the reason he himself had not gone down with those who drowned was that his life had been spared in repayment for his having saved the lives of the couple.

What a wonderful story! Tsunehachi heard it directly from the dealer himself.

In the castle of Lord Doi, governor of Yamashiro, in Kariya,[6] there was a cat about the size of a small dog, which people gave the name Big Cat. Sometimes the men on watch would catch sight of it, but it never did any mischief. When once talk turned to cats, I heard from my father that he had been told by Lord Doi himself that no one knew exactly when the cat had taken up living there.

It was spring, after some years had passed. The cherry blossoms were even more beautiful than usual and the skies so balmy that the samurai on duty got together and decided they would eat their lunch out on the grass in the garden, beneath the blossoms. As they went out, they found an indescribably beautiful little cat with a red collar, running around, frolicking just like a butterfly—such a beautiful sight that the men were all staring at it.

"It's got a collar, so it must be someone's pet," someone said. "But how could a little cat get so far into the castle? Something's not right."

Trying to get the cat to come closer, they threw it some food from their pot, and immediately it ran over. But no sooner had it eaten the food than it suddenly changed into their own Big Cat, which they had known for so long.

"Big Cat must be a shape-shifter!" someone said, and the cat fled, never to be seen by the guards again.

---

6. A small domain located in Mikawa Province (present-day Aichi Prefecture). Over the course of its history, many different lineages served as daimyo in Kariya, the Doi among them.

My father said that he heard this story from eyewitnesses who told him about it because it was so strange.

———————————

Sawaguchi Chūdayū, foster father of Kakuzaemon,[7] was a man of great courage. For ten years, he had wanted to get a look at the shape-shifters in Hosoyoko district,[8] hoping for a chance to grapple with one of them sometime. One winter night, when it was getting late, he was returning from somewhere. Snow had fallen, and there was just a little moonlight shining as he came to a place where he had a clear view of the area. He had three or four people with him, to whom he turned and said, "For a long time I have wanted to grapple with one of the shape-shifters who are said to come out here, and tonight is the night for my wish to be granted. But I want to go on alone. No offense is intended; all of you run on home. If we all go on together, we'll scare them off."

The men acquiesced and sent him off on his own, but they wanted to see, too, so they followed him and kept their eyes on him from behind.

After he had gone ahead a little way, Chūdayū squatted and stopped for a minute, walked a little more, again squatted and stopped for a minute, then went three or four *ken*[9] and squatted and stopped once more. But the last time, the men saw the glint of steel in the moonlight. Sure that Chūdayū had drawn his sword, they decided to see what had happened and all ran to where he was.

"What happened?" they asked.

"I've never had such bad luck," Chūdayū said. "The straw cords of the new snow sandals I put on this morning broke,[10] first one, then the other; and just as I had finally gotten them on again, I was broadsided. I got free and cut him, and then I saw him run down beneath that bridge. Go take a look."

7. The younger brother of Ayako's husband, Tadano Iga. He was evidently adopted by Sawaguchi Chūdayū.

8. In the city of Sendai.

9. One *ken* was equivalent to roughly six feet.

10. A note in a later version of this story included in Ayako's *Ōshū banashi* (*Stories from the Deep North*, 1817) says that the animal must have been responsible for breaking the cords. See *Tadano Makuzu shū*, ed. Suzuki Yoneko, Sōsho Edo bunko 30 (Tokyo: Kokusho kankōkai, 1994), 227.

They went to see and there was a big cat, about the size of a small dog, sliced open from belly to throat. It was unconscious, so they brought it up to show him.

Chūdayū held down the head of the beast and asked someone to finish the thing off, but the one who tried was so flustered that he missed and cut deeply into Chūdayū's own hand instead. He had the scar for a long time after, it is said. But he was calm enough to go on and apply the coup de grâce himself.

They rolled the animal up in some reeds and carried it back, with its neck and tail hanging out.[11]

Fukuhara Nuidono was a disciple of Chūdayū's and also highly skilled. Among his retainers was a man who excelled at handicrafts and made an amazing hunting flute that would attract shape-shifters when you blew on it. Once, Nuidono was in the mountains hunting, waiting for game to appear. At first daylight, he saw his wife standing at the entrance to his shelter in her bedclothes, and when he looked closer, it was a person, no doubt about it. Yet there was no way that a woman, all by herself and in her bedclothes, no less, should show up there, he thought: it must be a shape-shifter. So he shot the thing with his gun—but still it looked like his wife!

At this point, he went back to his house to see if his wife was all right, and she came out to greet him, just like normal. Since he was looking a little pale, people asked him if he wasn't feeling well, but he didn't explain.[12]

Calling one of his retainers, he said to the man, "This morning I shot something strange. Go look and tell me what you see."

When the man went to look, lying there dead was an old badger, which the man carried back to his master, who then told the whole story.

Another time, Nuidono went out hunting and was waiting for some game with five double loads all prepared when from a few yards away

11. A note here says, "Any story that tells about an especially big cat notes that when it was wrapped up in something its head and tail stuck out—making it sound as if it might have been a fox."
12. The original text reads as if it were the wife who was pale, but a note says that it was the husband.

a huge snake came at him with its mouth open, ready to devour him in a gulp. He shot the gun right down the snake's throat, which it couldn't well withstand and fell down into a gully. At the same time, however, the sky clouded over, a strong wind came up, the mountain groaned, and the earth shook in a most frightening manner—so the story goes. The snake thrashed about for three days in the gully and then died. It was nearly thirteen *ken* in length. People put one of the vertebrae from its spine in their courtyard as a conversation piece. It was about nine inches around.

In both cases, these beasts had been attracted by the hunting flute. Thereafter, they named the flute Princess and treated it as a treasure. Chūdayū had two flutes that he prized, one of which, when he was ill and dying, he handed down to his foster son, Kakuzaemon. It was this flute that sometimes attracted shape-shifters when it was blown. Kakuzaemon was ordered never to use it.[13]

A man named Kita Yūji returned to his house and opened the door of his sitting room to see a man at his desk. "Who could this be?" he wondered, noticing that the way the man tied up his hair, his robes, his sash—everything he was wearing was exactly like what Yūji himself had on. While he had never seen his own back, of course, it seemed to him that this man looked exactly like him.

Amazed at what he was seeing, Yūji stood there for a few minutes and then decided that he had to see the man's front side and began boldly to walk over, when the man—still with his back to Yūji—quickly ran out onto the veranda and disappeared from sight, gone to who knows where.

When he told his family about what had happened, his mother said nothing to him but seemed to be keeping something secret. Soon after, Yūji took sick and died the same year. Up until then, three generations had seen the same apparition, taken ill, and died—from what is called the shadow sickness. The mother and others in the household had known about this but had not spoken of it, or told the master of the house, so that he never knew.

13. A note here says, "Strange beasts also came when Kakuzaemon blew on it."

A man of my house named Sugano Saburōzaemon went deep into the mountains every day to collect firewood. When he was young, he went a little earlier than usual one morning and was picking up firewood just as the sun came up when he saw something moving around halfway up the slope opposite. Looking more closely, he saw a woman washing her hair. This makes no sense, he thought—for a woman to be alone early in the morning in such a deserted place, and washing her hair to boot. As he watched, she stopped directly across from him and turned to face him—a gorgeous woman, fair in complexion, with beautiful skin fairly shining in the sunlight. But there was something awful in her gaze, something he thought could not be human.

Hidden in the pines, he was out of sight himself, but he was so frightened that the hairs on his body were standing on end, so he dropped his load of sticks and went swiftly down the mountain without even looking back—and never went to that mountain again, it is said.

Thinking about it later, he remembered that the pines of that place, though still young, were more than ten feet high, which says how tall the thing must have been for her head to be visible above the trees. He also realized that the size of her head must have been twenty-four inches or so. Most strange. People said that perhaps she might have been what is known as a mountain woman.

When my father was still single, he would go along with his teacher to dissect bodies. Once, the teacher and four or five of his students went to Suzuga Grove at the end of the Tenth Month. A dry wind was blowing, and it was a cold night. After cutting up some bodies to study them, they all went to Shinagawa to drink rather than going straight home.

The women in the house where the group was staying were nervous and appeared ill at ease, and before they lay down to sleep, drank two or three tea cups of saké, which made my father conclude that they must like to drink. Then, after sleeping for a while, Father and his students awakened in the night to the sound of a cuckoo singing right above the bed, from so close by that it seemed to be either right at the eaves or perhaps inside. The women with them were so alarmed that they were clinging to the men.[14]

As soon as the new day dawned, all the men went home. Thinking about it later, Father realized that it wasn't the season for the cuckoo to sing and thought that the behavior of the women had been out of the ordinary. Perhaps there was something strange about the house, he said, and it may have been that the women had been unnerved by the fact that all the men in the group reeked of dead bodies.

[*TADANO MAKUZU SHŪ*, ED. SUZUKI YONEKO, SŌSHO EDO BUNKO 30 (TOKYO: KOKUSHO KANKŌKAI, 1994)]

14. Ancient legend identified the cuckoo as a harbinger of death.

22

Haikai Prose

NATSUME SEIBI

Natsume Seibi (1749–1816) was the son of a wealthy Edo rice broker (fudasashi) of the Asakusa district who, as an amateur haikai poet himself, encouraged his sons in the art. Seibi never studied under a teacher outside his family circle, but he composed haikai all his life and was acquainted with a number of other famous poets, including Ōshima Ryōta (1718–1787) and Kobayashi Issa (1763–1827). Tradition says that he was sickly, and the third piece included here confirms that he was unable to walk in his last years. Earlier, however, he undertook a number of journeys to see famous poetic sites.

In addition to his poetry, Seibi left behind a number of fine examples of haikai prose. The three examples translated here—"San'en no shin" (Three Monkeys), "Oretsue no ki" (Fragment of a Walking Staff), and "Sumika o utsusu kotoba" (Moving into a New House)—are from different times in his life: the first from his forties, the second from his late fifties, and the last from the very end of his life.

Three Monkeys

I have two little ones, a boy named Kyūji and his younger sister, Ito. Just when I get a little time to sit down at my desk, they come in squealing, "Papa, Papa," pick up my brush, and start scribbling. If I let this go on, they are so happy that they won't leave me alone; if I glower at them, they cry and make a fuss. That man of old may have thought of children as more precious than jewels or gold,[1] but not me: I am more apt to be cross with them, sometimes even wondering why I had them in the first place. But when they are waiting for me at the gate as I go out and begin pulling at my sleeves, I have to admit that I would not want to lose them. So we play Three Monkeys, the boy on my right knee and the girl on my left, and we make a fine sight. Kyū covers his eyes, Ito her ears, and I sit there between them, hands over my mouth.

The game is played always on the night of the monkey[2]—from which the name Three Monkeys derives—three times in the morning and four at night. It is better than the Five Beasts[3] game for raising children. Indeed, when he is all grown up and his gaze falls on a beautiful woman, my son may be reminded to close his eyes and not abandon himself to worldly desires. Likewise, my daughter may cover her ears when she hears the lies around her and not give heed to the vain words of untrustworthy men. The five colors[4] will blind you; the five sounds[5] make you deaf. I myself have argued with men over pointless matters and ended up feeling embarrassed or regretful too many times. A dog that barks too much is no good; a man who is overly prone to argument is never wise. Hereafter, I shall take the idea of saying nothing as my guide and, making my mouth more like my nose,[6] write out this piece on the Three Monkeys for my own instruction, with a resolution to share it with my children.

1. An allusion to a poem by Yamanoue Okura (660?–733?), in Man'yōshū (Collection of Ten Thousand Leaves, ca. 759), poem 803.
2. Kanoe saru. Literally, the night of the Chinese zodiacal sign "elder brother of metal/monkey" (kanoe saru), in the ancient sixty-day cycle that was in use in Japan until the late nineteenth century. According to ancient belief, on that night a bug living in the human body would leave the body while the person slept and tell the gods all the person's secret sins. To prevent this, people stayed awake that night, guarded by statues of the monkeys ("see no evil, hear no evil, speak no evil") as a talisman. This game was evidently a further development of ancient custom.
3. In this game, children mimicked the movements of five animals—tiger, deer, bear, monkey, and bird—in the hope of gaining animal strength and perseverance.
4. According to Daoist doctrine, the five colors—green, yellow, red, white, and black—had the effect of leading the eye astray. The character for "color" in Japanese is also used to mean "eros."
5. The five sounds—on an ascending scale from lowest to highest—were believed to have the same dangerous effects on the ears that colors had on the eyes.
6. A statement in Jikkinshō (Ten Maxims, 1252), a collection of folktales, says that if one only makes one's mouth more like one's nose, no mistakes will follow.

Fragment of a Walking Staff

In some foreign countries, there are rules that prohibit even people in their fifties from using a walking stick outside the house. Only after reaching sixty may a person use one out in the streets. A traveler's staff, however—now that's a different matter.

A traveler's staff must first of all be light; but it must also be strong. From the moment you cross your threshold, scattering prayer strips[7] from your pouch like so many flower petals, until the day you come home and make an offering upon return[8]—for all that time your staff must be ready to hand where you can lean on it to support your legs, never letting go of it, not even for an instant. This is why anyone going on the road is sure to carry a staff.

In the spring of 1807,[9] this old man took off on a pilgrimage to worship the god at Ise.[10] From there, with storm winds from the cedars in my sleeves, I continued on to Iga[11] and beyond in search of sites famous in haikai, getting a fair look at fair Yoshino,[12] dangling my feet in the waves of Waka Bay,[13] enjoying the new leaves on the plum trees at Naniwa, traveling to see the sights of Aki and Harima, and finally arriving in Kyoto after more than a hundred days on the road. What sustained me, however, was nothing like the wooden chair of Reverend Foyin[14] but rather a mere slender staff of bamboo. Having been such a support to me in my wanderings, it had a venerable air about it, but along the way the tip of the staff had gotten so worn down that it had lost a good deal of its length. Several times I was on the verge of throwing it away, in fact.

---

7. A way of petitioning the gods and Buddhas for safety in travel.

8. An allusion to a poem by Wakaomibe no Morohito (dates unknown), in Man'yōshū, poem 4350: "To the brush shrine / in my garden I will offer / prayers faithfully / until that future day / when you return to me" (niwanaka no / asuwa no shiba ni / koshiba sashi / are wa iwawamu / kaeriku made ni).

9. Seibi made his journey in 1807, but his haikai prose piece memorializing it was not written until the autumn of 1810.

10. Site of Ise Shrine, dedicated to the Sun Goddess.

11. The birthplace of Matsuo Bashō (1644–1694) and thus a site of interest, especially for haikai poets.

12. A mountainous area in Kii Province famous for its natural beauty that had attracted poets for centuries.

13. Located in Kii Province and likewise a popular stop for poets. Waka is the general term for Japanese poetry.

14. Foyin Liaoyuan (1032–1098), a Chan monk of the Song dynasty (960–1279).

But it had been a help to me for so many days that I thought better of it and kept using it just as I had been, going all the way to Kyoto, where I again made the rounds of the famous sights. After visiting the Great Buddha, however, I could no longer use it. This temple, Hōkōji,[15] had been erected at the request of the great Toyotomi[16] by the lord of Osaka,[17] and such a grand sight had it been—grander even than the Great Buddha in Nara[18]—that it was first on the list of places to visit in the capital. Ten years earlier, however, lightning had struck it, starting a fire that left not a building standing. Thus the glory of the place had long since faded away; nor was a favorable gaze likely to fall on it again.[19] The only thing remaining to attest to its glory days was a great hanging bell. And as I stood looking at this evidence of the End of the Law, holding the staff that was so reduced from its former self, I noticed how much thicker the metal of the bell was compared with my meager stick of bamboo. That is when I broke it into pieces and tossed most of them away, bringing only a fragment of it back to Edo with me.

Whenever I want to recall my travels, I have only to look at this fragment of my staff, which I have kept in my house for a long time as a way to bring to mind my experiences in the capital. Long ago, old Bashō spoke of making a wooden half pestle into a flowerpot.[20] My fragment of a staff holds no flowers and is a useless thing; yet still it stirs my emotions. I really must take good care of it—to ensure that it is never transformed into a dragon.

15. A Tendai temple located in the eastern hills of Kyoto famous for its large wooden statue of the Buddha.

16. Toyotomi Hideyoshi (1536–1598).

17. Toyotomi Hideyori (1593–1615), son and heir of Hideyoshi.

18. A reference to the statue housed at Tōdaiji in Nara.

19. Since Toyotomi Hideyori had been killed by Tokugawa Ieyasu (1542–1616) as part of his campaign to unify Japan under his own control, it was of course unlikely that a temple founded by Hideyori would ever be rebuilt.

20. In a piece dating from 1690, Bashō writes of something called a *kineore* (pestle made of a large block of wood, with a slender handle) that is now owned by a rich person who has named it "flowerpot." The tool was called a half pestle because it consisted of half a full pestle—two large wooden blocks connected by a slender handle that was used vertically rather than horizontally. See *Matsuo Bashō shū*, ed. Imoto Nōichi et al., Nihon koten bungaku zenshū 41 (Tokyo: Shogakukan, 1972), 554–55.

Moving into a New House

Suddenly I had to move, and the day was set for the sixth of the Fourth Month.[21] When I came to my place in Katsushika, in the shadows of Tada Grove, I thought that it would be for only a short while, but when I added up the years, I realized that I had been there a full decade.[22]

During my time there, I had made many friends in the neighborhood. Two among them—old Kawamura and Tokufu—had become for me like the other two legs of a three-legged kettle. Thinking that we would never part, I had stored up memories of them like so many chestnuts and could not get over the idea that we now had to say farewell.

> When again
> will we bask in the cool
> of a moonlit grove?[23]

sannin de / itsu suzumō zo / mori no tsuki

The people in my house were in a rush getting ready to leave, loading things in boats or hiring men to hoist things up on their backs. In the garden out back, the poppies I had planted were starting to bud, and it was touching to see a few blossoms appearing on the eggplants. It seemed as if the very plants themselves were reluctant to be left behind, and for the next two or three nights the moonlight seemed especially forlorn. As I looked around the area where I had grown so accustomed to living, I heard the pines murmuring to themselves.

> Mice will sing here,
> vines will spread over all
> —from this night on.[24]

nezumi naki / mugura shigeramu / koyoi yori

---

21. The year was 1814.
22. Katsushika was located on the far eastern edge of the city, far from Asakusa.
23. In the haikai collection *Arare kuyō* (*A Funeral Offering of Hail*, 1818), in *Natsume Seibi zenshū*, ed. Ishikawa Shinkō (Tokyo: Izumi shoin, 1983), 203.
24. Ibid.

The place I would be moving to was near the entry gate in Asakusa, where I had once lived long before. Located where the Sumida empties into the bay, along the Kamida River,[25] the place is entirely surrounded by shopping districts, right next to the famous Sensōji.[26] In my old age, I should have been withdrawing to a more tranquil place, although there are perhaps many who would prefer the opposite. But there was a specific reason behind the move. I have three sons. Tarō is already forty years old, and he and his younger brother Jirō are living in their own houses. But their younger brother, who just turned twenty, had been living with me in my little cottage. Recently, the older boys had said to me, "You're getting on now, and your legs are so bad you can't walk about on your own. We've been taking turns taking care of you, but our jobs have made it so difficult that we've been a bit negligent. What's more, if you should suddenly get ill, or if a fire should break out nearby, it wouldn't be easy for us to get here quickly. With these things on our minds, we're always worrying and feeling very depressed. And then there's our younger brother—out in the country like this, he's got nothing to do, and he needs to find a job, which he won't be able to do living out here. Therefore, we really must ask you to move someplace closer by."

What they said made complete sense. There are stories about how old people used to be left out on the mountainside, after all; for them to care for me so generously showed filial piety on the older boys' part as well as compassion for their younger brother. And so it was, yielding to their kind plans for me, that I left my old home behind on the evening of the sixth. The family welcomed me to my new dwelling that night, got out the saké cups, and we all got drunk celebrating the new home where they prayed I would live long.

As the new place was right in the middle of the city, there was no way to plant trees and shrubs, and no sound I heard resembled the soft sigh of the wind in the pines. Instead, my ears heard a raucous jumble—the sound of the chain as it brought water up from the well near the temple gate, the echo of pestle striking mortar as if it were right next to my pillow, the voice of mendicant monks begging for food. Yet it *was* nice

25. Now pronounced Kanda.
26. A temple located in the heart of Asakusa, one of the busiest sections of Edo.

to have fresh food so close by and to hear hawkers selling anything one could ever want, morning and night. For me, the people going back and forth on the street will for the moment have to stand in for trees in the deep forest, as I accustom myself to the bustling ways of the city.

All that I hear
I must hear anew—
even the cuckoo.[27]

kiku koto o / mina aratamete / hototogisu

Someone told me that having lived so long in solitude I would not be able to stand city noise, but I answered that I would act like an old silkworm and think of the time I had left as time to enjoy.

So short the night!
And do what you will,
still time goes by.[28]

mijikayo wa / totemo kakutemo / sugusubeshi

Here I sit, then, just amusing myself by jotting down these silly matters, using up the last long rays of the sun.

[*KINSEI HAIKU HAIBUN SHŪ*, ED. MARUYAMA KAZUHIKO AND MATSUO YASUAKI, NIHON KOTEN BUNGAKU ZENSHŪ 42 (TOKYO: SHŌGAKUKAN, 1972); *NATSUME SEIBI ZENSHŪ*, ED. ISHIKAWA SHINKŌ (TOKYO: IZUMI SHOIN, 1983)]

27. *Arare kuyō*, 203.
28. Ibid.

23

Clouds of Floating Grasses

Unpyō zasshi (literally, Clouds of Floating Grasses) *was published in 1843. Although often attributed to the eighteenth-century literati painter Yanagisawa Kien (1704–1758), it almost certainly comes from a later hand. Essentially a compendium of short essays and homilies, its tone is heavily moralistic, and most of the anecdotes included in the work end with a didactic lesson of some sort. The philosophical point of view is largely Confucian. Its straightforward and pithy style endeared it to the reading public, and the work continued to retain its popularity well into the Meiji period (1868–1912).*

A man wanted to get a clock so that he could tell the time, but his wife stopped him.

"It will cause you trouble day and night and use up time when it isn't working right. You'll lose more time than you gain," she said.

"Well, then, I'll get a rooster," the man said, but his wife objected to that as well.

"As human beings, we should all have a sense of time, just as the tides rise and fall. Resorting to a clock amounts to being lazy on the job."

In the end, he didn't get a rooster either.

As long as the courtesies[1] are maintained, relations between a man and a woman will remain fresh, and affections stay deep and strong. But when the courtesies are lost, affections wear thin, and separation isn't far off. Benevolence and deference work as go-betweens to keep the courtesies strong, and courtesy is the reverse side of flattery. Wisdom stands face-to-face with foolishness; truth and lie sit right next to each other. One must be aware that familiarity and disgust live in the same house.

Setting out to do good is no easy matter. The best course is to take care that one's actions result in no evil, and then pursue that course of action until death. Especially when it comes to women, the great mistake made by parents is to let them proceed according to their own understanding, leaving the learning of sewing and spinning until later on and instead letting them study music and the arts. For they then grow up without discipline, never learn sewing and spinning, and lose their femininity. Being less intelligent than men, they don't apply themselves to things wholeheartedly or hold themselves to a high standard, and thus become involved in improper behavior. Even if they think they understand what is right on their own, they should protect themselves by taking others as models.

"The small man withdraws into seclusion but gains nothing from it."[2] So the book says, but even those who are not small men often fail to benefit from seclusion. To enjoy solitude all by oneself is difficult. In the world today, most of those who go into seclusion have been forced to do so by circumstance. Those who leave the dusty world by their own choice, giving up on worldly ambitions, are in a different category; but those who still

1. *Rei.* The Confucian rites. Here the term seems to refer to common courtesies that help to maintain proper social relations.
2. "Moral and Social Programs: The *Great Learning* [*Da xue*]," in *A Source Book in Chinese Philosophy*, trans. and comp. Wing-tsit Chan (Princeton: Princeton University Press, 1963), 89. "Small man" is a Confucian term referring to a person of low rank and status, often in contrast to the "gentleman" (*kunshi*).

yearn for things while in seclusion and remain attached to the ways of the world only appear to be in retirement but are in truth not so. The fact that so many recluses have nameplates by their doors is enough to show this.

———————

Fools labor after useless things, while the wise enjoy creating things of value. There is no end to useless things, but things of value are scarce. If you use your limited life span to seek after so vast a variety of things, you will die before satisfying your desires. Wear yourself out gathering goods and you have already brought your life to an end, whereas things of value extend your life because they are good for something. Some say nothing is useless; I say anything that cannot satisfy one's everyday needs has no worth.

———————

Once when old Hikihyaku had Rikyū[3] over, he served him some watermelon with sugar on it. Rikyū ate only the parts where there was no sugar and then went home.

"Old Hyaku doesn't know how to entertain a guest," he said to a disciple. "He gave me watermelon, but sprinkled sugar on it. Watermelon is tasty enough on its own—what an atrocious thing to do to it," he laughed.

———————

Pepper has excellent medicinal properties. Medical books say various things about its good and ill effects but don't go into much detail. When you put it in saké or vinegar or soy sauce, or on clothing or furnishings, none of those things will get moldy and bugs won't touch them. Nothing is better against the humidity of mountains and fields and gorges or dampness inside a house.

———————

It is for their beauty that women are cherished and only rarely for their uprightness: people love them for their form rather than for their

———

3. Both Hikihyaku and Sen no Rikyū (1522–1591) were tea masters, the latter being by far the more famous.

attractive character. The wife of a certain man was known as a beauty, but she had an exceedingly jealous heart and was always exploding at him for his loose ways, which led to constant bickering. Finally one day, she was so jealous that while her husband was out she strangled herself. Then the man drank so much that he vomited blood and died as well.

The meaning of the woman's name was "long life" and of the man's "greatly blessed," which shows that actions say more about people than their names. In praying for a thousand years of life, we hail the pine and the bamboo, and liken ages to the crane and the tortoise, but it is harmony that maintains order in the home. We need to understand that a long life comes from taking care of oneself.

Once a man asked to learn painting from me, and this is what he said: "The reason I want to learn to paint is so I can paint Mount Fuji and Daruma[4] and nothing else. And I am not looking to become all that skillful: I just want my Fuji to look like Fuji and my Daruma to look like Daruma."

I had heard of such requests before but found it interesting. In all the arts, if one just understands this one point, everything else will fall into place.

I was taking the waters at Arima.[5] One day, before I had gotten into the water, I saw a skinny person in Buddhist robes without ears, eyes, or nose come shuffling in. Taken aback, I watched from the shadows as the figure got in the water for a moment and then quickly departed, looking exactly like a skeleton in a painting.

Some fox must be playing tricks on me, I thought, and went off to bed without ever getting in the water. The next day, I told the innkeeper about what I had seen.

"Yes, that woman—a nun, I should say—comes by once in a while. She went as a bride to the Fushimiya, a dealer in Chinese wares in Osaka, and was evidently a real beauty. But one day when her mother-in-law was

---

4. Bodhidharma, the legendary founder of Zen Buddhism.
5. A famous hot-spring resort located in what is now Kobe.

down with some ailment, a fire spread from next door and was bearing down on where the old lady lay. Since there was no one else to help, the nun went running in and brought the old woman out. After the wounds from the fire healed, all that was left were eyes the size of soybeans—although she could see—and a tiny little mouth, although she was able to eat. I hear she will turn seventy this year."

What an admirable person, I thought, and I often told people about her.

————————————

Kinokuniya Mataemon of Naniwa was a wealthy merchant. When he was a young man working for the main house, he was so honest and hard-working that the master of the house took a liking to him.

"It's more than ten years now that you've worked for me," the master said. "Day and night, you've worked hard, always avoiding waste and showing great dedication to the family business, and I'm more than satisfied. As a reward, I'm giving you a stake of one hundred gold pieces. Take it, go anywhere you please, open your own business, and don't come back here until you've increased your fortune to a thousand."

Most grateful, Mataemon took the hundred gold pieces, expressed his thanks, and went up to Kyoto. As he thought the matter over, he realized that while there were lots of ways to make money in business, those who crave huge profits almost always end up losing big, so the best thing was to sell something consumed daily, gaining only small profit but profit all the same. One such thing was paper, not a very profitable item, but one used a lot every day. So he set up shop on Nishinotōin Avenue, selling the sort of cheap paper that is usually cast aside. He would buy waste paper, clean it up, and put it on sale.

Within three years, he had made three hundred gold pieces in profit, which he used to expand his business, increasing his profit to one thousand gold pieces after five years. Then he went back to Naniwa to meet with the master of the house.

"I have taken the hundred gold pieces you gave me and made it into a thousand," he declared, explaining how he had done so.

Praising him, the master said, "I gave you this challenge because while you were in my house I realized that you had uncommon ambition. Now go off with your thousand and make it into ten thousand."

Mataemon accepted the challenge and five years later placed ten thousand gold pieces before his master, who praised him again and said, "Now bring me back a hundred thousand."

Again, Mataemon accepted the challenge: "At first I took the hundred gold pieces I received from you and made it into a thousand, and then worked hard to make that into ten thousand. So making ten thousand into a hundred thousand shouldn't be all that difficult."

Three years later, he had reached his goal, and the master was very impressed with his work.

"Now, you are so hardworking that I don't think you need any more direction. Go off, then, and this time make a million."

To this, Mataemon replied, "It will take more than a lot of effort to make a million pieces of gold, so there is something I must ask you. Just how much money have you yourself accumulated by now?"

"Why, there is no limit to my holdings now," the master said.

"And after you have that much saved up," Mataemon queried, "do you still find yourself wanting more?"

"I have never ceased to want more," the master said.

To this, Mataemon said, "I must ask you then to let me stop after this next round. Life itself is a treasure, after all, and wealth is possible only while one lives. Without life, wealth is of no benefit."

"I disagree with your way of thinking," the master said. "In my opinion, only wealth makes life in this world worthwhile, and to have life but no wealth would be pointless."

At this, Mataemon gave his master the hundred thousand gold pieces and said, "Until now, I have not wanted to go against your wishes because I was in service to you, but because I have desires of my own now, I will take my leave and ask you to forgo any further demands." Then he left and went back to his house.

At home, Mataemon divided up whatever little money he had left and gave it away to his associates, disposed of his goods, shaved his head, took the Buddhist name Enchibō, became a disciple at Taiyūji, and set up a hut for himself in Kyoto, where he went about begging for his food daily, eventually dying there. Some friends put up a grave marker, on which was inscribed his parting poem:

Look down below,
to those who tumble down
to the depths of hell:
then you will see how deeply
our desires dig their holes!

ochite yuku / naraku no soko o / nozokimin / ikahodo yoku no / fukaki ana zo to

---

Many people who keep cats don't know how to care for them. They put dried tuna in with their food, which adds fat, not knowing that if you give cats too much fat, they won't catch mice.

The thing to give cats is fried barley with miso on it. You shouldn't give them anything else. If they get used to eating meat, when you don't have any to give them, they are sure to steal from your neighbors.

It's the same with raising people.

Among the writings of Musō Kokushi[6] we read, "Anyone who wants to live a long life should not tell lies; for lies tire the heart, and even a small thing can tax one's energy. As long as you don't use up your energy, you will surely live a long time." In the inscription of a portrait of the sage Tekkai[7] is this poem:

Consider the sages:
they never fail to take care
of their bodies,
are never angry, and never lust—
and thus enjoy long life.

sennin wa / fuyōjō sezu / hara tatezu / mono hoshigarazu / sore de nagaiki

6. Musō Soseki (1275–1351), a prominent Zen monk.
7. A sage of the Sui dynasty (ca. 581–618).

A friend of mine named Hirasawa so-and-so was a samurai of great patience. One time, he was out on the road on important business with a large escort. A man on the second floor of a building along the way was brushing his teeth and spat out the window, accidentally hitting Hirasawa's robes.

The people escorting him got very angry and were about to go in and drag the man out into the street, but Hirasawa stopped them. "Pardon me while I use this house for just a moment," he said. Then he went in and got out a change of robes from one of his own linen boxes. As he was doing so, the people of the house apologized profusely.

"I'm sure it was just a mistake. Hereafter, be more careful," Hirasawa said, and left.

The people with Hirasawa asked him why he had let the man off so easily.

"I'm on an important errand today," he said. "I couldn't be spending my time on such a trivial matter. An event of this sort requires the kind of patience I always try to maintain."

Another time, Hirasawa was on an errand of a more personal nature. It was summertime, and someone had splashed some dirty water from a ditch onto the hem of his robe.

His men were about to start beating the man, but he stopped them.

"This makes no sense," the men complained.

"On the contrary," Hirasawa said. "I am on a personal errand today. To be cursing people out over private business is not appropriate for a samurai. One who shows patience will never be shamed before the world."

———————

A child who looked to be thirteen or fourteen was pulling a cart carrying a lame man, and along with them was a woman who appeared to be the lame man's wife, carrying an infant on her back and leading a child of six or seven by the hand. They were begging for food as they went along.

Laughing, a bystander said to me, "It's hard enough for people like that to make their way in the world; what sense is there in bringing so many children along?"

I told him that I saw things differently: "All sorts of things go on in life, and one never knows what will happen next. Sometimes parents and children, or siblings, or husbands and wives end up living far from one another in different places. Compared with them, these beggars can at least enjoy one another's company—which makes them better off, beggars or not. That child pulling the cart is a filial son, and that wife with a child on her back is a virtuous woman."

This stopped the man's laughing.

A man wrote out the word "patience" and put it next to where he sat, thinking that if he was looking at it all the time, the idea would naturally stick in his mind and give him a good attitude as he went about his daily work. But patience doesn't come unless you do training, and bearing up against things that are hard to endure is not so easy.

When I was trying to nurture patience in myself, I thought that nothing would work so well as taking a ride on a crowded ferryboat. So I took one servant and made a trip from Kyoto to Naniwa,[8] and then back from Naniwa to Kyoto, enjoying staying in the boat the whole time as a kind of training. For no matter how straitened your worldly circumstances, if you think back on the time when you stayed overnight on a ferryboat, nothing will seem beyond endurance. Living as a family in a little one-room house is still better than a ferryboat. The nights are especially unbearable. You have to bend your knees and pull your legs up against you, or use someone else's leg as a pillow. You try to settle down to sleep but get jostled awake. Then, just when you manage to nod off, snoring wakes you. Awake or asleep, you never feel relaxed. Even a single night spent that way is the same as a lifetime.

As a boy, already I loved poetry. Whenever I finished a composition, I would show it to my father, but not once was my work praised. "Worthless," he would say, and toss the paper aside. Others would look at my work and praise it, and I always wondered why he did not.

8. On the coast in what is modern-day Osaka.

Later, I married a woman who so excelled at sewing that she could make a full short-sleeved kimono in a day and still find time to do other things that had to be done. A woman who sewed for a living saw her work and was amazed at her skill.

Once when I praised my wife for her work as a seamstress, she told me this: "My mother died when I was three, so I was raised by my stepmother, who was of a strict disposition. From the age of five or six, I worked in the kitchen, and from the age of seven I began receiving instruction in calligraphy, reading, and sewing. She didn't want to be criticized later for not training me properly because I wasn't her own daughter, so I wasn't allowed to waste my time playing around. Sewing—that was all I had time for, and sometimes I thought Mother was awfully strict. But now, every time someone praises my sewing, I know there was nothing unkind in my stepmother's love."

Hearing this, I too became grateful that my father didn't praise my poems when I was a child.

Some words for those undertaking disciplines: "Blossoms after rain showers are of a richer red; willows battered by the wind are a deeper shade of green."

The ten virtues of drinking are Preserving the Proprieties, Recovering After Labor, Forgetting Troubles, Relieving Depression, Distracting the Mind, Warding Off Illness, Counteracting Poison, Solidifying Friendships, Forging Relationships, and Extending Life.

When Botanka Shōhaku[9] was living in the western hills, he was robbed of one hundred coins by brigands, and when Bechikan[10] had a hut in Yamashina, he was robbed by thieves of seventy *kan*[11] in coin that he had

9. 1443–1527. A master of linked verse.
10. Also known as Hechi and Hetsu, a late-sixteenth-century master from Mino Province who was patronized by Toyotomi Hideyoshi (1536–1598).
11. One *kan* was the equivalent of a thousand copper coins.

received from selling some tea utensils. Although the situation of people still in lay life is a separate issue, people living in seclusion after abandoning the world shouldn't keep fancy robes and money about—since that is what thieves and brigands are after. For household necessities, one should make do with earthenware and things made of paper. This is the best way to defend against thievery.

———————————

No matter what one is talking about, having few things is the basis of true abundance. Storing up lots of things just invites trouble and taxes the body. Rich people who live frugally can enjoy accumulating more things. But wearing thin robes when you are wealthy is to make sheer accumulation your only pleasure and to allow your treasures to consume your life. From the vantage point of those without many worldly desires, such people look like nothing so much as summer insects drawn to the flames.

———————————

Sitting beneath the window of my cottage, I would hear a sound all day long and wondered what it might be coming from. When I opened the shutter and looked out, there was an old man, wearing spectacles, sitting on a mat, and hollowing out a depression in the top of a mortar.

"How many days have you been cutting?" I asked.

"Some days I cut, some days I don't," he replied.

"And how old are you?" I went on.

"I'll be seventy this year," he said.

"Do you have children?" I asked.

"A daughter, who has taken in a husband, and I have three grandchildren," was the reply.

"If you have a son-in-law, you shouldn't need to work like this, should you?" I asked.

"To support a family of six, there's only my son-in-law, and he has no one to help him out," he said. "Even if I finish the mortar, it won't contribute much to the family finances, but rather than just whiling away the days doing nothing, I want to help some—even if I make only

enough to buy nose tissue. So I do this, dangerous work though it is," he
laughed.

Among both high and low, the way parents work to bless the lives of
their children is impressive, I thought.

[*MEIKA ZUIHITSU SHŪ*, ED. TAKE RYŪZŌ, VOL. 2
(TOKYO: YŪHŌDŌ, 1928)]

IV

THE MODERN PERIOD

In the mid-nineteenth century, Japan began to open its doors to the rest of the world after two hundred years of isolation. Predictably, great changes ensued. In the world of letters, traditional poetic forms like haiku and tanka (another word for *waka*) lost ground to free verse, and the novel gradually came to dominate literary discourse. Despite this, however, the *zuihitsu* continued to thrive, occupying a comfortable spot on the fringes of more "serious" genres. Indeed, the period from 1868—the year of the so-called Meiji Restoration, which inaugurated the country's rapid transformation into a modern industrial superpower—until the present rivals the mid-Edo period as a "golden age" for essayistic writing. The primary publishing vehicles for the form for the past hundred years have been magazines, journals, and newspapers—an immense discursive field that virtually demands participation by writers and intellectuals of all varieties. (When Tayama Katai describes his fear of an editor's appearing at his door demanding a manuscript, one cannot help but think that he is speaking for most Japanese writers in the modern age.)

Many of the writers presented in this section are novelists or literary critics. Also included, however, are essays by a physicist, a publisher (who was also a playwright and novelist), and a media critic, reflecting the broad demographic of the form. And it should be added that a good number of the authors presented here (Terada Torahiko, Kawamori Yoshizō, Mukōda Kuniko, Dekune Tatsurō, and Sakai Junko, most prominently) are specialists in the *zuihitsu* or the "essay" (*essei*), a loanword that is often used interchangeably with *zuihitsu*, although sometimes implying a more modern conception of the essay as a vehicle of empirical analysis or personal, psychological introspection and confession.

The subject matter of the selections is again diverse, offering musings on a broad range of humanistic topics—from heavy ones like individuality, the frustrations of the writing life, and dealing with the effects of drought, to lighter ones like laughter, life abroad, and the practice of "peeing by the roadside." Many writers hark back to the desultory and impressionistic habits of Yoshida no Kenkō and Tachibana Nankei, while others adopt more rationalist schemes of exposition and argument. As in the Edo period, the tone of the works is often quite personal, but references to historical events (the civil disturbances of the early twentieth century, the Great Kantō Earthquake of 1923, the American occupation of Japan in the late 1940s, and the Chernobyl incident, for instance) also occur. Finally, two of the pieces (by the novelist Dazai Osamu and the essayist Sakai Junko) offer musings (mostly amusing) on the *zuihitsu* genre itself in a way that returns our thoughts to the origins of the form in *The Pillow Book*.

24

Autumn Ensemble

HIGUCHI ICHIYŌ

The daughter of an erstwhile samurai, Higuchi Ichiyō (1872-1896) was born in the midst of the upheavals of the Meiji period and died before those upheavals were truly over. Despite a precarious financial situation, her parents sent her to a local teacher for poetry lessons, and in time she also apprenticed herself to a popular novelist. In 1895 and early 1896, she published a handful of stories that are now very much part of the modern canon, all of them about city people in the poorer areas of Tokyo. Praised by luminaries such as Mori Ōgai (1862-1922) and Kōda Rohan (1867-1947), Ichiyō was for a brief time a celebrity of sorts in the literary world and seemed poised for a stellar career. But then she fell prey to consumption, which had carried off her brother and probably her father as well. As she notes in one of the essays translated here, she was at first troubled with headaches and fatigue, which were followed soon by the more debilitating problems that hastened her death.

In addition to stories, Ichiyō left a diary, poems, and a number of essays, including the following four short pieces published as a group under the title Aki-awase (Autumn Ensemble) in the year of her death.

Ah, these headaches—they make these last days seem a dream. Outside, from summer growth as thick as the world's troubles, I hear the first cuckoo of the year. Yet here I am, putting together an ensemble from last autumn,[1] chagrined to see morning dew on the leaves of bamboo shoots shining new after casting off layers of bark.

Rainy Nights

How tall the leaves of the plantain in my garden have grown! Five feet above the fence, no doubt. I wonder how this can be, when earlier this very year I was saying how short the plant was; but then I recall my amazement last summer at how much it would grow over just two or three days of intense heat. Autumn winds begin to blow, the leaves start to fray at the edges, and as they appear more and more ragged, the sound of rain on the leaves seems all the more moving. So fine is the rainfall that it doesn't block out the sound of crickets in the grasses, but as the wind gains in intensity I am dismayed to think of the damage it will do.

Rain in any season makes me feel low; but it's in autumn that it strikes the hardest. Night deepens, the lamplight seems more somber, and on a night when I am unable to sleep it seems so futile to go to bed that I pick up the paper box I keep scraps in and end up taking out my needles. When I was small, the woman who taught me sewing used to complain about the stitching of my collars and skirts, and I was so afraid that I would never succeed in learning correctly that I went off to pray daily at a nearby shrine. But now that is a long time ago. The teacher is in her grave; the student has forgotten almost everything. On rare occasions when I do try to sew, my fingertips seem stiff and I wonder how disappointed my teacher would be to see how clumsy I look as I proceed.

Thinking back on those days, I am nearly moved to tears despite myself. The rain that seems to be walking toward me from so far away, the noise of shutters being closed nearby—how can such things not make one feel forlorn? And on such a night, how despondent I feel when, prepar-

---

1. The essays first appeared in a supplement of the *Yomiuri shimbun* in the autumn of 1895, and only in May 1896 were they put together as an ensemble.

ing to massage my mother's skinny shoulders, I reach out and feel her aging bones.

Moonlit Nights

If there are clumps of clouds, fine; if not, fine too. Sitting in moonlight so bright that it seems to have been buffed to a high sheen, one hears the sound of a flute—a delight if the musician is really good. Likewise if one hears a samisen. And when I hear a koto from across the fence in the direction of Nishikata-machi,[2] it seems so like something from an old romance that I want to get a glimpse of who it might be playing there in the moonlight.

How hard it is to find comfort in the moonlight after parting from a close friend! You think of the person looking up at the same moon far away, but since you can't go along, you feel only resentment, and then silly thoughts begin occurring to you, like making the moon for just a moment into a mirror. The reflection bobbing on the surface of the little pond in the garden seems to speak to you, and as you lean over the railing, staring down into the water, the image that before seemed to be floating on the surface now seems to be deeper and deeper down, leaving you feeling as if the pond had limitless depths and that the moon must reside at the very bottom. Then, after a long time looking down, you look up and find that you can't decide which moon is real—the one in the sky or the one in the water.

It was a foolish thing to do, but I once picked up a stone from our miniature garden and dropped it into the pond, which produced little waves for the moonlight to float upon. Seeing me do this, my little nephew decided to mimic me, so *he* took up an inkstone that he had managed to get his hands on, said, "I'm going to do just what Auntie did—I'm going to smash the moon!" and proceeded to toss it into the pond. The ink-

2. At the time, Ichiyō was living in the Hongō district of Tokyo, one area of which was called Nishikata-machi.

stone was something passed down from my dead brother[3]—something I had always treasured—and I feel guilty having lost it in such a senseless way. We talked about dredging the pond, but it remains as ever. The next day, the moon was gone into the sky, vanished without a trace. I think of what has become of the inkstone and wonder if every night it waits for the moonlight to appear.

On a moonlit night, one is happy to have a visitor—maybe someone one has not been all that close to who is kind enough to drop by. A man is all right, but one is happier if the visitor is a woman. And if it is difficult for her to come out, she can always send a letter. Someone trying to play the poet is tiresome, but on such a night the exchange of a single word can make a treasured friend. The sound of a peddler out on the street, the distant echo of a boat whistle—such things, too, somehow take one's spirit away.

Wild Geese Calling

Dawn moonlight lingers in the sky as you wake from a dream, still unsure whether you have returned to reality; and when you open the rain shutters, you see a sudden gust of wind strike the bamboo leaves, sending the dewdrops scattering and striking your body with a chill. And just then it happens: you hear, descending from above, the call of a wild goose, a forlorn enough thing when you spy a whole flock, but even more so if you see just one. If you are thinking of a loved one far off in the provinces, someone from whom you have been waiting day and night for some correspondence,[4] you wonder sadly about what he might be thinking.

How delightful it is to hear—out of sight—the voices of wild geese calling from gaps in the mists of morning or evening! How moving to imagine the shapes of the birds reflected on moonlit paddies while you lie on your pillow listening to the tolling of a temple bell! And in a traveler's inn or the home of someone living in quiet seclusion, the sound is sure to inspire the deepest thoughts.

3. Ichiyō's brother, Sentarō, had died in 1887.
4. An old Chinese story asserted that wild geese were used as messengers.

Some time back, I lived for a year or so in Shitaya,[5] involved in commerce, to my shame—selling little things in a shop to make a living. The eaves were in bad repair, but not enough to let through any moonlight, which I had only the barest glimpse of, at the edge of the second floor of the house opposite. One night when the autumn wind was blowing high and there was not a cloud in the sky, I went out into the street to gaze up. Thinking back to just such a night when my friends and I had met together to compose poems and ended up quietly chatting about our hopes and dreams, I was overcome with nostalgia and my eyes were filling with tears. And then, from somewhere in the distance, came the sound of a lone wild goose, calling for his lost companions. To say that I was sad at that moment simply does not suffice, for I almost despaired of life itself. What would it be like to hear those calls mixing with the sounds of a mallet striking a fulling block?[6] I wonder, and cannot but envy the innocence of little children running down the street chanting, "Three in a row."[7]

Insect Voices

Ever smaller bloom the morning glories on the fence, and as I look at one tiny blossom, all but hidden by the leaves, I think painfully back to when they started to appear. With time, the voices of the pine crickets[8] and bell crickets have grown thinner, and as one waits for the morning sun while attending to their frail calls, from beside a ditch, say, or by a wall, one wonders what sadness the voices must inspire in the old or the sick, who cannot but contemplate how little time they, too, have left. The time for the first frost has not yet come, yet already the insects are failing, their voices sounding withered and worn.

The giant katydid is full of voice and of sturdy mien, but even he loses strength over time: a pattern also seen among men, amusingly. The voice of the bell cricket rings out beautifully, to the envy of other insects, whose

5. For nine months, beginning in the summer of 1893, Ichiyō and her mother and siblings had made a go at trade with a small sundries shop in Ryūsenji, in the Shitaya district of Tokyo.

6. *Kinuta*. In autumn, it was the custom to clean robes with a wooden hammer and fulling block, a scene that is the subject of many classical poems.

7. A children's song about wild geese flying by in rows.

8. *Matsumushi*. "Pining" crickets. The word *matsu* (pine) is a homophone of the verb that means "to wait."

only satisfaction comes in saying, "Ah—but his life is short." The same is true for the pine cricket, who does not live up to the promise of his name.[9] For one expects the evergreen to withstand the withering on the moors, but the pine cricket fades away not long after the blossoms start falling from the bush clover. I would like to meet the person who gave him that name—who, knowing that he flourished for so short a time, must have chosen the name in the hope that it might extend his life by just a little.

One year I kept a pine cricket in a cage, taking care to protect him from dew and frost. It was when my older brother was ill in bed, however, and he so hated the sad song of crickets in the night that I thought he would sleep more easily if I let the bug out into the garden. I was worried that the cricket might call out nonetheless, but he did not, and we sadly concluded that he must have been so shocked by the cold of the dew that he lacked the strength even to cry out.

My brother passed away at the end of that very year.[10] Then the following year, just when I was recalling how he had died in exactly the same season, I heard, late into the night, the voice of a pine cricket—sounding just the same—from below our fence. It could not be the same cricket, I knew, but still the memories came over me, and I began to weep. How happy I would be, I thought, if like the insect, someone—not truly my brother, of course, but someone with the same voice and face—could come back to me. I would grab his sleeve and not let him go, I thought. Then my imagination got the better of me as I thought how happy my mother would be, so happy that she couldn't speak but could only weep, and further pondered how my father would react to it all.[11]

The insect sang for only two nights and then must have gone somewhere else, for we never heard from him again. Even now, when I hear a pine cricket, I think of those times and feel so forlorn that I have never considered putting one in a cage again. And whenever I hear insect voices withering in the fields, I am always reminded of the one who went away.

[*HIGUCHI ICHIYŌ SHŪ*, ED. WADA YOSHIE, NIHON KINDAI BUNGAKU ZENSHŪ 8 (TOKYO: KADOKAWA SHOTEN, 1970)]

9. In other words, who does not wait (*matsu*) long to die. The pine was a conventional symbol of longevity.

10. He had died in late December 1887.

11. Ichiyō's father, Noriyoshi, had died in the summer of 1889.

25

Short Works from Long Days

NATSUME SŌSEKI

Natsume Kinnosuke (known by the pen name Natsume Sōseki; 1867–1916) is among the most highly regarded of all Japanese novelists. After beginning a career as a professor of English literature at Tokyo Imperial University, Sōseki began writing serial novels for newspapers and eventually resigned from his academic position in order to become a full-time writer. Among his fourteen novels, I Am a Cat (1905), Botchan (1906), and Kokoro (1914) remain some of the most widely read and admired of all twentieth-century works in that genre.

In addition to novels, Sōseki wrote haiku, works of literary criticism, and essays. The short vignettes translated here, "Neko no haka" (A Cat's Grave) and "Kiri" (London Fog), come from a collection of twenty-five pieces that first appeared in the Asahi shimbun *in 1909 under the title* Eijitsu shōhin (Short Works from Long Days). *The first deals with the death of the family cat and the second with an experience that Sōseki had while living in London, where he studied English literature from 1900 to 1902 under the sponsorship of the Japanese government.*

A Cat's Grave

After we moved to Waseda, the cat gradually began to lose weight.[1] The children made no attempt to play with him at all. When the sun was out, he would be asleep on the veranda. Resting his square jaw on paws neatly paired in front of him, he stared out at the garden and never seemed to move. Even when the children were playing rowdily right next to him, he ignored them, and for their part the children from the beginning made no attempt to engage him. As if to say that the cat would never be any good as a playmate, they treated their old friend like a stranger.

This wasn't true only of the children. The maid put his three meals down in a corner of the kitchen every day, but beyond that paid no attention to him. To make matters worse, most of his food was eaten by a big tortoiseshell cat from the neighborhood. But still our cat showed no sign of anger, and I never saw him fight back. He would just lie there asleep, stock-still—yet with no sense of ease in the way he slept. Rather than stretching his body out in a leisurely way so as to take advantage of the sunlight, he seemed unable to find a comfortable posture. But no, that way of describing it isn't quite right; what I mean is that he looked as if he had reached a degree of misery where he had decided that being still was no more unpleasant than moving, and that therefore the best thing was to just hunker down and endure. Although his gaze was always focused on the garden, I doubt that he was aware of the leaves or the trunks or anything else. His greenish yellow pupils stared vacantly ahead. Just as his existence was not recognized by the children, he too seemed unaware of the world around him.

On occasion, however, he did go outside, as if he had something that had to be done—although when he did, he would usually be chased back inside by the tortoiseshell cat. In a fright, he would jump up over the veranda, crash his way through the nearly closed sliding door, and seek

1. The incidents described here took place in the fall of 1908.

shelter next to the hearth. These were the only times when we took any real notice of him. I would guess that it was only at these times that he had a full sense of his own being.

After this had gone on for a while, the long hairs of his tail began to fall out. At first, gaps would appear in his fur where the hair had fallen out, but later patches of red skin began to show through, and just looking at the way his tail hung there dolefully made one feel sorry for him. He had to contort his worn-out body in order to lick the places that hurt.

"Hey, something's wrong with that cat," I would say, and my wife would reply indifferently, "Hmm, I suppose he's getting old." Yet still I did nothing. Then it got so the cat would sometimes throw up his food. Big waves would rise up in his throat, and he would let out a distressed sound that was something between a sneeze and a sob. He was in pain, we knew, but there was nothing else to do, so we chased him outside because we couldn't have him soiling the tatami or the sitting cushions or our bedding. It was because of him that the fancy cushion we used only for guests was ruined.

"This is too much. He's got intestinal trouble, I bet. You'd best dissolve some Hōtan[2] in water and give it to him."

My wife did not reply. Two or three days later, when I asked her if she had done what I asked, she said it had done no good; he wouldn't open his mouth. "We give him fish bones, but he just throws them back up."

"Well, then, don't give him any," I said testily, and went back to reading my book.

After the cat was through vomiting, he would lie there quietly, just as before. By then, he began contracting himself into a ball, crouching on the veranda with all his might, as if it were the only thing he could rely on to support his weight. And something in his gaze had changed, too. Before, his eyes had focused on what was close by but still seemed to see something in the distance, as if he was able to relax somewhat, however despondent he had become. Gradually, though, his gaze grew strange and the color in his eyes began to fade away. To me, it resembled the way

2. The brand name of a patent medicine.

lightning flickers for a moment just after the sun has gone down. Yet still I did nothing, nor did my wife seem to be concerned. And as for the children—well, they had forgotten that the cat was even there.

One evening, he was lying on his belly on the fringe of one of the children's futons when he began to make a groan similar to the one he used to make when we tried to take away a fish bone he had gotten hold of. I was the only one who noticed anything different. The children were in bed, and my wife was intent on her sewing. After a few minutes, he groaned again. Then my wife finally put down her needle.

"What's wrong with him?" I said. "We can't have him biting one of the kids on the head in their sleep." As if to say, "Don't be silly," my wife just kept on sewing the sleeve of the under-kimono she was working on. Every once in a while, the cat groaned again.

The next day, he climbed up on the edge of the hearth and stayed there groaning all day. Whenever someone would fix tea or pick up the teakettle, he seemed put out. But when nighttime came, we forgot all about him. It was on that night that he died. The next morning, when the maid went out back to get firewood from the shed, his body had already gone stiff, lying where he had collapsed on an old earthenware stove.

My wife just had to go out and see the corpse. Indifferent as she had been before, now she was suddenly upset. Calling on the services of a rickshaw man who was often around, she had him buy a little wooden plaque and asked me to write something on it. On the front I wrote, "A Cat's Grave," and on the back I scribbled the verse

Of an evening
thunder may come rumbling up
from down below.[3]

kono shita ni / inazuma okoru / yoi aran

The rickshaw man asked if it was all right to go ahead and bury the cat as he was, to which the maid replied in jest, "What do you mean? . . . You think we ought to cremate the thing?"[4]

3. In his anthology of haiku, this verse is dated September and bears the headnote "On a Cat's Grave."
4. A note to the text quotes a letter saying that they buried the cat in a fruit crate.

Suddenly the children, too, were showing affection for the cat. In front of the grave marker, they set up two glass bottles and stuffed them both with bush clover.[5] Then they put some water in a teabowl and placed it there as well. Every day, they changed the flowers and the water. On the evening of the third day, I watched from the window of my study as my four-year-old daughter walked up to the grave, stood there looking at the unvarnished wood of the marker, and took out a little toy ladle with which she scooped water from the teabowl and took a drink—and not just once. There in the quiet of twilight, water into which tiny petals of bush clover had fallen moistened the throat of little Aiko time and again.[6]

On the anniversary of the cat's deathday, my wife always puts a bit of salmon and a bowl of rice topped with dried bonito shavings in front of his grave. Even now, she never forgets, although lately it seems she doesn't go out into the garden but just puts the offerings up on the bureau in the *chanoma*.[7]

London Fog

In my bed the night before, I had heard clacking all night long. It was coming from the large train station at Clapham Junction, which was located nearby.[8] More than a thousand trains passed through the junction every day. A quick calculation revealed that this meant a train was either coming in or going out once every minute. When the fog was thick, the trains set off some device that made a sound like a firecracker to signal that they were crossing the border into the train yard. This was necessary because in such dense fog, neither the green nor the red signal lights were of any use.

Crawling down from my bed, I pulled up the blinds on my north window and peered outside but found everything obscured. Beneath me, I

5. Putting flowers, water, rice, and other small offerings in front of graves was customary.
6. Aiko was born toward the end of 1905, making her four years old by the traditional Japanese way of counting but not yet even three in Western terms.
7. Literally, "tea room." Roughly equivalent to the parlor of a Western house, although usually smaller.
8. At the time, Sōseki was living at 81 The Chase, Clapham Common, South London.

could make out nothing until about ten feet above the ground—not the grassy yard below or the brick wall that surrounded it on three sides. Instead, the space was occupied by a thick emptiness, an emptiness that was deathly quiet, frozen motionless. The same was true of the garden of the house next door. This garden had a beautiful lawn where, as soon as the mild weather of spring arrived, a white-bearded old man would be out taking the sun. On his right arm, the old man always had a parrot that he would bring so close to his face that one feared he might get pecked in the eye—at which point, the bird would flap its wings and squawk repeatedly. When the old man didn't appear, it would be a young girl who came out, hitching up her long dress and running a mower over every inch of the lawn. Now, though, this garden, so teeming with memories, was buried in fog, standing there next to my rundown boardinghouse and the other houses on the street.

Across the alley behind my house was a Gothic-style church with tall towers. At the top of the gray, sky-piercing towers, bells were always ringing. They were especially bad on Sundays. Today I could see neither the narrow steeple—as one would expect—nor even the body of the structure below, which was made up of uneven chunks of stone stacked one upon the other. For a moment, I thought I could see something that seemed to be black, but there was no echo from the bells, which were chained back there in the same thick shadows that hid the bell from sight.

When I went outside, I could see only a few yards ahead. After passing through those few yards, another few yards would then open to view. For a moment, it seemed as if the world had been compressed into a space just four yards square, but as I walked, another space four yards square would always appear. Then, in turn, the little world I had just come through would vanish as I passed it by.

As I waited on the corner for the bus, the gray air parted and I suddenly saw right before me the head of a horse. The passengers from the upper deck had not emerged from the fog. Looking down after stepping forth into the fog to board, I saw that the horse's head had already become nothing but a blurry shape. When we passed another bus, I thought what a beautiful sight it was—but only for that moment, since before I knew it the passing shape would disappear into the muddy air. All was enveloped in a limitless, colorless expanse. When we were crossing over Westminster Bridge, something white flickered across my line of vision: once, then again. Looking hard, I followed the path of flight and saw what turned out to be gulls, faintly visible, flying dreamlike in that same enclosed space. Just at that moment, above my head, Big Ben grimly struck ten. Looking up, I saw that the sound was there in the sky, but nothing more.

After doing what I needed to at Victoria Station, I walked along the river past the Tate Gallery as far as Battersea, where the gray world I had been passing through suddenly went completely dark. A heavy, black-colored fog assaulted my eyes, mouth, and nose, as if peat moss had been reduced to liquid form and poured down over my body. My overcoat was so damp that it seemed like a weight pressing down on me. And I felt short of breath, the way one feels when breathing in the steam from kudzu broth.[9] Needless to say, my feet felt as if they were making their way over the floor of a cave.

For a moment I stood completely still, surrounded by this oppressive gray darkness. All around me, I sensed that people were passing by. But unless someone brushed my shoulder, I didn't feel convinced that anyone was truly there. Then, in the midst of this thick sea of blackness, a small point of yellow light just the size of a pea bobbed up. With that as my goal, I took four steps and found myself staring into the window of a shop front. Inside, they had the lamps on and things were fairly bright. People were going about their business as usual. At last I felt at ease.

Passing through Battersea, I fairly groped my way up the hill beyond, but there I found only houses. Street after street the homes stood in rows, looking so similar that one could easily get lost there even on a sunny day. It seemed to me that I had turned down the second street on my left and then walked straight ahead two blocks or so. But after that, nothing was clear. So I just stood there alone in the gloom, cocking my head to one side. From the right, the sound of footsteps approached—or so I thought; but then four or five yards in front of me, the sound stopped.

9. A broth prepared with kudzu (arrowroot) that was given to children or sick people in order to warm them.

When the sound started up again, it went fading off into the distance. In the end, I could hear nothing. All that remained was the stillness. Again I was alone in the gloom, wondering what to do. I had no idea how to get back to my house.

[*SŌSEKI ZENSHŪ*, VOL. 16 (TOKYO: IWANAMI SHOTEN, 1979)]

26

Snow

Tokutomi Roka

Tokutomi Kenjirō (better known by the pen name Tokutomi Roka; 1868–1927) was the brother of a famous journalist, for whom he worked in his early career. After the publication of his best-selling novel Hototogisu (The Cuckoo, 1900), *however, he became a professional writer. An advocate of various progressive social causes, he was greatly influenced by Tolstoy—whom he met on a trip to Russia in 1906—and other Western idealists and for a time enjoyed a high public profile as a popular novelist and a moralist. His most famous novel is the semiautobiographical* Omoide no ki (literally, A Record of Memories, *translated as* Footprints in the Snow, 1901). *In 1907, he moved into a small estate in Senzaimura (otherwise known as Kasuya) and lived the life of a gentleman farmer, for two more decades. His house, with its two adjoining studies (shoin), was preserved after his death and is now maintained more or less as it was in a garden open to the public called Kōshun'en (Garden of Enduring Spring, in Setagaya Ward, Tokyo).*

The essay translated here, "Yuki" (Snow), describes a snowy day spent at Senzaimura with only his wife and the housemaid, Tsuruko, for company. It first appeared in 1913 in the collection Mimizu no tawagoto (Ramblings of an Earthworm).

It was at year's end, on the twenty-eighth. Rain began to fall after lunch-time, and it rained on into the night.

Around two in the morning, there was a sound near my pillow and I sat up with a start. Putting on a robe, I stood there on my futon for a while, but there was no hint of anyone prowling about, and from outside I heard only rustling sounds.

"Ah—it's snow!"

The sound I had heard earlier was snow slipping off the leaves of the oak trees. I chuckled and went back to bed.

At six o'clock, I got up. When I opened the rain shutters, my eyes were pierced by bright sunlight. Everything right up to the verandas was pure white. Already there were four inches on the ground, and it was still coming down strong.

Last year had been warm, and in the end we had nothing you could call a snowfall. This was the first time since coming to Senzaimura that I was seeing four inches of snow before the end of the year.

I opened the door into my study,[1] which provided a full view to the southwest, and was presented with an unframed painting of snowy fields. In my garden were ten or twelve pines, of all heights and sizes, bent low with all the snow they could bear, their branches trembling as if to say that any moment they would let it drop. The leaf-bearing trees, all completely naked, calmly submitted to the growing burden. My one clump of withered bush clover was bent to the ground in the perfect shape of a bow. Without thinking, I laughed out loud. Seen from the back, my stone Jizō[2] was adorned with the sort of white hat that nurses wear, his attire grandly topped off with white epaulettes on both shoulders.

I closed the sliding door and went inside and wrote two letters before getting down to work—one letter to a certain physician called Tsukuba Sanka, the other to the owner of a bookstore in the Ginza district

1. The property boasted a main house (*moya*) and two detached studies, the *okushoin* (back study) and *omoteshoin* (front study).

2. Statue of a bodhisattva revered as a protector of women, children, and travelers. The statue was located just outside the *okushoin* to the left, facing forward into the garden, and is still preserved, now with a wooden roof over its head.

of Tokyo. Before my eyes, I saw, like phantoms, snow scenes from lands of abundant water and woodblock prints of the city in snow at year's end. After finishing the letters, I set myself to writing. The light coming through my sliding doors became more and more intense, and every once in a while falling snow would produce a thud big enough to startle me. Next to my chair, my brass pot was hissing away.

Tsuruko came in to tell me that lunch was ready. When I left the cottage, snow was still coming down, but all around it was not snow but sunlight that shone brightly, and the grass in front of the main house was full of spots melted by water dripping from the oak trees.

"Is this all, you think? Looks like spring snow," I mumbled, sitting down to my meal. On my lacquer tray sat three snow sculptures: a rabbit with the red fruit of the nandina for eyes, a quail with eyes of blue berries from the dragon's beard bush, and a little snow Bodhidharma,[3] likewise with leaves from dragon's beard for eyebrows and eyes from the same plant.

My wife had made them for Tsuruko.

"This Daruma is a European; it's got blue eyes," said Tsuruko.

With the snow, there was no newspaper. In the morning the milkman came, and in the afternoon the old mailman, who was nearing seventy; that was all. As we had asked him to make *mochi* for the days ahead,[4] the man from next door dropped by to pick up the *mochi* rice. While he was at it, he gave Tsuruko two sweet potatoes, just steamed.

I went back to my morning's work. It was cold, so I was continually putting coals in the brazier. The glass panels in my sliding doors were not so bright now—admitting just the right amount of light. I would hear a soft sound and then a hard sound that echoed. The wind seemed to have come up. Around four o'clock, I put tea on and Tsuruko brought in some roasted chestnuts.

"I used melted snow," my wife said. I put my pen down and took time for a sip. The occasion called for a silver teapot, but we had the usual iron kettle. Still, there was a finer taste to the tea. As I shelled the chestnuts, I opened the sliding doors and took a look outside. Wind was blowing from

3. J. Daruma, the legendary founder of the Zen sect.
4. *Mochi* (rice cakes) were eaten at the New Year festivities.

the north. It was a white wind, blowing down in gusts, one after another, grazing the tops of the cedars bordering the rice paddies. In my garden, snowflakes, large and small, some looking like moths, others like flower petals, blew about in the sky—jumping, weaving crazily, like dragonflies; it was as if they were dancing, abandoning themselves to the excitement, letting body and spirit frolic at will. The snow was melting, but the hat on the Jizō had gotten taller. From the branches of the red pine that lorded it over all else in the garden, snow descended like a waterfall.

"It's going to snow more tonight," my wife said, as she and Tsuruko left the room.

I continued working, listening to the sounds of wind and snow outside. By the time I had finished a page, the words I was writing were getting blurry. I put the pen down, stood up, and opened the sliding door.

It was dusk, and the snow was a bluish white. As far as my eyes could see or my ears reach, there was no one about and not a sound to be heard. Only snow coming down, snow coming down, everywhere. I stood and gazed out for quite some time. Unexpectedly, something dark passed by just beyond the veranda, and it turned out to be the stray dog that had taken up residence in my house last month, a female, still quite small, with big ears. We didn't know where she had come from, but she was determined to stay and showed no sign of leaving even after we had chased her away. Since I already had a male and a female, keeping another female was sure to cause trouble, so I had leaned on a friend to take the dog to the other side of the Tama River and let her go, but she was back again the next day. Then I decided to have her taken away by train, and had him take her from Ogikubo out to Kichijōji and leave her tied up in the woods, but about a week later she came waltzing back, the rope dangling from her neck. Finally, I had asked a neighbor to take her to a house of dog lovers who had two dogs as it was, but when I had him chain her at his house before going, she returned again, dragging the chain along behind her. So it seemed that nothing could be done. I whistled, and the dog looked up at me, surprised, and ran around back with her tail between her legs, leaving deep little footprints in the snow.

The snow was still falling steadily.

For no special reason, I began thinking over the events of the last year. Much had transpired—in my own life, the life of my family, the life of the village, in the nation, in foreign lands. In my mind's eye, sundry reflections on things that had happened at various places in the world, things that tried men's hearts, unsettling events—all these passed by once again, in a dark and misty vision.

How would things turn out in the end?

For a long time, I gazed out blankly at the snow. Thus the twenty-ninth day of the first year of the Taishō period[5] drew to a white conclusion.

Each one of us
dances his own crazy dance—
leaving no trace.
The whole world is one color
on an evening in winter.

onogajishi / maikuruitsuru / ato mo nashi / yo wa hitoiro no / yuki no yūgure

[*YUKI*, ED. KATŌ SHŪSON, NIHON NO MEIZUIHITSU 51
(TOKYO: SAKUHINSHA, 1989)]

5. 1912, the last year of the Meiji period (1868–1912) and the first of the Taishō period (1912–1926). Emperor Mutsuhito (known as the Meiji emperor) had died at the end of July and was succeeded by his son, Yoshihito (known as the Taishō emperor).

27

Desk

TAYAMA KATAI

Tayama Rokuya (known by the pen name Tayama Katai; 1871-1930) was born into a samurai family in Gunma Prefecture just after the Meiji Restoration. After his father was killed in the Satsuma Rebellion in 1877, he was sent to Tokyo and for a time was an apprentice in a bookshop. After being let go, he returned home but then moved back to Tokyo with his entire family in 1886. There he began studying poetry and making friends among the major writers of the time, who were mostly men of his own age. Eventually, he established himself as a newspaper reporter and travel writer, later becoming one of the most popular novelists of the Meiji period. Through his novels Futon *(The Quilt, 1907) and* Inaka kyōshi (Country Teacher, *1909), he cemented a reputation as a writer of the naturalist school. Although his career was marred by scandal—first by an affair with a young woman admirer and later by involvement with a geisha—he remained an important literary figure in the* bundan *(literary establishment) until his death.*

The following essay, "Tsukue" (Desk), comes from his long memoir Tōkyō no sanjūnen (Thirty Years in Tokyo, *1917) and depicts a typical day in his life as a writer.*

I sit down to write—at my desk, in my study.

Brush in hand, I spread a sheet of paper out and try to start writing. One word comes, then two. But I am not in the mood. My subject is boring, and I just don't feel like writing. I don't think that I can produce anything satisfying. I have a deadline approaching, but I think to myself, "No need to worry—I'll think on it for another day." I get up from my desk, which I had just taken pains to arrange for writing, and head for the parlor.

"No luck again?" my wife asks.

"It's no good. Just no good."

"That won't do."

"I'll do it tonight—tonight, for sure."

I stroll about in the sunlight on the veranda, and then through the trees in the garden. Hands pulled inside my kimono against my chest, I wait for some interesting idea to arise.

I am afraid about what will happen when my editor from the magazine comes. He is sure to show up, and he will make it clear that he won't leave without a manuscript in hand. "You are always so punctual," he will say, but for me that phrase is full of complicated feelings. Let's say that I *do* write—but that what I write turns out to be boring; it goes out into the world and is criticized. . . . When I start thinking that way, I feel myself, body and spirit, being pushed back into the corner of a corner of a corner.

Now I feel like I will never be able to write. I get irritated. I can't believe I ever succeeded in the past. My subject matter—it all seems a confusing mess. What I had thought was interesting before now seems to be dull as dull. Why, I ask myself, did I ever think it was something I could write about?

"No good, just no good."

"There's nothing you can do?"

My wife has a worried look on her face.

"Watching you walking about like this—you're a tiger in a cage."

"That's the truth."

My wife is suffering, too. She can't stand seeing me upset. And then again, she knows that it's at times like these that I get in a foul mood and I take it out on someone—grousing at her, grousing at the children.

"I can't stand it. I hate writing."

"Well, if you can't do it, you can't do it," she says. But she doesn't say, "You've tried—just give it up." Which makes it all the more painful.

At this point, my editor shows up.

"Sorry, I'm stymied. I don't think I'm going to be able to produce anything."

"We can't have that. We're depending on you. We'll have a gaping hole to fill in."

"But I'm stuck."

"All right, then—we'll wait one more day."

With that, he leaves.

I sit down at the desk again, but to no avail. It gets to the point that it's painful even to look at brush and paper. It feels like some demon has taken over my brush, my paper, and my heart.

Worried, my wife peeks in—but stealthily, knowing I'll be angry if I notice. When I take up my brush and sit quietly, she leaves.

"Any luck?"

"No—it's just no good."

"But you were writing—I just saw you."

———————

Then, in the middle of the night, an idea comes to me. I get up all alone and pick up my brush. My brush and my heart start running along, together. Ah, what happiness! What a sense of power! What an enjoyable sensation! As I look on, first two pages, then three, four, five pages come out, all in short order. At such a time, any complaints about my awful chosen profession are forgotten. My heart is again the heart I had as a student: those days when, in the dim light of a lamp, my hair long and unkempt, I gave myself entirely to my writing. Back then, there was no literary establishment, no editors, no outside world. Only my brush, my paper, and my heart moving forward as one.

[*TŌKYŌ NO SANJŪNEN*, GENDAI NIHON BUNGAKU ZENSHŪ 97
(TOKYO: CHIKUMA SHOBŌ, 1958)]

28

Fireworks

NAGAI KAFŪ

Nagai Kafū (born Nagai Sōkichi; 1879–1959) began his career as a student of French literature. Among other things, he was famous for his translations of symbolist poetry and for his attempts to write in the style of the French naturalists. In his twenties, he traveled to America and Europe, returning to a Japan that he regarded as engaged in petty mimicry of Western ways. After publishing several collections of stories based on his experiences abroad, he taught literature at Keiō Gijuku, one of the most important colleges of the early twentieth century, and was involved in editing important literary journals. From the very beginning, however, he had been drawn to the Tokyo demimonde of beer halls, dance-hall girls, and prostitutes, as well as to the old Edo traditions that were still alive in various nooks and crannies of the modern city, and in the late 1920s he largely withdrew from public life. During the years of the Pacific War, he published little but kept a diary chronicling his meanderings around Tokyo and occasionally expressing his disgust at the military regime that was stifling intellectual and artistic life. After the war, he played the part of bemused cultural hero to those searching for someone in the literary community who could claim to have actually resisted the militarists.

Kafū is as well known for his essays as for his fiction, the two sometimes hard to tell apart. The essay translated here, which deals with noteworthy civil disturbances covering a thirty-year period, is typical of his work in the way it strikes a nostalgic and whimsical pose reminiscent of that of Yoshida no Kenkō.

"Hanabi" (Fireworks) first appeared in the December 1919 issue of the journal Kaizō.

I was about to pick up my chopsticks and begin eating when I heard the sound of fireworks. It was a cloudy day near the end of the rainy season. A cool breeze gently swayed the window blinds. Looking outside, I saw national flags lined up on the eaves of the houses in the alleyway, except for my own lattice shutters, that is, where no flag was flying. Only then did I remember that Tokyo was celebrating the peace treaty ending the European War.[1]

After eating, I tied up my sleeves with a piece of cloth and picked up my brush in order to paper the walls of my closet.

Ever since moving into my house in the alley at the end of the previous year, on a day when the snow was barely coming down, I had been concerned about plaster flaking off the walls, but somehow six months had gone by and I'd done nothing about it.

Several years ago, my mother had still been in good health and my wife was still with me. On the broad veranda of our second story, I had sat basking in the spring sun, repairing books. Ever since then, whenever I wanted to relieve my boredom, I would turn to the maintenance of my library. The older I get, the stranger my habits become.

Picking up scraps of paper I once used for calligraphy practice, pages from manuscripts I had tossed away sometime in the past, and pages from old letters from friends, I looked at each one to see what was written there and then pasted it onto the wall.[2]

Outside, the fireworks continued, yet the alleyway was strangely silent. Usually when something was going on out on the main street, I would hear from here and there the sounds of doors sliding open and clogs running

---

1. July 1. Fighting had ended in November 1918, but the Treaty of Versailles was signed in 1919.
2. An allusion to *Tsurezuregusa* (*Essays in Idleness*), section 29, and to an old but apocryphal story about how that medieval work consisted of stray thoughts that Kenkō had jotted down on paper that he then pasted on the walls of his hut. See Yoshida no Kenkō, *Essays in Idleness* (chap. 2).

along the pavement, but that day I heard no children's voices, no wives talking with one another. Even the file of the metal worker on the corner was silent. No doubt, everybody was off in Hibiya or Ueno. Straining my ears, I could make out the faint sound of people shouting along with the fireworks. As I read the words of a manuscript I had just pasted on the wall, I was suddenly aware of how removed I was from the social world, to a degree amazing even to myself. I felt sad somehow, and dejected. It wasn't that I had intended to withdrawn from human affairs out of sheer perversity, after all; I had just become more and more isolated as time went by, hardly realizing it. Now there was not a single connection left between myself and the world.

A cool breeze continued to sway my dirty blinds, and beyond the blinds the cloudy sky loomed so dark that it seemed more and more like a dreamscape. Gradually, the fireworks display shone brighter. I began to imagine the scenes to myself—schools and factories on holiday, arches of greenery decorated with cedar boughs on street corners, shop fronts on the thoroughfares clad with striped curtains of red and white, flags and lanterns hanging here and there, newspaper headlines proclaiming glad tidings in thick, black Chinese characters, people thronging the streets toward Hibiya and Ueno. Perhaps there would be geisha troupes marching in ranks or people with lanterns passing on parade. And, of course, some child or old woman might be trampled to death. This new kind of celebration is of recent vintage, a phenomenon of the Meiji period, based on Western models. Neither in form nor in spirit is it anything like the old shrine festivals or Buddhist unveilings of the sort that have come down to the citizens of Tokyo rather innocently from the Edo period. At shrine festivals, the young men of a district could drink to their heart's content, shop boys and apprentices could have their fill of rice and red beans. But lurking behind modern festivals are political designs.

And so I began to think back on all the new festival days I could recall since my youth.

———————

In February 1890, there was a celebration to honor the newly promulgated constitution.[3] This is probably the earliest public celebration I can

3. The celebration actually took place in 1889, when Kafū was eleven.

remember. Counting back, it would have been in the spring of my twelfth year, when I was living in the house in Koishikawa. It was so cold that day that I didn't go outside, but I am sure that this was the first festival for which there was a parade of lanterns, and I also remember that this was when people first learned to shout "banzai" in praise of the state. The reason I remember is because my father, who was teaching at the Imperial University then, went out with a red cord tied to his shoulders right over his Western clothes, carrying a red lantern, and didn't return until very late. He said that he had led his university students to Nijū Bridge,[4] where they shouted "banzai" three times. "Banzai" came from some English word, and he said that far away in the West scholars and their students would often march in parade for one reason or another. To me, the whole business seemed rather bizarre, and I didn't really comprehend what he said.

Yet that morning, from next to my house in Koishikawa, which stood on the banks above the river, I had watched as flags and banners passed by on the street along the outer moat. And somehow, I had sensed from the words written on the flags and banners that these parades were something different in nature from those I was used to seeing by members of the Fuji or Ōyama sects.[5]

———————————

After the Russian crown prince was attacked by a policeman in Ōtsu city, the whole country was on tenterhooks.[6] Although still a child, I remember being afraid, without really knowing why. There were rumors that Katō Kiyomasa[7] was still alive in Korea and that Saigō Takamori[8] had been in hiding in Hokkaido but would now come to save the nation. Being children, we did not understand that these were just outlandish rumors and found ourselves frightened and upset. Looking back on it now, I think of

4. Located near the main gateway of the imperial palace.
5. Religious groups that worshipped Mount Fuji and Mount Ōyama (southwest of Tokyo).
6. On May 11, 1891, a policeman attacked the Russian crown prince when the latter was passing through Ōtsu, near Kyoto. The Meiji emperor visited the crown prince in person to offer his apologies, and the attacker was executed.
7. 1562–1611. A famous warrior of the Warring States period, three hundred years in the past.
8. 1827–1877. One of the heroes of the Meiji Restoration who later died in a rebellion against the new government.

Tokyo in those days as a gloomy backwater much like Edo had been under rumors about the Black Ships.[9] It seems like the only sounds were those of people in snow clogs walking on the street, dogs howling forlornly, and the west wind blowing in the trees.

Festivals and disturbances resemble each other in that both make the world into a noisy place.

In the summer of my sixteenth year, I often went swimming at a pool next to the Sumida River. One evening, I saw a man with a special edition of the newspaper running down the street along the river, shouting. This was the beginning of the Sino-Japanese War [1894–1895]. The Treaty of Shimonoseki[10] was signed the next year, when I was in Ashigara Hospital in Odawara, where I had gone in hopes that a change of climate might improve my health. The voices raised in protest over the return of the Liaodong Peninsula[11] did not reach into the halls of a hospital so far from Tokyo. I heard about it only when a shop boy in the pharmacy read a newspaper editorial aloud. At the time, I was immersed in reading *Taikōki*,[12] the first volume of the Imperial Library published by Hakubunkan.[13] That time I spent in the old post town of Odawara, where plums ripened in the summer and *mikan* turned yellow in the winter, left me with the most peaceful and happy memories of my life.

In 1898, a celebration marking the thirtieth anniversary of the establishment of Tokyo as the capital was held in Ueno. As I recall, the cherry

9. A reference to the American ships that arrived in Japanese ports in the 1860s demanding free entry. Since the mid-seventeenth century, foreign contact had been strictly controlled by the Japanese government.

10. The treaty that ended the Sino-Japanese War in 1895.

11. After the Treaty of Shimonoseki had been signed, Germany, Russia, and France—in what is called the triple intervention—prevailed on Japan to return the peninsula, which it had won in the war, much to the consternation of the Japanese government.

12. A popular novelistic work portraying the exploits of Toyotomi Hideyoshi (1536–1598). The version Kafū was reading was *Shinsho Taikōki* (*The Grandee: The True Story*), published in the late eighteenth century.

13. One of the most active publishers of the day. The Teikoku Bunko (Imperial Library) series eventually included one hundred volumes.

blossoms were in bloom, so it must have been at the beginning of April. Rumor had it that hordes of people were trampled to death on the avenue outside the celebration stand.

I was in Tacoma, in the United States, when I learned about the war between Japan and Russia [1904–1905]. Reading about it in a newspaper extra, I was very excited—by which I mean that I was elated. It didn't occur to me that foreign enemies might lay waste to my homeland and cut down my countrymen, as in the days of the Mongol invasions.[14] Even if the worst were to happen, I thought, the spirit of modern civilization and international relations would not allow any one country to be thrown into so pitiable a state. I was convinced that the Christian religion and the laws that had been passed down since Roman times were still strong enough to be relied on, and that, wartime or not, no one born a human being need suffer the kind of treachery that the Germans had recently worked in Belgium.[15] So when I read the extra, I was moved, but I did not feel any intense worry about the safety of my father and mother. What's more, the news was of nothing but victory. And since one by-product of the war was that I was able to extend my pleasant stay in foreign parts, I spent that year completely unaware of how the citizens of Tokyo at the height of the summer heat were burning down police stations and Christian churches, or how policemen were cutting down citizens in the streets.

In 1911, when I was teaching at Keiō,[16] I happened to be on the street to see paddy wagons, five or six of them in a row, go rushing down the street at Ichigaya toward the Hibiya courthouse.[17] Nothing that I had seen or heard of in a public setting had ever inspired me with such an indescrib-

14. Troops of the Mongol dynasty attempted to invade Japan twice in the late thirteenth century.
15. A reference to the German invasion of Belgium, a neutral state, during World War I.
16. Kafū taught in the Literature Department of Keiō University from 1910 to 1916.
17. The paddy wagons were carrying the men accused of conspiracy against the government in the Kōtoku Shūsui Incident of 1910, which ended with the execution in 1911 of Kōtuku Shūsui (1871–1911) and eleven others for treason.

ably unpleasant sensation. As a writer, how could I simply remain silent in the face of such an intellectual challenge? Had not the novelist Zola suffered banishment from his own country because he had taken a courageous stand in the Dreyfus affair?[18] Yet along with the other writers of my time, I said nothing, and the pangs of conscience I felt as a result were almost beyond enduring. Being a writer now became cause only for shame. There seemed no other course but to lower the level of my own writing to that of the frivolous hacks of Edo times. It was from that day onward that I began wearing a tobacco pouch, collecting ukiyo-e prints, and playing the samisen. Late Edo writers of frivolous fiction and painters of woodblock prints felt that such things as the appearance of the Black Ships at Uraga or the assassination of a high shogunal minister at Sakuradamon[19] were none of their concern—indeed, that these were things about which they had no right to speak—and I resolved that rather than being scandalized by their decision to savor the experience of writing erotic stories or painting erotic prints, I would admire it.

———————

So time went on, and then in March 1913[20] I was having a samisen lesson at the house of a certain woman in a backstreet of Yamashirogashi. (Despite its location, the house had a low-entrance gate,[21] a little garden space, and, next to a washing cistern, an unexpected old camellia frequented by sparrows and warblers. How often one finds, in the most unlikely places, down alleyways hemmed in on all sides by the city, quiet little retreats and Inari[22] shrines!) Suddenly there was an uproar in the alley, first the sound of people running over the wooden planks across

18. In 1894, a French army officer named Alfred Dreyfus (1859–1935) was accused of spying for the Germans and sentenced to banishment to the penal colony on Devil's Island. The prominent French novelist Émile Zola (1840–1902) publicly denounced the action as motivated by anti-Semitism and was himself convicted of libel against the French Army. Zola fled to England in order to escape imprisonment but was granted amnesty eight months later, and Dreyfus's conviction was eventually overturned.

19. Ii Naosuke (1815–1860), a senior adviser to the shogun, was assassinated by political enemies outside the shogunal castle gate Sakuradamon in Edo in 1860.

20. The public disturbances that Kafū describes here came in response to the formation of the Tarō Katsura cabinet at the end of 1912. The rioting actually occurred in February.

21. *Kugurimon.* A wooden doorway through which one had to stoop to gain passage, of the sort used at the country cottages of literati and tea masters.

22. The Shinto deity of rice, agriculture, and fertility.

the ditch nearby, and then the rattle of police sabers. In response to this, I assume, the drone of the printing presses at the *Chūō Newspaper* plant ceased, as if they had been switched off. I opened the door of the low entrance and gingerly stuck my head out. Four or five men wearing *tabi* of the sort used by milk-delivery men, clad in knit undershirts and head-bands, were running through the alley and out toward the canal. At the kitchen door of a house across the way, a deliveryman from a local eatery was saying that someone had set fire to the *Kokumin Newspaper* building. But when I straightened up to look, I couldn't see any smoke, so I went back inside, lay down, and took a nap. The coal heater had warmed things up nicely. Later that night around eight o'clock, after I had finished din-ner and was on my way across Sukiya Bridge hoping to make my way home before it got too cold, I saw a police box on fire. There were no streetcars. Ginza was more crowded with people milling about than at New Year's. And there in the middle of it all were police boxes set ablaze. A kerosene can had been tossed right into the middle of the street.

When I arrived at Hibiya, the police were standing in line like a black wall blocking the road. I heard that a few minutes ago, rioters had been throwing rocks at police headquarters. Recalling rumors that many people had been attacked by the police during the disturbance back in 1905, I changed my route, heading toward Sakurada Hongōchō. Finally, I succeeded in hailing a cab outside Toranomon. When we attempted to go from the pitch-black of Kasumigaseki into Nagatachō, the road was again blocked, this time by soldiers protecting the various government ministries, so we went back toward Miyakezaka and around to the av-enue through Kōjimachi. It was after midnight when I arrived back at my house on the outskirts of Ushigome.

After this, things were peaceful for a time.

I think it was midway through November 1915. The newspapers of the capital reported that geisha from the various districts of the city had dressed up and formed parades shouting "banzai" as they made their way toward Nijū Bridge in celebration of the imperial ascension.[23] Now

23. The formal ascension ceremony (*sokui*) of the Taishō emperor took place in November 1915.

that I think about it, it was after I had advanced to middle school that elementary-school students began to parade toward Nijū Bridge on the occasion of national celebrations or public holidays. And it cannot have been more than twenty years since the prefectural office had first commanded people in the alleys to display national flags. One measure of the success of this direct government involvement was to enlist even women from the entertainment trade to go marching down the street in broad daylight. What strange turns the trends of the times seem to take! On the day of the geisha parades, so many people came out to watch that the police were unable to control them and confusion ensued. I heard various stories from people who were there to witness what happened. At first, spectators waited quietly on both sides of the street for the geisha to pass by, but as time went by people in front were gradually pushed from behind, and just about the time the geisha arrived on the scene, the crush of people gave way on both sides and collapsed onto the women. Geisha and spectators were all mixed up together, and the pent-up resentment of the common people toward the extravagance of the geisha, along with animal lust, led to the most unseemly acts of violence being committed in the middle of a crowd and in open view. Screaming, some geisha fled for their lives into the company offices around the Imperial Theater, followed by crowds as fierce as wolf packs that smashed down doors and threw rocks through windows. Some geisha went missing, and others lost their senses over the humiliation they experienced on that day. The geisha union completely suppressed the story, however, and placated the injured parties by taking up a collection among themselves to pay them off.

At festivals in the old days, gamblers would get into fights. Nowadays, women get trampled to death.

––––––––––––––

It was midway through August 1918, just four or five days after the beginning of autumn, the hottest time of the year. Having just finished up work for the journal *Kagetsu*, which Inoue Aa[24] and I were editing at the time, I was seeing him part of the way home. To cool off, we went as far as Kagurazaka. When we got off the streetcar at Sakanamachi, there were

24. 1878–1923. A novelist and haiku poet.

as many people as usual out on the streets in search of a cool breeze, but for some reason the shopkeepers had gotten upset and closed all the doors that had been open a moment before—and not because of an approaching thunderstorm, I noticed, but because police were coming and going all around. Turning into an alley, I saw that the fronts of the geisha houses were silent, their doors all shut, their lamps all out. Going back out onto the main street, we went into a beer hall to wait for a few minutes, and a young man who looked to be a student was saying that shops in Ginza and geisha houses in Shinbashi had been ransacked.

This was how I learned of the rice riots.[25] The next day, newspaper articles on the matter were censored, but I later learned that the riots always began after it had cooled off in the evening. Just then, there was a beautiful moon every night. When I heard that rioting students would wait to attack the houses of the rich until after it cooled off and the moon had come out, I couldn't help but think that there was something rather casual about it all. The riots calmed down after five or six days, as it began to rain. I had not yet moved from my old house in Ushigome, and when, along with the rain, I heard more insects crying from the garden and the echo of the wind blowing in the shrubs, I realized that autumn was progressing.

In November, I lost my house and had to go out looking for a place to shelter my sorry bones. As I was walking by Hibiya Park, I saw a group of laborers wearing pale-indigo workers' clothes marching in close formation behind a union flag. Then I remembered that that day was the anniversary of the cessation of hostilities in Europe [November 21, 1918]. To the eyes of someone who had been cut off from the world by illness for some time, the sight of the workers' clothes that I had so often seen in France now parading down the streets of Tokyo made me feel as if the world had truly changed. It was as if my eyes had been opened.

Rumors about rice riots I could dismiss as troublemaking by political groups, but the image of workers marching silently along in Western

25. Late in the summer of 1918, in reaction to volatile rice prices, rioters attacked rice merchants, police boxes, and the homes of the rich. Rioting began in Toyama and soon spread nationwide.

clothing seemed to me an undeniable revelation of the energy of the age and of the sorrows of life at that time. Again, I found myself recalling various problems that I had first noticed when I had returned to my home country after a long absence some years before.[26] Were events before my eyes informing me that the time had come for me to wake from the nostalgic dreams of Edo days that I had indulged in for so long? If so, then I could only lament my unhappy fortune.

The fireworks continued. I put my brush down to smoke a cigarette and looked out the window. Despite cloudy skies, the summer sun was as bright as before. A quiet afternoon at the end of the rainy season, a hazy evening late in autumn—there are no better times than these for moments of quiet thought.

[NAGAI KAFŪ SHŪ, ED. SAKAGAMI HIROICHI, NIHON KINDAI BUNGAKU TAIKEI 20 (TOKYO: KADOKAWA SHOTEN, 1970)]

26. Kafū had been traveling in the United States and Europe between 1903 and 1908.

29

Laughter

TERADA TORAHIKO

Terada Torahiko (1878-1935) was born in Tokyo but grew up in Kōchi on the island of Shikoku, the ancestral home of his father. He went to the Fifth Higher School in Kumamoto before going on to Tokyo Imperial University. In his teens, he had met the prominent haiku poet Masaoka Shiki (1867-1902), and in Kumamoto he took classes from Natsume Sōseki (1867-1916), who was then a teacher at the Fifth Higher School. Over time, Torahiko became a member of a group of young literati surrounding Sōseki, who eventually left the academic life to become a professional novelist. After his mentor's death, Torahiko served as the editor of Sōseki's complete works.

Unlike Sōseki, Torahiko chose to stay in the academic world after receiving his doctoral degree in physics—also from Tokyo Imperial University—in the autumn of 1908. After a trip to Europe for further study, he returned to Tokyo to take up an appointment at his alma mater. In 1916, he became a full professor and went on to have a distinguished career in the scientific community while remaining an active poet and literary figure.

Torahiko is particularly famous for his essays, which range widely over literary and scientific subjects. "Warai" (Laughter) was published in the January 1922 issue of the magazine Shisō.

Since childhood I have been sickly, and I have vague recollections of going to see the doctor from as soon as I started to be aware of the world around me. Even now, after having the good fortune to survive several serious illnesses, I feel as if there has never been a time when I wasn't ill with something. There are occasions when I am not suffering from things to which Latin names are easy to attach, but the days when I don't feel my body to be a painful burden are rare—although thanks to long habit, I am not conscious of having to drag it after me as I walk along. In that sense, I sometimes think that I am one who cannot *conceive*[1] of the usual, pleasant sensation of having a healthy body, in the same way that a person who is color-blind lacks the ability to see the color red. But then, since for a healthy person that sensation is only the usual way of things, he would not feel it as a pleasant or happy state, unless he happened to have recently recovered from an illness. I suppose this means that the effect of one's own awareness of one's physical state on anyone—whether it be someone like me or a healthy person—is probably not substantial. Yet I do believe that something as fundamental as differences in physical well-being must manifest itself somehow.

Having said all that, then, I am sorry to note that I do not know just how much of what I am now going to say about my rather bizarre personal experiences will be shared with those happy souls who have *normal*[2] good health and how much of it is the product of my own sickly constitution. Indeed, one could say that my motive in writing this piece derives from my own irresolvable doubts about that very point.

Ever since I was a child, I have had the strange habit of feeling like laughing whenever I am being examined by a doctor. No matter how old I get, I haven't gotten over this tendency. Even now the vestiges of it remain.

1. Terada uses the Japanese words *shiryō suru*, glossing them to the right with the katakana word "conceive."
2. Terada uses the Japanese word *seijō*, glossing it to the right with the katakana word "normal."

Of course, one can't indulge in such a thing when one has a high fever or something causing unbearable pain. On those occasions when my symptoms aren't so severe and I am not flat down on my back, however, this strange phenomenon does occur.

From the very beginning, when the doctor is looking at his watch to check my pulse, I feel a strange sensation that portends laughter coming on. And the feeling is not the same as what one gets when something is amusing. I feel a certain tension building from having to hold my hand out in one position, and at the same time I sense in my body a vague kind of ticklishness beginning to circulate all through me. One might compare it to the way a finely balanced *mechanism*,[3] when even the smallest degree of surplus weight is applied to it, loses its balance and begins to shake this way and that. My body quite literally starts to wobble strangely, and as I try to steady it, my hand suddenly starts to twitch.

One could attribute this to *weak nerves*[4] and be done with it, I suppose, but the problem is that whenever this happens, it is only a prelude to laughter.

Perhaps it's because precisely at the time I am losing my equilibrium in this way, I have to stick my tongue out, say "ahh" in such a stupid-sounding voice, and roll my eyes around—who knows? But sometimes it seems that I feel a certain *impulse*[5] that almost topples me off into laughter just from those things alone. The doctor moves on, from tapping to listening with his stethoscope, and as he does so, the vague feeling of powerlessness that has been building in my body only gains in strength and clarity. The climax comes when I fill my lungs with air as I try to take deep breaths, and then exhale—explosively. It's then that it all comes out as a proper laugh.

Laughing at such a time, in the absence of a proper stimulus, is illogical, and even as a child I felt acutely ashamed for being so rude toward the doctor, while at the same time feeling even more sorry for my mother, who would be sitting right there next to me. So I would try to

---

3. Terada uses the Japanese word *kikai*, glossing it to the right with the katakana word "mechanism."
4. Terada uses the Japanese words *yowai shinkei*, glossing them to the right with the katakana words "weak nerves."
5. Terada uses the Japanese word *shōgeki* (usually translated as "shock" or "impact"), glossing it to the right with the katakana word "impulse."

restrain myself by stealthily biting my lips or pinching my leg, but even if this succeeded in bringing tears to my eyes, it was not enough to overcome my irrational need to laugh. In fact, the effect of such efforts was to make me feel even more the need to resist. To my surprise, though, the doctor would react with nonchalance and just laugh with me. And at the moment when I was reassured that I could laugh with abandon, my feeling of wanting to laugh would swiftly disappear.

One might conclude that the cause of the ticklish feeling was being touched on the skin of my chest, but that doesn't explain it. I have concluded myself that there is some intimate relationship between my reaction and the effort involved in taking deep breaths. For when it was my belly being probed, I had no desire to laugh at all.

When I was seeing the family doctor, I didn't feel so awful, but when it was a new doctor, I was worried even before he began examining me, and the more I worried, the worse things would get. All I could do was have my mother there to explain for me right from the beginning. If she could only do so, then I would not feel that I had to laugh.

My father had taught me that a man shouldn't be moved to laughter by just anything, and I believed this myself. To laugh when there was no proper object of laughter was illicit behavior of a sort that was unforgivable. So when the mother of another household once kindly said that my problem must come from a weakness in my stomach of some sort, I heard it as the best of Good News.[6] It was as if a spiritual sinfulness that I could not withstand had now been attributed instead to my body—something over which a person had no control.

My propensity to laugh at times when there was nothing to laugh about was not limited to the doctor's office.

The worst times were when I would go to visit a relative or someone else and have to say my greetings. This was especially true if the person had suffered some misfortune and I had been taught the proper words of condolence at home. I would memorize the words, but as I tried to recite them just as I had learned them, my strange laugh would come popping

6. Fukuin. The Christian gospel.

out. The pain I felt at such times I cannot forget even now. There was nothing funny about it.

Yet the old ladies I was talking with at such times didn't seem in the least concerned when I laughed in this way. On the contrary, they too would smile and say things like, "Oh, what a big boy you're getting to be!" After that, I wouldn't feel the need to laugh anymore, but I would usually be assaulted by an indescribably wretched feeling of humiliation.

Even when I began junior high school, I was still not cured of my habit, which caused me more and more pain and humiliation. When I was seated for a very dignified Shinto ceremony, listening to sacred music being performed or a solemn salutation being intoned, I would make a special effort to be serious and keep my body properly under control—only to have my urge attack me. It was the same thing when I was sitting in the barber chair being shaved, although in this case it was the feeling of danger that induced laughter.

As I took on years and learned to examine the workings of my own psychological phenomena, I attempted countless times to find an analytical explanation for my habit. But the problem was far beyond my abilities to resolve. In the end, I usually came to the exceedingly unpleasant and forlorn conclusion that there must be an abnormality somewhere in the workings of my nervous system.

For me, somehow there was a gap between *what should induce laughter and the laughter itself.*[7] For instance, I would watch a demented man famous in the village for his antics doing comic stunts and pratfalls on the street and not feel like laughing at all, instead feeling rather uncomfortable and sad; or I would watch people doing funny parlor games at a drinking party and feel only that it was all fearsome or terrible—and never once feel like laughing. One can attribute this to the temperament of a *pessimist*,[8] I know, but still somehow . . .

Come to think of it, in the midst of a violent storm, I would be looking out on the sight of trees swaying in a frightening sky as leaves were torn and scattered on the wind and suddenly feel laughter welling up. What's more, I felt that my laughter, coming forth with the other sounds of the

7. This phrase is rendered with the equivalent of italics in Terada's text.
8. Terada uses the katakana word "pessimist," with no Japanese gloss.

passing storm, was entirely natural. Again, when the river in front of our house overflowed, flooding the streets, and I would go out walking in water up to my knees that gradually chilled me from my thighs to my belly, until my whole body began to shiver—even then I would burst out laughing.

In all these cases, I was not able, in terms of normal reason, to make sense of why laughter should burst forth when I could see nothing to laugh at.

Another thing that would call laughter forth was that difficult predicament where I was trying to defend myself against a misunderstanding—one in which someone felt that I had offended him, and it gradually became apparent that my defense was having no effect. This was the most unhappy of situations, which I found more difficult to overcome by force of will than anyone on the outside could possibly imagine.

I had thought that this kind of irrational instinct to laugh was a mental phenomenon distinctive to me alone, but as I paid attention over time, I learned that I was not alone. Two or three people told me of cases in which they had cracked up when paying a sympathy call, or burst out laughing during a formal banquet, and so on.

On one such occasion, a family had been burned out of its house, and the middle-aged housewife was watching over the family treasures that had been taken to the precincts of a Shinto shrine. As she was chatting with the people who came to offer their sympathies, she saw someone glaring at her with a surprised and dubious expression when she broke into laughter from deep down inside, as if something hilarious must have happened.

I have also read somewhere about people on the battlefield being overcome with the abnormal phenomenon of laughter at the most horrific of moments.

Of course, these cases may be very close to insanity, but thinking about all these things together, I think we may get some hint, at least, of the functions and basic nature of what we call laughter.

In physiological terms, the phenomenon of laughter results when, after muscles in the abdomen undergo spasmodic contractions brought about by some stimulation of the nervous system, air in the lungs is brought forth sporadically, in a cyclic fashion. It appears that it amounts to an interplay between the actions of drawing the air in and trying to put a halt to it. At least, it is with such actions that a laugh is first produced, according to the theory of one psychologist.[9] In other words, we are amused because we laugh, rather than laughing because we are amused.

The first time I heard this theory, I felt as if I had finally gotten hold of what for many years I had been searching for.

While it may be impossible to think about a proper reason beforehand, and then laugh about it, I thought it was unacceptable that one could not discover the reasons for the behavior at least *after* it happened. Now I felt that an explanation for that difficult problem was possible. And it seemed that when I combined this theory together with that woman's reassurance that my problem must come from a weakness in my stomach of some sort, I had come up with a good explanation.

Looking at the instances I noted above, each case involved an occasion in which one felt a kind of tension, mental or physical. If one only had the vitality, or was in other words of strong constitution and could resist the tense situation, then all would be fine. But at times when, due to physical illness or a lack of spiritual vitality, one could not withstand such tension, that tension would, before one was even aware of it, find a way to relieve itself. Furthermore, these intermittent shifts in levels of tension have a close relationship to the phenomenon of laughter in physiological terms. Which would lead to a feeling much like laughter, and then to true laughter itself—or at least these are the conclusions to which I came. It seemed to me that this explanation described my case remarkably well. The most obvious fit was with the case of inhaling and exhaling while being examined by the doctor, but I felt that the explanation was for the most part suitable for all the other situations as well.

Of course, accepting this theory was unpleasant and humiliating because it also meant admitting that I had weak nerves, a weak body, and a timid nature. At the same time, however, I was also overwhelmingly pleased, since now a primary cause for my problem had been established in scientific terms, a means of treatment might follow.

9. Probably a reference to the American philosopher William James (1842–1910).

Even in the case of someone like me, it is rare for such anomalous laughter to burst forth as long as I am healthy and able to maintain my vitality, and when one considers that the most pronounced cases of the problem occur after an illness or some excessive mental stress, the theory seems to have great promise.

———————

The next question that arises is, of course, what the results might be if one were to study the general phenomenon of laughter in these terms.

What about the laughter of people who are mad or suffering from *hysteria*?[10] Since I have no direct experience in this area and no resources to examine near to hand, I can't say much, but if one were to characterize the sorts of hysteria that tend to accompany the change of life in women as arising from an inadequate release of pent-up energy, one would not be far outside the boundaries of my definition.

Putting that issue aside, however, I would like to consider *normal*, healthy kinds of laughter. Among these, the most pure and fundamental must, of course, be the kind of laughter that is shared between both barbarian and civilized, both children and adults. As much as I wanted to know what barbarians laugh at, I couldn't get the materials together to study the issue, so I had to focus my research on children. And there the most typical case is, first of all, laughter arising from the occurrence of something unexpected yet not terribly frightening, the tension of which laughing attempts to dissipate—some examples being when a doll's head comes off, or a balloon bursts, or something on a shelf falls down. Second would be a situation quite similar, in which grand expectations are betrayed in some way so that the result is trivial—as when the jack in a jack-in-the-box is broken and doesn't spring out, or when fireworks fail to work and end in a tiny sputter. These two kinds of situations for laughter are possible even among those with little knowledge of the way the world works and are in that sense instinctive and primitive, but one can characterize both as resulting from the sudden release of either mental or physical tension of a temporary or continuous nature. And if one considers them carefully, one realizes that after the release of that tension comes

10. Terada uses the katakana version of the German word *Hysterie*.

a ripple effect involving both stretching and relaxation—although this doesn't seem to be the case when the tension is released very gradually.

In the physical world, when something in a state of inertia is moved out of its proper position and effort is expended to return it to that position, oscillations occur—a common phenomenon. In most cases, figuring out the equation for movement is easy because the inertia is constant and elasticity is in direct proportion to *displacement*.[11] But there are problems associated with applying such a model to the workings of the nerves. If one were to try to calculate the effect on "release" in the case when displacement is *plus* and stress *minus*,[12] for instance, one would have to define clearly what physical thing caused the situation, or else one would not be able to determine either mass or elasticity. And one would still be far from being able to render the situation in mathematical terms.

Nevertheless, these models taken from the science of dynamics appeal greatly to my imagination when I try to think about laughter in physiological or psychological terms, and I can't help but think that in the context of this problem of laughter we see the possibility of a bridge uniting physiology and psychology.

Adopting this as a *working hypothesis*,[13] certain probable conclusions can be deduced. For instance, when it comes to making distinctions between people who laugh easily and those who do not, one can posit the existence of physiological factors corresponding to viscosity and friction in dynamics. Indeed, the very word "viscosity" has a revelatory power, making one consider a possible relationship between physical/temperamental types and the intermittent periodicity of laughter. Also, if we posit that laughter is a phenomenon distinctive to human beings, can one not wonder whether it is because in other animals the distribution of mass, elasticity, and friction somehow fails to produce periodicity and that oscillations therefore become *aperiodic*?[14]

11. Terada uses the Japanese word *hen'i*, glossing it to the right with the katakana word "displacement."
12. Terada uses the katakana words "plus" and "minus," with no Japanese glosses.
13. Terada uses the English term, with no Japanese gloss.
14. Terada uses the English word, with no Japanese gloss.

There are various types of laughter, from the laughter of children to the kind of adult laughter that is beyond the ability of children to comprehend. One cannot dismiss as mere *Schadenfreude*[15] laughter that comes at the expense of someone's dignity (A) or laughter arising when some person's weakness is exposed (B). Here, too, a release of tension is involved.

Laughter of the happy variety that comes when a hope is realized (C)—this, too, falls within the boundaries of the definition.

More difficult to deal with are the proud laugh of someone who has triumphed (D) and the sneering laugh used to deride (E). Yet (D) involves a mixture of (A) and (C), and there is both (B) and (D) admixed in (E).

There is also the wry laugh (F). This is a combination of (A) and (B) that comes about when one looks at oneself from a third-person perspective and is mixed with the pain of recognizing oneself as oneself.

I suppose that one could go on this way and adduce various other kinds of laughter as well (L, M, N, and so on). But such questions are the province of psychology and go well beyond relations to the body and thus beyond my own concerns.

This hypothesis is something that I conceived in order to come to terms with the peculiar kind of laughter that I had experienced in childhood and is not something for which I would claim universality. Yet it would bring me no reassurance if it did not promise some degree of application for large numbers of people.

People who are fond of making taxonomies are liable to be blind to realities not accounted for by their systems, and I cannot deny that that tendency may be at work in my case. Yet although I have not thought the problem through to final understanding as yet, I still think that my theory has promise of developing into something.

If among my readers there are some specialists, they may be kind enough to correct my amateurish ideas. Furthermore, there may be an

15. Terada uses the German word, which refers to laughing at someone else's misfortune, with no Japanese gloss.

amateur out there who has been through the same experiences and can add his efforts to mine in working through the same problem. It was actually on the basis of those two ideas that I wrote this piece, which is neither confession nor treatise. If what I have included here should itself become the object of laughter among readers, however, there is nothing I can do about it.

––––––––––––––––

Addendum:
After I had written this manuscript, I received a copy of a book by Bergson titled *Laughter*,[16] which I read with great interest. The author thinks that all laughter has an object and does not touch on laughter that has no object. He also believes that, directly or indirectly, the object of laughter is always human and lists something like formulas or rules defining what strikes a person as funny based on factors such as facial expressions, movements, environment, personality, and the like—rules that I must say seem rather audacious in scientific terms—and then gives concrete examples of each. With this as a basis, he then argues various points concerning the significance of laughter not just in comedy but also in tragedy, and considers the social and ethical significance of laughter from an ontological viewpoint.

As I was reading the book, I came upon many valuable insights but also felt dubious about one or two of his points. Yet I didn't feel any need to delete or revise anything I had written based on Bergson's book. I had begun with the problem of "laughter that has no object" and was seeking a key to laughter lurking somewhere between physiology and psychology, whereas Bergson considered only pure psychology and did not treat physiology at all.

Among the cases of laughter that Bergson raised, there were none that were inconsistent with my hypothesis; on the contrary, there were many that fit the hypothesis rather well. And I felt some reassurance when, at the end of his book, he touched briefly on the relationship between laughter and spiritual relaxation.

16. Henri Bergson (1859–1941), a French philosopher who wrote *Laughter: An Essay on the Meaning of the Comic* (1900).

After reading the book, I do have some impressions that I would like to record, but since they don't harmonize well with the subject of my essay, I have decided to put them off to another time.

[*TERADA TORAHIKO SHŪ*, ED. KADOKAWA GEN'YOSHI AND OGIKUBO YASUYUKI, NIHON KINDAI BUNGAKU TAIKEI 34 (TOKYO: KADOKAWA SHOTEN, 1973)]

30

Various Thoughts on
the Great Kantō Earthquake
and My Moral Precepts
for Everyday Life

KIKUCHI KAN

Kikuchi Kan (1888–1948) was born in Takamatsu. After a brief stint in normal school and Tokyo First Higher School, he moved on to Kyoto University, graduating with a degree in English literature in 1916. Now he is most remembered for founding the magazine Bungei shunjū *(which began publication in 1923 and is still being published) and establishing the two most prominent of Japanese literary prizes, the Akutagawa Prize, for "pure literature" (jun bungaku), and the Naoki Prize, for "popular literature" (taishū bungaku).*

Kikuchi was an extremely prolific author himself, writing numerous plays, stories, novels, and essays. The first essay translated here, "Saigo zakkan" (Various Thoughts on the Great Kantō Earthquake), originally appeared in the magazine Chūō kōron *in October 1923, not long after the events it describes; the second, "Watakushi no nichijō dōtoku" (My Moral Precepts for Everyday Life), was published in 1926 in* Bungei shunjū.

Various Thoughts on the Great Kantō Earthquake

The Great Kantō Earthquake[1] was—in terms of its effects—a social revolution. Wealth, position, traditions—all of these were thrown into confusion, and the world became a place where practical ability was paramount; that is, the ability to do useful work. The change was temporary and not universal, but among all the awful results of the disaster, this effect alone was salutary.

If officials and the general populace can only remember the lessons of the disaster, I believe it may be possible to avoid the ruin of the social revolution that was in the making.

———————

For professional writers such as myself, the first shock was the vivid demonstration of how, when it comes to matters of life and death, our writings are leisure goods, like antiques or calligraphy or paintings. Of course, we already knew this, but it was painful to have it demonstrated so graphically.

It goes without saying that from the disaster we learned what was most necessary in life. In a life-or-death crisis, food and shelter are the only necessities: something to eat, somewhere to sleep. Sasaki Mosaku[2] joked that we should launch a new literary movement—the "food and shelter school."[3] For the first four or five days after the disaster, we thought of nothing but food and shelter. Ideas like "Man does not live by bread alone" are an indulgence for more peaceful days.

Among the many ways of making a living, only those of greatest necessity remained—only stores that sold food. Even clothing shops and

1. On September 1, 1923, a magnitude 7.8 earthquake struck Tokyo and the surrounding provinces, destroying more than 50 percent of the buildings in the city. More than 100,000 people died in the quake and the fires that followed, and more than 50,000 were injured.

2. 1894–1966. One of Kikuchi's closest associates, a writer who later became the editor of *Bungei shunjū*.

3. The 1920s and 1930s were the heyday of literary schools—the naturalist school, the neo-impressionist school, the Japan romantic school, and so on.

shoe stores were not quick to reopen. Shops that sold art objects and fancy goods, photography studios, and antique dealers were for the time being left in ruins. At the music shop near my house, they were serving miso soup. A sad situation for the arts.

———————

Even in this world of "food and shelter," there was of course more to human existence. Nonetheless, we did see the visage of life in its extremity. And the fact that in such an extremity, art was a useless old cart—that fact was for us as artists an unhappy truth. For us, the first blow was a loss of confidence in our own work.

———————

As for me, I pondered having to do all my own labor. For someone of my physique, muscular labor was impossible. Something like cutting hair, I thought I could perhaps do. No matter what happens in the world, I figured there would be a demand for barbering. When I saw that barbershops were the first places to open again after the disaster, I chuckled at my own prescience.

———————

But at the same time, I was well aware that when it came down to it, the most important work was being able to provide and prepare one's own food. The person who can make his own food is truly the strongest sort of person, I mused. In that sense, the finest and strongest kind of worker is the farmer. At such a time, I thought all the more keenly of the lifestyle of Mushanokōji Saneatsu.[4]

———————

To me, there seems no doubt that literature will lose ground because of the disaster, the first reason being that we writers have lost faith in our writing. Moreover, the demand for writing will doubtless decline drasti-

———

4. 1885–1976. A prominent writer of the White Birch school (Shirakabaha) who in 1918 established a utopian commune named New Village (Atarashiki Mura) in Hyūga Prefecture dedicated to self-sufficient farming.

cally. In the immediate aftermath, bookstores remained closed for a long time. Another reason will be the reduction in printing capacity, one effect of which is evident in the decline of magazine production. I think we can say that in terms of quantity at least, the golden age of literature is over.

If you write novels, you need only a brush and paper, so there is no reason not to write something. But the situation for playwrights is more miserable. Even for someone of great ability, it will feel hopeless to go on writing plays when there are no theaters. The world of Japanese theater, which was just beginning to thrive after so much labor, is bound to be set back at least for the next four or five years.

There are people who say that because of the disaster, writers will have a deeper sense of themselves and that their writing will therefore become more serious. They may be right. But that is a writer's perspective, I think: we refrain from saying anything too depressing. But that is just the writers' side of things, rather than what will be demanded on the consumers' side. Instead, I would wager that popular writing of the sort that puts entertainment first will thrive. I think that readers will chase after entertainment literature as a way to escape the dire state of reality. In that sense, too, writing will go into decline.

Even if the literary world is in for decline, people like me will accept that the time for reckoning has come[5] and withdraw to the countryside, but the situation will be hard for new writers. Terms like "proletarian writers" and "bourgeois writers" no longer matter.[6]

All we can do is be still and endure, and wait for the arrival of new opportunities.

5. *Nengu no osamedoki* (literally, "the time for accounting for taxes due"), here with the sense that writers must now pay for their sins.
6. Kikuchi was a critic of the proletarian movement and thus belonged to the "bourgeois" category.

I suffered only slightly at the time of the disaster. When the ground began to sway, I ran out into the garden. After waiting for the first shaking to subside, I went to look in on relatives near Nihonbashi. On the way back, I was headed toward Manseibashi, but that way everything was engulfed in black smoke. Realizing that I would never get through, I turned back. The area behind Mitsukoshi Department Store was on fire. Kanda was on fire. But through the smoke between Marunouchi and Kanda I could see a patch of blue sky, so I headed off in that direction. The streets were crowded with refugees and carts. When I got to the area between Youth Hall and Kandabashi, the other side of Kandabashi was burning. I was barely able to escape by making my way along the riverbank between Kandabashi and Hitotsubashi. I was brought to a standstill two or three times because people had piled their things next to the water, and there were so many people and carts in the way. Ash was falling down from the sky. There were children crying, sitting between futons and wardrobes. I slipped through between the carts and felt that I had made it back to life only after crossing over Hitotsubashi. The next day, when I heard that there were lots of dead bodies between Kandabashi and Hitotsubashi, I shuddered. Had I been just twenty or thirty minutes later, I realized that I, too, would have been engulfed in smoke. I could understand how people ended up getting burned to death.[7]

The one surprising thing was how upbeat people were just the next day. They were not downcast. I realized that even those who had escaped the fires were happy at having escaped death during the earthquake. At the same time, though, I also thought that there must have been many people who burned to death because they had let their guard down after surviving the earthquake.

7. All the places mentioned here are located in central Tokyo, not far from Kikuchi's home in Komagome.

In books, I had read accounts of the awful events of the Ansei Earthquake[8] and the Meireki Fire,[9] which were heartrending even a hundred years later, but never had I thought that I would see something even more tragic in our own times.

I have read that at the time of the Meireki Fire, thousands of people were crushed in front of the closed gate of Asakusa Temple and then burned to death, but the tragedy at the Clothing Delivery Center exceeded even that.[10] Yet human beings are strong and will, I am sure, stand up to every trial.

I had thought it unlikely that people in modern times would ever use passwords, but for the first four or five days after the disaster, I too carried my identification and used passwords as a precaution. The prompt was *Koma* and the reply was *Three*. In my neighborhood, there was an association called the *Three* Trades Association of *Komagome*.[11] I think it must be something unheard of before or since for restaurants, waiting lounges, and geisha houses to have created passwords.

What made the disaster fairly easy for me was that I was living alone. Among my acquaintances were two or three people who, after being burned out of their rooms, went scurrying around among the ruins. The more relatives you had, the more painful this was. It truly makes sense that the first step in taking the tonsure is to cut all ties of love and affection.

This is an announcement: the Ninth Month issue of *Bungei shunjū*, the magazine for which I am managing editor, was reduced to ashes in the

8. The Ansei Earthquake refers to thirteen quakes that occurred during the Ansei era (1854–1860), the most devastating of which was on the second day of the Tenth Month of 1855.

9. More than 100,000 people died in a fire that swept through Edo on the eighteenth day of the First Month of 1657, the third year of the Meireki era (1655–1658).

10. After the earthquake, many people gathered on the opened grounds of the former Army Clothing Delivery Center (Hifukushō) for safety, but were later surrounded by fire and engulfed in firestorms. More than 35,000 people died from the intense heat of the maelstrom in that one spot alone.

11. Sangyō Kumiai. An organization of restaurants, waiting lounges (*machiai*), and geisha houses.

fire, and we have decided to resume publication with the November issue, so please wait until then. I am using my space here to make this announcement to our readers.

On the second day, when the fires had burned all the way to Ikenohata,[12] I too left my house and fled to the evacuation site at Iwasaki,[13] intimidated by the ash flying overhead and the waves of people fleeing into the Komagome area. "Fleeing for one's life" was an awful business, particularly for those shepherding the young or the elderly. I pray that I will never again experience such a disaster in my lifetime.

My Moral Precepts for Everyday Life

I am always pleased to take any kind of gift from someone who is richer than I am. Nor do I hesitate to let them treat me to dinner. Indeed, I never show any hesitation when people give me things. The pleasure we get from giving and receiving is something that brightens our lives. I receive things happily and try to give in the same spirit.

Whenever I am treated to dinner, I eat as much as I can. At such times, I do not feel the need to comment on things not to my taste, but I always mention explicitly whatever I think is delicious.

When I eat out with someone, if that person's income is considerably smaller than mine, I pay, even if it means insisting a little. If the person is someone with considerable income, I let him pay if he insists.

---

12. The area around Shinobazu Pond in Daitō Ward.
13. The grounds of the Iwasaki estate, also in Daitō Ward, southeast of Shinobazu Pond, were opened for use by refugees.

When someone asks me for money, I decide whether to agree or not depending on how close I am to the person. No matter how desperate the situation may be, if it's someone I have just met, I turn him down.

I do not lend money to anyone for anything but living expenses. If it is for living expenses, I will lend. However, I have already decided inwardly the appropriate amount for each of my friends and acquaintances, and I lend only the amount that I have decided I will not mind giving to each person. After lending the money, I have never once thought of being repaid, nor has anyone ever paid me back.

I strive to keep my promises at all costs, because if people did not abide by their promises, social existence would become impossible. Therefore, I have never broken a promise except in cases when I truly had no choice. Come to think of it, though, there are some promises I have broken—specifically, promises to finish manuscripts. In this one area, I do not seem able to always keep my word.

When a person tells me something that someone else has said about me, I give it no heed. The fact is that in private, people are going to say bad things about others, even though they may inwardly have respect for the person they criticize. In many cases, only the bad things they say get reported to you, while the praise they offered at the same time does not.

I am not reserved. I am quite confident of my own value, and I expect others to respond to that by treating me with respect. No matter who else may be riding, when I get in an automobile, I will not sit in the rumpus seat if there is any room inside the car.

_____

Even if someone is kind in the way they tell me about it, I will not listen to criticism or vicious gossip about myself. If knowing about it allows for some kind of immediate response, that is one thing; otherwise, I would simply rather not know.

_____

When I am out on the street, the belt of my kimono often comes loose, but I hate it when people feel they have to point it out to me. If I myself have not yet realized that my belt is slipping, it doesn't bother me, and I hate someone else's drawing attention to it. After all, it's the sort of thing you will eventually notice on your own, even if no one tells you. It may be that one can say the same about some of the more important things in life.

_____

The kindness I show others I want to do out of pleasure; I do not want to do it out of a sense of duty.

_____

To people who show me goodwill, I show goodwill in return. To those who show me ill will, I will return the same.

_____

If I am asked to critique a work that is bad, I will die before I will say it is good—no matter how much it may hurt the person who wrote it. But if there is even a little good in the thing, I will give it exorbitant praise as a way to encourage the writer.

[KIKUCHI KAN BUNGAKU ZENSHŪ, VOL. 6 (TOKYO: BUNGEI SHUNJŪ SHINSHA, 1960); KIKUCHI KAN, CHIKUMA NIHON BUNGAKU ZENSHŪ 27 (TOKYO: CHIKUMA SHOBŌ, 1991)]

31

Master Hyakken's Idle Fantasies, Bumpy Road, *and* A Long Fence

UCHIDA HYAKKEN

Uchida Hyakken (born Uchida Eizō; known by the pen names Hyakken and Hyak-kien; 1889–1971) was born into a merchant family in Okayama. Already in his youth, he was a devotee of haiku and an avid reader of the novelist Natsume Sōseki, whose disciple he became after enrolling in Tokyo Imperial University to study German. Beginning in 1913, he served as editor and proofreader for Sōseki and later became a member of the editorial committee for Sōseki's complete works. At the same time, he began teaching German in various higher schools, including the army and naval academies.

In his thirties, Hyakken began writing stories and essays, many of them humorous, while continuing to teach. Much beloved by his many students, he became the model for the teacher portrayed in one of Kurosawa Akira's final films, Māda da yo! *(Not Yet, 1992). He is one of the most highly regarded Japanese essayists of the twentieth century.*

The pieces translated here—"Hyakken Sensei no gensōroku" (Master Hyakken's Idle Fantasies), "Dekoboko no michi" (Bumpy Road), and "Nagai hei" (A Long Fence)—appeared in collections published in 1933, 1935, and 1938, respectively.

Master Hyakken's Idle Fantasies

Traveling by airplane is all very fine, but if it crashes, you're in a fix. No matter how kindly someone standing next to me assures me that things will be all right, I just can't feel at ease. For human beings, who don't have wings, after all, to think of flying through the air is an invitation to trouble—and an act of defiance against the will of the universe. Yet it is not a certainty that if one gets on a plane one will end badly, so one can of course put off thinking about such things until facing an actual crash. Which means that one *does* want to try a ride.

Once as a merchant was about to get on a boat, he asked a boatman there how his father had died, and the boatman said that both his grandfather and his father had died at sea. Surprised to hear this, the merchant asked the man if he wasn't frightened to venture out onto the water. To this, the boatman replied by turning the tables and asking how the merchant's grandfather and father had died, to which the merchant replied, "In their beds, of course." At this, the boatman feigned surprise and asked, "So, are you afraid to get in bed at night?" Dangerous though they may be, by that comparison airplanes are much safer than one's own bed.

I hear it was the German engineer Lachmann,[1] of an aircraft-manufacturing company in Ishikawajima, who invented the slotted wing. Rumor has it that this device is an absolute guarantee against crashing, so if you travel by an aircraft equipped with it, you need have no fear, I guess. Let's say, then, that you go flying off into the skies over Tokyo. Looking down on the dusty world below, you exercise your wizardry while thinking of your poor friends scurrying around down there like so many fools. But let's say that the slotted wing—which I have to admit I have never seen and know nothing about—let's say that it works too well, and you are

1. Gustav Lachmann (1896–1966) began his career in Germany, where he developed the slotted wing in 1918, after having served as a pilot in World War I. In the late 1920s, he spent several years in Japan, working for the Ishikawajima Aircraft Manufacturing Company.

unable to descend. Now, wouldn't that be a problem? When it comes to crashes, you might have one chance in a thousand of surviving; if you could never come back down, though . . . then you would have to spend the rest of your life up there in the sky.

"Oh, but that wouldn't be a problem," someone says. "Even if you couldn't descend, you could just fly horizontally and land on the side of Mount Fuji or Mount Tsukuba,[2] climb down, and come home by train." But I'm afraid that this person has been too clever for himself and forgotten that the earth is round.

Now, if you get on an ordinary airplane not equipped with the slotted wing, you never know when a wing might break or the engine stop, sending you down to earth. In such a case, you could strap yourself into a parachute to get down, but if there were a lot of birds migrating, as there are at this time of year, you couldn't be sure of not meeting an unhappy fate in midair. The shrikes that live here and there all over the mountains might come in droves, and there you would be, dangling in the air and so constrained in your movements that you would be helpless.[3] With their curved beaks, they would bite at your armpits or your crotch, or perhaps peck at your back or tear out your guts. Hanging there, you would present a scene little different from the one a caterpillar makes falling from a tree in the garden, only to be set upon by ants—a caterpillar that can do no more than writhe against the pain to which he is subjected.

So rather than seeking reassurance about riding in an airplane, I think it's more interesting to think about how you might use it as a suicide device. You could lie down on the grass of the airfield, which is broad as the sea. If you didn't want to be alone, two or three friends could come along with you. Around your necks you would tie ropes, loosely, which would then be fastened to an airplane on the runway far off in the distance. Before long, you would hear the roar of the engine starting up, and the plane would taxi and take off. Then, quite suddenly, the ropes would tighten around the necks of you who are so weary of the world, and off you would go, suspended in the air over Tokyo, until out over the sea the

2. Mount Fuji, southwest of Tokyo, is of course well known; Mount Tsukuba is located in Ibaraki Prefecture.
3. Shrikes are notoriously fierce and ill-tempered.

ropes would be cut free so your dangling remains could be cast off and the plane could return—with no fuss at all.

───────────

Listening to baseball on the radio is fun, and I think it lets us intrude on pleasures usually reserved for the blind. I have heard that when a blind person goes to see sumo matches, he can tell who is winning or losing by the calls of the referee or the reactions of the crowd, enjoying things just as much as sighted people. So when sighted people enjoy broadcasts of baseball or sumo, staying right there in front of the radio, it's as if they were snatching a bit of what is enjoyed only by the blind, whom we normally think of with pity.

Putting aside the topic of blindness for a moment, I cannot help but think that since we enjoy such broadcasts with our ears alone, there really is no need to take the microphones out to the baseball field or sumo arena. After the announcer has accumulated some experience, he could broadcast rain or shine, no matter what the season. All he would have to do is say, "Ah, there's a hit!" convincingly, and that would do. Coming up with equipment to produce background noise and the roar of the crowd would be no problem. Nor do I think that listeners would object to such staged contests. Don't they end up laughing and crying at the movies, completely taken in by moving images that appear only to disappear, knowing all the while that there's really nothing there behind the screen? Were a match to be cancelled, a true genius of an announcer could go ahead with the broadcast and gain a reputation as a kind of artist, provided only that he had the courage to take advantage of his listeners' expectations that the match would take place as planned, using artificial effects—sound, voices, echoes—to keep their attention.

The way telephones are shifting more and more toward self-dialing systems is truly unfortunate for the blind. With the old-style system, if a blind person could get hold of the receiver, he could proceed just as sighted people do, but the new system requires him to search out the holes and dial the ten numbers.

Of course, it appears that the fingertips of blind people are more sensitive than those of the sighted. Miyagi Michio, the composer of *Music from*

Heaven,[4] is blind, and he reads music scores set in braille with his fingers, playing Bach preludes on an eighty-string koto of his own design. At the end of this last year, he told me that books written in braille are really handy. Even if you're in a train, you can put the book on your lap and read by just running over the text with your fingers—and without spreading the newspaper out right into the face of the person sitting next to you. And when you're sitting at a *kotatsu*,[5] you can put the book under the quilt and read one page at a time, keeping your hands warm all the while and still getting the sense of what you're reading. What's more, he said, it seems that sighted people have a lot of trouble reading in bed, while the blind don't read with their eyes and so don't need the light left on, which means that they don't have to bother with getting up and turning it off before going to sleep. On a winter night, they don't have to expose their elbows to support the book, or complain about their shoulders getting sore from reading facedown. A blind person can lie on his back, with the paper underneath the quilt, resting it on his stomach, and understand the text just fine while moving along with warm hands. And if he gets sleepy, his fingertips will also lose their sensitivity, and he can just drift off to slumber. He read Bakin's *Eight Dogs*[6] that way, he said, with the text sitting right on his belly.

I was so envious when I heard this that I determined to start studying braille, but after I tried it for a while, I found that the way the dots were arranged vertically or curving to the right or left was something I could grasp with my eyes but not distinguish with my fingertips alone. That being the case, even if I could "read" braille, it would be no different from reading with my eyes. Still I would have to leave the light on at night, and still I would not be able to go to sleep while reading with the pages on my belly. So my attempts to learn braille stopped there.

---

4. 1894–1956. A composer and concert artist who combined Western and Japanese elements and instruments in his compositions. *Etenraku* (*Music from Heaven*) is one of Miyagi's most famous works, based on an ancient Japanese folk song (*imayo*).

5. A low table with a heater underneath, covered with a quilt.

6. *Nansō Satomi Hakkenden* (*A Tale of Eight Virtuous Dogs*, 1814–1842), by Takizawa Bakin (1767–1848), one of the longest and most popular of Edo-period *yomihon* (didactic romances).

Things come before names. First you have a thing, and then you can decide on what to call it. To confirm this, just give the name Cat to your pet dog and watch how he comes running up wagging his tail when you call out, "Hey Cat!" "Come, Cat!"

Once I heard that there was a shop in Kagurazaka selling Canton cats for seven yen, so I put ten yen in my pocket and went to see. There, on top of a box, was a cat with a funny-looking face. The proprietor could not recall quoting anyone the seven-yen price, though, and said that the price was really fifteen yen, which he would reduce to thirteen. In the end, he said that he would let it go for ten yen, but by then a lot of time had gone by, and I was getting more reluctant to part with the money. First of all, if I spent the ten yen, I would be left with no spending money, and I also realized that even if he went down to ten yen, there really was no law that said I had to have the experience of owning a Canton cat. So that evening, I came home without a cat. However, someday I still intend to find an opportunity to call a dog a cat, or drink saké as if it were water, or try to use a fallen leaf as paper money.

Bumpy Road

When I think back on friends from my childhood years who have passed away, more come to mind than I can count on five fingers. I think to myself that this may be true of anyone about my age who thinks back on old friends, but then I feel that this may not be true.

Hayashi Ken'ichi was a friend from my grade-school days. We were also together in junior high, graduating at the same time and both succeeding in gaining entrance to Okayama Sixth Higher School. His father was a judge who was transferred to Mito. For spring vacation in our first year at Okayama, my friend went home to his father's house in Mito and never came back again.

I heard something about what had taken his life so suddenly, but the impression I got was rather vague. At that time, my heart was rather easily wounded, and there was a protective membrane of reluctance over it that made me hesitate to ask for more clear information.

The Number 6 train that left Okayama at 7:22 in the evening was the only direct express that went straight through from Shimonoseki to Shinbashi.[7] Hayashi was going to leave for Mito on that train, so I set out on my bicycle to see him off at Okayama Station. When I was almost there, however, my bicycle lamp, which I had switched on as dusk fell, went out on a bumpy patch in the road. I got off and began to walk, pushing my bicycle by the handlebars and hurrying as fast as I could out of worry over the time. When I came to a police box located at the intersection around a curve, a policeman called me over.

"Why are you riding without a light?"

"I'm not riding at all."

"Don't lie to me. It's no good riding without your light and then getting off when you get near a police box."

"My lamp went out, so I got off."

"Then why don't you just light it?"

"I didn't bring any matches, so I got off and started walking."

"Liar. You no-goods are a real nuisance. Come on over here."

"My lamp just now went out. I'm seeing someone off at the station, so can't you please let me go?"

"Do you have any proof that it just went out?"

"Touch the lamp—it's probably still warm."

He touched the lamp and took a peek inside at the candle. That seemed to convince him, so I thought that I would be able to go, but he said to come with him. Under the streetlamp, he pulled out his little notebook and took down my name and address.

I didn't think that it was taking all that long, but when I arrived at the station, the express had just left and they wouldn't let me through the gate. I jumped up onto the fence and saw the train, just beyond the edge of the platform, the red light on its last car swaying as it picked up speed and moved off into the distance. In the lamplight, I could see vividly as

7. Shimonoseki is at the very southern tip of Honshu. From Shinbashi in Tokyo, Uchida's friend would have transferred to a train that would take him to Mito, located in Ibaraki Prefecture.

a clump of white smoke, hovering around the carriage storage shed in front, dissipated into the rough shadows.

Hayashi had been a friend for a long time, ever since childhood, so I frequently remember the bumpy road that prevented our saying farewell long ago.

A Long Fence

It's still cold out, so the time for peeing on the roadside hasn't even come around yet; and probably I shouldn't be talking about doing such a thing in the city, no matter how balmy the weather. But even if I myself don't indulge, the fact is that on occasion I do catch sight of other men doing so. Which must be why on every fence of any length there is a sign carrying some message enjoining people not to pee there.

There is a comic poem that goes,

A long fence:
suddenly I feel the urge
  to pee.

nagai hei / tsui shōben ga / shitaku nari

Very insightful, I find myself thinking—though I must admit that if I happen to remember the poem when I am walking by a long fence, the memory in itself awakens that certain urge.

Next door to the house I recently moved into is a large old-style residence with a very long fence, which does tend to bring all of this to mind.[8] Before I moved, I sent out notifications by postcard, which I asked a friend to make up for me. In addition to the message, he put in a map in relief and drew a fence next to my house. Probably thinking that it wouldn't do for people to mistake the fence for something else, he added a note that said, "white fence." When I was first searching for a house, I

---

8. Hyakken had recently moved from Yotsuya to Ichigaya, both in Shinjuku.

had seen the place in the evening and thought that the fence was white myself, but when I saw it later in the daytime, it turned out to be not white but yellow. In fact, however, I didn't care much about the color, although I had thought it was unfortunate that he hadn't written "long fence" instead, which would have been more tasteful.

Evidently, long fences create not only the urge I mentioned before but also—among city janitors, that is—the desire to use them as a place to leave their trash cans. In front of the fence of an old-style residence in Kappazaka where I used to live, there would always be cans stacked up one night a month or so. And along the fence next door to my new place, the cleaners from the ward office did the same thing every so many days, too—something that could be annoying, depending on which way the wind was blowing.

After going out the door of my house, I stroll along the fence, but no matter how long it gets, it is broad daylight after all, and I *have* just left the house—so I don't get the urge mentioned in the poem. At the corner, the road runs along an embankment, on the curve of which hangs a wooden plaque that I stop to read:

"Respect public morals—do your peeing in the privy"

What a silly thing to write, I think to myself. But rather than rewrite the sign, I think it would be more fun sometime when the need arises to step inside the gate into the gravel-covered compound, go up to the door, and ask if I might please have the use of their convenience.

In a country town, I saw a sign hanging from the wood-plank wall of a dry-goods store down an alley that said this:

"Anyone urinating here will be swiftly prosecuted"

I was amused imagining the look on the face of the owner as he wrote the warning out. Considering the nature of the activity he was attempting to prevent, I felt the diction was a little too blunt.

I have heard stories about people who, when looking around at fences to find a place to put up a flier or a poster, see a small sign that says, "No

Posting," and because it feels wrong to hang anything there, end up looking somewhere else. But while such injunctions may work against other things, when it comes to peeing by the road, they don't appear to do any good at all. Either people don't notice the sign at all, or they pretend not to, or they just stand there staring right at the sign while they take care of business.

Here and there I also see injunctions that read,

"Well Within—Peeing Forbidden"

Sometimes there is a drawing of a well curb above the words, but in this case it seems as if they are trying to appeal to one's moral sense about just this one particular place, leaving one open to interpret the message as saying, "Anywhere else is fine—go ahead!"

I also come across signs that have a drawing of a Shinto torii, beneath which is written, "Shrine to Inari[9] inside." But try though such believers may to impose their beliefs on passersby, the effort won't do much good if the one stopping there happens to be a Christian.

Among all these illustrated signs, the one that impressed me the most had beneath the words "Peeing Forbidden" a drawing of a long, sharp pair of pruning shears, which made me much more fearful than the threat of being "swiftly prosecuted."

Among the many signs—and the strategies behind them—I think the best one is one that you see all over: "Peeing Forbidden—Except for Dogs," though these days one doesn't see it as much as one used to. It may be that people got so used to the stock phrase that it lost its effectiveness.

In spite of all this, it still happens that you are on foot somewhere and there is no public lavatory and there are lots of other people walking by, but you have to go so bad that you almost wish you could become a dog. And at the moment when, having found an out-of-the-way corner, you are at last able to take care of things, you aren't really worrying anymore about being a dog or anything else. Viewing things from that perspec-

9. Inari-sama, originally a god of grain who later became a patron saint of merchants, in particular. Small Inari shrines are located in many neighborhoods.

tive, in fact, none of the old injunctions I have listed is likely to have any effect at all.

Some years back, I was riding along through the streets at midday with a white-bearded old gentleman who had the driver stop the car at an unexpected place. The driver quickly opened the door, and the old man went trotting off toward an empty lot outside the fence at the corner of a certain foreign-government compound located on the side of the road.

What could he be doing? I thought curiously, but the driver appeared to be unconcerned and just said, rather casually, "He's just taking care of a little business."[10] In a while, the old gentleman returned, said "Sorry!" and then sat down beside me again and had the driver proceed.

A young office worker told me that when he and his friends were out gallivanting in Ginza and had to go, they would pop into the first floor of any nearby department store or other building and use the facilities there—which they already knew about. Good thinking, I mused to myself, feeling very impressed, and imagined that when you are really feeling the need, a department store looming up in front of you would begin to look just like a huge public lavatory. Of course, a stay-at-home sort like me won't ever experience the new sensation coming from the idea "A tall building: / suddenly I feel the urge / to pee." But one can even wonder whether department stores might in the end be putting up signs that say, "Peeing Forbidden—Except for Customers."

I once had the experience of peeing not by the roadside in a town but from the sky in an airplane. In a Fokker 3M model, there is equipment for such a purpose. In the early days, I understand that there was just a hole gaping there in front of you, but when I had my own experience, there was metal netting fastened underneath. My knowledge of airliners is limited to the Fokker, but as various new models have come out since then, the technology has no doubt progressed. Basically, though, the fact remains that you are raining water down on people from above. At the time, that idea bothered me, I must say, but I was told that the water would immediately turn to mist and dissipate, and so I went ahead. Yet as I looked down through the netting on the bright landscape

10. *Yō o tasu.* A phrase that is still used as a euphemism for visiting the toilet.

stretching out right in front of my eyes, the feeling I had wasn't all that pleasant.

In airplanes and buildings, facilities are in place, anticipating a need, so I must accept criticism for straying from my topic of long fences. But when I think once more about my own case in relation to fences, or when I see others making use of them, I first note that we all begin by looking around, right and left. No doubt, we do this partly out of a certain reserve, thinking that we mustn't do it in front of other people; the more immediate concern, however, is bound to be that a policeman might be about, which is something that will almost unconsciously pop up into the mind of anyone who is about to relieve himself in this way. Perhaps this is a sign that the indoctrination of urbanites that began in the Meiji period has actually succeeded, and one must hope that we will continue to respect this instinct to take a look around. But the effects of this indoctrination have been limited to the spiritual realm, I believe, for I can't imagine that the numbers of people peeing by the roadside since the establishment of the various categories of criminal behavior are that different from what the numbers were before. However discreetly and with whatever care, people still do what they must—an outcome that to me seems just about right.

From time to time, I hear stories of drunks peeing on the wall of a police box, supposedly because when they get drunk they lose their self-control and their usual inhibitions turn against them. But to claim that in such circumstances the man has mistaken the police box for a public lavatory is a bald-faced lie. In his own drunken way, a drunk understands that a police box is a police box. To go ahead and pee on the police box even when his companions try to stop him, even when it takes some effort to do so—that is the inner working of a drinker's mind. What he is really doing is taking an opportunity to relieve the intense feelings of tension that come with having always to look around right and left in his everyday life.

Please understand, though, that I say this because I have had the experience of *being out* with drunks of that sort and not because I have ever done such a thing myself.

[*UCHIDA HYAKKEN ZENSHŪ*, ED. HIRAYAMA SABURŌ ET AL., VOLS. 1–3
(TOKYO: KŌDANSHA, 1971–1973)]

32

The Image of an Author

DAZAI OSAMU

Tsushima Shūji (known by the pen name Dazai Osamu; 1909-1948) was born in Aomori Prefecture to a wealthy landowner who was a member of the House of Peers. He did well in school and enrolled in the French Literature Department at Tokyo Imperial University in 1930. For a time, he was involved with the Communist Party, but his writings reveal a life preoccupied less with politics than with his personal experiences. Tuberculosis saved him from military service during the war years, but not from his own dissolute habits. After writing a number of stories and novels that are highly prized as expressions of the ennui and nihilism of the years after the defeat, he committed suicide with a lover in 1948. He had attempted suicide four times before.

The essay translated here, "Sakka no zō" (The Image of an Author), first appeared in the Miyako shimbun *in April 1940. It reveals his characteristic narcissism—which he rather freely admits—and his thoughts on the* zuihitsu *as a literary form.*

There is no reason I should not be able to write a ten-page *zuihitsu*, but for three full days I have been working at it, to no avail: I write something but soon tear it up, write something again but then tear it up. Paper is in short supply in Japan just now, and I realize that I shouldn't be wasting it in such a way. No matter how timidly, though, I still end up tearing everything up.

I cannot say it—I cannot say what I want to say. This writer is simply unable to make the proper distinction between what is acceptable to say and what is not. It appears that I have not yet developed what might be called a moral aptitude. I have a mountain of things that I wish to say— things that I truly do want to say. But at the crucial moment, I hear a voice: "No matter what you say, aren't you just trying to justify yourself?"

"No! It is *not* just self-justification," I say, rushing to my own defense; but in a corner of my heart, I do rather sheepishly admit that that may be what it comes down to. And so I tear in half the sheet of paper I had begun to write on, and then tear that in half again.

I begin: "I think that I must be no good at writing a *zuihitsu* of this sort," and write a little more; but then I tear it up. Again, I write, "In a *zuihitsu*, fabrications are not allowed. . . ." But I hurriedly tear that up as well. I do have something I wish to say, but somehow I just cannot express it.

I want to hit my target audience squarely, yet without getting even a speck of dust on innocent bystanders. I am so clumsy that when it comes to making an assertive statement, I always wound people pointlessly. Among my friends my name is Bear Claw.[1] I reach out to pet but always end up scratching.

When I was reading Tsukamoto Toraji's "My Memories of Uchimura Kanzō,"[2] I came across this passage:

One summer, at Kutsukake Hot Springs, Uchimura splashed some water on one of my children in fun, and the child started to cry. "This is what always happens with me. I try to be nice, and end up being the bad guy," he said.

When I first read this, I could hardly stand it. If I want to throw a rock to the other side of the stream and move my arm to do so, I hit the person

1. The common noun corresponds to the popular name for a bamboo rake.
2. Uchimura Kanzō (1861–1930) was a famous Japanese Christian thinker and minister. Tsukamoto Toraji (1885–1973) was one of his disciples and a prominent Christian missionary.

next to me with my elbow, and he cries, "Ouch—that hurt!" I'm in a cold sweat trying to apologize and explain myself, but no matter how much I try, I get back a sullen look. It may be that my arms are just longer than other people's.

A *zuihitsu* is not fiction; the writer's words are supposed to be "raw." Yet if one is not careful as one writes, one may unintentionally injure someone nearby. So it is not that I mean to refer to that person at all. To put it in grandiose terms, I always just think of myself as reporting to the heavens the true features of the human story; it has nothing to do with any personal grudge. When I say this, however, people laugh and refuse to believe me.

I think that I may be a rather indulgent sort of man—what is called a stupid idealist. When I set out to write or do something, it is the idea that comes first. Even if it's just drinking, I have to drink with a rational justification.

Just yesterday I went drinking in Asagaya, and this is how it transpired: I was writing a *zuihitsu* to send to this newspaper [*Miyako shimbun*], but I had failed to come up with anything to say. Had it been a work of fiction, I would have been able to write all sorts of things. In fact, I stopped to ruminate for a while about a short story I had been working on for about a month, and actually enjoyed it. So, I thought: if I'm going to write something, it should be something fictional through which I can dispel my current feelings of gloom. Until I was done with that, therefore, I thought it might be best to look the other away. Were I to publish my little fragment as a *zuihitsu* now, I thought, my words would come up short, I would be misunderstood, people would find fault, and I would get pulled into arguments—a useless proposition. After all, I did want to be prudent. For a moment, I thought to myself that I should be able to get through this by dissembling, putting a good face on things by writing something along the lines of "Today the weather is fine, so I determine to go out for a stroll, as usual. The rose plums are already blooming, the heavens are full of feeling—yes, there can be no doubt that spring has come!" But I am too clumsy for that; I am the sort of person who cannot succeed at concealing his true feelings. When something fortunate happens, I am all smiles; when I make a stupid mistake, the gloom shows in my face. I cannot dissemble. So this is what I wrote:

The thing about me is, whether others are kind enough to acknowledge it or not, I'm determined to walk my own path. The result is that every day I must engage in a host of futile labors. Sometimes this seems stupid even to me. Sometimes I get red-faced about it.

This way of doing things is not at all in vogue, but I myself persist in it, by fits and starts, writing and living as prudently as possible. Even the most insignificant matter requires care. One mustn't stumble over something slight. Always, waking or sleeping, even in the face of unpleasant events, one must fortify oneself and remain smiling. In grand tones, I think, "Who knows? Anytime now I may write a masterpiece!" and continue on expressing my foolish ideas. I wonder if maybe I am wrong in the head.

Lately I was asked for a *zuihitsu* by a newspaper, so I took courage and set myself to the task. But I kept tearing up whatever I wrote, and even after working on ideas for three or four days, I had ten pages at the most. It seems that I wanted to write a *zuihitsu* so brilliant that I would have readers thinking, "That's it—he has it right!" But after working at it so long, I no longer knew what was what; I didn't even understand what a *zuihitsu* was supposed to be.

I rummaged through my book box and took out two books: *The Pillow Book* and *The Tales of Ise*. I thought that I could use these books to search out the *zuihitsu* traditions of Japan. What an imbecile I am.

So far, nothing too awful here, I thought, and went on and produced another page, starting with, "However . . ."—but then I realized it would not do and tore it up—for I knew that I was bound to drop my guard and make a big mistake. For one thing, I have a short story that I want to write. Until I've finished with that, I don't want to give anyone any impressions of myself. *That* is the truly formidable task I must face. I know full well that this is a rather extravagant hobby, but if at all possible, I want to remain hidden until I'm finished. I cannot pretend otherwise. That is an impossible task for a man as simpleminded as I am. Yesterday, too, I suffered in the same way. "How can it be so hard to come up with materials for a *zuihitsu*? Couldn't I write about a friend who has passed on? Or about travel, perhaps? Or a diary?"

But I have never kept a diary. The fact is that I am unable to keep a diary. All the events of a day: What is one to leave out, and what is one to record? I don't understand where the limits are. If one approaches the task with vigor, writing down everything, one will write the whole day long and be breathless at the end. You think that you should be accurate, so you want to leave nothing out, right up until when you go to sleep—a truly annoying business, to be sure. Moreover, it is no easy task to decide whether a diary should be written with the idea that the day will come when others will read it, or whether it will be just between yourself and God. So even if I bought a diary, I would doodle in it or use it to record the addresses of my friends and be unable to record the details of my days.

And yet . . . my wife[3] did seem to keep a diary in a little notebook, so I decided that I would borrow it and just add my own private commentary to it.

"You keep a diary, don't you? Let me see it," I said, quite casually, but for some reason she refused me outright.

"All right—don't let me see it, then. But that means I'll have to go out drinking."

Now my logic here may seem obtuse, but I assure you it is not. The thing is that I had no other way to escape writing my *zuihitsu*. So I did have a perfectly proper reason. And I never go drinking without a reason. It was because I had such a reason yesterday that I went off drinking at a place in Asagaya with a righteous look on my face. And at that establishment in Asagaya, I did my drinking with the greatest care. I had serious things on my mind and could not afford to be careless. Adopting the manner of an elderly gentleman, I drank quietly. After I got drunk, though, it was no good.

With two rubes as my companions, I began to spout off:

"What is love? Do you think you understand? Love is the accomplishment of duty. A sad idea—surely. Or again, we might say that love is the defender of morality. Or, yet again, that love is a physical embrace. All

3. Dazai married Ishihara Michiko, his second wife, in 1939. The couple had three children together, the last—who would later become the writer Tsushima Yūko—born in May 1947, just a year before Dazai committed suicide with his lover, Yamazaki Tomie.

these statements are worthy of attention. They may be true; they may be accurate. But there was one other—what was it? Love is . . . I guess I don't know. But if I *did* understand, now . . ."

I was sodden by then, it appears, and talking nothing but nonsense.

[*DAZAI OSAMU ZENSHŪ*, VOL. 10 (TOKYO: CHIKUMA SHOBŌ, 1975)]

33

Baby Sparrow, Turtledoves, and Morning Glories

SHIGA NAOYA

So great was Shiga Naoya's (1883–1971) reputation in the literary world of the second two decades of the twentieth century that he was popularly called Bungaku no Kamisama (God of Literature). Coming from a wealthy background, he attended the Peers' School and later Tokyo Imperial University, where he mixed with the intellectual elite of his generation. While still a university student, he collaborated with a number of friends in putting out the journal Shirakaba (White Birch), which introduced avant-garde European art and culture to the Japanese intellectual world. In 1910, he began to write short stories, many of them confessional, and garnered a high reputation almost immediately. After completing, in 1937, his long, semiautobiographical novel An'ya kōro (A Dark Night's Passing, begun in 1921), he wrote very little, instead enjoying his position at the very pinnacle of the literary world.

Many of Shiga's stories are indistinguishable from essays. The pieces translated here—"Suzume no hanashi" (Baby Sparrow), "Yamabato" (Turtledoves), and "Asagao" (Morning Glories)—originally appeared in literary journals in 1949, 1950, and 1954, respectively.

Baby Sparrow

My five-year-old granddaughter, Midori, caught a baby sparrow. Its tail was still short, but it had all its feathers and would not take food from human hands. At the time, I had a cat about a year old, so I hung a cage from a branch too slender for the cat to climb up and left it to the bird's parents to bring it food, taking the cage inside only at night. My daughter Kimiko was fond of such things, and since my grandchildren were staying with me at the time, I thought that our little group could enjoy looking after the bird as a plaything. When you took it out of its cage and held it in your hand, the baby bird would move its little tail and sing, but when surprised it would suddenly fly up, crash into the window, and fall to the floor. It had two parents, and they were always bringing it food. It seemed to grow better that way than when being cared for by human hands alone.

One day, I heard birds making a racket in the garden and went to see what was going on. The two parents were clinging to the cage, looking inside, and crying wildly. The baby was not on its perch. The parents noticed when I got within a few yards of them and flew off in confusion. The baby was on the bottom of the cage, wrapped in the clutches of a rat snake.[1] I took the cage down and put it on the ground, and when I did, the snake quickly escaped from the cage. I grabbed a hoe that was there and cut the snake in two. As if it had no idea what had just happened, the baby bird returned to its perch and began calling for its parents, just as always.

When my granddaughter came outside, I said, "Time to turn the bird over to its parents, I think," and she agreed.

I returned the cage to its place in the tree, took the bird out, and put it on top of the cage. A little later when I went out to take a look, the baby sparrow was gone, and the cage was hanging there empty.

1. *Jimoguri.* A small constrictor.

The next day, a young man I had hired to make me a desk came walking up with his hands cupped together next to his chest, holding something, which turned out to be the baby bird from the day before. He had found it nearby, its wings not strong enough to make it back to its nest, and had caught it with the idea of giving it to my daughter. I took out the cage I had just put away and had him put the bird inside.

This time, so I would know right away if a snake was after it, I hung the cage from the eaves outside the room where I usually spend my time. But now the parents were afraid to come so close to people, which left the parents and the baby just calling to each other. The baby would look out at its parents and grab onto the bamboo slats of the cage and struggle, while the parents would fret in the pines but never dare to come as far as the cage.

I had an idea: I whittled a plum-tree branch down to a sharp end, which I then arranged in the branches of the pine so that the cat couldn't get at it, and hung the cage on it. Now the parents could bring the baby food.

A few days later, we had a windy, rainy day. I took some cardboard and brown paper and fashioned a roof for the cage, but still the bird was sopping wet and looking dejected. It still looked so cold that after I took it inside that evening, I made a nest of cloth for it in a cardboard box, cutting slits in the lid so that it would have no trouble breathing. At night, I took it upstairs to where I sleep, so that the cat wouldn't get at it, but the next morning, as soon as the light started to show outside, it started crying and woke me up. Such a small thing, and such a big voice! It kept on raining that day, too, so I took the bird in the next night as well, but the third night I had had enough of its crying, so I put the cardboard box on the ledge above the sliding doors of my downstairs room before I went up to bed. I thought that the cat wouldn't be able to get at it there.

The next morning, I heard a strange sound coming from my downstairs room, a low sound like something bouncing around. I got up and went to take a look. The cat was hopping around with the dead bird in its paws. The slits I had made in the lid had been too wide, and the bird had gotten out and been killed by the cat.

Turtledoves

Turtledoves are pretty, and I like their throaty, doltish call. I used to hear them at my home in the Shinmachi area of Setagaya and when I would go to Ōhito Hot Springs.[2] They always fly in pairs. The house where I live now in the mountain resort of Ōhoradai is on the heights above Atami,[3] so I often catch sight of a pair of them flying at eye level and have become used to seeing them there.

This spring, on the last day of hunting season, Fukuda Randō, who lives in a place called Kajiya in Yoshihama, showed up with his hunting gun on his shoulder, saying that he had just been out shooting and carrying some pheasants, turtledoves, and bulbuls. It was the first time I had had birds of this sort since the end of the war, so I was pleased with the gift.

"Shall I go out and get a few more?" he asked.

"No," I said, "let's go duck hunting in Atami instead."

Fukuda is an expert at bird hunting, fishing, and abalone gathering, as well as at mahjong, which he beats us at regularly. What I meant by hunting in Atami was going to see Hirotsu Kazuo,[4] who lives there. Fukuda's face lit up, and he agreed right away.

"What time's the next bus?" he asked, and I told him.

"That leaves us thirty minutes," he said. "While you're getting ready to go, I'll do a little shooting." He changed into his rubber-soled working shoes and headed off up the mountain behind the house.

After twenty minutes or so, Fukuda was back. I hadn't heard any shooting, so I figured he hadn't gotten anything, but he handed over a turtledove, a bunting, and a bulbul, still warm. He had bagged them all in the space of twenty minutes.

I was all ready to go. After Fukuda changed into regular shoes, we went down the hill together and headed off toward Atami by bus.

The next day, I saw a single turtledove flying by. They have a lively way of flying. First one will dart ahead four or five yards, and then the other

2. Located on the Izu Peninsula in Shizuoka Prefecture.
3. Located above the coastal town of Odawara.
4. 1891–1968. A prominent novelist and close friend of Shiga's.

will quickly come from behind, not to be overtaken. I had watched this day after day, but today there was just the one bird, going back and forth before my eyes, over and over again. I hadn't thought much of it when I was eating the bulbul and pheasant, and I hadn't been bothered about eating the turtledove that Fukuda had shot somewhere else, but it didn't feel right now that I saw just one of the pair I had gotten used to watching over the past few months.

A few months later, I saw two turtledoves flying by, and I thought happily that the remaining bird had finally found another mate. But I was wrong: these two birds had come in from elsewhere, and that single bird was still flying alone. This goes on even as I write.

Recently, the hunting season has started again. Among my friends in the neighborhood is Mr. S., who has a pair of expensive, purebred English setters, and I often see him prowling around in his hunting gear. I hear that you have to watch out for his dogs, but that he's not a good enough hunter for the birds to worry about.

The real danger is Fukuda Randō. When he came by a few days back, I said that maybe this year I would ask him to forgo hunting here.

"If it's bothering you so much, I could go take care of the other one, too," he said, laughing.

That's the sort of man birds have to watch out for.

Morning Glories

For more than a decade now, I have planted morning glories every year and kept them growing—not to look at the flowers but because the leaves produce a medicine to use when you've been stung by noxious insects. It works well not only against mosquitoes and gnats but even against centipedes and bees. You just crush three or four leaves between your hands until a sticky juice appears, and then rub the juice and the leaves on the place where you've been stung. The pain and itching stop right away, and afterward there is no oozing from the wound.

On the hill in back of the house where I live in Atami, I have put up a little hut to use as a study. The space is not very large, and the slope in front of the window is quite steep, so to be safe I built a latticework fence there and scattered some tea seeds about. My hope is to have a hedge of tea plants someday, but since that time is still a long way off, this year I bought some morning glory seeds at a department store in Tokyo and scattered them down there, too. As summer approached, the vines began to wrap themselves around the latticework fence, and any that started crawling the other way I forced back. Some tea-plant seedlings were beginning to show themselves, too, but sadly the thick morning glories didn't allow them to get much sun.

This summer, my house was so full of children and grandchildren that for more than a month I ended up sleeping in my study on the hillside. Perhaps because I'm getting older, I would wake up at five in the morning and, even though feeling drowsy, not be able to get back to sleep. So until the family got up in the main house, I would just wait there, gazing out at the scenery. The view from the main house is quite good in itself, but because it's higher up, the study opens up on a broader vista. Looking southwest, one sees Mount Amagi, Mount Omuro, Mount Komuro, Kawana Point, and, continuing on, Nii Island; then, just off Kawana Point lies To Island, and even farther off, Miyake Island. But one can see this only on a clear day two or three times in a year, and then ever so faintly. The more immediate view is of little Hatsu Island and Ōshima behind it, with Manazuru Point to the left, and beyond that the peaks of the Miura Peninsula—a scene of rare beauty. In the past, I have lived in many places blessed with fine scenery—in Onomichi, Matsue, Abiko, Yamashina, and Nara—but I think the scenery here surpasses them all.

Every morning I would get up, sit down cross-legged in front of the bay window, and enjoy a smoke as I looked out at the view and at the morning glories on the latticework fence right in front of me.

Until now, I hadn't thought of morning glory flowers as being all that beautiful. One reason is because I am usually a late riser and so had never seen the flowers just after blooming, but only at midday, after they had been out in the sun too long. In their vanquished form, the blossoms produced an anemic impression that made it impossible for me to like them. But this summer, waking at dawn, I was able to see the flowers just after they opened, fresh and new, and it was then that I realized how truly exquisite they are. Compared with canna or geraniums, this fresh beauty is something remarkable. The blossoms last only an hour or two, really.

When I first recognized the fresh beauty of the flowers, I was for some reason reminded of my childhood. In my youth, I must have already recognized freshness as a quality but simply hadn't been much impressed by it. It was only in old age, I think, that I came to appreciate its great beauty.

———————

Hearing the sound of voices from the main house, I went down. But before leaving, I picked one azure flower, one red one, and a russet one the color of adzuki beans, thinking that my grade-school-age granddaughter could use them in her collection of pressed flowers. As I walked down the wooden steps with the flowers in one upturned hand, a horsefly[5] started buzzing annoyingly around my head. I swatted at it with my free hand, but it wouldn't relent. I stopped for a moment on the stairs. Just as I did, the thing stopped flying and went upside down into the center of one of the flowers and began to suck up the nectar. The tip of its round striped bottom began to make a motion much like breathing.

After a moment, the horsefly emerged, the way it had come in, this time a little clumsily, and went to the next flower—and again on to the next, once more going in upside down, sucking out the nectar. Then, without any hesitation, it flew off to who knows where. To him, the morning glories were just morning glories, and he didn't take any notice of me, a human being, at all. As for myself, I felt a certain kinship with the insect and was happy.

I told my youngest daughter, who has more interest in such things than I do, about all of this, and we got out an insect identification manual to look at together. It appeared that the insect had been a horsefly or, if not, a bumblebee. Insects of the horsefly group have just one wing on each side, with no small wings underneath them, while bees have small wings connected to the primary wings from below. I wonder which variety it was that came after the morning glories. When I saw it, I thought that it was a horsefly, so that's what I wrote down. Even now, though, I don't really know which one it was.

[SHINPAN SHIGA NAOYA ZENSHŪ, ED. AGAWA HIROYUKI ET AL., VOLS. 8 AND 9 (TOKYO: IWANAMI SHOTEN, 1999, 2001)]

5. *Abu.* A large flying insect, resembling a bumblebee, that is known for its painful sting.

34

Esprit and Humor

KAWAMORI YOSHIZŌ

Born into a merchant household in Osaka, Kawamori Yoshizō (1902–2000) gradu-ated from Kyoto University with a degree in French literature and began his career as a lecturer at several universities in the Kansai area. After studying and traveling in Europe from 1928 until 1930, he returned to Japan and continued his academic career, eventually becoming a professor in the Literature Department at Tokyo Uni-versity of Education, where he established himself as a scholar, critic, and translator of French literature. His best-known work is a study of the French poet Baudelaire, Le spleen de Paris: Baudelaire and His Era, *which garnered him the Osaraji Jirō Prize in 1978. Among his close friends were the writers Hori Tatsuo (1904–1953), Miyoshi Tatsuji (1900–1964), and Ibuse Masuji (1898–1993). In 1970, he became a member of the Japan Art Academy and later received the Order of Culture.*

In addition to his literary criticism, Kawamori is noted for his journalistic works and essays. The essays translated here are from the collection Esupuri to yūmoa (Esprit and Humor), *published in 1958.*

A Room to One's Self

Although it doesn't seem to be true anymore, there was a time when the novels of Dostoevsky were banned in the Soviet Union. When an

American journalist asked a writer—I think it was Ehrenburg[1]—why this was so, he said, "Dostoevsky's novels put people's nerves on edge. Take *Crime and Punishment*, for instance: after you read that book, you have to move to some other room or you can't sleep peacefully at night. But because of the housing shortage in the Soviet Union these days, almost no one has both a bedroom and a study. That's why we don't allow the masses to read Dostoevsky." An unlikely story, I think, but in Japan too, few people have enough space in their homes for both a study and a bedroom. The reality is that most people can't even provide a separate study space for their children. In the days to come, it will doubtless become even more difficult for each individual in a family to have any sort of room of his own.

Yet all of us have an intense need to be alone from time to time. The desire to be away from everyone else in the house is something that everyone in a family feels inside. Being all together as a group is pleasant, of course, but we can't be all smiles all the time. At such times, having no room to withdraw into, a place where you can be alone, makes you feel sad and desolate. It is a hard thing when family members always have to sit staring at one another, all for a want of more rooms.

Now, the man of the house, who spends his whole day outside the home at his job, is bound to experience a lot of unpleasantness at work, and though one cannot praise him for bringing his troubles home with him, the fact is that if the house is too cramped, his sullen mood can dampen the spirits of the whole family. This may be one reason—or at least one excuse—why so many men stop off at a bar to throw back a few instead of going directly home from work. If we can't find solitude at home, aren't we bound to seek it outside?

The poet Hagiwara Sakutarō[2] liked to walk among the crowds in rundown districts of the city. I think he must have been seeking some rest for his spirit. A composer I know says he gets on the Yamanote rail line[3] in Tokyo and goes around the same route two or three times because the monotonous rhythm of the cars going over the rails gives him such a pleasant feeling of calm that ideas for tunes come to him.

1. Ilya Ehrenburg (1891–1967), a Soviet journalist and writer.
2. 1886–1942. One of the most prominent free-verse poets of his day.
3. Then, as now, the busiest loop in Tokyo's vast system of trains and subways.

Lately, children listen to jazz on the radio while doing their math, using what seems to me the same method as my composer friend to get their minds working. Listening to jazz, they can separate themselves from everyone else and work on their math problems in solitude. No matter where you are, if you can never be alone, you will start thinking of ways to separate yourself from those around you. So I cannot but think that the housing shortage will have a profound impact on the minds of the Japanese.

Saving Money

The other day, a group of us the same age got together, and someone said, "Now that I'm getting on in years, I can't get over how stingy I've become."

This seemed to strike a chord with everyone. Most of them said they felt the same way—that lately they'd become stingy almost in spite of themselves. Their children were getting older, and they were always hard-pressed because of the money needed for schooling, marriage, and so on.

One man said that he didn't feel bad about spending money for drinking, but did begrudge money spent on clothing, even for a single shirt. To this, another countered, "You don't know what you're talking about. Just go to the department store once in a while. See how cheap you can get kitchen things and even clothing there, and you'll start feeling bad about the money you spend at bars."

In the end, we all agreed that you can't have too much money, that we all wanted more, and that it was a shame that we didn't have any talent for investment.

The famous French actor Sacha Guitry[4] wisely said, "They say that money can't make you happy, but I think that must mean 'other people's money.'" I agree: it's other people's money that can't make you happy. And the reason we dislike those who say you can't buy happiness with money is usually because people who say that have more money than

4. 1885–1957. A writer, director, actor, and producer.

they know what to do with. That such declarations are no more than a rich man's way of hiding his embarrassment is apparent from the fact that we don't see them throwing their money away.

In France, there's a proverb: "Patience is the miracle cure of the poor." But the idea of noble poverty must have been concocted by someone trying to console himself for having no money. If there were truly such a thing as noble poverty, there ought to be noble wealth, too: For what's the reason we don't use the phrase "noble poor" if not because those who live noble lives don't ever accumulate any money?

I don't care what people say—there's no one who doesn't want more money. Yet there are some people who can't seem to save money no matter how much they want to. They work hard and deny themselves luxuries, but still the money seems to flow away. I'm one of those people, and in my case it's because I'm wasteful. When I buy something, I don't choose carefully, and then I end up not liking what I bought and have to go back and buy something else; I want to impress everyone over a little thing and leave a two hundred–yen tip when a hundred yen would do; I don't take good care of things and can't seem to get good use out of them long term. I worry about appearing stingy, so I look for ways to be generous; but because I really do begrudge spending the money, in the end it's really no different from being tight. Since I've never been able to shake the habit I acquired when I received an allowance from my parents during my school days, I always feel that if I don't use up all the money for one month before the month ends, somehow the next installment won't be coming—and that's no way to accumulate a bank account. Now it's too late for me to be frugal even if I want to, since saving money requires being on your guard all the time.

On Awarding Medals

I understand that six attendants accompanying the Shah of Iran on his visit to Japan who had been awarded medals as a courtesy from the Japanese government later returned them through the Ministry of Foreign Affairs, explaining that the medals were too low to be commensurate with the rank of the awardees. They must have been displeased because men of first rank had been awarded medals of only third rank, to put it in Japanese terms.

No doubt, this was an insult to the awardees, and one for which our government must bear responsibility. But had they been Japanese, I wonder whether the men would have returned the medals—even if they *had* thought them inappropriate to their rank. Or, depending on what country was involved, if they would have gotten angry, feeling they had been insulted. I suppose it may even be that the Iranians sent the medals back because they were from an insignificant country like Japan.

I believe it was a good thing that at the time of the defeat, Japan did away with the peerage and official ranks, but in recent years, when a politician or high official dies and the National Diet bestows letters of commendation on him, one fears that the old ways are coming back to life. If we are spared reinstatement of the peerage, we should count ourselves lucky, I guess.

Yet it seems that human beings have an instinctive desire for medals or, in other words, that we want to have our achievements recognized publicly. Particularly in the military ranks, courageous warriors would cease to exist without medals, I think. As evidence, I cite the fact that even countries like America and the Soviet Union, which don't bestow medals on their citizens, do give them to their soldiers.

The fondness of the French for medals is well known. The famous Legion of Honor, for instance, was established by Napoléon I. Thereafter, the country went through many changes of government, first being a monarchy, then an empire, and later a republic, but the Legion of Honor survived it all. Seeing this, one can understand how enamored the French people are of medals.

There are five different ranks in the Legion of Honor, but even those who are appointed to the lowest level—*chevalier*—seem quick to host a banquet for their friends and make a big to-do of it all. For the bourgeoisie to behave this way is one thing, but one hates to see that it's the same with writers and artists—though, of course, one can note this as proof of how innocuous the whole business is and be done with it.

It is certain, however, that French writers are not indifferent to the attractions of ceremony. For example, there is the Académie française, which is similar to the Japanese Art Academy but has a longer history and is much more highly respected in the wider world. It would not be an overstatement to say that among French writers there is not one who does not hope to be chosen as a member of the academy. Moreover, since one nominates oneself for election—something not true in the case of the Japanese Art Academy—the degree of self-promotion involved is obvious. And those who have become members of the Académie française never forget to note that fact next to their name on all their books—as if they were always wearing a little insignia of the award on their collar. If a Japanese writer were to do something like that, the world would laugh him to scorn, but no one thinks the practice strange of the French—which shows the degree to which they are fond of medals.

The Season for Naps

When a journalist asked the famous French dramatist Yves Mirande[5] what sports he liked, he is said to have replied, with no hesitation, "Taking naps." Whether napping counts as a sport is a moot point, but if the role of sports is to reduce nervous and physical stress, then I think it can be said that napping accomplishes the same end.

My whole life, I have needed lots of sleep, at least eight hours every day. If I get more than that, so much the better, and even if I slept all day it wouldn't be too much. On the other hand, if I am short even ten minutes of my eight hours, my head feels heavy all day, and if the pattern goes on for four or five days, I get attacks of diarrhea and end up down in bed. For me, lack of sleep is my worst enemy, and for that reason I don't get up to see anyone who comes calling when I'm asleep, no matter how close we may be. Conversely, I am particularly cheerful when I have had plenty of sleep, so much so that at such times I usually agree to grant favors to people on the second request.

I also fall asleep easily, and I have never in my life taken a sleeping pill, because I truly wonder how long I would sleep if I did so. Now, needless to say, one who likes sleep so much is bound to like naps. In a magazine,

5. 1875–1957. A writer of more than seventy film scripts and the director of *Moulin Rouge* (1941) and other classic films.

a man named Uwabayashi wrote in an essay on napping that when he began dozing off, he would feel so good that he would decide to take a nap and get out the futon, only to find that the pleasant feeling had disappeared. I feel the same way. The pleasure one feels when dozing off while being rocked along on a train or subway car or when taking notes in a lecture hall is quite beyond price. When I was in college, I took Professor Shinmura Izuru's[6] course "A General Theory of Linguistics" from one to three in the afternoon, the sleepiest time of day, and without fail I would fall asleep for about ten minutes in the middle of the lecture. When I was looking over my notes in preparation for exams, I was frustrated to find that there was always an empty space for that period, but while I have completely forgotten the professor's lectures, I remember the pleasant feeling of those naps still today. The warm feeling one gets when napping or dozing in this way cannot be compared with anything else—although the pleasure of taking out the futon on a summer afternoon, getting down on it, spreading out one's arms and legs, and drifting off to sleep while listening to the faint sound of a hanging scroll gently clacking against the wall in the breeze is also difficult to describe.

In hot countries such as Italy and Spain, in the summer, from just after noon to three o'clock, companies and government offices shut their doors so that everyone can take a nap. Walking through the quiet streets during those hours, one feels as if the whole town is at peace taking a pleasant nap, like being in heaven on earth. Wouldn't it improve the energy level of the people in Japan, also a hot country, if we were to follow the same custom?

Either way, it's the season for naps now, and so as not to wear myself out working too hard, I think at this point I'll just take a little time out myself.

Foreign Doctors

Nothing makes one feel more forlorn than taking ill in a foreign country. Big cities like Paris and London are nice because there is always a

6. 1876–1967. A prominent linguist.

Japanese doctor studying there who can look at you, but if you become ill in the sort of small city to which Japanese rarely travel, you won't be able to find anyone.

When I was in Grenoble, during the first summer I ever spent in France, I was suffering in the heat and having trouble getting accustomed to the food, so I lost my appetite completely and got very weak. Just looking at anything fatty made me feel like vomiting. The symptoms were exactly like those of jaundice, which I had had before. So I thought I should see a doctor.

In France, doctors don't generally practice from their homes, with a sign hanging out front, as they do in Japan. Instead, they are in apartments, which makes finding one a task in itself. Fortunately, though, before leaving Paris I had asked a friend what to do if I needed medical attention, and he told me I should ask at any big druggist's shop. Since in France doctors don't dispense medicines themselves, they form cooperative relations with druggists, my friend had said, who are therefore happy to introduce you to a doctor. So I set off to ask for help at a druggist's shop in the business center of town.

Just as my friend had told me, I was kindly given the name and address of a doctor in the area. As the doctor was a Frenchman, I had to go prepared with enough French vocabulary to describe my condition, for I couldn't very well barge in and try to get things across by gesturing with my hands and feet. So I went back to my hotel, got out my dictionary, and looked up the French words I thought I would need—words for lack of appetite, vomiting, jaundice, and so forth—and then set out. After not having any appetite for some days, my legs were a little shaky. It was only with great effort that I was able to make it up the stairs to the apartment. Had it been typhus that I was ill with, I would doubtless have gone to my final reward halfway up.

The doctor said that I was the first Japanese person he had ever seen and showed great curiosity, in fact forgetting about examining me as he asked me questions about various things. To my amazement, he brought out a bunch of objects—collected where, I don't know—to show me: a Japanese sword, a seal case, an iron-ribbed fan, and the like; then he asked me how much each of them might be worth. I was so weak that I barely had the power to speak.

At that point, I asked him if he would please put the appraisals off until later and get on with examining me. "Oh, why of course, of course" he said, and gave me a very thorough looking over. As I had feared, I was showing the first signs of jaundice, and he gave me instructions about what to eat and wrote me out a prescription. For right now, though, I asked if the best thing might be for me to return to Paris and get some Japanese food, and he immediately said, "Yes. Surely that would be best of all." However, when it came down to it, he perhaps didn't know anything about Japanese food, because he appeared completely in the dark. When he began asking me questions about Japanese cooking, though, I decided to get out of there quickly.

Since I had not yet spent a full month in Grenoble, it was really too bad, but the next day I returned to Paris and immediately headed for a Japanese restaurant. After eating there for a week, I rapidly regained my appetite, got better—and gained a new appreciation for rice meals.

Retorts

In every country, writers as a group are skilled at the art of retort, but it seems that, as one might expect in a country of great élan, the skill is something for which French writers[7] have a particular talent. When the Catholic novelist François Mauriac published his novel *River of Fire*, one critic attacked it mercilessly. "This is no river but a passing drizzle," he wrote, probably meaning to say that the book was vague and hard to understand. Mauriac immediately wrote him a letter in which he said, "Perhaps you should have read the book under an umbrella."

The painter Émile Blanche was very proud of always being finely dressed, with never a crooked seam. One time he said to the poet Henri Régnier, "My, but those slacks of yours are nice. Who made them for you?" To this Régnier replied, "A tailor."

7. Kawamori goes on to give anecdotes concerning a who's who of French intellectual figures: novelist François Mauriac (1885–1970), painter Émile Blanche (1861–1942), poet Henri Régnier (1864–1936), actor-director Jacques Copeau (1879–1949), novelist André Gide (1869–1951), poet Laurent Tailhade (1854–1919), and playwright Pierre Beaumarchais (1732–1799).

When actor and director Jacques Copeau staged a production of *Saül* by Gide, the play didn't do well, and the director sent a letter to Gide expressing his surprise. The reply he received was this: "I'm not surprised that the play didn't ring any bells, since I really didn't push any buttons."

The same Gide was once waiting on a train platform. When he tried to get on the train, the conductor came and said that it was too soon to get on and restrained him.

"No, it's all right," Gide said, "I'm very used to doing this," and tried to force his way by.

"What do you mean, you're used to doing this?" the conductor asked.

"Why, I'm used to doing this so that I can get a seat!" Gide replied.

The poet Laurent Tailhade got so tired of an old society lady who persisted in following him around that he was quite at a loss. One day, she came up to him and said in a very coquettish way, "Now, Mr. Tailhade, don't I inspire any feelings in you at all?"

"On the contrary, Madame," he said, "when I look at you, I can't help having the most intense of feelings—intense feelings of horror, that is, at the idea of original sin."

Seeing Beaumarchais, the author of *Le mariage de Figaro*, all decked out in splendid clothing as he made his way conspicuously down a corridor at Versailles, a courtier approached him.

"Say now, Beaumarchais, I'm glad you happened along. You see I'm having trouble with my watch. Might I ask you to take a look at it?"

Beaumarchais, it should be explained, was the son of a watchmaker.

Beaumarchais quickly replied, "It looks very cheap, I should say. But I must tell you, as I have in the past, that I am really quite clumsy when it comes to such things."

"That may be so, but it is the profession of your house, is it not?" the man said with evident disdain, and handed the watch over.

At this, Beaumarchais dropped the watch on the ground and smashed it to pieces under his foot.

"Oh, I'm so sorry," he said. "But then I did tell you I was clumsy."

Laughter and Nationality

According to Westerners, the Japanese are so serious that they don't understand humor and seldom laugh. Consequently, when you tell them a joke, if you don't explain that it's a joke beforehand, you risk a misunderstanding—so they say. This is an exaggeration, of course. There are plenty of Japanese with a good sense of humor, and as a people, we laugh a good deal. It may be true, however, that when we are with Westerners we get so tense that we forget to laugh.

As an example of how the Japanese lack humor, a Frenchman wrote this story about when Mr. Hackin, head of the Guimet Museum in Paris,[8] was staying in Tokyo. One day, he wanted to buy a fountain pen, so he took his translator and went to a department store in Ginza. He wanted a large pen, but the salesgirl was showing him only small ones that were not to his liking. Then he suddenly spied in the show window a row of pens that were just what he wanted. He was ready to purchase one right away, but as a thundershower happened to be passing by at the time, he saw through the window that people on the street were running around trying to escape the rain, and with this in mind he said to the salesgirl, jokingly, "Might I ask for a fountain pen with an umbrella attached to the end?"

"Please wait a moment," the girl said, and then went off somewhere and didn't appear to be coming back.

Tired of being kept waiting, Mr. Hackin asked his translator to go hurry things and learned that the girl was contacting the manufacturer to see if such a model was available, so the story goes. A true example of someone being overly conscientious.

But according to André Maurois,[9] the French can't match the English when it comes to sense of humor. He writes about standing in the British Museum, waiting to check out a book, when next to him appeared an old maid who said this to the librarian: "I wonder if I might ask a question. You see, I am single, and in the past I have always written my own

---

8. A museum dedicated to Asian art and founded in 1879 in Lyons. It became part of the Musées nationaux and was later moved to Paris. Joseph Hackin (d. 1941) was its director in the 1930s.

9. 1885–1967. The pen name of Émile Herzog, an essayist, critic, and biographer of Hugo, Balzac, George Sand, and others.

family name on my library card, but for the past four or five nights Lord Nelson[10] has been appearing in my dreams. And finally, last night, he asked me to marry him and I accepted. So I am wondering which name I should write on my card. Will my maiden name do, or must I now write Mrs. Nelson?"

All this time, the librarian had been writing something on a piece of paper, and now she didn't even lift her head but said, "As your marriage is of a purely spiritual nature, please continue to write your maiden name, just as before."

Standing there listening to this, Maurois was quite taken aback. "Had this happened in France," he writes, "they would have contacted the police or the mental hospital immediately."

The old lady was deranged, no doubt, but the way the librarian remained unperturbed was truly humorous.

I hear that Marcel Pagnol,[11] author of *Marius*, says, "What humans laugh at reveals their true character." I wonder if one can say the same about nationalities. It's certain at least that laughter differs from place to place.

[*WATAKUSHI NO ZUISŌ SEN*, VOL. 7 (TOKYO: SHINCHŌSHA, 1991)]

10. Horatio Nelson (1758–1805), a famous British naval hero who died at the Battle of Trafalgar.
11. 1895–1974. A French playwright.

35

Sleepless Nights *and* A Bed for My Books

OSARAGI JIRŌ

Nojiri Kiyohiko (known by the pen name Osaragi Jirō; 1897–1973) was born in the port city of Yokohama. He studied at Tokyo University and worked briefly in the Japanese Foreign Ministry before becoming a full-time writer. By the late 1920s, he had achieved fame as one of the most prominent of Japanese popular novelists, known especially for his works of historical fiction, set in both Japan and the West. He also wrote contemporary novels, short stories, and plays. Many of his works were produced as movies, thereby expanding his audience and reputation. Two of his novels set in postwar Japan—Tabiji (The Journey, 1948; trans. 1954) and Kikyō (The Homecoming, 1952; trans. 1960)—were among the first in their genre to be translated into English after the Pacific War. In his later years, Osaragi became an advocate for the preservation of traditional Japanese culture and received many prizes and awards, including the Asahi Cultural Prize, the Kikuchi Kan Prize, and the Order of Culture.

For many years, Osaragi lived in Kamakura, a haven for artists and writers. The name Osaragi in fact derives from an alternative reading of the characters for Daibutsu, the Great Buddha in the Hase district, which had become an international tourist attraction. The essays translated here, "Nemurenu yo" (Sleepless Nights) and "Hon no shindai" (A Bed for My Books), date from his later years.

Sleepless Nights

Young people have the most enviable ability to fall into deep and unin-terrupted sleep as soon as they lie down. Old folks like me, on the other hand, wake up in the middle of the night for some reason and often can't drop off again no matter how sleepy they feel.

If I get up, turn on the light, and start reading, soon I'm so wide awake that I can't get drowsy again, so instead I just lie there in the darkness, quiet and still. Usually I think about something. On bad days, all that comes to mind is my mistakes—things I've done that I wish I hadn't—and I end up berating myself and feeling assailed by a keen sense that I must look like a fool, that I am lazy and a failure as a human being. All I can see is my faults. That kind of sleepless night is hard to endure. Having lived more than fifty years, I have made many blunders and been careless many times. Am I alone in this?

On other nights, I think of friends who have died. Or sometimes of my parents, who passed on more than twenty years ago. Or else I follow my memories back into childhood. People lose all sorts of memories with the years. When I was an infant, I must have been living in a dream world, for nothing of that time remains in my memory now. The oldest of my memories are from when I was about five years old, and even in that case I have forgotten day-to-day things and remember only events of special importance, such as how I had to have endless moxa treatments because I was sickly, or how once, when I went out on an errand with the maid, I stumbled on a brick road and cut my forehead so badly that we had to go to a nearby grocer and borrow a copper pan to wash the wound and then staunch the blood, with me of course crying loudly all the while. I suppose I remember this even now because the injury was a significant event, but everything down to the ginseng and the color of the vegetables at the grocer's remains vivid in my mind. I also remember how one time when my brother was flying a kite in front of our house at New Year's time, and the kite was about to get entangled in the bamboo near the decorative pine on the front gate, I called out without thinking (no doubt mimicking my mother's voice), "Hail Amida!"[1]—after which my brother scolded me and I felt greatly ashamed, child that I was. Perhaps because I was born with a weak constitution, the memories of youth that I have retained to the present day are all about being humiliated or breaking into tears. Strangely, I have no memories of anything interesting or fun—something equally true of later years. Maybe this is because when I lie alone in the gloom of night, my thoughts get colored by the darkness around me. If I could just exchange my memories of regret and shame with more cheerful recollections, my sleepless nights might be more enjoyable.

There are also nights when I am awake and entirely preoccupied with things I'm writing at the time or with research plans. On such occasions, I can at least feel a certain vitality welling up inside me, however painful being awake is in other ways. Sometimes I'm even up when the sky begins to brighten outside my window, and I hear the sound of the great drum at the nearby Tsurugaoka Hachiman Shrine. The sparrows begin to chirp, and morning sunlight illuminates the pine branches, first in the topmost ones and then moving down. The footsteps of the paperboy run through my alley. Night has moved aside. But I am by nature likely to slack off before reaching my goals for writing and research, so I have to crack the whip. It's daytime now. If I am to make my sleepless nights more pleasant, I must live without cause for regret while the sun shines.

With such thoughts on my mind, I stop working and sit looking blankly out into my garden.

A Bed for My Books

Night and day, I spend my time in a big bed, so big that it may be no exaggeration to say that it's the biggest in all Japan. I would bet it's even bigger than the bed of Napoléon.

---

1. A prayer, similar in resonance to "God preserve us!" Osaragi's brother evidently felt that it was sacrilegious.

All around my bed, at head and foot and then close on both sides, are bookshelves, which give me enough space to satisfy my reading habits. The shelves are so full of books that I have only to stretch out my hand and it will fall on something I like. Furthermore, so covered are my quilts with books that I want to read that even on this huge bed that I'm so proud of, I'm cramped for space to lie down. Organize your books, and you lose the opportunity of finding what you want to read by rummaging. So I live in a flood of books and make no attempt to organize them, not even every year or two. Over time, I've lost any sense of whether the bed is there for me or for my books.

I live a busy life, always pursued by the obligations of work, but my happiest time is when I'm lying in my bed. I look around, planning out what to read next. Some books I've read over and over again, but I also read newly published works. Books I hate or inferior attempts, of course, aren't given the honor of being up on my bed. Many of the books I put there are ones that friends have sent me. Book in hand, I imagine the face of the author or his or her way of talking, and—rude though it is to do so while lying down—say a greeting in my mind. As I am just as discourteous to Goethe and Plato, I figure the authors will just have to forgive me.

Outside the window near my bed is a big sweet olive tree that is one of my treasures. I believe the experience of reading on a clear autumn day when the sweet olive is in bloom is something anyone would envy. When that season comes around, I remember what I was reading the year before at the same time, surrounded by the scent of flowers carried on a faint breeze. For some reason, I don't usually notice the progress of the seasons throughout the year, but the happiness of these autumn moments is something that was not marred even during the war years. Food may have been scarce, but the scent of the sweet olive was still there, and the books I loved—however much I had resented having to evacuate—were where I could reach them. What I read during the war was primarily foreign literature, of course, going again through books that I had read before.

I am terribly sensitive to the cold, so when winter comes, my quilts gradually become my whole world, my bed the place where I feel most comfortable. Because the hand I use to hold a book gets cold, I keep a little bed warmer[2] or a small hand warmer[3] nearby. Or sometimes I put a glove on just one hand. My bed never needs to be made; indeed, it's a perpetually unmade bed—and how grateful I am to the person who came up with that idea.

In French, they refer to a book one never wants to part from as a *livre de chevet*, a "bedside book." The phrase is similar to *zayū no hon*[4] in Japanese, although it doesn't carry with it the same connotation that *zayū no hon* does, of sitting formally in front of a desk, in the Eastern style—since in France, people are literally sitting in bed and not at a desk. But what an innocent pleasure it is to experience the delight of nodding off while reading a difficult book! Rather than feeling guilty about being irresolute, the way one would feel wearing formal clothes and sitting in front of a desk as if straightening up to begin rowing a boat, one feels instead that the experience of dozing off in this way can be counted among the most pleasurable that the world has to offer. Ah, the delights afforded by works of philosophy and weighty ideas!

When I am doing research or writing, of course, I do get up and sit down properly at my desk. According to my family, the expression on my face when I am working there is frightful and forbidding. Maybe that's why a number of vertical lines have formed between my eyebrows that never go away. But even an infant is out of sorts when he's forced from his bed, so I suppose it's not unusual that I would rather sit on my bed and read whatever I want than get up to write or do research. For many years, one of my desires has been to spend more time reading what other people write and less on writing things of my own. I'm sure it's my fault, but this is one goal I have not been able to reach. Occasionally I allow them to be tidied, but the mountain of books on my bed just gets taller, accumulating layers of dust rather than snow.

[*OSARAGI JIRŌ ZUIHITSU ZENSHŪ*, VOL. 3
(TOKYO: ASAHI SHIMBUNSHA, 1974)

2. *Yutanpo.* A small container made of metal or porcelain filled with warm water and put in the bedding to warm it before retiring.
3. *Teaburi.* A small hibachi used for warming the hands.
4. Literally, "a book just to the right of where one is sitting."

36

On Being Down with a Cold

KAWAKAMI TETSUTARŌ

Kawakami Tetsutarō (1902-1980) came from a family of samurai background in Nagasaki. He began his career as a music critic, later becoming a literary critic as well. Along with Kobayashi Hideo, Kamei Katsuichirō, and Miyoshi Tatsuji, he was one of the most influential intellectuals during the war years and on into the postwar era. In addition to his work as a translator of French literature, he is known for his critical writings on modern Japanese literature, most particularly Nihon no autosaidā (Japanese Outsiders, 1960), his essays on modern poets, and a study of the Meiji-period political thinker Yoshida Shōin (1830-1859). Many of his more casual essays, such as the one translated here, deal with personal matters, including illness, a topic he knew much about from personal experience, as the essay illustrates.

The essay translated here, "Kaze netsu dangi" (On Being Down with a Cold), first appeared in the Asahi shimbun *in 1969.*

This past January, I caught a cold and—unusually for me—ran a high fever. For some days, I was down in bed. I hadn't been through that sort of thing for years.

As a child, I was frail and spent a lot of time in bed every winter. In the throes of a fever, I would drift off into a drowsy state and then suddenly awaken to see the sunlight on the paper doors fading away. From the street would come the horn of the tofu seller; in the kitchen, my mother would be cutting something up on the chopping board. Listening to this, a child thinks, "Ah, the day is coming to an end," and feels as if engulfed in a sweet dream. He may feel some guilt over his own inactivity, but in a child's own way he also has a sensual feeling of intoxication at having surrendered to the allure of idleness.

Now, more than fifty years later, I went through the same experience again, and savored the same thoughts. The memory of childhood was sweet, and not sweet just because it was a memory, for this kind of experience is sweet whenever one has it.

When you catch cold, you get to lie in bed under clear skies. I wonder why people don't take more advantage of this privilege. You can sleep whenever you wish, and there is no particular time you must get up. That so antimodern yet so publicly tolerated a prodigality, so unrestrained a physical indulgence, should be waiting right at hand for city people like us is perhaps a little too difficult to imagine.

Of course, a person can cut work and laze around at home anytime. But the feeling I am talking about is something quite different from that, and I don't mean that it is just a question of whether the behavior is illicit or not. It goes without saying that the difference is the difference between health and illness, yet I would not want to call sleeping with a cold an illness in any but the strictest medical sense. This kind of sleep is a normal human activity, after all, and I should like to think of it as healthy.

For this, we must give sole credit to the assistance of a fever, since it is the fever that does the preparation, animates the project, and assumes all responsibility. It is for this reason that one is made completely free. Indeed, the "freedom" that people these days are always shouting about and searching for in the most unlikely places is available right nearby.

By contrast, the sleep of someone cutting work is blessed with no such sense of freedom. Even while sleeping, one must take the responsibility of searching out that freedom for oneself. In other words, in such a situation being asleep is like being wide awake.

Being asleep with a fever is like sport. It is painful, to a degree, and physically wearying as time goes by—that much is obvious. But just who is it, then, who plays the part of one's opponent? Who, in other words, is the enemy? Oneself, and no one else. That is what makes the match seem so long, as if it will never end. On the positive side, however, it is also for the same reason that, no matter who wins, there is no trouble afterward and one is not left wounded in any way. All is neat and clean.

———————

But I have digressed—a trifle ostentatiously, I fear. The gist of things is that thanks to my cold I got a high fever. My life was not in danger, nor did I suffer terribly; rather, I lapsed into a trancelike state and was able to go to bed in the middle of the day, with no concern for the opinion of the world around me. And what I want to say is that this special privilege granted to the chosen few is, in fact, given to all of us. Most people who seek it usually use alcohol or drugs. But the effectiveness of those substances is far from perfect.

In the case of alcohol, one's goal is not always to get drunk. One can also claim that some people drink because being tipsy makes them more sociable, or because they are seeking to be more awake—in a special sense—than they are when sober.

It appears that when it comes to drugs, the goal—whether it's drugs of the old days like opium or hashish or new drugs like paint thinner—is to get high. Unfortunately, I have no experience in this area, so I may be laughed at by users, but if we can subsume everything under the topic of getting high, then I think what I'm talking about amounts to the same thing. Over a hundred years ago, Baudelaire, imitating Thomas De Quincey, wrote an exquisite prose piece titled *Les Paradis artificiels* [1860]. Although never tempted by a desire to experiment with such things myself, I read the book and was impressed by it.

I know even less about the kind of drugs that have appeared recently, especially since the war. Sometimes I read a novel in which they are alluded to, but even when events involving drugs are described, they don't teach me anything about the physical experiences of users.

So I don't really know whether fever can serve as a substitute for such people. But even if not, at least I am sure that in the trancelike state of a fever I feel a kind of intoxication—something that releases me, enthralls me, takes me to play in Daoist heaven. Is there any other drug that is so ready to hand, so cheap, so reliable, both in terms of effectiveness and in terms of safety? Using it, people can get away from it all, vanish, gain freedom; and yet the return trip is 100 percent guaranteed. What's more, after a fever, their physical bodies are cleansed like beings of superhuman powers and then placed right back in their original ranks, reborn and refreshed. Could any state be more healthy?

So the state of being I am describing might more correctly be seen as that ideal situation we call luxury. The misery of spending hectic hours with the kids at some playground in the suburbs on a rare day off, jostled by crowds of people, has been the subject of many a comic strip. Of course, if one foists that burden off on someone else, one *can* experience the sorts of luxuries that used to be reserved for the aristocracy and the rich—long trips by train and hotel stays, for instance. But aside from a sort of warped sense of superiority or vanity, what sort of intoxication is there in that? Moreover, now that tour buses are lined up in front of the gates of once-obscure temples and famous restaurants have to accommodate thousands of customers a day, such pleasures inevitably become so routine that they lose their appeal. In other words, in such an age, everyone is part of the elite, and no one can take any pleasure in feeling superior. Just how much relaxation and liberation can one gain in busily chasing after luxury? All you are doing is tying yourself in a knot that is the reverse side of your working life, diligently pursuing a course in order to maintain a norm.

People are always saying that we moderns, while thinking that we have gained domination over the material world, have on the contrary ended up being dominated by it. I believe the same can be said of time. What a pathetic thing it is to feel at loose ends while waiting two minutes for a train to come, just because one doesn't happen to have a magazine! In the old days, people were leisurely in the way they pulled out their purses to get coins or bills, because to them time was something of their own to make use of. Come to think of it, there was wisdom in the decision to divide the hour up into sixty units rather than, say, ten. Sixty is divisible by two, four, five, or six. And it is in the way we individually apportion out each of those units that the differences between labor and leisure and enjoyment and temporal poverty emerge.

[*KAWAKAMI TETSUTARŌ CHŌSAKUSHŪ*, VOL. 7
(TOKYO: SHINCHŌSHA, 1982)]

37

The Road

SHŌNO JUNZŌ

Born in Osaka, Shōno Junzō (1921-2009) was raised in an academic household, his father being the head of Tezukayama Gakuin, which was at the time a women's college. His older brother, Eizō, became a writer of children's stories, and Junzō showed an interest in literature from a young age. After first college and then brief service in the navy during the Pacific War, he began a career as a school-teacher but was soon publishing fiction and essays. He won the Akutagawa Prize in 1954 and spent time at Kenyon College in Ohio on a Rockefeller Fellowship later in the 1950s. His stories and essays—which are often difficult to distinguish from each other—tend to concentrate on his home life. He won a number of other liter-ary prizes and became a member of the Japan Art Academy.

Several of Shōno's stories and his novel Evening Clouds (Yūbe no kumo, *1964) have been translated into English. The essay translated here, "Michi" (The Road), first appeared in the April 1962 issue of* Shōsetsu shinchō.

Just before summer vacation, the whole family bought straw hats, which we've worn a good deal. In order to avoid confusion, we wrote the first letters of our names on them. Mine has a *J* on it.

Our house is on top of a mountain (just 295 feet above sea level, but a mountain all the same), and as it's a twenty-minute walk in the blazing sun to the train station, you really do need a straw hat. It's not a matter of style.

The sun beats at you from all around. Not just down onto your head, but up from your feet. It feels as if it's coming from all quarters.

So, whether I'm just going to mail a postcard or buy a watermelon at the grocer's, I put on my hat. The same when I play catch with the kids in the evening. The hats truly serve us well.

Yesterday, I walked to the station with my oldest son, who is in middle school. A silver crown from his tooth had come off, and he was headed to the dentist; I was off to the doctor to have him look at a scrape on my foot that was beginning to fester.

As we were walking along on the sidewalk, we came upon a dead sparrow.

"Let's move it off the sidewalk," I said to my son, and he picked it up, walked down into a rice paddy by the side of the road, and put the sparrow down there in a cool, shady place.

The sparrow was already dead, so we couldn't leave it just anywhere. Cars used this road constantly, and ever since the sidewalks were put in, they go awfully fast.

As we continued on our way, my son said, "I wonder what happened to it."

"Hmm—I wonder. Probably got hit."

"But it didn't look like it got hit."

"I wonder."

The next thing we happened on as we walked on was a dead frog—belly up on the sidewalk. It was a tiny frog. It looked so funny in that posture that both my son and I laughed.

"Wonder what happened," my son said.

"Hmm—I wonder."

We started walking again, and came upon a dead beetle—also belly up.

"A beetle," my son said. "I wonder what happened."

"Hmm. I wonder."

"Hit by a car, maybe?"

"Could be."

We went a little farther and found a dead scarab.

"It's a scarab," my son said.

"From smaller to smaller."

"Next it'll be an ant!"

"Probably right."

We both laughed.

———————

When I came out of the doctor's office, there was my son across the way, walking toward me.

Just as he always did when we bumped into each other on the road, my son raised his hand. It was funny how we had gone to different places but ended up returning home together.

"And it isn't as if we'd planned it," I thought to myself.

He was holding some writing paper, rolled up. When we left home, my wife had asked him to buy some. He hadn't forgotten: after the dentist, he had dropped by the stationer. He had done well.

I drew up next to him, and we began to walk. Then I remembered.

"Where's your hat?"

"Oops. I must have left it."

"At the dentist's?"

"Uh-huh."

He gave me the paper and ran back. Next to the road there's a low spot, where a bridge crosses the stream that flows down from the mountain. In spite of the bridge's being there, however, on the other side the mountain rises steeply and there's no path going anywhere.

Whenever I come to this place, I always think it would be nice if there were a path up the mountain from the other side of the bridge.

I wondered why a bridge had been put up if there was no path on the other side. If it wasn't built so people could cross, then why was it there at all? Had someone put it up for some other purpose?

In either case, it was a shady spot, and there was a breeze, so I stepped down and decided to wait there.

At night, if you were standing in a place like this, you might be taken for a person of suspicious intent. Fortunately, though, it was midday and sunny, so there was no danger of that. It was so hot out that people would probably see me as someone taking a moment to get out of the sun.

What made him forget his hat, I wondered. No one, adult or child, is happy about going to the dentist. After his treatment was done, when he was free to go, he may have been in a hurry to get away.

He had only had a new crown put on, so there probably wasn't much involved. At least that machine—the one that makes such an awful noise and comes at you without a fare-thee-well (what is that thing called?)— had probably not been employed.

Still, maybe the dentist had used it some. It was a dentist's favorite instrument, after all. Using it was his forte.

But even if in the end that thing hadn't been used and the dentist had just put the crown on, during the time you're sitting there in that chair you never know what's going to happen, or when; so when the dentist says, "Okay, all finished," you're so relieved that you just want to get out of there as fast as possible. The straw hat my son was wearing when he arrived might have been sitting there on the chair in the waiting room, but he wouldn't have seen it, wouldn't even have given it a second thought.

Then, again, maybe he was remembering that he had been told to buy that paper on his way back home and was so focused on the paper that he forgot about his straw hat.

He wasn't back yet. What was keeping him? He had taken off running, but it was so hot that halfway there he might have slowed down and walked. There was a railway crossing on the way. He needn't run. It wouldn't do for him to be so anxious to retrieve his straw hat that he got hit by a train.

It was true, though; such things did happen in life—boys died like that.

But then suddenly, there he was. He saw me on the bridge and waved. Earlier, when things had turned out so that we would be walking home together, I had thought to myself, "And it isn't as if we'd planned it." But something had been missing from the calculation and that had thrown us off—the straw hat.

Once again we set off walking, shoulder to shoulder. This time, we did the opposite of what we had done on the road there. Going on the right side was awkward. Although we were used to it, when you walk along a country road your feet want to go over to the left side.

But a rule is a rule. And since there were cars going by, you had to take care. If you weren't obeying the law and got hit, you would have no case. So we walked on the right side.

After going a little way, my son caught a lizard. He had picked it up before I even noticed it was there.

Lizard in one hand, he walked along, putting a finger from his other hand in the lizard's mouth to let him chew on it.

"Hey, don't do that."

"It's all right."

"No, it's not all right. It's a stupid thing to do."

He pulled his finger away.

"Doesn't it hurt?"

"No, it doesn't."

"But doesn't it have teeth?"

"Yeah. But it bites down just hard enough so you know it has teeth—that's all."

A nice way to put it, I thought.

"Wanna give it a try, Dad?"

"I think not. Why don't you let the thing go."

He let the lizard go. Living things give you a good feeling. The way it had opened its mouth wide to chew on my son's finger had been beautiful.

"If you had to catch either lizards or caterpillars but not both, which would you choose?" he asked.

"Lizards, I would say."

"Me, too. What about between caterpillars and centipedes?"

So we walked along on a sunny road that offered hardly any shade, father and son, both wearing our straw hats and talking nonsense. And we weren't even halfway home.

[*MICHI*, ED. FUJIWARA SHIN'YA, NIHON NO MEIZUIHITSU 90
(TOKYO: SAKUHINSHA, 1990)]

38

Kitchen, Raindrops,
and A Memento of the Season

KŌDA AYA

Kōda Aya (1904-1990) was the daughter of the prominent novelist and scholar Kōda Rohan (1867-1947). Her mother died when she was six years old, and she took on household duties from a young age. She married in 1928 and had one child, a daughter, but divorced in 1938 and remained single thereafter, returning to her father's house. It was only after her father's death that she began to write, and in the early days she wrote primarily memoirs about her complex relationship with him. In time, however, she went on to establish herself as a major literary figure in her own right, writing a number of highly regarded short stories and novels, mostly autobiographical, for which she won the Yomiuri Literary Prize, the Japan Art Academy Prize, and numerous other awards.

She is particularly well known for her essays, many of which deal with domestic life and the roles of women in the Japanese household. The essays included here—"Daidokoro" (Kitchen), "Shizuku" (Raindrops), and "Kisetsu no kitami" (A Memento of the Season)—appeared in 1966, 1967, and 1978, respectively.

Kitchen

Counting up the years, I am amazed at how much time has gone by. Since I first stood in the kitchen, forty-eight years have passed. I was thirteen when I started helping, and by sixteen I had become a full-fledged cook, continuing on ever since.

I wonder how long I shall continue to stand here, washing vegetables, wielding a knife, using the stove, doing these same little tasks. "You're getting older—doing kitchen work is too hard on you to keep going on like this," my daughter says, as if pleading my case. Although happy for her concern, I just shake my head and smile. True, there have been times when I thought the work hard, but those days are in the past. The feeling I have as I stand here now, doing these tasks, is one of relaxation and calm—of enjoyment. I don't want a divorce.

Over the past fifty years, I have neglected kitchen duties only two times. The first was when I was still young and, unable to suppress my egotism, became so dissatisfied with my husband that I couldn't take it any longer; the other time was in middle age, when suddenly I underwent the changes associated with taking on a job. The first time I returned to the kitchen almost immediately, but the second time I stayed away for quite some time. Then at a certain point, I suddenly realized to what a great degree I had actually grown up in the kitchen.

The kitchen is a mysterious place, public in some ways yet one's own private space in others. Moreover, it is a place furnished with appliances that use water and fire, where there are sharp knives—the sort of place where one is not surprised by a little blood flowing. So I ask myself, "What is it you've been doing here?" Of course, I have been moving about, handling fish and eggs, doing the chores involved in cooking. But is that all?

No. Surely not.

For the human heart is also a mechanism of strange workings, somehow public, somehow private. What was my frame of mind, then, as I worked in the kitchen? That I *do* remember, and can't deny that I used the public work of the kitchen to hide my own feelings of desire and resentment, my jealousies and transgressions, my indifference and anger, behind the activities of a normal woman. But was it not also in this way that I learned of the calm that follows perseverance, the relief that follows grief, the guilt that follows anger, the emptiness that follows jealousy? While I was preparing fish or radishes, I was also doing the woman's work of the heart. The kitchen was a schoolroom.

Now the kitchen is a quiet place. It has taken forty-eight years for me to get here. It is quiet, yes, and also peaceful. The work will last the rest of my life and never be done, but I am grateful to the kitchen for allowing me this sense of tranquility.

Raindrops

February is the month when things settle into a quiet calm.

Rain was falling. No wind came with it, but it was a cold rain that struck hard. The temperature in the hospital room had dropped, too. The young woman was lying in her bed, quiet and still. Only her face was turned, so that she could look at the crape myrtle just outside the window. There was not a single leaf left on the tree. The bare branches were drenched. The rain kept on falling. She was looking at the raindrops.

Rain would fall on a bare branch, collecting on the tip before forming into round drops; then when the round drops were fully formed, they would sparkle for a second and fall. How many branches might there be? I wondered—some large, some small. The droplets fell in great numbers, descending here and there, sparkling off and on.

"It's so cold, and so gloomy, until a moment ago I was really hating the rain—but those raindrops are so pretty."

She had graduated from high school, gotten a job: a cheerful girl who was becoming more lively all the time. But then almost immediately, she had to go to the hospital. Summer passed, autumn passed, then even the New Year. Worry over the future, resentment toward her healthy friends, concern about love and marriage, the loneliness of being on a sickbed— all these things can only have caused her great pain.

"Grandma, lately I've hit on a way to be at peace."

Poor thing, I thought. But it was a good sign. There's nothing shallow about her; she's smart. But what kind of technique could it be? Using the beauty of the raindrops to dispel her resentment of the nasty weather? I had been feeling sorry for her, but this made me more hopeful.

February—the month when things settle into a quiet calm. A year is a collection of twelve months, and as the months go by the seasons come around, everything changing, each month with its own peculiar features, peculiar features that come around only once a year. If you live for sixty years, you experience each month just sixty times. So we mustn't waste the time but learn well the peculiar features of February. The brilliant leaves of autumn, then the sudden cold of the winter wind following hard after an excursion to see the chrysanthemums, then the end of the old year and the bustle of the New Year—all of it enjoyable, however much a trial for both body and spirit.

February is a month for calming down, taking a rest, feeling deeply. Since that time, I have taken that young girl and the raindrops as my model.

A Memento of the Season

This year, the summer heat was relentless. Day after day, the temperature stayed over 85° Fahrenheit, the nights went on like nights in the tropics, and there was not a drop of rain. Water levels in the reservoirs dropped, water pressure was reduced, and water conservation measures were enacted. We can only count ourselves fortunate that we didn't experience the awful things they did in Fukuoka, where water had to be rationed according to the time of day. It was a summer that left one tired out, gasping for air. Both strong sunlight and intense heat are invigorating things that one can enjoy only in summer, of course, but nothing feels invigorating when you're short of water.

I am not wasteful when it comes to water, I think—not a fanatic, but someone who tries not to be careless. To be more precise, I seem to always use water with a clear sense of what I am doing. This is because of the training I received as a child. Perhaps one should call it the custom of those times, but then again it was also the custom of the region and the custom of my house: all us children, if we were careless with water, were scolded and told that we should beware the "water punishment." I was raised in a town east of the Sumida River, which is now within the Tokyo city limits but was then in the country, and we weren't connected to city water. To get water, one had to go to the family well or to a neighborhood well and fill a bucket—by letting a line down or using a hand pump—and then carry it back to the kitchen. Filling buckets and transporting water is backbreaking work, especially in rain or snow. What's more, since we lived in the lowlands along the dike of the Sumida, the streams and ditches would overflow in typhoon season each autumn, contaminating the wells so that we could not use their water. Surrounded by water, we had none for drinking or washing.

Things being what they were, everyone understood how precious water was and how difficult to handle. I think we realized that it was not something man-made but a gift of nature. That must be why the term "water punishment" came into being: as a way to express the commandment not to waste water. Every girl naturally learned the convoluted sequence of rinsing the dish towel out over a bucket, then using that water to ring out the floor cloth, and finally tossing the water out beneath the shrubs. I was raised that way myself and handled water as part of my chores all through my youth. Then came the great earthquake of 1923.[1]

With so much shaking, there was no way that water currents beneath the ground could remain unaffected. The water from some wells continued on as pure as before, but there were also problems: some wells dried up; some were polluted. The well at our house was contaminated by something metallic in nature, so that if you let water sit in the bucket for a few minutes, a garish film developed on its surface, and we were afraid to use it even for washing. The only thing to do was borrow water from a good well in the neighborhood, which I had to haul by pole on my shoulders. When there is no drinking water in the house, you can't worry much about appearances. I quickly got the knack of how to manage the bucket, but still the weight of the water bearing down on my shoulders was so great that it felt like what must have been meant by the water punishment. If it was the water punishment, though, I had lots of company, and those of us without wells developed a certain camaraderie as we huffed along under our loads of water.

No matter what we tried, the well at our house never again produced good water. But just about that time we moved into the city, and—in a

1. On September 1, 1923, a magnitude 7.8 earthquake, which came to be known as the Great Kantō Earthquake, struck Tokyo and the surrounding provinces, causing widespread damage and making normal life impossible for a time.

flash—we were on the city system. Turn a tap, and there was water free for the taking, water ready to hand, demanding no labor, almost to the point of disappointment. All the trouble I had gone through for water until I had left my old house that very morning seemed like some fantasy, and I found it all unsettling. Rather than feeling relieved or happy, for some reason I couldn't help but feel reluctant to let go of the water that I had hauled from the well by my own hands at such great expense of labor.

The very next day, as I was passing by a neighborhood shop, I saw the lady of the house get a tub out to rinse some washing next to the stream that ran in front of the place. Since she had left the water running, there it was, overflowing the rim of the tub right in front of my eyes! I had never wasted water in such a profligate way before, so I had conflicting feelings: I was surprised and reproachful, yet also impressed with how exhilarating it all was. The old way, using well buckets and pumps, you couldn't get away with such a thing—although you couldn't be stingy with water or labor either, having to change the water constantly while rinsing until you got the soap out. But how impressive it was to just let the water run over as you worked! The way they used water in the city seemed a luxury to a country girl like me. By that time, in the city, the term "water punishment" seemed already to have disappeared.

Since that time, I have lived in the city, enjoying a tranquil existence using city water that demands no exertion. However, still, from time to time, I am thrown into a dither. The faucet breaks and the water stops, or the tank overflows, sending water down in a sudden waterfall from the second floor, and I have to scurry around. To my own mind, I don't seem to be guilty of any carelessness, yet at such times I feel as if I might be getting the water punishment. And I do recall some offenses. For instance, while filling a bucket, I will go out to get the evening paper, returning just at the time the bucket is full. But sometimes I pick up the paper and stand there reading for a moment and forget about the water. Flowing over the side of the bucket, the water raises a faint cry of protest. This has happened any number of times, and the result is the same as if I had been negligent.

Then came this summer. Although we never got to the point of water rationing, we had been asked to conserve and were obliged to refrain from sprinkling. But the ground beneath the plants in my little garden space dried out and turned so white that I decided to empty the bathtub water there. Getting the water from the tub and carrying it out through the house was a considerable task for me,[2] but when I looked at the thirsty plants, I felt I had to persevere. As I was trying to slip into my garden sandals, however, I tripped and dropped the bucket.

Suddenly a sound rose up from the ground—a sound like something popping. I looked down and saw that the dry earth had already drunk the water up, and that thin, shallow cracks were spreading out in a random pattern. I was stunned. The parched, hot earth must have contracted when the water hit it and hardened into little blocks, separated by cracks. When you put water into a heated cooking pot, the pot angrily spurts out drops of water, but the drought- stricken ground had cracked instead. After this, I couldn't very well give up, so I brought out seven buckets of water from the bathtub. I was getting weak in the knees by the end but was feeling a little more at peace. I felt that the trees, the ground, and I had all met the drought straight on. Summer was going off down the road. Next year, too, there might be a summer drought. But the way the parched earth made that popping sound and cracked when I spilled the bucket— that would be my vivid memento of the season.

[*KŌDA AYA ZENSHŪ*, VOLS. 15, 16, AND 21
(TOKYO: IWANAMI SHOTEN, 1994-2003)]

2. The author was in her mid-seventies at the time.

39

On Surgery *and* Rainy Day

KŌNO TAEKO

Kōno Taeko was born in Osaka in 1926 and graduated from Osaka Women's College in 1947. She started writing stories in the immediate postwar years but established a reputation for herself only after winning the prestigious Akutagawa Prize in 1963 for her story "Kani" (Crabs). Since then, she has won a number of other literary prizes—the Yomiuri, the Tanizaki, and the Noma among them—and is now widely recognized as one of the finest living Japanese novelists. She served for a time on the selection committee for the Akutagawa Prize and is a member of the Japanese Art Academy. Her stories often blur the line between fantasy and reality and contain shocking scenes that seem more so for being presented in the most everyday settings and situations.

Kōno was sickly in her youth and has battled tuberculosis since her early twenties. The essays translated here, "Shujutsu to iu mono" (On Surgery) and "Ame no hi" (Rainy Day), appeared in 1974 and 1976, respectively.

On Surgery

It must have been close to midnight, last night. Before going to bed, I thought I would watch a little television, so I switched the set on and saw the beginning of what appeared to be an open-heart surgery. As soon as

I realized what it was, I felt such revulsion that I had to quickly turn to another channel.

In the past, too, I never liked looking at photos or watching television programs involving surgery. If I should ever need to have an operation myself, I thought, it would only add to my anxiety if I remembered scenes from photos or television programs as I lay on the surgeon's table. That is why I had no desire to see such things. What's more, I imagined myself being plagued by doubts as I lay on the surgeon's table, berating myself for having ever watched such things. Sometimes I even found myself assailed by the superstition that if only I hadn't done so, I never would have needed surgery. This, of course, made me resist the idea of viewing surgery all the more.

Last night, though, I had a different reason for not wanting to watch a program that showed surgery. Early this summer, all my efforts to avoid any dangerous contact with surgery through photos or television programs had come to naught when I had to go under the knife myself. It was an emergency: not feeling well, I went to a doctor in my neighborhood and was told to get to the hospital and have surgery immediately. Since my pain increased greatly just during the time I was going through the paperwork and the preparatory procedures at the hospital, it appeared that there was indeed a need for urgency. I even got to the point where I *wanted* to have the procedure done—and right away. Even my blood pressure, which as a rule is low, had gone up to the normal level when they checked it. (After being released from the hospital, when I went to see a doctor I had known a long time, for recovery therapy, I told him that that day my blood pressure had been higher—which was unusual for me. "Oh," he laughed, "that's just because you got scared.")

While I was waiting to begin admission procedures in the hospital, I thought to myself, "If they don't get a move on, I may die," but then I remembered how I had always feared that surgery might kill me, too. During the operation, I was so frightened that I kept breaking out in a cold sweat. Yet never for a moment did I think, "I'm sure glad I didn't watch any surgeries on television." On the contrary, I feel now that even if I had watched such things in the past, I would not have had any time to consider their effects on me in the face of the very real fears I was facing at the moment.

In the past, I had often been sick but have never had to undergo an operation. As a child, I was about to have my tonsils out, but while we were waiting for good weather, the crisis passed. Then in my early twenties, I came down with tuberculosis and was going to have the "Ping-Pong ball treatment"[1] but got away without having it done because a new medicine was discovered—which I ended up not taking, because just hearing that the new medicine was effective was evidently enough for me. We postponed the surgery, and while I was waiting to get the new medicine, I experienced an amazing recovery. Just after I turned thirty, I developed tuberculosis again, but because my condition wasn't something that surgery could do much for, I escaped once more. So although I've had teeth pulled and that sort of thing, this was the first time I had ever gone through an actual operation.

For the operating surgeon, my surgery was of the most common sort, something as simple as a fishmonger carving up a fish. But when it was over, I felt very grateful to have lived through it—that is, until about four or five days after the operation, when I began to succumb to the strange feeling that through the surgery my life had been prolonged beyond its natural limit.

Until now, I have always blithely accepted advances in medical science. When the scientific cure for my second attack of tuberculosis proved itself effective—like when the intense stomach spasms caused by an injection I had received passed within only ten minutes or so—I thought to myself, "My, but I'm glad to live in a time of medical progress," and was able to go on my way. But this time, while I was still happy not to have died, I was not able to proceed so easily to a feeling of uncomplicated gratitude.

During the surgery, I heard the words, "Get ready with the distilled water—lots of it!" While my insides were being cleaned out, I felt sick two times. And aside from the pain, I was able to feel the pressure in spite of the anesthetic, which felt exactly like the inside of a nylon bag being scrubbed. Remembering that sensation, I look at my scar and think that I have been opened up and then closed again, and that I could have

1. Ping-Pong ball plombage. A therapy involving extrapleural insertion of a plastic Ping-Pong ball "plombe" to collapse the lung.

decided to pursue some other course and chosen not to go through surgery—in which case, I know that I would have died; and then I start to feel that there is something terribly unnatural about my still being alive.

Having a tooth pulled is one thing; so is having medicine introduced into your body from the outside in order to heal you. Nor is there anything wrong with disinfecting and sewing up a wound. But if you have to be cut open and operated on in order not to die, might it not be better not to undergo the process?

It's not that I think of opening up the human body as a desecration. And although the surgery was painful, it wasn't so bad that I felt like saying, "If it's going to hurt this much, please just kill me." It's just that I can't help feeling that my life, which had to undergo surgery in order to be saved, was supposed to have come to its end. For example, there are indications that cesarean sections have been performed since Roman times. But if you were born in an age when all they could do for a headache was whack you on the head with a stone hammer, it seems to me that it would be better to accept your plight as a curse from the gods, like everyone else around you, and go ahead and die. Respect for human life is all very fine, but when the face of the surgeon appears on the television screen, wearing his big mask and surgical gown, as confident and free of doubt as if he were standing beneath a brocade battle flag, it puts me off.

I have heard about people who returned home after surviving the war who felt that thereafter their lives seemed so superfluous that they didn't care what happened to them. As one who at the end of the war felt only a sense of liberation—as if my life were just beginning—I could not understand this. Now, though, I think I have at least a small sense of how they feel. Maybe I don't feel that my life is superfluous or that I don't care what happens from here on out; but I do have a strong feeling that I have already experienced the end of my life, that the life I am living now has been sent to me from some other frightful realm. I feel an indescribable perplexity—but something that is beyond my power to express. If I were to put it in the form of a manga, it would be as if my existence as a human being had ended, with my space now taken over by something that is a mixture of ape and robot.

That being said, I'm quite sure that if something happens again, I will run straight to the hospital and, if necessary, have myself operated on again.

Rainy Day

I am incompetent in everything I do and, for all that, strangely impatient, too. For instance, I don't like the escalators deep down in subway stations. I just don't feel like standing there doing nothing as I move tediously from floor to floor. Even when I'm going up, I end up taking the stairs. In department stores, when I have a few floors to travel, I take the elevator. Only when it's right in front of me do I take the escalator; otherwise, I use the stairs. But I do hate going up and down the stairs to use pedestrian overpasses—I suppose because I feel like I'm being forced to take the long way around to something right in front of me. . . . And when I'm walking down the street, people don't overtake me; more often *I'm* the one who passes *them* by.

That time, too, I wanted to pass by the couple walking right in front of me, but there was a guardrail that made it too tight to pass. It was the summer rainy season, and it had just started to rain. What's more, I had my umbrella up, but the couple did not, so passing them seemed too much like an act of aggression.

The two were walking forward at a slant, and from behind I got the impression that he was a man of retirement age, and she his wife. The man was protecting his head from the rain with a weekly magazine—not open, but closed. The woman had one arm through the handle of a handbag and was holding a handkerchief over her head. The rain wasn't coming down all that hard, but it was more than a sprinkle, so their headgear was getting drenched. Still, I would have felt strange inviting just one of them under my umbrella, and, besides that, I'm not in the habit of asserting myself through acts of kindness.

"Think we should buy an umbrella?" I heard the woman in front of me ask.

We weren't passing by an umbrella shop, nor were we even in a shopping district, but there were stores here and there, one of which might carry umbrellas. But the man answered, "No, we're fine."

Soon the woman asked again:

"Think we should buy an umbrella?"

"No, we're fine."

The man gave the same reply.

I was restraining myself from passing them by but was nonetheless walking close behind them, poised to do so at any moment. If they had noticed me and made any gesture of invitation, I would have quickly left them behind, but they just kept blocking my way. After a moment, they talked again.

"Think we should buy an umbrella?"

"No, we're fine."

Then once more, I heard the two of them say the same thing.

All four times the words were the same, and always with the same intonation. Neither one would agree with the other, yet I didn't feel that either of them was just being obstinate.

I had thought of them as husband and wife, but that was a little hard to imagine. I wanted at least to get a look at their faces, but I never got past them.

[*YAMAI*, ED. ŌKA SHŌHEI, NIHON NO MEIZUIHITSU 28
(TOKYO: SAKUHINSHA, 1985); *AME*, ED. NAKAMURA TEIJI,
NIHON NO MEIZUIHITSU 43 (TOKYO: SAKUHINSHA, 1986)]

40

Looking for Gloves

Mukōda Kuniko

Mukōda Kuniko (1929-1981) was born in Tokyo, attended Jissen Women's College in Tokyo, and then worked in the world of publishing and writing all her life. From 1950 to 1960, she worked for a publishing house and then a film magazine. She made her reputation writing radio and television dramas, turning out 2,500 scripts in all. In 1975, she published her first novel and went on to gain fame for her essays and short stories, one collection of which earned her the Naoki Prize in 1980. In 1981, she died in a plane crash while on her way to visit China. Posthumously, the Mukōda Kuniko Prize was established to honor screenwriters.

Many of Mukōda's essays are autobiographical—indeed, confessional—as is the one translated here, "Tebukuro o sagasu" (Looking for Gloves). It first appeared in the periodical PHP *in the summer of 1976 and later was published in* Yonaka no bara (Roses in the Night, 1984), *a collection of Mukōda's essays.*

I think it was when I was twenty-two that I spent a whole winter without any gloves.

At the time, I was working for a company that produced educational films, located in Yotsuya. Although not very high, I'm sure my salary was enough to take care of basic needs. I was going without gloves because I couldn't find any that I liked.

It seems to me now that it was much colder in those days, probably because it was just after the war and nutritional standards were not that high. Heaters were not as widely available as they are now, and inside trains and buses it was frightfully cold. Over several layers of clothing, people would wear thick overcoats, with gloves on their hands. These days, it's considered fashionable to go without coat and gloves, but back then people had so little money for clothing that to go without was a sign that you were short of cash and having a hard time.

I didn't like looking destitute, so I wouldn't rub my hands together or blow on them for warmth but instead stick them in my pockets and strut around airily, as if to say, "I'm not cold—in fact, I like things this way." But inside my pockets, my gloveless hands were dry and chapped and always numb.

It's funny, but as I look back now, I can't recall what kind of gloves I wanted enough to brave the cold that way. I must have thought that rather than wear gloves I didn't like, I would be happier going without.

People around me thought it was a joke to begin with, but when I caught a cold, my mother lost her patience and scolded me in earnest.

"Stop this foolishness. What will you do if you really take ill?"

I insisted that gloves had nothing to do with catching a cold and then became so stubborn that I never took a day off work, even when I came down with a fever. By then, people were watching to see when I would finally buy gloves, and I was determined not to give in no matter how much I suffered.

Then one day, one of my superiors who had always been kind to me at work came over to me on the pretext of talking about overtime work to offer a word of advice. He was thirty-five or thirty-six, I suppose. He brought with him two bowls of noodles that he had bought and while we were eating, slurping up the steaming hot noodles, he said this:

"The problem you're having now may go beyond gloves."

I was taken aback.

"A man can get away with it, but not a woman. A woman would be endangering her chances for happiness."

And then he spoke very frankly:

"If you don't solve the problem soon, you may regret it the rest of your life."

I had two feelings—first, that I should meekly say yes, but also that yes was what I could not say. That night, I didn't get on the train but decided to walk until I had come up with an answer I could accept within myself. At the time, I was living in Kugayama on the Inokashira Line, so I began walking away from Yotsuya in the direction of Shinanomachi. Almost immediately, my fingertips, recently warmed by the bowl of noodles, went numb in the cold.

———————

Since childhood, I have been picky and had a vain heart. I liked only the finer things, and often I wanted what was beyond my reach. Never satisfied with what I had, I was always on the lookout, thinking that if I just searched for a while longer, I would get hold of something better. Whether it was a toy or a sweater, I wanted the best, even if it meant having fewer in number, and I remember adults frowning at me and saying that a child should not be so obstinate.

Furthermore, although still a child, there was something in me that was secretly proud of my high attitude. In a word, then, I think I was thoroughly disagreeable—a truly detestable child. Even after reaching twenty, I still bit my nails and embraced my high ambitions—indeed, if anything, those feelings intensified. Thinking about it now, it seems undeniable that a Freudian analysis would see my nail biting as from my frustrated desires, my impatience over unrealized hopes. When I was eight, sometimes I would try to calm my feelings by reading, only to realize after a few minutes that drops of blood were falling onto the book.

I was impatient, no doubt about it.

The company where I worked was small, but we had a cameraman, a painter, and a musician who all taught me many things I could not have learned in school. The head of the company and his wife were kind to me and even gave my name to their new daughter. In other words, a bystander would doubtless have called a still-unmarried young woman who complained about such a working situation picky indeed.

I was young and healthy. I was blessed with parents and siblings and knew no want. I had young male friends, and had even received two or three marriage offers. Now that I look back on it, these men were all entirely worthy both as men and as human beings, and I could have married any of them and doubtless been happy in the conventional sense.

Yet each and every day, I was truly unhappy.

"What do I want to do?"

"What would be best for me?"

"What should I do, and how?"

"What could I do to remove my discontent?"

Even without answers to these questions, I vaguely knew that I hated things as they were, that something wasn't right; and I was angry at my persistent but unrealizable dreams, at a reality that even on my tiptoes I could not quite reach.

Yes, the problem of the gloves was surely not just a problem of gloves.

What a disagreeable sort you are, I had to admit to myself.

If I went on that way, I knew that the complaints and discontent would only persist. I knew that it wouldn't be only this winter that I went without gloves; it would go on and on. And I knew that for someone without more talent or appeal, and with a personality that failed to comprehend lofty notions or feelings like gratitude or peace, marriage was not likely to work out.

Which reminded me of what my father had once said to me:

"While you're young, you'll be all right; people will naturally be kind to you and forgive you. But as you get older, that disposition of yours will make you suffer."

So I decided to think things through.

If I was going to change, now was the time.

That very night, that instant.

I was walking in a back alley in Yotsuya. Mixed in with the smells of evening cooking came the sound of a baby crying and music from a radio, and from the gutter rose the somehow lonely smell of bathtub grime, probably because someone had just drained the tub. With a lifestyle like mine, what was there to complain about? I thought to myself that anyone—even me—with normal looks and talents, who found an appropriate job, chose a proper companion, and walked on, looking not beyond but down and ahead, would doubtless find the normal sort of happiness. And to do so would also be to fulfill my duty as eldest daughter to my parents, who were looking forward to my marriage.

In the end, though, what I decided was to keep on going as I had been.

If I was a disagreeable sort, always wanting what I didn't have and being full of grand ambitions, then that was that, I concluded: I would accept myself as I was. From the time I was two or three years old until my current age of twenty, I had been cautioned by my parents and my teachers, and I had tried to change myself without any success. My conclusion was that these traits would be mine until death.

Had I compromised at this point and made do with just any sort of gloves, I still would not have worn them unless I truly liked them. To pretend that I liked them would have been nothing more than a sham drama staged for myself alone. The discontent within me was still there, and no matter how skillfully I pretended to be happy by hiding it, I knew that I would only be telling lies—layers of them.

It's embarrassing to admit it, but I am a person whose worldly desires are quite strong. I want to wear fine clothes and eat good food. I want fine paintings. If I find myself wanting a black cat, I've got to have one. Until I do, the complaints will just go on and on.

When I was young, I was embarrassed by this fault of mine and resolved to live on a higher, more spiritual plane. But compared with the spiritual qualities of the famous people I read about in books, I seemed to be made of earthier stuff. When I was not content with my clothing, food, and living arrangements, it had a negative effect even on my spiritual being. I had even gone so far as to think that somehow I had to do something about myself.

But then I made up my mind: I would simply stop trying to reform myself.

Although a perfectionist by nature, there was something in me that shied away from putting effort into truly examining myself. I was clever enough to make do with the readiest solution. Even if I wasn't sorry, I would think that the best thing for both myself and those around me was to quickly apologize, and then deceive myself into thinking that I had made up for my offense by some soul-searching—thus never truly feeling any guilt, forgetting the content of my soul-searching in a single day, and going on to commit the same offense over and over again.

To go on doing this would be no different from holding my conscience up to a trick mirror that produced a flattering image. The little figures of my existence might add up in the day-to-day accounting, but when looking back over the whole of my life, there would be no change at all, I realized. All that would remain was the record of how I had examined myself every day in order to satisfy my own vanity.

I am sure that there are people who truly examine themselves from deep down and then try to convert the results into action. But for me, self-reform was a thing of the moment.

So I decided that I would change and no longer engage in self-serving, halfway kinds of soul-searching. To examine oneself from the bottom of one's heart, even if no one was watching, even in the darkness—if it didn't result in remorse that made your body shake with embarrassment, then was it the real thing? I concluded that to write down one's confessions in a diary, to examine oneself in a ritual fashion to prepare for sleep, was no more than hypocrisy.

Try your hand at flower arranging, and you will learn how difficult it is to make a branch bend. Even when you spend a lot of time in the process, making sure not to break it, with the first lapse in attention the branch will revert to its natural shape, as if mocking the vanity of human efforts to change it. That being the case, I concluded that even if the branch wasn't an especially beautiful specimen, the true way was for a person to let it grow according to its own nature.

I don't like the term "virtuous poverty."

And I just can't warm up to the word "modest."

Around me, there sometimes hasn't been anyone who made these words appear beautiful. To put the matter harshly but state my feelings honestly:

"Virtuous poverty" means "grin and bear it."

"Modest" means—I can't help but say it—"pompous and hypocritical."

By nature, I am closer to being greedy than to embracing virtuous poverty, and whenever I sensed that someone acting modestly was really only hoping to be recognized as a person of good character, that was enough to make me dislike him. The ones I liked were my friends who cared nothing for reputation but admitted honestly that they wanted money, wanted social position, and were proud to proclaim they could speak English.

That night, I ended up walking as far as Shibuya Station, where I got on the Inokashira Line. It was while I was riding the train that I decided on my course of action. Beginning the next day, I determined, I would give a try to anything that until then I had rejected as coming from something in my personality in need of reform.

The next morning, I ran my eyes over the help-wanted ads in the newspaper, and the morning after that applied for an editorial position listed in the "women wanted" section of the *Asahi Newspaper* and got the job. When I was told at the place where I had been working in Yotsuya that I couldn't just leave them without notice, I began working in Nihonbashi in the daytime and tying up loose ends in Yotsuya at night.

In this way, while working in the editorial office of a magazine specializing in Western films, I reclaimed my last twenty years.

I quit making do with the normal sort of thing just because I would be accused of being picky. It was around this time, for example, that I spent three months' salary on an American-made swimming suit. Of course, because my salary was very low, my taste for luxury meant not drinking tea, carrying a lunch to work, and making do without any new Western clothing.

I had seen the swimming suit in an American magazine—an elastic one-piece made for competitive swimmers, black, with no decoration; the kind of suit one wanted to wear swimming in a clear blue sea. The privations I had to bear in order to quench my desire for it would have seemed foolish to an outsider, but they didn't bother me; indeed, I found them refreshing. For ten years, I wore the suit every summer and then finally gave it to a swimmer friend who said she just had to have it. I think she got good use out of it, too.

Patience and pain come along with getting what you want. But since I was not bending against my will, I had no complaints, no discontent, no excuses, and in the process I believe I discovered that what I was doing could be said to lead to spiritual improvement.

The swimsuit was just one example. During the time I was working at the movie magazine, my desires and high expectations seemed only to intensify.

Not satisfied with the work of introducing other people's movies or running other people's movie reviews, I even spent a year taking private lessons on how to make hats, just out of a desire to make something on my own.

It was in my late twenties that, through a chance opportunity, I began a job writing copy for a radio disc jockey. Until then, I had worked in the world of print journalism, and music had been only a hobby, but now the two came together—and I spent three years so fascinated by how words became sounds and bounced around in complete freedom that I paid attention to nothing else and put all my effort into my new job. But in time, I got used to the work and tired of the strictures of five-minute segments. The usual dissatisfaction and high expectations began to rear their heads, so I took a job working as a reporter for a weekly magazine.

For a time, this was my life: at nine in the morning, I would go to my job at the publishing office and work hard until noon, read drafts while eating lunch nearby, then go to the coffeehouse in the basement of the *Asahi Newspaper* building (where they charge you by the hour, just for sitting) to write radio copy, finally putting in an appearance at the weekly magazine office in Tsukiji before making soup for myself at a little inn not far away, where I worked at my writing until about midnight.

Around this time, I got so amused at how harried I was that once, when I was crossing a street in Ginza, I started asking myself just what I thought I was doing and laughed out loud. A friend who happened to see me said, "What's so funny?" with a straight face.

Couldn't I find something even more interesting?

It was with that kind of pure curiosity and the hunger of a wolf on the prowl that I spent my twenties. But it was my own doing, and I *was* receiving a salary from three different jobs—which meant that I went without any sleep at all if I wasn't careful, but it also kept me in such a state of constant tension that I did not fall ill. After that, I let the waters take me into the river (that's how it felt to me) and quit my editing jobs, quit the radio station, and concentrated solely on what interested me most— writing television dramas, which I have been doing now for seven years.

That winter night when I was twenty-two.

What if I hadn't been treated to those noodles?

And what if I hadn't received that kind warning?

I don't think I would have gotten so upset and given such thought to my personality. After all, I am by nature the sort of person who is realistic and not given to ideas and abstractions.

The result of my supervisor's warning was thus the opposite of what he had intended.

Yet I realize that his words prophesied what I have become today. Midway through my forties, still unmarried, I work as a scriptwriter for television dramas, a job with no security and a tenuous connection to the real world.

What's more, I still am not satisfied enough to say, "This is fine." Still I writhe about, unable to resign myself, always thinking there must be something more interesting somewhere else, that for me there must be something other than this.

It was seven or eight years ago that I read something in a book by Ishikawa Tatsuzō.[1] I can't give the exact quote, but the gist of it was, "In modern times, we call a woman cornered an evil woman."

Well put, I thought.

I discovered something looking through photo albums from my childhood. There wasn't a single photo of me smiling that cute way that little girls do.

I was either glaring at the photographer in anger or sulking—one or the other. And already I had an uncertain look on my face, as if I were searching for something.

If back then I had repented of my haughty attitude and my greediness, been grateful for the usual kinds of happiness, and lived every day in peace, without questioning, then what kind of face would I have now, and what kind of life would I have lived?

Not being a god, these are questions I cannot answer.

Short of a rebirth, is there no such thing as reconstructive spiritual surgery?

It's what I most despise about myself, but the force of my narcissism and conceit made it so painful for me to correct my faults that I made up my mind to take these things as my spiritual "least common denominator."

There is a positive side, however: at least I have been able to have a little success living on my own as a woman. And in terms of the market ledger, since I don't have a husband or children, there will be only me when I die. Whether this is a happy situation or not probably depends on who is looking at it. I'm not sure what to answer when I'm asked myself.

But there is one thing I *can* say.

1. 1905–1985. A popular novelist.

Thinking back on that night when I was twenty-two, and knowing my own disposition, I think that if I had compromised even a little bit, I would have had complaints about my life.

Of course, even now I have negative feelings:

Anger at how cautious and sly I become as the years go by.

Impatience at how my body won't go along even when my heart is full of excitement.

Contempt for myself because I am too lazy to make the effort, even though I have a list of things I say I want to do—to study music, to learn a language, and so on.

And a feeling of inferiority concerning my meager talents.

Yet one thing I still count as a treasure: that I am still searching for gloves.

What kind of gloves do I want?

I don't know.

I have never come across a book that I would not tire of if it was all I had alone on a desert island, or a record that would make me feel I had no need of any others. And the same can be said regarding a man to be my life's companion.

Of course, I am probably just holding out for something I can't have—something like Don Quixote's windmill that you can't reach even after wearing out your feet over a lifetime. But lately, as I stay on the lookout, eyes turned up or gazing all around, for the gloves that even at my age I still haven't found, I feel a certain pride in having lived the life of a scavenger, trying not to toady to the god of my fate as I keep on searching just a little while longer for what I want, in a slight posture of defiance.

I realize that what I have written here might be called self-justification. All I wanted to do was, by telling the story of my own perverse pride, to show how I nearly bent out of shape the branch of my own individuality—which more and more I think of as an act of weakness rather than of strength—because in the innocence of youth I took the business of self-reform too seriously.

[*YONAKA NO BARA* (TOKYO: KŌDANSHA, 1981)]

41

One, We Count, Then . . .

Takenishi Hiroko

Before becoming active as a writer, Takenishi Hiroko (b. 1929) worked for some years as an editor at two major publishing houses, Kawade Shobō and Chikuma Shobō, where she developed a broad acquaintance with Japanese literature of all periods. Her own first published works were critical essays on classical Japanese literature written from the perspective of a modern woman, most of which appeared in literary journals. A collection of her essays received the Tamura Toshiko Prize in 1964. Her first important short story, "Gishiki" (Ritual), appeared in the journal Bungei *in 1963, and since then she has continued to pursue an active career in both fiction and literary criticism. For her fiction, she has been awarded the Women's Literature Prize and the Kawabata Yasunari Prize.*

Takenishi's fiction often concentrates on events related to the Pacific War—in particular, the suffering of people in her hometown of Hiroshima—whereas her essays tend to focus on everyday experience. The following examples—"Sora" (Sky), "San'yū" (Three Friends), "Iriai" (Evening Bell), "Ari" (Ants), and "Me" (Eyes)—are taken from the collection Hitotsu to ya (One, We Count, Then . . . , *1983), the title of which refers to an old "counting song" used to teach children. As is true generally with so many short essays of the type Takenishi writes, they all appeared first in a periodical: the* Mainichi gurafu (Mainichi Graphic).*

Sky

Some mornings, I entrust my eyes to the sky. No matter how unsettled my feelings, never once has the sky hindered my eyes from floating freely and reveling as they will.

Moreover, when in the evening I look to the sky thinking to erase some sadness, to rid myself of some pain, to ask that a prayer be granted, never—not even once—has it turned me away.

There are times when the sky does seem to be fading into the distance, just as by contrast there are times when it seems to be slowly bearing down on me from above. Strangely, however, my forebodings at such times are never realized: always I feel that I am in the midst of a process that has just begun, not at its end.

One morning, I looked out into the still-murky light of a spring dawn and felt like singing quietly. Knowing all the while that the happiness I felt in my passion for a certain person must in the end lead to loneliness, still I felt that I should express my gratitude for what had come my way. Rather meekly, yet quite naturally all the same, I felt like pronouncing a blessing upon all the lovers in the world.

To eyes that were more sensitive than usual, the spring sky, hazy even after the break of day, appeared serene, and that serenity seemed to be gently encouraging me to spend the day with my lover, making me happy beyond words.

Another time, in the night, as I stood before a winter sky aglow with moonlight, I prayed that someone dear to me might be allowed to live longer, if only for a day. As I prayed, unknown to anyone else, I felt a tremendous tension concentrating my thoughts.

The wind was cold, and the cold made the moonlight brighter. It was a night when every time I looked up, I saw stars—a small one here, a big one there—emerging one after another from depths where the moon bobbed as if on the sea.

Why did the person I cared for have to suffer so? For what offense? I asked, but the sky did not answer, and suddenly I was inexpressibly sad.

Then I realized: all around me, there might be others whose eyes were likewise fixed upon the same moon and the same stars. At first I doubted my supposition, but gradually my doubt changed to strong conviction.

Consider: from long ago, before they possessed words to express themselves, how many people must have cast their thoughts out like bridges toward the sky? And the sky, while never turning away, has replied only with its silent depths, with a vastness that may have incited people to cast their thoughts even farther out into its emptiness.

There are moments when this sky—which has no voice to speak to men—frightens us with the thought that its silence might be intentional. In a storm, for instance, when violent winds have banished all hope of sleep and one follows the sound of mighty black clouds and rushing rain, one cannot help but think that off behind the wind and the rain, behind the clouds, there lies an even stronger will. And a blinding sunset communicates a stern warning of complex and subtle designs.

Needless to say, in times when the world is happy, but also when some corner of it has been burned to ash by human wickedness and vanity, the sky has always remained the sky, deep and cold.

It may be that, like us, the sky has its life span. But I think it fortunate that our knowledge has yet to extend that far. It is our ignorance in this regard that keeps us humble.

Three Friends

Six or seven years ago, I greeted the New Year in the hospital. The other patients in my room having all gone home to be cared for by their families during the holidays, I was left alone in a cavernous room recovering from surgery, part of my body bound in a plaster cast that reduced me to doing little more than staring at the potted plants—a pine, a bamboo, and a plum[1]—kindly brought by someone who had come to visit. Mixed into the generous mounds of dirt in the pots was some white sand.

---

1. This combination of plants—referred to in the Sino-Japanese compound *shōchikubai*—is often given as a gift in winter. The combination of strength and beauty offered by the plants in the desolate landscape of the season is felt to symbolize hope and good fortune.

As well as being long-lived, the pine, the bamboo, and the plum matched one another nicely in height; but the colors and scents of the three are of course different, making me realize how even as they set one another off so well, they still preserved a harmony by which the pine was more like a pine, the bamboo and the plum more like themselves. Circumstances being what they were, they would ever after remain a fresh image in my memory.

Bo Juyi[2] called poetry, the zither, and rice wine the Three Friends, but the pine, the bamboo, and the plum are sometimes referred to in the same way.[3] Long ago, in Heian times,[4] someone had called the pine and the crane millennial companions,[5] I knew: but as I gazed at the three plants, I wondered who it was that, at some auspicious event, had first put the three of them together as an ensemble? As I did so, I began to reminisce about an old man I had not remembered in quite some time.

If he is still alive, he would be over a hundred by now. In my youth, when I lived in the countryside, he was in and out of our house often, especially at New Year, when pine boughs and *mochi*[6] were being prepared. Usually he was the sort who hung back in the shadows, only coming forward to do menial tasks like raking up the leaves or cleaning out the bamboo water pipes.

At the end of the year, or at New Year or the equinox, however, he came to the fore as the one we all relied on.

He was like a living dictionary who knew how high to stack the rice steamers, how long the bamboo shafts on the pine decoration attached to the gate should be, the proper dimensions of mirror *mochi*,[7] and many other such things.

My mother and father also consulted with him often, leaving many things up to him altogether and probably making other decisions only after checking with him first. For myself, I went further and concluded

2. 772–846. A Chinese poet who has been especially popular in Japan since ancient times.

3. *San'yū*. The combination of the three is particularly prominent as a topic in painting (*gadai*).

4. 794–1180. The golden age of the Japanese imperial court.

5. A reference to a poem in *Tosa nikki*, the travel record of Ki no Tsurayuki (d. 949?): "Gazing out, I see / cranes perching in the tops / of all the pines. / Millennial companions are they, / so it truly seems" (*miwataseba / matsu no ure goto ni / sumu tsuru wa / chiyo no dochi to zo / omou bera naru*). A slightly different version of the poem also appears in Tsurayuki's personal anthology.

6. Pounded rice cakes, a traditional New Year food.

7. Round, flat *mochi* cakes displayed during the New Year season.

that if he did not appear, there would be no doll display. Likewise, I thought that he was the one to decide on which day the *kotatsu*[8] should be brought out. Thinking back on it now, I know the old man could not have been correct all the time. Rather, it was a matter of my family and others in the neighborhood looking to him with unswerving confidence.

Once one begins probing into the meaning of such observances, there is no end to it. In many cases, people end up following established ways just for peace of mind: one finds it hard to decide the matter by oneself, yet lacks the courage to dispense with tradition. If one accepts the notion that for ritual forms to have continued so long, there must be something behind them, then they settle down into what feels like truth.

In this process of settling into truth, there are some hesitations, however—even if one still has not the courage to dispense with traditions altogether. And one cannot deny that at such times one unconsciously misses that old man, wondering at where such confidence, such stubbornness, could have come from.

Ancient people also did not comprehend the meaning of such ritual forms completely, but all the same they constructed them, protected them, and proceeded with them step-by-step down a road the end of which could not be seen—and in so doing, I believe, preserved harmony in a universe full of mysteries and unknowns. Perhaps my plant ensemble, too, deserves to be called a thing of wonder.

I enjoyed many conversations with those Three Friends who visited me. At times, I even relied on them to lead me down unexpected and happy trains of thought. When I was discharged from the hospital three months later, it was with those three unforgettable gifts in my hands that had helped me through a hard time.

Evening Bell

Once, back before the rail lines were well established, I was riding in a bus on the coastal road in southwestern Shikoku.

8. A low table with a heater underneath, covered with a quilt.

There were so many cars getting on and off the road and the road was so bumpy that I was unable to peacefully enjoy the scenery. Not without cause, I was a bit fearful for my safety from time to time, but a few scenes along the coast do stand out in my mind, particularly a view of the Pacific one evening that stretched out from the cliffs below my window—that and the wondrous combination of the sky as it changed color and the beach pines and the white sand now appearing, now disappearing from view.

Traveling somewhere that you can get to by rail or by bus is a fine thing, and there are even good things about sightseeing tours of temples and shrines where you stay in hotels. But when I remember bouncing along on that bus seat, my mouth covered with the sand and dust of the coastal cliffs, I think to myself that it truly is a little selfish to be so readily satisfied with pleasant views that have been too easily obtained.

Ōhara in Kyoto and Murō in Nara are quite different in appearance, yet both are unpretentious enough to be called villages, and I am fond of early morning and nightfall in both places. Especially in the evening, when there is almost no movement in one's field of sight and the colors recede ever so gradually into various shades of darkness, one feels oneself also becoming just another object in that landscape, unable to forget how useless one feels, body and soul, standing there in the empty sky.

Among the poems of the monk Nōin, who is well known for his many trips into the northern hinterlands, is this one:

To a mountain village
at nightfall, on a spring day,
I came—and saw this:
blossoms scattering on echoes
from the vespers bell.[9]

yamazato no / haru no yūgure / kite mireba / iriai no kane ni / hana zo chirikeru

The poem is not one that poses any difficulty for the reader to understand. Most readers will readily respond to the invitation to visit a

---

9. The most famous poem of Nōin (988–1050?), in *Shinkokinshū* (*New Collection of Ancient and Modern Times*, ca. 1205), poem 116, with the headnote "Written when he was visiting a mountain village."

mountain village at evening. But the poem is in fact very ingeniously conceived.

The impression the poem creates is of a quiet mountain village. Yet that stillness is revealed by the *movement* of echoes from the vespers bell and the falling blossoms, so that rather than by silence itself it is through things in motion—the sound, the falling petals—that the silence is expressed.

The reverberations of the bell sound cannot actually have caused the blossoms to fall from the branches; rather, it is a scene in which the bell is ringing and the blossoms are falling at the same time. Yet it does not seem strange to interpret the lines "blossoms scattering on echoes / from the vespers bell" to mean that the slight motion of the echoes sends flower petals dancing into the air. In fact, one might even claim that such a reading brings out the depths of the silence that the author, in straightforward and unadorned words, probably wanted to evoke.

Thus I believe that Nōin's poem indirectly shows us that we need not always use movement to express movement, instead relying on stillness to do so—although this is an effect of the poem that may go beyond the poet's intent.

Mishima Yukio[10] left us distinctive approaches to writing, not only in his novels but equally in his plays and criticism. Among his plays is one called *The Wife of the Marquis de Sade*.

In the play, a number of women speak of de Sade, though de Sade himself is not in the cast. This method can probably be traced back to the story "In a Grove" by Akutagawa Ryūnosuke.[11] One thing that links Mishima and Akutagawa is the question "What is truth?" but I also think that, while at different times, Nōin, Akutagawa, and Mishima all felt exactly the same thing and for a single moment expressed themselves in exactly the same way.

10. 1925–1970. A novelist.
11. 1892–1927. A novelist. His story "In a Grove" became the basis for the famous film *Rashomon* (1950), directed by Kurosawa Akira. The story treats a single event from the perspective of many characters and puts the nature of "truth" into question.

Ants

One big solitary ant was crawling effortlessly along the edge of my veranda.

He was so big that I could see his features clearly without bringing my face any closer. From time to time, he would stop, exactly as if he were thinking.

It was on a summer afternoon, before the sun had started to go down, and I was in the house, taking in the laundry, all of it quite dry. After lightly misting the bathrobes and white *tabi* stockings, I stretched the wrinkles out, folded them neatly, and then put them between flower mats[12] and spread them out on the veranda. Only women and children sit on flower mats—although I am talking not about the present but days gone by.

I thought back to one of the many summer afternoons I spent in the countryside when my mother was still quite young and my children still infants. It must have been the ant on the veranda that brought it back to mind. A big ant had come in from the garden onto the edge of the flower mat and down the vein of a board in the hallway floor, moving and then stopping now and then, in exactly the same way. The ears of the Chinese lantern plant had turned red, signaling that it was time for Obon.[13] (In the countryside where I grew up, we celebrated only the old Obon.)

Just two or three days before this, in the morning, I had opened the rain shutters and looked out into the garden, for no particular reason. Suddenly, while I was looking over at some low-lying grass, I noticed something pitch-black, about an inch in diameter, clinging to a fallen leaf. The dark sheen of the thing engulfed by the surrounding greenery and the yellow cast of the fallen leaves had caught my eye.

I stepped down into the garden.

Wondering why I had noticed this when I just as easily might not have, I drew closer to the black object and realized that it was slowly wriggling.

It was a cluster of ants.

Within the cluster were smaller clumps of tiny ants.

---

12. *Hanamushiro.* Rugs decorated with floral patterns.
13. The Festival of the Dead, held midway through the Seventh or Eighth Month, depending on the locale.

Something pale green in color was there in the midst of the ants. It looked like a bowler hat—or like an airplane that had crashed into the ocean with only its tail section exposed. But it turned out to be a green insect, already half devoured, trembling only slightly in response to the movement of the ants.

Reacting against the sight, I looked away, up into the sky.

Then I lowered my eyes to what was taking place down on the ground.

Morning trains were going by frequently on the tracks close by—just as always. Birds were chirping. I could hear the light step of the paperboy.

Adjust your point of view, people say. If you get too attached to one point of view, you will make mistakes, not seeing things for what they really are; we must be flexible enough to change our perspectives.

That is an easy thing to say, of course. But the most difficult task of all may be that of remaining flexible enough to change one's view of oneself.

These days, it seems perfectly acceptable to use the phrase "that other person inside me" at certain times. Yet, for me at least, adopting someone else's view of myself—no matter how important it may be to do so— is never easy.

In the same way, I wonder about those who say they see others as clearly as they see themselves. Probably most of the time such people are only deluding themselves into thinking they can look at someone else the way they are looked upon, while only imagining the other person based on what is most easy to apply from their own experience.

When I read a fine book, I am unfailingly impressed with the author's ability to look at both himself and others impartially. Surely, this must come from training. But training alone may not be enough.

Eyes

After mailing off a manuscript I had promised someone, I took some extra time and stopped in at the park on my way home. Being conscious that I am of an age when eyestrain becomes inevitable, I always take a little time each day to look far up into the sky or gaze at the green of trees and grasses. It is my good fortune to have a wooded park nearby.

The park has both a baseball diamond and tennis courts. Although I have no talent for any kind of sport, I do like to watch people playing from time to time, drawn by the pleasant feeling I get watching young people looking so intent on their games.

No one swinging a bat or a racket can afford to look away, so the expression in the eyes of people as they throw and hit and run around is full of life and completely focused. Even though I do not know where they come from or whose children they might be, what they do is still impressive—and beautiful.

On that day, the sound of tennis balls was producing such delightful echoes that I walked over to take a look. Four young women, doubtless university or high-school students, were enjoying a fast-paced game of doubles. At midcourt was a group of younger girls, teasing the players as they chased down balls that went out of bounds. These girls seemed to be younger sisters or friends who had been invited to watch the four girls on the court.

Soon I was standing right behind the younger girls. As I looked briefly away from the blur of bodies in motion out on the court, one of the young girls turned to look at me, and suddenly I knew that I had seen her somewhere before. I remembered her face; of that I was sure. Perhaps she felt the same thing, for she turned once again to glance back at me, as if she were trying to place me. But then she ran off after a loose ball, evidently giving up on remembering who I was.

It had happened two weeks or so ago.

After doing my evening shopping by the train station, I was standing in front of the crossing gates waiting for a train to pass, my shopping basket dangling from one hand, when suddenly the handlebars of a bicycle that had come up beside me lightly struck my basket. At just the same moment, the girl who got off the bicycle asked me,

"Ma'am, is there a doctor nearby?"

She was breathing hard, and there was sweat on the end of her nose. She was perhaps an older grade-school student or maybe just into junior high. One look at her told you she was in a panic.

"A doctor? What kind of doctor?" I responded.

"A surgeon. We need a surgeon. Grandma told me to go and get one right away."

Unfortunately, the only doctors that came to mind were internists or pediatricians or ear-nose-and-throat doctors.

"A surgeon? Well, let me see. The nearest one I know of is . . ."

Just at that moment the train passed by, drowning out every other sound. The look on the girl's face said that she could wait no longer.

"A police box, then—is there a police box nearby?" she asked.

"Up at the top of the hill."

This time, I replied quickly. The girl bowed deeply and sped off, her hair flying behind her in the wind. I had no idea what had happened at her house. From the expression in her eyes, I could only tell that she must be facing something serious, going through something she had never experienced.

Looking at the girl as I stood there at courtside, I felt relieved—doubly so that she seemed not to remember who I was.

[*TAKENISHI HIROKO CHŌSAKUSHŪ*, VOL. 4 (TOKYO: SHINCHŌSHA, 1996)]

42

Sunday Musings

Hiraiwa Yumie

The only child of the head priest of Yoyogi Hachiman Shrine in Tokyo, Hiraiwa Yumie (b. 1932) had a very traditional upbringing and education, which included dance and music. After graduating with a degree in Japanese literature from Japan Women's University in 1954, she apprenticed herself to popular novelist Togawa Yukio (1912–2004) and attended the workshops of Togawa's mentor, Hasegawa Shin (1884–1963), one of the most popular writers of the day who was famous for his samurai novels.

In 1959, Hiraiwa was awarded the Naoki Prize and since that time has been a highly prolific and popular writer. Her long-running series Onyado kawasemi (Kingfisher Inn)—detective stories set in the Edo period—has been made into several television dramas, and she has been active writing scripts for plays and other television dramas, as well as historical fiction and romance novels. She has won the Yoshikawa Eiji Prize and the Kikuchi Kan Prize, and served on the selection committee for the Naoki Prize from 1987 until 2010. She is married to Itō Masateru, who succeeded her father as priest at Yoyogi Hachiman Shrine, and has two daughters.

The essays here—"Mibae" (Good Looks), "Sanjū sū nen mae no ichidoru" (That Dollar Thirty-Odd Years Ago), "Inu to ame" (Our Dog and the Rain), "Ningengirai" (Misanthropy), "Konchū no koto" (On Insects), and "Majo no ichigeki" (The She-Devil Strikes)—first appeared as a column in the weekly Sunday edition of the Mainichi shimbun.

Good Looks

Someone gave up a seat to me on the train.

It was a young woman about the same age as my daughter.

"Please, come ahead," she said. I quickly looked right and left. Somehow I didn't think she was talking to me.

But there were only students on both sides of me. They were chatting noisily together.

Since it was clear that it was me she was yielding her seat to, I said thank you and, a little flustered, sat down. But still, I could not accept the idea.

I *was* relieved to sit down, physically, that is. The night before, I had been up late writing and was feeling exhausted. I had intended to go by taxi, but hearing that there had been an accident on the Metropolitan Highway involving a cargo truck, and that traffic was all backed up, I felt better going by rail. I had started on the subway and then transferred to the National Railway.

So I was grateful, but on the other hand I was left thinking to myself that I was at an age now when people would give up their seat to me.

I was getting more farsighted, and the white in my hair was showing more and more, so there was really nothing to be surprised about, but it was dispiriting to think that I would now be sitting in Silver Seats.[1]

Just a week later, I had a phone call from a grade-school friend. We discussed what she had called about, and then she added, "My daughter says she ran into you the other day—on the train."

"Your daughter?"

"Yes. She said you looked really worn-out standing there, but when she gave you her seat, you didn't seem to recognize her. She thought your eyes must be getting pretty bad."

So that was it, I thought. The face of the girl from kindergarten days and grade-school days floated up before my eyes. But the images didn't mesh.

---

1. Seats on Japanese trains, usually near the door, that are reserved for senior citizens.

"I must not have recognized her," I said.

Then I realized that I hadn't taken a good look at the face of the person who had been so kind to me. No doubt, it was because I had been self-conscious about being offered a seat.

"Tell her I'm so sorry."

"Not to worry. But when you're out, at least, you should try to look feminine. We're at an age where we can't get by on beauty or reputation."

After a few minutes, we promised to get together soon and hung up.

So that's what happened, I thought, with a sigh of relief.

The young woman had known me since she was a child, and I wanted to laugh it off by concluding that that was why she had offered me her seat—which allowed me the reassurance that I still had my looks.

I had thought myself resigned to becoming an old lady, but if there was one way in which I didn't want to be thought of as an old lady, that was it—in my looks.

Appearing feminine was no easy task, but there were appropriate looks for each period of life, I thought to myself—and that's fine. Then I began thinking about when I would go to get my hair dyed.

That Dollar Thirty-Odd Years Ago

Lately it seems that the number of foreigners on the streets has increased.

I get on the subway and end up sitting right across from a group of them, and in the supermarket it is no longer unusual to encounter a foreign woman buying tofu.

Just yesterday, when I was going out to walk the dog, I saw some young people playing in the courtyard in front of the shrine painfully trying to explain to some foreigners who had asked about the stone guardian dogs there.[2]

This reminded me of something that happened more than thirty years ago. It was just after the end of the war, and three American soldiers showed up at the office of the shrine where my family lived. They had

2. *Komainu.* Two such guardian figures are usually placed next to the steps of shrines to ward off evil.

a little piece of paper with an address written on it and were asking if someone might be so kind as to give them directions.

With considerable labor, I was able to pick up that they were going to visit a Japanese friend on a private matter.

My parents and our live-in students wouldn't put themselves forward but were waving their hands, telling me that some foreigners had come and pushing me out to speak with them because I was studying English at school—although it wasn't as if my grades were very good.

So it fell to me to show them the way. I may have wanted to show off to my parents a little, and probably I felt that it just wouldn't do to deny a request from Americans once it had been made.

Unfortunately, the address written on the piece of paper was in a troublesome area to navigate, a fire-ravaged spot that was a jumble of shanties and shacks with only a few houses poking up out of the ruins, and the house numbers were not in any order.

The American soldiers were in high spirits now that they had a Japanese child to guide them, and they began to talk to me, though what they said sounded like gibberish.

I just went haltingly along, occasionally saying "yes" and "no." First I asked at the police box and then at a shop, and some people were so concerned to see "the young lady from the shrine" (that's what they called me in those days) going off with some American soldiers that they came out to make sure I was all right. But somehow, the whole gaggle of us did in the end arrive noisily at the friend's house.

Even a child like me knew what sort of woman it was who opened the door after I pushed the buzzer, and the truth is that I was disgusted.

I said a quick "good-bye" and was about to run home when one of the American soldiers came after me and, before I knew what was happening, pushed a dollar bill into my hand.

When it dawned on me that it was a tip, I was mortified.[3] I thought about going back to return it, but I didn't know what to say, and with my pitiful language skills there was nothing I could do.

And then, too, a dollar bill was something unusual.

---

3. Even today in Japan, tipping is not standard practice. Being offered a tip is considered demeaning.

As I stood there, the gaggle of noisy people who had been coming along with me began talking.

"What's that?"

"Is that American money?"

The bill was passed around the group and then was back in my hand.

After everyone had left, I made my way home, thinking about what to do. I tossed the money into the prayer box in front of the outer shrine.

Even after more than thirty years, I still wonder what finally happened to that dollar bill.

Our Dog and the Rain

Our family dog is a tough Shiba,[4] but he does hate the rain. He's especially bothered when his paws get wet or dirty, and he painstakingly licks them in his doghouse. Unusually for a dog, the area around his toenails is pink, which is touching somehow.

We were told that before coming to us he had lived for a while as a stray, but his fastidious habits make us imagine that he must have been kept inside a house when he was a puppy.

He likes to keep his paws clean, but still he is a dog, and he loves going for a walk. Although not all that clever, he knows the words "walk" and "food," and at least once every morning he whines fawningly when someone is getting ready to take him out for a walk. I'm the one who's supposed to take him in the evening, but we seldom end up going.

He understands that an evening walk is something extra, and when we do go on one, he shows more joy than he does in the mornings.

For this reason I, too, feel good about taking him, and in the afternoon, when he is lolling around in the garden, I'll end up making him a promise, saying, "Later on we'll take you for a walk." When evening comes, he's practically menacing in the way he pesters me to go.

The other day, the weather was fine and I had finished what I had been working on after lunch, so I promised to take him out. When the time

---

4. A Japanese breed similar in characteristics to the more famous Akita breed but considerably smaller. The breed was created for hunting and is known for independence and spirited behavior.

came, however, a light rain had started to fall. Our garden is quite small and is covered by the canopy of a zelkova tree, underneath which you don't notice a light rain. And so the dog was wagging his tail, urging me to keep my promise. There was nothing for it, so my husband got out the umbrella and they headed out.

As soon as they left the shrine precincts, the dog started fussing about the rain. To avoid getting wet, he would walk under the trees, and when they left the front street on the usual course, he still tried to avoid the rain by bounding from beneath the eaves of one house to the next, one after another.

After a while, they came out onto a road where there were no trees and no eaves anywhere in sight. When he realized this, the dog tried to get under the umbrella, walking clumsily in a way that brought him up against my husband's legs. This made walking very difficult for my husband, but he couldn't very well shoo him away, so they continued on their happy journey. People passing by looked back at them in wonder.

When the rain started coming down hard, they took refuge for a time under the eaves of a house. As he stood there, my husband felt someone pushing at his knees from behind—pushing him out from under shelter. Because he had his umbrella up, he was not getting wet, but when he turned around, the offender was none other than our dog, who had moved into the space my husband had vacated and was crouching down to escape the rain. Not a very loyal dog, surely—but he showed no sign of being aware of it as he fussed about his wet paws, which at the moment nothing could be done about.

Out of sorts because the rain kept on coming down no matter how long they waited, they dashed back home, and the dog jumped into his doghouse and began his cleanup regimen.

I had heard on television that there was a strong likelihood that rain falling in Tokyo for the next few days would contain radiation carried from the Soviet Union because of atmospheric conditions, and that we should wash our vegetables and not drink rainwater.[5] Could it be that our dog somehow knew this? No, surely . . .

5. A reference to the Chernobyl disaster of April 26, 1986, in which a meltdown at the nuclear power plant in that city in Ukraine released large amounts of radioactive vapors into the atmosphere.

Misanthropy

The older one gets, I have heard, the more one prefers insects and plants to people.

Lately I feel as if I see this tendency in myself.

When I was younger, I loved people.

Family and friends were always warning me that good-natured people end up looking foolish, but on numerous occasions I trusted people too readily and committed myself too totally, thinking that a person was really nice, only to have the tables turned on me in the end.

Each time I would be downcast, wondering why someone could not understand my feelings, until I gradually got used to feeling that way.

As the years went by, I became very cautious about getting close to anyone. No matter how friendly a person was toward me, I would be careful not to get too intimate. I was particularly careful when it came to women.

I was a woman, after all, so it was not hard to keep a certain distance from men. The problem was with women: someone would begin leaning on me, and finally I would feel unable to move. Then the other person would say something like, "I don't need you propping me up," and I would be shocked. I would get angry and complain, and as a result, end up disheartened by my own lack of spiritual resources. Recovering from my self-loathing was not easy.

If it was someone involved with my work, the person would of course be dependent on me, and, to that extent, we could work together with complete trust and sincerity. In private matters, though, I tried to keep things light and aloof.

Of course, I did have a group of friends from grade school with whom I had shared my feelings over all that time. We could be open and unselfish with one another and enjoy one another's company.

Some of my friends think of me as the solitary type, and there is some truth in that, but as an only child, I am used to doing things by myself. It was because I don't mind being alone that I became a writer. Even now, I don't mind riding all alone for a long time on a train or whiling away my time on something entirely for myself.

I prefer working at home to working outside among other people. In recent years, this tendency has become even more pronounced.

My interest in flowers and plants is also much greater compared with when I was young.

I thought the *matsumushi* flowers[6] that I saw last year at Takahara in Hachigatake[7] were so pretty that I am thinking of visiting there again this year.

When I mentioned this to one of my mentors, he laughed and said, "So you're still at the flower and plant stage—not to rocks yet." According to him, it is when you develop an interest in rocks that you know you are truly old.

I almost said that I had nothing to do with rocks, but then stopped short. Last year, I had gone to a stone dealer with some friends associated with my mentor and teacher, Hasegawa Shin, in order to arrange for a commemorative monument. We decided on a wonderful blue Iyo stone[8] and were very happy with our choice, and then I saw another stone, not so fine and smaller but still similar, and thought that I would like to get it because it was like the one we got for Hasegawa Sensei. I would not be using it as a monument but thought I might look at it in my garden and perhaps share in his good fortune. But thinking such a thing was so embarrassing that I dropped the idea. I'm glad that I didn't buy that stone.

On Insects

This summer, it was later in the year than usual that I heard the cicadas singing.

My house is in the grounds of a shrine, so from childhood I have had a close relationship with summer insects.

Cicadas, scarabs, butterflies, grasshoppers, bell crickets, crickets, grasshoppers, and in the pond, whirligigs and skippers.

At night, when I was sitting at my desk doing my homework, scarabs would fly in through the open window, knocking themselves silly bumping into the lampstand.

6. Literally, "pine-cricket grass" (*Scabiosa atropurpurea*), a purple wildflower that can blanket whole fields in alpine or subalpine regions.
7. Hachigatake is located in Nagano Prefecture.
8. *Iyo no aoishi.* A greenish blue stone originally found in the riverbeds of the Iyo region that is widely used in ornamental Japanese-style gardens.

In the daytime, it was *jiijii* cicadas, *minmin* cicadas, *ooshiikku* cicadas; in the evening, the sound was *kanakana*.[9] And at night, the sky was given over to grasshoppers.

During the decade or so after the war, insects began to vanish, one by one. Only the cicadas fought to the end.

Most years, the *jiijii* cicadas started to sing—not a very pleasant sound—about the end of the summer rainy season. Only later, when summer was in full swing, would you hear the *minmin* cicada, and finally, at the very end, the *ooshiikku* and *kanakana*.

But this summer, even though I was listening for them, there was no singing.

I thought that it might just be me, but when I asked the other people in the house, they all said that they hadn't heard anything either.

The cicada song may not be that pretty, but it was unsettling not to hear something one was so used to hearing, and I couldn't help wondering what was going on.

When I mentioned this to an acquaintance on the phone, he laughed and said that it must be because of more buildings in the area or because we had cut down trees in the shrine precincts, but I said that neither of those things was true. Then he got serious and said, "You know, it must be because of that Chernobyl business."

It is true that radioactive rain had fallen on Japan after the nuclear accident.

In Europe, rabbits had been born without ears, and radioactivity had been detected in reindeer meat.

According to him, the insect population of Yoyogi had been completely wiped out by the fallout.

"Nonsense," I laughed to myself, but then I began to worry. It was midway through July, and still the cicadas weren't singing.

My daughter said it was because it had been cold so far into the year.

One night just two days before the beginning of August, I was bent over my paper, writing, when I heard it: the weak voices of *minmin* and *kanakana* cicadas. But what about the *jiijii*?

9. Different kinds of cicadas, characterized by the different sounds they make.

The next day, I heard the same thing. The songs sounded frail and strained.

"Finally!" I thought, all the same.

Minmin cicadas are the stupidest ones, the ones I had most often managed to catch as a child.

They would cling to the tree trunk and not fly off, even when you approached. From the window of my workroom, I looked out at them and said, "What's with you, anyway? Has the radiation gotten to you?"

This summer, it seems to me there weren't many cicadas singing around my house. The "cicada showers" that used to be almost an annoyance I never heard.

The She-Devil Strikes

When I told my friend that I'd thrown my back out, she quipped that I had probably been carrying some heavy book.

That image was better than the truth, which is that I had opened the refrigerator door and peeked in, looking for something to snack on. That's when it hit me: a pain so bad that I stood bolt upright, unable to speak, let alone move. And what everyone I told about it said came down to the same thing: "God is punishing you."

Why should I be punished? Why, because I had been warned that I was too fat for my health and that I should refrain from eating so much. I had not heeded the warning but gone on eating whatever I could get my hands on, day after day. This is your punishment—you're getting what you deserve, my friends all said. No one showed me any sympathy.

The intense pain—called the strike of the she-devil—was finally brought under control, thanks to the efforts of a masseur, but for some days I was hampered in my movements, unable to bend. Bowing became an ordeal.

As fate would have it, we were dealing with a number of troubles around that time, and I was not able to use my body efficiently—bowing clumsily and feeling irritated with myself.

Almost every time I explained that I had thrown my back out, there were one or two people in the group who said that they had done the same thing some years before. One would say, "You should use ice," and another, "Heat will fix it." "You should stabilize your back by wrapping it in bleached cloth." "Acupuncture will work." "Massage therapy is best." "Your best chance for avoiding a relapse is a chiropractor." I was amazed at how everyone had such informed opinions.

It appeared that the world was full of people who had experienced back pain.

The circumstances in which people were stricken were various, but the most common were bending over to wash one's face first thing in the morning or to get a pack of cigarettes from a vending machine.

I had one acquaintance who was a real authority and said that if it concerned throwing your back out, he had all the answers. According to him, the cause was fatigue, cold, and stress all hitting together.

That described my case perfectly.

I had not had enough sleep for some days, and the night before, I had been sitting in a place too close to the air conditioner for a long time. In addition, this summer, my schedule had not worked out as I would have liked. My work had been going slowly and I had had no time for a summer holiday, while other people kept telling me about the fun they had been having on their vacations. Enough, I would think, and get angry.

So according to the authority on back pain, I had thrown my back out because—well, because it was simply inevitable.

On top of that, I realized myself that lack of exercise and being fat had been the triggers.

According to a graph displaying the proper balance between height and weight among Japanese people—which I really didn't need to look at in order to know—I was just over the line between plump and fat.

A friend had said, "There's more to life than clinging to your desk—you should get involved in sports . . ."

But then she burst out laughing.

"Come to think of it, though, you've never been any good at anything you could call a sport. You'd probably try something you weren't used to and—and throw your back out!"

Then she laughed again.

[*SUIYŌBI NO HITORIGOTO* (TOKYO: BUNSHUN BUNKO, 1995)]

43

Not Much of a Book, but Please . . . and Just Be Sure You're Not a Bother to Anyone

DEKUNE TATSURŌ

Dekune Tatsurō was born in 1944 in wartime Japan, in Ibaraki Prefecture. In his early teens, he went to Tokyo to serve as a shop boy in a used bookshop, and in 1973 he opened his own place in the Kōenji area of the city. In his spare time, he wrote essays and stories, much as his father—a persistent, if unsuccessful, writer—had done as Dekune was growing up.

In 1992, Dekune won the Kōdansha Essay Prize and the next year received the prestigious Naoki Prize for one of his novels. He has gone on to become a major figure in popular literature, writing many volumes of essays—often chronicling his experiences in the world of used bookshops—as well as historical novels portraying Edo- and Meiji-period popular culture. Most of his essays appeared first in various periodicals, subsequently being published as collections. The essays translated here come from two collections published in the early 1990s: the first three from Hon no okuchi yogoshi desu ka *(Not Much of a Book, but Please . . .), and the latter three from* Hitosama no meiwaku *(Just Be Sure You're Not a Bother to Anyone).*

Dust Mogul

When I opened my used bookshop, I put a sign up in front saying,

In Business *ZERO* Years
Giving Top Dollar for Old Books,
So Bring 'em In—Dust and All!

One customer showed up with books covered with dust and asked, "Do you really want them 'dust and all' "? He must have jumped to the conclusion that the books would be more valuable with their dust intact, and when bringing them in he took great pains not to let any of it fall. But what surprised me even more was when a customer showed up one day asking if I would *sell* him some dust.

I had gone to buy books at an old house so grand that in an earlier day it could have been the home of a feudal lord. There I was shown into a storehouse, which had doubtless never known the touch of a broom. The dust that had piled up on everything was like so much fine spring snow. I was so excited that I snitched a pinch of it from far at the back, where things looked the oldest. I put it in an empty cigarette box and back in the shop showed it off to some customers, explaining that it was something from the Edo period.

The dust was very fine textured, like high-grade flour. In the shade, it gave off a black luster; in the sunlight, it glowed like silver. It truly seemed to be something of noble provenance.

As word gets around, exaggeration sets in. Some people even came from far away to get a peek, asking if the dust was really from the Heian period [794–1185]. One time I was amazed to receive an inquiry asking if it was true that I had dust from the Shōsōin.[1] There was even one crazy fool who took a pinch of the dust, then licked his finger, and was about to give it a taste before I stopped him.

Finally, someone showed up wanting to buy some. He suggested a price of five thousand yen. I was completely taken aback and turned him down immediately. He persisted but in the end left the shop quite disappointed. It appeared that he hadn't been joking. Later someone told me that the man must have been an antiques dealer. They apparently use

---

1. A famous storehouse dating to the Nara period (710–794) that contains a large collection of ancient Chinese and Japanese artworks and artifacts.

dust to make objects look older. "You should have sold him some!" my friend laughed.

He was right: if I had had any business sense, I would have turned all the dust in that storehouse into gold, and by now I would be known as the Dust Mogul. I had an unbelievable opportunity to make money, and I let it get away.

In the Graveyard

In my hometown, the Obon Festival[2] was held according to the ancient calendar, and we always visited the graveyard in the evening. After lighting beautiful paper lanterns, people would take their offerings and go off together as a family. Everyone wore newly made *yukata*,[3] and the children carried lanterns that we called Chinese plant lanterns because of their special shape and color. As there was no recently deceased ancestor in our own house, I was full of envy for the other children. I made myself such a nuisance whining for a lantern that my father got angry and said, "Don't court bad luck."[4]

Then recently my father died, and we had to put up a grave marker.

For a variety of reasons, it fell to me to make the arrangements. The place was very bright, with a lawn so broad that it could be mistaken for a park. But it was not very conveniently located for someone like me, living in Tokyo. Visiting took up a whole day.

My wife and I arranged our flower offerings before the grave and then stretched our legs out on the lawn and began eating the boxed lunches we had brought along. The feel of the wind on my face was pleasant, but perhaps because of the surroundings we ended up talking about life after death.

"After I die, I'll be looking out on this scene from this very spot every day. It's peaceful and all, and you couldn't really ask for finer

2. The Festival of the Dead, held midway through the Seventh Month of the old calendar. The primary activity associated with the event is visiting the graves of ancestors as a family to present offerings in hope of their salvation.

3. Light summer robes.

4. *Engi demo nai.* In other words, "Do you want someone to die, then?"

surroundings, but the fact is, I've never been that interested in scenery. So within a few minutes, I'll be bored. It's really awful that after death you can't read books," I said as I set about breaking up the inner shell of my pickled plum to get at the pit.

"Then I'll bring you books once in a while," my wife replied. "Make up a list of what you want and leave it for me."

So I began considering one by one the books I would read after I died.

It was then that I remembered a short essay I had read sometime before by Takamine Hideko.[5] As she was getting on in years, she began to put her affairs in order, she had written. She had no children, so when the time for death came, she and her husband were planning to jump off a boat. She went so far as to write rather blithely that the two of them had made a pact to strap encyclopedias to their backs and jump in the water together. Reading this gave me the chills. The image of the encyclopedias on their backs was too vivid. For her, the books were no more than aids for suicide.[6]

"What kind of encyclopedias were they?" my wife asked.

"What does that matter?" I replied, evasively.

We don't have children either. We will be wandering as unmourned spirits. And after death, the only books I will be opening will have to be ones strapped to my back when I go.

One of the Superrich

One year, snow fell on Christmas Eve. I decided to close up early and was out front taking the sign in when a really drunk man in his thirties came bursting in, asking me to buy a book.

When I quoted him a price, he begged me to give him just a little more for it, saying that tomorrow was payday and he would come and buy the book back. At first I said that I wasn't running a pawnshop and refused, but then he began listing his troubles. It turned out that he had drunk away the money he should have used to buy a gift for his child.

5. B. 1924. A famous actress who appeared in films such as *Twenty-four Eyes* (1954) and *Floating Clouds* (1955).
6. *Jisatsu no dōgu*. Literally, "suicide instruments."

"I just can't go home empty-handed," he said, bowing over and over again—then he started to cry.

I detest people who get drunk and lose control of themselves, but I surmised that what he said about getting a gift for his child wasn't altogether a lie. So for the child's sake, I gave in and handed over what he wanted. He quickly recovered his spirits and shouted out in English, "Thank you very much! Jingle Bells! Merry Christmas!"

As I had expected, there was no sign of him the next day. The lousy bastard used his own kid to get to me, I thought. As time went on, I was more angry with myself for being such an easy mark than I was with him.

On the evening of the last day of the year, a couple came into the shop, with a little girl in tow. The man bowed to me. Taking a close look, I saw that he was the drunk from Christmas Eve. He was so reserved and looked so serious that I hadn't recognized him.

He thanked me for the other night and then apologized, saying that he had had such a hangover the last few days that he hadn't been able to go out.

"Yeah, you were in a pretty cheerful state," I said sarcastically, and he became silent.

"When he gets drunk, he's another person—I don't know what to do with him," his wife laughed.

At that point, the husband asked, "Do you still have that book?"

"Yes," I said, and took it out. When he asked how much it would be, I quoted the price we had agreed on that night.

"No, that's ridiculous. A bookstore has to stay in business, after all," he said, red-faced.

As we were haggling, the wife butted in. "Wait a minute. Don't we already have this book?"

Flustered, the man explained that it was a different book. But then she said that the book was awfully expensive and wouldn't back off.

I tried to throw him a line. "It's a rare book, so the price is high."

The little girl, who had been quietly watching all this time, said in a loud voice, full of pride:

"Today, Daddy's one of the superrich!"

At that, we all broke down and had a good laugh.

Inexplicable

As customers go, he was nothing unusual, just a stout fortyish gentleman who showed up from time to time. He purchased a complete set of books on flower arranging that was too heavy and cumbersome to carry, so I delivered it to his house the next day.

On the nameplate outside—a rather large one—his wife's name was inscribed next to his.

"Please have some tea before you go," he insisted. The house was oddly cold.

I was invited into the study. As I walked, I heard the sound of something crunching under the soles of my slippers and looked down to see beans scattered all over the floor.

"The kid did that—got worked up and scattered far too many," the man explained.

So that's it, I thought, remembering that last night had been the equinox.[7]

The books in the study were all by women. I wondered if the gentleman might be doing research on women's history. He was taking a long time getting the tea.

He was standing in the kitchen calling, "Miriko, Miriko," but Miriko didn't materialize, and he brought in the tea himself, wearing a white apron.

"The wife seems to have gone out on some errand," he apologized, obviously embarrassed.

For some reason, the conversation went nowhere.

As it had begun to rain, I borrowed an umbrella when I left. It was pink, a lady's umbrella, evidently his wife's, and the man was a little chagrined.

I wondered what the Chinese characters for the name Miriko would be, and checked the nameplate as I left. When I got home, I looked up the characters in the dictionary but couldn't find that reading. It must have been a special way of reading them used in names. Or perhaps it was a nickname.

---

7. Setsubun, celebrated on February 3, around the beginning of the lunar year. By custom, the head of the house threw roasted soybeans out the front door or at a family member wearing a demon mask in order to drive evil from the house.

Some days later, I bought some sweets as a thank-you gift and went to return the umbrella, and—wouldn't you know—the house was empty. Even the nameplate was gone.

When I asked next door, the people seemed a little put out and only said, "Yeah, it does seem like they moved out in a hurry." They had never heard of Miriko, however, and said rather guardedly that the man had lived alone. I insisted that there had been a child as well, but in fact I hadn't ever seen one. By then, the people were getting a little impatient, so I gave up and left. It was the wrong time of year for ghost stories, but to this day I still don't know what was behind it all.

The umbrella I had borrowed, at least, was real.

Mice

One day, I was approached by a classy-looking older lady who had a question.

"I have something a little unusual to ask you," she said, and what she asked was indeed unexpected.

"Do mice like old books?" she said.

Just about every night, they were appearing in her late husband's study, no matter what steps she took to stop them. She could only conclude that their target was the books.

I told her that mice do in fact damage books and encouraged her to use one of the very effective poisons that were around, but she quickly waved her hand and said that she didn't want to kill them.

What she did want was for me to inspect the place, so I went—out of curiosity, really. It was a Western-style room eight mats in size, with bookshelves on three walls. On the floor in front of the shelves sat a box the size of a minispeaker that, she explained, was a mouse-repulsing instrument. Someone had told her that it sent out strong electric waves that kept the mice away, and she had put it in just a few days before but didn't yet know how effective it was. Since the device didn't kill the mice but only kept them at bay, there was really no way to judge.

Her husband had died six months before, and since then she had left the study just as it was. "Cleaning it up would seem as if I were tormenting him," she said. "I just can't stand to do it."

There was nothing unusual about the room, and it didn't seem the sort of place that mice would want to take over. She said that her husband had been a diabetic.

When the lady was out of the room, I picked a book at random. Pulling it out, I discovered a paper bag there behind the bookshelf.

It was a bag of candy. As I looked behind all the books on that row, there they were—lots of bags of candy, all chewed on, with their contents scattered about. The husband must have liked to enjoy a little candy while he was reading, I thought. And he had been hiding it from his wife.

It wasn't the books that the mice were after, but the candy.

While the lady was out of the room, I hurried and cleaned everything up. I imagined the husband enjoying a moment of happiness there eating candy as he read his books.

"They won't trouble you anymore," I told her. "I've put a spell on them."

"Ah, I guess I was right to go to a used-book dealer," she said happily.

"But if they stop coming, I will be a little sad," she chuckled. "One of those mice might be my husband reincarnated, after all."

Man of Leisure

Obon and equinox holidays aren't the only times that one can visit graves. Some people go at New Year.

For many years, Mrs. K. had gone herself at that season, but as old age came on, she was having a harder time getting around, and making the trips became a chore. So she came to me, asking if I would find someone to go in her place, for a full day's pay.

In the past, I had been to her house to buy books. Her late husband had collected them as a hobby, and I had been amazed at the number he had accumulated.

"Myself, I hate books," the lady said, "they're so dirty. My husband and I were always arguing about it." She spoke rather spitefully, with her hand under her mouth.

Her husband was a strange sort who would bathe only about twice a year and never washed his face. All day long, he stayed locked up in his study. Mrs. K. hated dirt and wouldn't go near the place.

I don't know how he made his living, but the house I visited was very luxurious and well appointed by today's standards, so he must have inherited a fortune from his parents.

There beneath one roof, the two of them lived together, hardly setting eyes on each other—a strange sort of existence for a man and wife. Yet they had four children. When the father died, all the children left and never came around, not even to visit his grave. They were scattered hither and yon, living as they pleased. It seemed that the selfishness of their parents had been passed down.

Mrs. K. said they were all like him and had only harsh words for her husband, and yet every New Year she visited his grave.

"He hated bathing so much that I just enjoy washing him. I can just see him cringing right there in front of me as I pour ladle after ladle over the gravestone—just for the fun of it," she said, with a weird-looking smile on her face.

"But I'm afraid that I'll have to turn over the pleasure to someone else now."

When I questioned why she had come to a used-book dealer to ask about finding a substitute, she answered, with a straight face,

"I figure people who read books must not have much to do."

[*HON NO OKUCHI YOGOSHI DESU KA* (TOKYO: KŌDANSHA, 1991);
HITOSAMA NO MEIWAKU (TOKYO: KŌDANSHA, 1993)]

44

Myna Bird

KIZAKI SATOKO

Kizaki Satoko (the pen name of Yokoyama Masako) was born in 1939 in the Japanese puppet state of Manshū-koku (Manchuria) and witnessed the defeat of the Japanese forces there as a child. After the war, she returned to Japan, living in Toyama, where her father was a college professor. In 1960, she graduated from Tokyo Women's College and went to work in an office. She married two years later, spending ten years abroad (in France, then California, then France again) with her husband, an academic. From 1976 to 1979, she was in France again, studying comparative literature.

Kizaki began to write stories after returning to Japan in 1979. She was awarded the Akutagawa Prize for "Aogiri" (The Phoenix Tree) in 1985. In 1982, she was baptized into the Catholic Church, and many of her works have Christian themes. Her novel Shizumeru tera (The Sunken Temple, 1987; trans. 1993) received the Geijutsu Sensho New Writer Award from the Japanese Ministry of Education in 1988. The essay translated here, "Kyūkanchō" (Myna Bird), appeared in the June 1993 issue of the magazine Kaien.

I think it was at an exhibition. Had it been in Japan, it would have been at a department store, but it was in Paris, so it was at a hall in the Salon de Something-or-other. The surroundings remain murky in my mind, fading away even as I attempt to remember, but there was an old man standing there, rather sullenly, and in a cage next to him a myna bird was methodically belting out "La Marseillaise."

First the bird would introduce himself ("Bonjour, Claude!"), and then he would sing "La Marseillaise"—not all of it, of course, just the first few lines. But he got the melody and the rhythm right, and it fit perfectly with his glossy black feathers, his bright yellow beak, and most of all with those wide-open, expressionless eyes.

After shrieking out the French national anthem, the black bird would abruptly close its beak and withdraw into silence, becoming no more than a black clod, entirely inert, that wouldn't sing no matter how you poked it. I stood gazing at it, feeling truly amazed, but the old man showed no more sign than did the bird of accommodating onlookers or prompting another performance. I did figure out, though, from how the old man said, "Claude—hey you!" that it was his own name that the bird was calling out. The old man had a very arrogant look and demeanor, but then the bird was so impressive that I suppose arrogance was to be expected of the one who had trained him.

It may be that even before this, I had had within me a desire to own a myna bird, but it was on that occasion that I clearly realized that that was what I wanted. My husband loved birds and was always ready to adopt one, of any kind; in fact, he said the reason he had wanted to marry me was because he thought I walked like a duck. Since getting married, we had never been without a bird in the house. We had had about ten birds, I think, but never a myna bird. We did have a duck, just once. We put a board out in the middle of our little pond as a place for him to eat, and the rest of the time he was in the water, so I'm glad to say that I never had a chance to observe closely this way of walking that was so like my own. But whenever I looked at him, I had an image of myself seen from behind, awkwardly tottering along—not a happy feeling.

Our encounters with animals are like our encounters with people; it's not that we go out seeking them, but if we're looking, one day we just happen upon them. Thinking plays a role, but you can't just stand there staring, making appraisals and comparisons. One simply feels that *this* is the bird, *this* is the dog, *this* is the fish—and if you aren't certain that you must have it, then you will never gain its trust. One's resolve must be just right. That was the case when I met Leo. It was at an unexpected place, in a nearby supermarket. I had gone to buy groceries and happened to peek at gardening supplies on a different floor, where there was a "pet corner." And there he was. His dark black feathers and bright yellow beak had a fresh sheen to them, and as he cocked his head, his face was almost childlike. I knew nothing about birds, but even I could see that he was still quite young, perhaps even young enough to be called a chick.

It happened to be a Sunday, so I had my husband take a look at him, and then we joyfully took him home.

We put his cage—the same color as his beak—in a sunny spot facing the veranda, and he hopped in, his head cocked to one side. "What am I doing here?" he seemed to be wondering, and after letting out a loud squawk he appeared to be thinking that even his own voice was strange. It seemed as if he were paralyzed, not understanding himself but not conscious of his own doubts. Yet for some reason, this inspired affection. And I wasn't the only one feeling fascinated. My husband, too, was already behaving like a pet owner, claiming that the bird seemed especially smart, even before he had made an intelligible sound. Then there was my elderly mother, who usually sits on the couch all day long with the dog on her lap, reluctant to move an inch, but would now struggle to her feet to give the bird food or water—a very effective form of therapy for her, as it turned out.

It may offend them to say that their feathers are black as crows; but a myna bird's feathers do have that black, wet look. And the bright yellow arc of color that runs from their eyes to the back of their head is as dramatic as the makeup of a Kabuki actor.

We labored over choosing a name. For the man in question—or, rather, the bird in question—it should be a name that was easy to say, so we called him Leo, just two syllables, and the last one a vowel. Although it had been a long time ago, the memory of Claude was still vivid in my mind, and I was hoping that our bird would one day say, "Bonjour—Leo!" Then I thought better of that idea, asking myself, "But why in French?"—as would anyone, including the bird himself. Yet "Konnichi wa—Leo!" seemed too ordinary. For a time we considered "Ni hao—Leo!" since the bird seemed to have been born in China, but there was no one in the house who could teach him correct Chinese pronunciation. So we decided on "Arigatō" [Thank you]. As we repeated "Arigatō" each time we fed him, however, it was not Leo who was grateful, but Mama and I.

As I write this, I suddenly realize that Claude may have been the name of that old man himself. Probably he gave his own name to his beloved bird so that they could enjoy their days calling out to each other. When I remembered the old man's proud manner, I decided my conclusion could not be wrong. For someone with low self-esteem like myself, though, it would be impossible to repeat my own name over and over again as I tried to teach him to talk.

Then I remembered something else. Some years back, I had written a radio drama for *NHK FM Theater* titled "Myna Bird." It was a one-person drama about a middle-aged single woman harking back to her memories of childhood, and this now made the myna bird seem like "another self" inside myself, to whom I should be calling out. I wondered if being a myna bird might be a little more attractive than being a duck. The story had it that the woman had been born to a scholar in Manchuria, which was the case with me; and we were also similar in having complex feelings about the rise and fall of states and our relationship to those things.

I thought to myself how fortunate that old man was, teaching his beloved bird a song that symbolized his nation and listening to it at odd times every day. The myna bird in my radio drama would sing Barbara's chanson, "Le mal de vivre."[1] The idea of a myna bird singing "Kimi ga yo"[2] was beyond imagination, I thought to myself, and burst out laughing.

[*NAKAKURAI NO TSUMA*, ED. JAPAN ESSAY CLUB
(TOKYO: BUNGEI SHUNJŪ, 1993)]

1. A song by Barbara (Monique Andrée Serf; 1930–1997), a French singer. The Japanese title is "Kodoku" (Solitude).
2. The Japanese national anthem. A very solemn, sedate, and low-pitched tune that would indeed seem absurd if sung by a myna bird.

45

Concerning the Order of Culture

SHIROYAMA SABURO

Sugiura Eiichi (known by the pen name Shiroyama Saburo; 1927–2007) was the son of a Nagoya merchant. He began his professional life as an economist, earning his degree at Tokyo Shōka University, which would later become Hitotsubashi University. After a short career as a university lecturer, he began writing fiction, and in 1959 won the Naoki Prize for a fictional exposé of the world of stocks and stockholders. He was known mainly for his realistic "business novels" and his biographical novels based on the lives of important financial and political figures such as the Meiji-period entrepreneur and business leader Shibusawa Eiichi (1840–1931). His novels won him numerous other awards, including the Yoshikawa Eiji Prize, the Kikuchi Kan Prize, and the Asahi Prize.

As the following essay, "Kunshō ni tsuite" (Concerning the Order of Culture), reveals, however, there is one prize that Shiroyama refused to accept—the highly coveted Order of Culture (Bunka Kunshō), awarded each November by the Japanese government to leaders in the sciences, literature, music and the fine arts, architecture, and scholarship. As a young man, at the very end of the Pacific War, Shiroyama (then Sugiura) had enlisted in the navy and was in service at the time of the defeat in the summer of 1945. His experience at that time so disillusioned him with government in general that he remained highly skeptical of all national institutions until the end of his life.

A call from my wife came while I was at work.

"I just had a phone call—*the* phone call. What will you do?"

The tone of her voice told me that the news was nothing gloomy or serious. Yet neither did it seem like anything we had been waiting for.

She was intrigued and half anxious about my reaction.

"What phone call? What are you talking about?"

"It was from some office in the Ministry of Culture—an unofficial notification, but they are hoping you will accept."

"No," I said. "Tell them I will not accept."

"But they were so nice on the phone. Why are you so ready to say no?"

Her labored breathing seemed to say, for thirty-five years we've been living this way, always on a tight budget, beaten by wind and waves, and I'm tired of it.

"All right, then. I'll think about it for a bit. See you tonight."

I really didn't need to think about it, but that's what I said, and then I hung up.

———

A Western-style restaurant in the train station.

I got there first and ordered two dishes and drank some *shōchū* liquor with warm water.

I already had my reply to the government ready:

"I have done no work that would qualify me for such an honor."

But what was I going to tell my wife?

I considered appealing to the example of characters from my novels, but thought better of it. The point was that I didn't want to be subject to any judgment by the government, or to end up feeling muzzled by them.

I was still adding up my reasons when my wife arrived. I wasn't prepared enough, not drunk enough—just dangling in midair.

"I'm going to turn it down."

"But why?"

"What do you mean, 'Why?' They say writers who get medals die a dog's death, always at the government's beck and call."

Suddenly I had blurted out the real issue, but as usual I had gotten bothered and jumped right to the worst way of putting it.

"Don't you understand what I mean?"

She was silent. Then I put a final coat of paint on it.

"I thought I knew you better."

She wouldn't even pick up her chopsticks.

I hurried to say something and brought things to the worst possible finish.

"And listen, now. If the government comes around after I die, you aren't to accept anything."

"Bossing me around after you're dead—that's a little autocratic, don't you think?"

I thought about that and had to nod my head.

I thought of saying, "If you accept it, I'll come back and haunt you," but I could already imagine her answer:

"You don't say. Well, you just go right ahead."

I changed the direction of the conversation.

"Going to accept it would be such a pain. If only they would send it by special express or something, but . . ."

Now she gave me an angry look.

"The way you talk about it is a little rude to those who do accept it, don't you think?"

"No, no—I'm talking only about myself. When it comes down to it, I just don't have any faith in governments. From back when I was a soldier in my youth . . ."

That was all I could get out.

I gulped down some *shōchū* and picked at my boiled squid, and thought, gratefully, that this might work.

"This squid is enough of a medal for me."

No doubt my words surprised even the squid, but then I remembered the most important thing.

"My readers and you and the children—you're my medals. I don't need anything else."

Those words even surprised me a bit, but that was truly the way I felt.

I should have said this at the beginning.

The war clouds began to clear from my wife's brow.

"*To know one has enough . . . ,*" I said.

The quote was from a note on the white door of our refrigerator.

Mostly she put cooking recipes on the door, but the other day she had heard the phrase "To know one has enough is to be ever happy"[1] and written it down and told me about it.

––––––––––––––

My wife didn't know it, but I already had a medal. Or, rather, I *had* had a medal in the past.

I hadn't been awarded it, though—I had bought it.

It was in the city, in the dark days just after the defeat.

Above, blue sky stretching far and high; below, packs of people crawling around.

In the dust of the grass at the roadside, a pan and a kettle—and squeezed in between them what looked like a painted tin toy but was in fact a medal.

There was a military decoration next to it. When I thought of the soldiers and the nobility, I could only close my eyes and ponder.

If it was the usual sort of medal, it was probably something some official had awarded himself and was of the right sort of value to be sold at the roadside.

To test whether our new society was truly one in which there were no more social distinctions, I asked the old man in the shop how much. His complexion was the color of winter melons.

The price was what it cost to buy a couple of used books.

1. *Chisoku wa jōraku.* A Chinese proverb the origin of which is probably two statements in the *Daodejing*: "He who knows contentment is rich" and "Hence in being content, one will always have enough" (Lao Tzu, *Tao Te Ching*, trans. D. C. Lau [Baltimore: Penguin, 1963], 81, 92).

I didn't even ask what level of medal it was.

It felt liberating to buy it. I put it in a corner of the room where I stored books and lost track of it.

Either it had been mistaken for junk and tossed out, or it was still there in the old house, probably covered with dust.

Even now, when I think about it, the blue of that sky—that sky beneath which heaven has not created one person above another[2]—is still there in my eyes.

[*SHITENCHŌ NO MAGARIKADO* (TOKYO: KŌDANSHA, 1996)]

2. The first words of "An Encouragement of Learning," by the Meiji-period educator Fukuzawa Yūkichi (1834–1901): "Heaven never created a man above another nor a man below another" (*The Autobiography of Yukichi Fukuzawa*, trans. Eiichi Kiyooka [New York: Columbia University Press, 1966], 391).

46

On *Zuihitsu*

SAKAI JUNKO

Sakai Junko was born in Tokyo in 1966. She graduated from Rikkyō University with a degree in sociology and worked for a time in an advertising firm before becoming a prominent columnist and essayist, writing primarily for a variety of magazines. In 2003, she won the Kōdansha Essay Prize and the Fujin Kōron Literature Prize for her book Makeinu no tōboe (The Howl of the Loser Dogs), *a wry portrait of unmarried middle-aged women in Japan, whom she encourages to take charge of their own lives and contribute more to the Japanese economy and Japanese culture. She continues to write on social issues, from public manners and demographics to gender and the workplace. She is among the most widely read of present-day Japanese essayists.*

The essay translated here, "Zuihitsu to iu mono" (On Zuihitsu), comes from the series "Makura no sōshi REMIX" (The Pillow Book Remix), which appeared in the journal Shōsetsu shinchō *and in which Sakai records her own musings on that famous book and engages in a mock conversation with its author.*

As the sun rises higher, dew weighing heavy on the bush clover falls and the branches recoil though no hand has touched them—a truly captivating sight. Having said that, though, I think it equally interesting that to other people this may be of no interest at all.

Thus concludes section 124 of *The Pillow Book*, describing the beauty of a dewy garden at dawn in the Ninth Month after a rainstorm that lasted through the night.[1] After expressing her own enjoyment while she gazes at bush clover branches swaying as dew falls from them, Sei Shōnagon says she finds it fascinating that something she has just called "interesting"[2] may not be interesting to other people at all. It is here that I sense Sei's strong personality and individuality as an essayist.

First her lens shows a close-up of just the bush clover; then she shifts to the bush clover and herself; and then she expands the shot to include the bush clover, herself, and what is on the "outside." The ease with which she handles perspective and the high degree of objectivity that makes it possible for her to include herself in the scene—that is what makes Sei Shōnagon, Sei Shōnagon.

Sei Shōnagon is said to be Japan's first essayist. One wonders why she decided to write essays rather than tales. Thinking about that question as I read *The Pillow Book*, I conclude that she clearly has the disposition of an essayist.[3]

I believe that the difference between the disposition of the essayist and the disposition of the novelist is something like the difference between sushi chefs and chefs who prepare meals for formal dining—*kaiseki* chefs. To a sushi chef, ingredients are life itself, but he also thinks to himself, "I'm going to arrange them in such a way that guests won't know what they are." Not that ingredients are not important to *kaiseki* chefs as well; but to them, it is often the method of preparation and composition that are paramount.

In other words, what someone with the disposition of an essayist desires is for guests to enjoy the taste of the various ingredients. As I peruse Sei's lists of things like "Mountains," "Market Towns," "Depressing Things," and so on—the sections that in textbooks used to be called compendia—I savor the combination of ingredients and the keen edge of the kitchen blade she uses to serve up her dishes.

1. Sei Shōnagon, *The Pillow Book*, sec. 124 (chap. 1).
2. *Omoshiroshi*. A word that is at the very center of Sei's aesthetic vocabulary.
3. Here Sakai uses the older term, *zuihitsuka*.

Examining the lists, I feel an almost painful instinct in Sei to gather things into categories. Natural objects—"Seas" and "Grasses"—along with other things like "Illnesses," "Houses," and "Amusements" combine to make ninety-six lists. And then come her lists of "things"—"Graceful Things," "Distressing Things"—seventy-nine of them.

The idea of organizing things by name categories did not originate with *The Pillow Book* but appears to have already been used in both China and Japan. But that technique—for someone who had within her already a mania for categorizing and collecting—suited her perfectly, so much so that for us the idea of lists has come to be synonymous with Sei Shōnagon.

For example, in Sei's book we encounter lists like "Things that suffer when sketched" (things that are inferior to the real thing when one draws them) and "Things that give a bad impression, however pretty in appearance" (things that however beautiful on the surface are still ugly on the inside). I feel that Sei must have felt a close to biological sense of pleasure in the act of stipulating such fine distinctions—which she then makes the basis of her groupings—among things and feelings of which ordinary people are only vaguely aware, if at all.

There may be some who say, "So, I get that you have divided things up into lists, but what's the point?" But drifting among her more than 170 lists is a compelling answer. "Well, I just made the lists because I wanted to. What's your complaint?"[4]

The sensation the sushi chef has when he sees the ingredients he has brought together lined up neatly in their case, pondering how things will work out: I think that this is the very spirit of the essayist.

The question of how to read the essays is left up to the reader. Unless asked by a guest, a sushi chef will say nothing about how much effort went into combining the ingredients and will give no directions about how to eat or in what order. Yet sushi chefs do pay careful attention to what and how guests eat. Sushi may be fast food, but it is a kind of food that assumes a certain ability in those who eat it. Depending on how a guest eats this most simple of foods, the distance between guest and chef

---

4. In the concluding section of *The Pillow Book*, Sei says that in her lists of things she has merely written "whatever occurred to me, for the pleasure of it" (*onozukara omou koto o tawabure ni kakitsuke-tari*). See Sei Shōnagon, *The Pillow Book* (chap. 1).

may be either reduced to intimacy or extended to something hopelessly remote.

———————

I think Sei's disposition as an essayist also has its origins in her demure nature. There may be people who wonder how this could be true of someone so adept at dealing with people of high rank and men at court, but I think she truly was shy.

In the passage with which I began my essay, for instance, she could have restricted herself to describing the beauty of the garden after the rain had lifted. In the immediately preceding passage, she had after all offered something truly exquisite: "The way raindrops cling to half-ravished spider webs in the open-weave fences and the eaves above, look-ing like so many strings of white pearls—that is also charming and beau-tiful." And yet, in closing, she has to note how interesting it is that she is the only one who might find such a scene interesting. Certainly she is "in the moment" and thoroughly enchanted by the beauty of something, but she is too self-conscious to forget herself and remain enthralled to the end.

The way she becomes self-conscious at the end of things is apparent here and there. In section 98, she says something witty but then con-cludes, "This is terribly self-serving, but I have been told to leave nothing out, so I can't very well not include it."[5]

In section 134, "Things with nothing to recommend them," she lists "A person who has not only bad looks but bad character as well. Cleaning starch that has gone rancid . . ." but then concludes, "People will hate my mentioning such things, but at this late date I cannot restrain my-self from recording them. I never thought anyone would ever read my jottings, so I decided to just write down whatever occurred to me, even things that are vulgar or odious."[6]

Sometimes Sei is even coy about her own writing. After using the word "again," she says, "Ah, another 'again.'" And after recording some gossip, she says, "Too many gossip sections in a row."

5. This is Sakai's paraphrase. A more literal reading of the first phrase would be "This should be listed among 'embarrassing things,' but . . ." In standard texts, the section is 97, not 98.
6. Sei Shōnagon, *The Pillow Book*, sec. 134 (chap. 1).

What's more, she sometimes makes excuses. When she does so, how-ever, she appeals to her readers for understanding. "I have not recorded gossip or self-serving stories[7] unwittingly, but rather knowing fully what I was doing."[8] Indeed, she makes it a matter of pride to show that she knows what she is doing each time she is captivated by beautiful scenery or love or when she is thinking something mean or spiteful. A major fac-tor in why we forgive her self-serving comments—which are many, as I have pointed out—is that her comments are interesting of themselves, of course; but it also helps that she is so conscious of her own vanity.

So Sei employs her own vanity to good effect. And, occasionally, she also uses self-reproach. When one reads her disparaging comments about her own looks, particularly, one realizes that already in her time female essayists had established the tactic of always being modest about their own looks. As I have written elsewhere, self-reproach is also a special technique of urban people.[9]

Self-reproach is an easier tool to wield than self-congratulation, and in essays of recent times I sometimes feel that people are competing to see who can produce the most eccentric sort of self-deprecation, but Sei's cases are not so extreme. It is not just that she did not like the idea of flowing along in the easiest current; I believe that as an aristocrat, she felt that self-reproach was not as stylish as self-congratulation and that therefore she should not be too ready to deploy it.

Sei's gaze remains objective, but neither does she show pride in her faults. Which is worthy of one who does not tolerate fools well—at least, that is my conclusion.

---

7. Sei's word, in section 126, is *warebome* (literally, "self-praise").

8. A reference to section 259, in which after describing an occasion on which she was clearly favored by Teishi (976–1001), consort to Emperor Ichijō (980–1011; r. 986–1011), she admits that what she writes appears to be boasting but says that she is merely recording the facts as they are (*aru koto wa mata ikaga wa*). See Sei Shōnagon, *Makura no sōshi*, ed. Watanabe Minoru, Shin Nihon koten bungaku taikei 25 (Tokyo: Iwanami shoten, 1991), 304–5.

9. Sakai Junko, *Makura no sōshi REMIX* (Tokyo: Shinchōsha, 2004), in which a chapter is titled "Tokai to iu mono" (In the City).

INTERVIEW

SAKAI: The first thing I felt when reading *The Pillow Book* was, "This is like a women's magazine!"

SEI: Meaning?

SAKAI: Your lists seem like gravure pages—a little travel, a little fashion.[10] And your lists of "things" are, well, just like columns.[11] Your memories of life with Lady Teishi, your anecdotes about experiences with men, your boastful accounts—sometimes they read like gossip pieces, sometimes like short stories.

SEI: Yes, well, I did think it best to include different textures. Certainly I owe readers a little entertainment. Although I'm the sort who, as I was compiling words for my lists, would suddenly think of something from the past and end up mixing it in.

SAKAI: But that is what makes it easy to take your writing as a woman just chatting—it's impressionistic; topics suddenly just pop up. Although in your case, I'm sure this was done intentionally.

SEI: Whatever you say. I haven't thought much about it.

SAKAI: Obviously, you have great talent as a writer, but I think you also have editorial ability. You didn't just put *The Pillow Book* together all at once—I think it must have been enjoyed by readers as a sort of "Sei Shōnagon Magazine."

SEI: Now that you mention it, as I wrote I guess I was thinking about how readers would react.

SAKAI: If one reads *The Pillow Book* more carefully, it involves political matters too, such as the death of Fujiwara no Michitaka, father of Empress Teishi, whom you served, and the rise of Michitaka's younger brother, Fujiwara no Michinaga.[12] One can also find meaning in those episodes.

SEI: I am happy having people read it either as a mirror of those events or simply as a miscellany decribing things that happened around me. But

---

10. *Gurabia pēji.* The term comes from the French word *photogravure* and refers to the glossy photo montages often found in the first pages of magazines, which feature famous people (including writers) or popular topics.

11. Sakai uses the English word.

12. Fujiwara no Michitaka (953–995) and Fujiwara no Michinaga (966–1027) were rivals. Teishi took the tonsure after her father's death.

rather than trying to pass something down to posterity, or because there was something I wanted to say, I really just enjoyed writing—I wrote *The Pillow Book* because I simply could not *not* write. If readers understand even that much, I am happy.

SAKAI: The thing I like most about you is your masculine spirit of restraint—of leaving things unsaid.

SEI: There are many things in the world that are best left unsaid, I think. If readers will be attentive not just to what I *did* include but also what I *did not* include, I will be even more happy. But wait—perhaps I have just broken my own rule and said too much.

[*MAKURA NO SŌSHI REMIX* (TOKYO: SHINCHŌSHA, 2004)]

Permissions

The translator and publisher acknowledge with thanks permission granted to use the following material.

Yoshida no Kenko, "Essays in Idleness," from *Classical Japanese Prose: An Anthology*, edited by Helen McCullough. Copyright © 1990 by the Board of Trustees of the Leland Stanford Jr. University. All rights reserved. Used with the permission of Stanford University Press, www.sup.org.

Translations of various sections of *Shōtetsu monogatari* from *Conversations with Shōtetsu* (*Shōtetsu Monogatari*), translated by Robert H. Brower with an introduction and notes by Steven D. Carter, Michigan Monograph Series in Japanese Studies, Number 7 (Ann Arbor: Center for Japanese Studies, The University of Michigan, 1992). Copyright © 1992 The Regents of The University of Michigan. All rights reserved. Used with the permission of the publisher.

Uchida Hyakken, "Master Hyakken's Idle Fantasies," Bumpy Road," and "A Long Fence," translated and used with the permission of the estate of Uchida Hyakken.

Shiga Naoya, "Baby Sparrow," "Turtledoves," and "Morning Glories," translated and used with the permission of the estate of Shiga Naoya.

Kawamori Yoshizō, essays from *Esprit and Humor*, translated and used with the permission of the estate of Kawamori Yoshizō.

Osaragi Jirō, "Sleepless Nights" and "A Bed for My Books," translated and used with the permission of the estate of Osaragi Jirō.

Kawakami Tetsutarō, "On Being Down with a Cold," translated and used with the permission of the estate of Kawakami Tetsutarō.

Shōno Junzō, "The Road," translated and used with the permission of the estate of Shōno Junzō.

Kōda Aya, "Kitchen," "Raindrops," and "A Memento of the Season," translated and used with the permission of the estate of Kōda Aya.

Kōno Taeko, "On Surgery" and "Rainy Day," translated and used with the permission of Kōno Taeko.

GPSR Authorized Representative: Easy Access System Europe, Mustamäe tee 50, 10621 Tallinn, Estonia, gpsr.requests@easproject.com